Enduring
Controversies in
Presidential
Nominating Politics

Enduring Controversies in Presidential Nominating Politics

Edited by

Emmett H. Buell Jr.

and

William G. Mayer

UNIVERSITY OF PITTSBURGH PRESS

PUBLISHED BY THE UNIVERSITY OF PITTSBURGH PRESS,
PITTSBURGH, PA., 15260
Copyright © 2004, University of Pittsburgh Press
All rights reserved
Manufactured in the United States of America
Printed on acid-free paper
10 9 8 7 6 5 4 3 2 1

Library of Congress Cataloging-in-Publication Data

Enduring controversies in presidential nominating politics / edited by Emmett
H. Buell, Jr. and William G. Mayer.
    p. cm.
  Includes bibliographical references and index.
  ISBN 0-8229-4233-X (cloth: alk. paper) — ISBN 0-8229-5849-X (pbk. : alk.
paper)
  1. Presidents—United States—Nomination. I. Buell, Emmett H. II. Mayer,
William G., 1956-
  JK521.E53 2004
  324.273'15—dc22
                          2004003483

Contents

Tables and Figures

Figures

Acknowledgments

We dedicate this book to the memory of James W. Davis, whose pioneering work, *Presidential Primaries: Road to the White House*, awakened students of the 1960s to the importance of primaries in presidential nominations. We are also indebted to our editors at the University of Pittsburgh Press, Niels Aaboe, Nathan MacBrien, Deborah Meade, and Jane Flanders for their encouragement and fine work in bringing the book out. Thanks, too, to the two anonymous reviewers who evaluated our initial proposal, and to James E. Campbell and Rhodes Cook for thorough and insightful critiques that greatly improved the final version. Emeritus historian Clarke Wilhelm and Denison University political scientist Paul Djupe helpfully commented on drafts of introductory essays. Leslie H. Southwick, author of the invaluable *Presidential Also-Rans and Running Mates*, furnished valuable details on the ethnic and religious backgrounds of defeated nominees. Emmett Buell thanks Denison provost David Anderson and the Robert C. Good Fellowship committee for granting time off to complete this project. Christy Trager, Political Science Department secretary at Denison University, helped enormously by scanning and reformatting the readings selected for republication. Mary Prophet of the Denison Library tracked down sources no longer readily available; Sarah Torrens and Joyce Ford cheerfully responded to myriad requests for reproducing copies of the manuscript in its various manifestations; and, hardly least in appreciation, Tim Chiappetta, August Gramaglia, Nathan Manning, John Romito, and Keith Vessell—all students in Buell's course on presidential selection—scoured the manuscript for typographical and other mistakes.

Acknowledgments

Enduring
Controversies in
Presidential
Nominating Politics

PART I
Introduction

Emmett H. Buell Jr.

ILL MAYER and I put this book together in the shared conviction that historical perspective is essential to understanding presidential nominating politics. Excellent studies of recent nominating struggles have found their way into college classrooms, but for all the skill exhibited in these analyses, they provide limited insight into the past of presidential nominating politics. Readers of the next round of postelection books, for example, will find extensive analysis of recent developments such as the "front-loading" of presidential primaries and the latest innovations in campaign finance, but the same works will devote only a few pages (if that) to what transpired at the national party conventions. This is understandable, owing to the decline of the convention's importance, but even a bare-bones account would hold greater value if readers knew more about how much power these mass assemblies once exercised. A similar deficiency exists with regard to the congressional caucus method of making presidential nominations, as well as the complex scheme of presidential selection worked out by the Framers of the Constitution. Lack of historical perspective also handicaps the discussion of how best to cure the ills of the present system. Remarkably few proposals to improve the current system are truly new; the idea of national primary, for example, has been on the table since the turn of the twentieth century.

If history teaches us anything about these subjects, it is that selecting an American president has never been a simple undertaking. Likewise, critics will always find fundamental faults with whatever system is in place. Nominating systems always change in ways that are neither anticipated nor desired. However idealistic the rhetoric, the most likely reforms will benefit some factions and ambitious politicians at the expense of others. Perhaps this explains why controversies over representation, popular participation, and the role of parties endure from one nominating system to the next.

This book has a secondary purpose, which is to acquaint today's students with important writings on presidential nominating politics that have been forgotten or are no longer readily accessible. Accordingly, our readings include James W. Ceaser's overview of nominating politics from the Framers to the late 1970s, Samuel Eliot Morison's account of the first national nominating convention, William G. Morgan's history of the congressional caucus; Lord Bryce's explanation for why great Americans do not get elected president; M. I. Ostrogorski's dyspeptic commentary on the old-fashioned convention at its height; Eugene B. McGregor's analysis of how delegates might have voted rationally at supposedly irrational conventions; Sig Mickelson's delightful account of how network television coverage in 1952 changed campaign journalism forever; George W. Norris's spirited defense of the direct primary; E. E. Schattschneider's attack on the concept of party "membership"; William C. Carleton's analysis of how profound changes in American society and politics reshaped the nominating power of conventions; Kenneth E. Bode and Carol F. Casey's defense of Democratic reforms in the 1970s that further affect convention power; Michael Walzer's unlikely proposal to revive the old-fashioned convention; Thomas Cronin and Robert Loevy's call for a radical overhaul of the nominating process; Michael Nelson's advocacy of a national primary; and a proposal by the National Association of Secretaries of State to create a system of rotating regional primaries. We have arranged these selections chronologically to highlight the development of nominating institutions and the enduring controversies associated with each stage of development. Following this introduction and Ceaser's overview, the remaining sections cover (1) the preconvention period of presidential nominations, (2) nominations during the time when conventions exercised most or all of the power of choice, (3) nominations increasingly determined by presidential primary outcomes, and (4) proposals to reform the current system.

We also offer six original essays, including William Mayer's analysis of how the Framers at the 1787 Constitutional Convention settled on a complex process of presidential selection. The other essays review the literature and otherwise set the stage for the sections listed above.

Our readings commence with James W. Ceaser's overview of nominating history. Drawing on the writings of selected Founders, Martin Van Buren, and Woodrow Wilson, Ceaser highlights changing perspectives on personal ambition, political parties, and popular participation in the process. He also elaborates on the theme that nominating systems differ not only in objectives pursued but also in types of candidates nominated.[1] Although his account pre-dates the massive front-loading of the current system, it helps us to understand how and why the process has developed as it has.

Ceaser wrote in the late 1970s, when many election analysts believed that American political parties had entered an era of serious decline. No work did more to advance this argument than *The Party's Over* (1971) by David Broder, which set the mold for related writings well into the 1980s.[2] The literature that built on Broder's work maintained that parties no longer controlled the nominating process or had the resources to wage successful campaigns. Moreover, the failure of parties to advance programs for change supposedly undercut their influence in government.[3] Parties were said to have suffered a substantial erosion of their core supporters. In 1976, for example, the authors of *The Changing American Voter* concluded that the "most dramatic political change in the American public over the past two decades has been the decline of partisanship."[4] Ceaser, too, claimed that party organizations no longer determined presidential nominations, that nominating races had become plebiscitary contests among individual contenders, that parties no longer structured the voting behavior of large numbers of citizens, and that the national electoral process had taken on the characteristics of nonpartisan competition.

Subsequent research has modified or negated many of these conclusions, and in retrospect it is clear that many scholars underestimated party resilience. Signs of recovery appeared as early as the 1980s, when party organizations assumed greater responsibility for fund raising, candidate recruitment, and innovating campaign technology.[5] The 1980s also marked the beginning of an ideological polarization among voters and elected officials that moved both parties much closer to the "responsible parties" model once idealized by political scientists.[6] Similarly, party elites regained some of their leverage over the nominating process.[7]

No tenet of the party decomposition thesis has provoked more challenges than the claim that party identification has declined. Much of the dispute turns on measurement issues, such as how best to gauge partisanship and what to do with so-called independents that lean toward one party or the other. Bruce E. Keith and his coauthors in *The Myth of the Independent Voter* make a strong argument for classifying independents as partisans, in which case the loss of party followers appears much less pronounced.[8] When he limited partisans to strong and weak party identifiers, the late Warren E. Miller found that partisanship had fallen off in the late sixties and seventies before rebounding in the eighties. Age breakdowns showed that older voters recovered their partisan identity sooner than younger ones. Miller also discovered that much if not most of the decline occurred among *nonvoters* rather than voters. "In other words," he wrote, "the cry of alarm that the partisan sky was falling, with all of the strong implications for the future of the electoral process, was occasioned by indicators emanating primarily from nonparticipants in presidential politics."[9]

The claim that fewer people voted consistently with their professed party loyalty has also been negated by more recent evidence. As James Ceaser and Andrew Busch note in *The Perfect Tie,* parties structured the vote to an unprecedented degree in the 2000 presidential election.[10] But an important remnant of the decomposition thesis survives in the floating vote that is said to determine election outcomes. From 1952 to 1964, according to Miller's analysis of National Election Studies data, self-designated independents constituted less than one-quarter of all voters in presidential elections. Their number increased to 35 percent in 2000. This development occurred simultaneously with a dropoff in voters identifying themselves as Democrats, from 45 percent in 1968 to 36 percent in 2000.[11] In this vein, Joel H. Silbey notes that analysts impressed by the consistency of voting along party lines in 2000 tended to overlook "a large and growing middle group" that voted for reasons other than partisanship.[12]

While compiling these readings we were continually impressed by the recurrence of basic discontents in the history of presidential nominating politics. Consider today's litany of complaints that too many Americans are shut out of the contemporary process, that those who participate in the primaries do not represent those who abstain, that big money and special interests exercise undue influence on presidential selection, that the process discourages leading politicians with the highest potential for greatness from seeking the presidency, and that those who do run seldom address "real" issues.[13] Critics of national conventions voiced every one of these objections with similar or greater vehemence a century or more ago.

We were also struck by the extent to which each new method of making presidential nominations sprouted from seeds planted in local and state politics. The congressional caucus originated from local and state caucuses, the national convention from state conventions, and presidential primaries from state primaries. Similarly, the roots of today's caucus-convention process used by a few states to choose their national delegates go back to the mid-nineteenth century.[14]

Any contested nomination divides a party to some degree, and parties are frequently tested by the difficulty of uniting factions behind a contentious choice. A serious failure to achieve unity subjects the process to intense criticism; repeated failure sets the state for systemic collapse, as happened to the congressional caucus. Early critics of the current system saw merit in a "divisive primary" thesis, which held that bitterly contested primaries reduced the nominee's chances of carrying the same states in the presidential election. More

CHAPTER 1

Political Parties and Presidential Ambition

James W. Ceaser

A ccording to political scientists of the last generation, party competition was an essential feature of any form of popular government. How dismayed they would be, therefore, to learn from contemporary students of American politics that our parties are "decomposing" and that our national electoral process is increasingly taking on the characteristics of nonpartisan competition. While the labels of the two traditional parties continue to exist, the institutions bearing these labels have lost many of their previous functions. Parties no longer structure the voting behavior of large numbers of citizens. They have ceased to play a major role in constraining presidential decision-making, and presidents now place little reliance on them in their efforts to generate public support for policy initiatives. Perhaps most important of all, party organizations have lost their influence in determining the outcome of presidential nominations. Under the "open" nominating process that has emerged since 1968, the races have for all practical purposes become plebiscitary contests among the individual contenders. Candidates create large personal campaign organizations and devise their own programs and electoral strategies, very much as if they were establishing national parties of their own. These personalistic features of the nomination contests continue into the final election stage, as the parties become the extensions of the organizations of the victorious nominees.

Journal of Politics 40 (August 1978): 708–39, reprinted with permission from Blackwell Publishing. James W. Ceaser teaches in the Department of Government and Foreign Affairs at the University of Virginia and has authored or coauthored numerous books on presidential selection and American politics.

What are the implications of this decline in the role of traditional parties for the presidential selection process and for the presidency itself? Is it a positive development, as many reformers argue, or does it pose a serious threat to moderate republican government, as many of their opponents contend? Addressing these questions today is of more than academic significance. The recent changes in the presidential selection process have resulted not primarily from forces beyond the control of political actors but from the decisions of practicing politicians in party commissions and state legislatures. These decisions have been made under the influence of a theory of the selection process that has yet to win general acceptance, and even some of its original proponents have now begun to have second thoughts.[1] Any clarification, therefore, of the basic purposes and functions of the selection process could influence prevailing theoretical views and thereby the direction of future institutional development.

The reform theory of selection on which the current open system is based was introduced to national politics at the 1968 Democratic Convention. In its original formulation, the theory attacked the legitimacy of the influence of the regular party organizations and called for "direct democracy" in the selection of presidential nominees.[2] As the theory evolved within the official reform commissions established by the party in 1968 and 1972, the ideal of "fairness" emerged as the single most important value for the nomination process. By fairness was meant procedural regularity and the placation in the selection of delegates of the expressed candidate preferences of the participants. While the reform commissions did not expressly call for direct democracy in the form of more primaries, the emphasis reformers placed on popular participation and the individual's right to the expression of a candidate's preference certainly encouraged the subsequent adoption of presidential primaries in many states.

The reform view of presidential selection should be compared with the very different perspective of the Founders and the originators of permanent party competition. For these statesmen the concern was not so much with the procedural goal of fairness as with the substantive results of how power was sought and exercised. After satisfying themselves of the compatibility of their systems with the basic requirements of popular government, they turned their attention to regulating the behavior of presidential aspirants with a view to preventing dangerous political divisions and leadership styles that might undermine the intended character of the presidency.

To speak of a single perspective on selection that includes the Founders with the originators of party competition might seem like a serious misreading of the historical record. The Founders, after all, were opponents of national parties and sought to establish a nonpartisan selection system. Yet if one focuses on their objectives rather than on the institutional forms they established, it is plausible to argue that by the 1820s permanent party competition was the solution that was most compatible with their goals. The key to this last argument is an understanding of the theme of presidential ambition in the thought of each group.

For the Founders, a major objective in selection was to prevent the creation of factions that form around "different leaders ambitiously contending for pre-eminence and power."[3] By their electoral institutions the Founders sought to deflect the great force of presidential ambition from its possible manifestations in demagoguery or "image" appeals and to channel it into conduct that would promote the public good. This also was the goal of Martin Van Buren and his followers in the party school of the 1820s and 1830s. They held that the non-partisan system that emerged in 1824 encouraged the very kind of leadership appeals that the Founders wanted to avoid. Only by instituting party competition between two parties of moderate principle could leadership be circumscribed within safe limits. The answer to personal faction for Van Buren was party, though party of a different sort from that which the Founders had feared. Whatever differences exist between the views of the Founders and Van Buren—and these, as we shall see, are not insignificant—they both accepted the premise that the electoral process should be considered as an institution that controlled candidate behavior.

This premise went unchallenged until the rise of the Populist and Progressive movements at the turn of the century. According to Woodrow Wilson, the most thoughtful spokesman of the Progressive view, the selection system should be designed to elevate a dynamic leader above the political party and make the party serve his will. In Wilson's thought, party is transformed from an institution that constrains leadership to an instrument that enhances it. "Leadership," the central theme of Wilson's proposed revision of the constitutional system, could best take root in an open nominating process in which each contender presented his program directly to the people. The winners would then earn the right to "own" their parties. Wilson accordingly proposed national primaries, making it clear that contenders might appeal beyond traditional partisan followings to form new constituencies. Wilson was satisfied that the problem of dangerous leadership appeals could be avoided in an open selection process: the wisdom of the people along with the self-restraint of the leaders obviated the need for any institutional guidance.

A balance of sorts existed throughout most of this century between institutional elements representing Van Buren's theory of selection and those representing Wilsonian ideas. This system, known sometimes as the "mixed" system because of the presence of both candidate-oriented primaries and organization-dominated selection procedures, was overthrown after 1968.[4] Although there are some differences between the Progressive and the reform views, the reformers have accepted the crucial Progressive premise about the safety of an open nominating system. The use of institutions to influence the character of what V. O. Key called the "echo chamber" has been abandoned in exchange for the right of the people to hear each aspirant shout what he pleases.[5]

THE FUNCTIONS OF THE PRESIDENTIAL SELECTION SYSTEM

To facilitate discussion of the theories of the electoral process noted above, it will be helpful first to identify four major objectives or "functions" of the selection system. By the selection system here we are referring to the nomination and the final election stages, since both are part of the same general process. The treatment that follows will be very general, as the purpose is not to resolve the issues that are raised but to indicate some of the major considerations that any legislator of the selection process should keep in mind.

First, the selection system should promote the proper character of the presidential office in respect both to its powers and to the style of presidential leadership. This implies that, at least up to a certain point, the office should be thought of as the end and the selection process the means. Many today might take exception to this assumption. Two recent defenders of reform theory, John Saloma and Frederick Sontag, argue that the goal of the selection system should be increased participation, which they see as a means of building citizen virtue.[6] Pre-reform theorists, though no less concerned about citizen virtue, looked elsewhere for its cultivation. They focused instead on more directly related issues such as the effect of the selection system on the presidency, realizing that the way in which power is sought will have a profound influence on how it is subsequently exercised. Many of the important historical debates on the role of parties in our system have centered on this issue. The Founders and John Quincy Adams opposed party competition because they thought it would compromise the president's independence, while Woodrow Wilson sought to transform parties into candidate-centered organizations in order to increase the president's power.

Second, the selection system should ensure an accession to power that is unproblematic and widely regarded as legitimate. By unproblematic we refer to the "mechanical" aspects of the process, most notably to those that relate to its capacity to determine a winner without confusion or delays. Legitimacy refers to whether the people accept the process as being in accord with their understanding of republican principles. A system that is widely regarded as corrupt or undemocratic imposes a heavy burden on its choice, whether at the nomination stage, as Taft learned in 1912, or for the final election, as John Quincy Adams discovered after 1824. It is important, therefore, for the selection system to conform to a well-established conception of republicanism. This must be distinguished, however, from calls for change in response to ephemeral inter-

pretations of republican principles which may be championed by some particular candidate or faction seeking a temporary advantage. Since the selection
system is an important "teacher" of the meaning of republicanism, such
changes present a danger that the regime will be altered without sufficient attention to long-term effects. These changes are most likely to occur at the nominating stage which lies outside the sphere of direct constitutional regulation.

Third, the selection system should help promote the choice of an able executive. What transforms this concern from a meaningless expression of hope
to a legitimate institutional question is the reasonable assumption, backed by
comparative research into selection in various liberal democracies, that different systems affect the type of person apt to compete and succeed. A plebiscitary
nomination system would seem to place a greater premium on those qualities
that appeal to a mass audience, such as vigor, appearance, and the aura of sanc-
timony; "closed" systems will value to a greater degree those qualities esteemed
by the narrower group empowered to select, for example, "keeping one's word"
in the case of American politicians or trustworthiness in the case of British par-
liamentarians.[7]

Of course what constitutes an able and good person is, beyond broad
agreement on certain basic qualities such as honesty and intelligence, a matter
of great dispute. After a long period of neglect, some political scientists have returned to this kind of normative issue, especially since Watergate. The predominant contemporary school in the study of presidential character classifies
character according to different "personality types" defined primarily by reference to psychological attributes. Apart from considerations of the adequacy of
this approach for assessing political qualifications, there is the additional question of whether it can be of assistance in informing the debate over the institutions of presidential selection. One well-known scholar who recently made use
of this approach seems implicitly to have conceded its irrelevance in this respect. In the article entitled "What Manner of Man?" Erwin Hargrove develops
a profile of the ideal presidential personality, which he chooses to call a "democratic character." Persons of this description, among other things, would "give
every sign of so loving themselves in the biblical sense that they are free to
have concern for others." Unfortunately—and, one might add, paradoxically—
Hargrove finds that the extremely democratic system now used to select the
president does little to promote democratic characters. Indeed, the only institutional device by which to encourage this character type would be to establish
a board of "elite gate keepers" to screen the candidates. But Hargrove recoils
from a solution that is so obviously undemocratic, and the best he can offer is
the noninstitutional recommendation that we "emphasize democratic styles of
leadership in all organizations of our society . . . so that the selection of leaders,
including presidents, will be implicitly guided by a search for 'democratic char-

acters.'"[8] From the difficulties Hargrove encounters with this approach, it seems that in a popular regime no single personality type could ever be mandated by law or institutional arrangement. The most the selection system can do is to influence character choice by indirect means—by determining who has the power to select, and thereby which political and character attributes may be favored, and by certain general injunctions regulating candidate eligibility, such as the Constitution's age requirement.

Finally, the selection system should prevent the harmful effects of the pursuit of office by highly ambitious contenders. Almost every major politician will at one time or another fix his attention on becoming president and adjust his behavior to improve his chances of being considered. For those who enter the select circle of legitimate contenders, the tendency will be to adopt whatever strategies are legal and acceptable—and even some that are not—if they promise results. It is reasonable to assume, therefore, that the ambition of contenders, if not properly guided, can lead to strategies and appeals that threaten the public good. Such in fact would seem to be the "natural" tendency of ambition, for the ambitious seek first that which is advantageous for themselves. It is this problem which led some of the past legislators of the selection process to look for institutional arrangements that could create a degree of harmony between personal ambition and behavior that promotes the public good. Every student of American politics recognizes this principle as it applies to officeholders, but it is surprising how many ignore it or deny its applicability in the case of office-seekers.

The problem that presidential ambition can create may be classified under two broad headings. The first is the disruption of the proper functioning of an office or institution: office-holders, using their positions to further their presidential aspirations, may perform in a way that conflicts with their intended constitutional role. One striking instance of this problem is discussed by James Sterling Young in his account of the effects of the caucus system of nomination in the early nineteenth century. Young shows how that system led cabinet members who were interested in becoming president to court favor with congressmen, with the consequence that the unity and independence of the executive branch were undermined. The failure in this case to structure presidential ambition in accord with the intended character of the Constitution very nearly led to a transformation of the entire political system.[9]

The second problem, by no means exclusive of the first, is the attempt of candidates to build a popular following by the "arts of popularity"—by empty "image" appeals, by flattery, or by the exploitation of dangerous passions.[10] The general term for such appeals is demagoguery, although one often finds the term restricted today to harsh utterances that evoke anger and fear. It is a mistake, however, to fail to recognize the demagogic character of a "soft" flattery that tells the people they can do no wrong or of seductive appeals that hide behind a veil of liberality, making promises that can never be kept or raising hopes that can never be satisfied.

The approach usually relied upon today to control candidate abuses is the imposition of legal restrictions. This approach was used in the campaign finance legislation of 1972 and 1974, which was designed to protect the public interest from candidates' granting special privileges or favors to large contributors. Thus while one arm of the modern reform movement makes the selection process more open, the other attempts to prevent certain excesses, in some cases encouraged by that very openness, by means of new legal limitations and regulatory procedures. But whatever the merits of this legal approach for curbing certain kinds of abuses, it cannot reach those which by their very nature cannot be classified as criminal or proscribed by statute. Into this category fall most of the abuses discussed above.

If ambition in these instances cannot be checked by law, it might nevertheless be controlled by the institutional arrangements of the selection system. Institutional regulation of behavior consists in establishing certain constraints and incentives—not criminal penalties—that promote desired habits and actions and discourage unwanted behavior. The selection system, conceived in this sense, is the institution that structures the conduct of presidential aspirants and their supporters. By marking out a certain path to the presidency, it influences the behavior of the nation's leading politicians and, by their example, the style of politics in the regime as a whole. Regulation of presidential ambition is likely to work most effectively where it relies on the candidates' own strongest impulse: if matters can be arranged such that undesirable behavior will detract from the chance of success, candidates will turn "voluntarily" to other strategies. Properly channeled, ambition can be used to curb its own excesses.

THE FOUNDERS

The Founders' two main objectives for presidential selection were to help secure the executive independence from Congress and to prevent the kind of campaign that would undermine the constitutional character of the office. The first objective, which has been identified by nearly every scholar of the Founders' thought, was to be accomplished by giving the president an electoral base outside of the legislature. The second objective, which has been almost entirely overlooked in the literature on the founding, can only be understood after treating the more general question of constitutional authority and the threat posed to it by the claim to popular leadership.

One of the distinguished features of constitutional government for the

Founders was rule based on institutional authority. Officeholders, in their view, were to rest their claim to govern on the legally defined rights and prerogatives of their offices. This kind of authority was threatened by claims to rule on informal grounds, such as personal heroic standing or assertions of embodying the will of the people. The latter claim was particularly dangerous to constitutional government in a popular regime. The people were already recognized as the source of ultimate authority for the system as a whole, and it would involve but one small step for an enterprising leader to activate the principle of popular sovereignty and make it the immediate basis of political rule. Popular authority was thus identified by the Founders as the likeliest grounds on which attempts would be made to throw off constitutional restraints and to concentrate power in the hands of one person. It was the most probable source for what the Founders called "encroachment" or "usurpation" and for what we refer to today as institutional "imperialism."

The Founders' analysis of the problem of popular authority appears in *The Federalist* in the context of their discussion of the House. Here Publius warns against the danger that the House, urged on by some of its "leaders," might seek to "draw all power into its impetuous vortex." But it is crucial to observe that it is not the House itself that the Founders fear, but the claim to informal popular authority. Any institution asserting power on the basis of "its supposed influence over the people" is properly suspect on the Founders' grounds. Although the Founders did not emphasize this problem in the case of the executive—probably because their opponents, fearing only the monarchic tendency of the presidency, never made an issue of it—their concern is evident from their discussions of the possibility of an executive "demagogue" at the Convention and from their occasional references to the danger of a presidential "favorite" in *The Federalist*.[11] The prospect that the president might emerge as a leader in this sense was especially alarming to the Founders, for they intended the executive in particular to check any tendency to popular authority and protect the constitutional tone of the government.

The general name we have given to this kind of noninstitutional rule is "popular leadership." "Popular" refers to the source of the authority and "leadership" to its informal character. Although the Founders conceded the need for leadership in establishing the regime—twice they speak approvingly of "leaders" of the revolution—elsewhere the term is used disparagingly. The establishment of the Constitution, they doubtless thought, obviated the need for leaders, as authority would henceforth rest on the institutional foundation. This foundation was also understood to protect the possibility for the exercise of statesmanship by providing the president with a margin of discretion free from the immediate constraints of public opinion. Though leadership on rare occasions could be statesmanlike, as at the time of the Revolution, the

Founders held that admitting it as the normal means of seeking and exercising power would promote demagoguery. Where authority rests on the leader's supposed representation of the popular will, competition for public favor ensues and with it the tendency to cultivate whatever currents of opinion that can provide a following. Power that is generated in this fashion might well be formidable, but its scope and discretion are apt to be circumscribed. The popular leader follows public opinion rather than directs it, and it is in this sense that popular leadership is antithetical to statesmanship.

Besides serving as a claim to authority, popular leadership is a way of soliciting power. The Founders refer to it in this context as "the popular arts." Where the popular arts are employed in seeking office, the danger increases that informal authority will be claimed as the basis for governing. The popular arts accustom the people to the style of popular leadership and train aspirants to generate support and power by this means. To protect the constitutional character of the presidency, the Founders accordingly thought it essential to discourage the use of the popular arts in the selection process.

The Founders identified two basic forms of the popular arts. The first was issue arousal. From their experience with elections for state legislatures after the Revolutionary War, the Founders became deeply concerned about demagogic issue appeals directed against property and merit.[12] These same prejudices, they feared could be tapped at the level of national politics, either directly or through attacks on the allegedly undemocratic branches of the government. The other form of the popular arts was the use of appeals that played upon certain passions relating to the personal qualities of the leader, what we might call today "image" appeals. Of course the Founders wanted the voters to focus on character qualifications, but they drew a distinction between character assessments based on a calm consideration of the candidates' merits and those influenced by strong emotions or flattery. Madison called attention to the danger of factions forming around "persons whose fortunes have been interesting to human passions," while Jay stressed the importance of closing the door to "those brilliant appearances of genius and patriotism, which, like the transient meteors, sometimes mislead as well as dazzle."[13]

The general principle the Founders followed in attempting to discourage the use of the popular arts was to make the election turn on personal reputation, not issue appeals. Personal reputation, the Founders believed, would serve as a rough approximation for merit: those who became well known at the national level would most likely have had to earn a reputation by distinguished service to the state.[14] The institutional means for favoring reputation over issue appeals was sought in the first instance by creating large electoral districts, a principle referred to by Hamilton as "the extension of the spheres of election."[15] The Founders reasoned that since all elections pose the problem of name recognition for the candidates, persons with established reputations begin with a decided advantage. The larger the size of the district, the more difficult it becomes for one using issue arousal to overcome this advantage—an assessment that might need to be reversed today in light of modern communications and of the extended campaign which gives a greater chance to the "outsider." As Madison observed in a note made to himself at the Convention: "Large districts are manifestly favorable to the election of persons of general respectability and probable attachment to the rights of property over competitors depending on personal solicitation in a contracted theatre."[16] Applied to the case of the largest possible district, a nationwide constituency, there was all the more reason to expect a safe result. As Gouverneur Morris argued, "If the people should elect, they will never fail to prefer some man of distinguished character or services, some man, if [one] might so speak, of continental reputation."[17]

The Founders were thus not the inveterate foes of direct popular election that some of their democratic critics have charged. But it is equally important to observe that their qualified approval of this method was based on the belief that it would normally produce a "conservative" result. Their position can thus in no way be construed as an endorsement of the concept of a "people's president" brandishing the sword of a popular electoral mandate. The selection process, in their view, was to be neutral with respect to presidential power, neither detracting from the independence of the executive branch nor providing it with an added source of extra-constitutional authority.

The proposal for direct election failed to gain the support of most delegates at the Convention. The opposition came from a number of quarters, including some who objected on the "practical" grounds that there would not normally be persons with a sufficient national reputation to command the votes of the people in the face of competition from strong regional candidates. This opposition obliged the direct election advocates to search for another plan, and they readily shifted their support to the proposal of an election by specially chosen electors. Along with providing the same guarantee of presidential independence, this plan increased the likelihood of selecting a continental figure, as the electors would be more knowledgeable about national affairs and could practically be given two votes for the presidential contest. The system also had the advantage of allowing for a certain degree of indirectness in the choice of the president. It therefore provided further insurance that the election would turn on reputation rather than the use of the popular arts. The electors, it was thought, would be less likely than the people to be swayed by popular appeals and might even resent them, even as—to cite an analogy that is only partly apt—convention delegates who formerly had discretion resented attempts by candidates to go over their heads to the people. By making the use of the popular arts unnecessary and perhaps counterproductive, the Founders sought to close the door to direct popular appeals and induce the ablest candidates to "campaign" by establishing a record of distinguished public service that might earn them a reputation for virtue.

From a cursory reading of the one paper in *The Federalist* that is devoted to presidential selection (number 68), one might receive the impression that the Founders viewed the pursuit of the presidency as a gentlemanly affair conducted among reluctant participants. Yet nothing could be further from the truth. There was a sense, of course, in which they expected that the immediate campaign would appear in this light, just as it was formerly the practice for aspirants to wait for their party to confer the nomination upon them. But this kind of campaign would conceal, even as it controlled, the powerful ambitions of the candidates. No more "realistic" analysis of political motivation exists in American thought than that which Hamilton provides in *The Federalist*. Hamilton begins with politicians as we find them: high-spirited, ambitious, and in some cases committed to achieving a noble fame. Hamilton's aim is not to make politicians into "democratic characters"—an objective he doubtless would have considered as undesirable as it was utopian—but to make them serve popular government. Ambition, the dominant force that drives most major politicians, is a neutral quality that leads them to seek out the path to success. Properly channeled it can divert politicians from destructive behavior and lead them to act for the public good, even to take risks and incur momentary displeasure for the sake of long-term glory. Hamilton's understanding of virtue admits and allows for the desire for reward: it can best be described as conduct on behalf of the public, even if that conduct is undertaken for self-interested reasons. The office of the presidency was designed by the Founders to attract persons of the highest ambition or virtue, and the selection system was meant to point their ambition in the proper direction.

MARTIN VAN BUREN

Martin Van Buren began his national political career as a senator from New York in 1821, during the Era of Good Feelings. Competition between parties had ceased at the national level, and the dominant opinion in Washington was hostile to any manifestations of partisanship. President Monroe called parties the "curse of the country" and his successor, John Quincy Adams, pledged to "break up the [last] remnant of party distinction."[18] Van Buren quickly became the leading opponent of this view, calling immediately on his arrival at the capitol for a "resuscitation of the old Democratic Party" and later, after the election of 1824, for a renewal of two-party competition.[19] To promote his unorthodox position, Van Buren first had to convince others that permanent party competition was not the evil that most believed, but a positive constitutional doctrine that would promote the well being of the regime. Beyond this, he had to show the way to an actual partisan division in the nation, a step he undertook by re-establishing the Democratic party and forcing its opponents to organize in response. Van Buren was thus acting at one level as a disinterested legislator and at another as a committed partisan. Despite the appearance of a tension between these two postures, they were in fact perfect complements for effecting the same goal: the doctrine of party competition was necessary to justify a partisan stance, and a partisan stance was necessary to create party competition.

Van Buren's justification for the doctrine of permanent party competition is very different from the kind of defense one is likely to hear today. Van Buren developed his case for parties in response to an impending crisis in the presidential selection process. His objectives were to ensure the legitimacy of the choice of the president by keeping the election from the House of Representatives and to prevent a dangerous politics of personal factionalism caused by non-partisan competition. These objectives are a far cry from the abstract defense of competition of the modern responsible party government school in which the need for parties is adduced from a general theory of democracy. In contrast, Van Buren begins from the particular and subordinates the question of party competition to the concrete problems of presidential selection. Yet before one dismisses Van Buren's views as mundane and untheoretical, one would have to ask whether the current thinking about party competition has not overlooked an important aspect of the entire question by divorcing the study of parties from the issues of candidate selection.

To understand the difficulties connected with the House election plan, a word must be said about the development of this part of the selection system. The advocates of a strong, independent executive at the Constitutional Convention fought the idea of selection by Congress on the grounds that it would make the president, in Morris's words, "the tool of a faction of some leading demagogue in the Legislature."[20] They won their main point with the adoption of the system of electors, but an auxiliary election by the House, voting by states, was also included for the purpose of breaking a tie or making the choice where no candidate received the required minimum of electoral votes. Madison strongly opposed this plan, fearing that the undemocratic method of voting by states would conflict with the people's understanding of republican legitimacy. Moreover by the end of the convention, he began to have doubts, along with Hamilton, about the existence of a steady supply of candidates with continental reputations.[21] Thus while the authors of *The Federalist* were on record as opposing regular selection by the House, they were in fact worried that their plan might produce this very result.

The likelihood of an election by the House increased with the adoption of the Twelfth Amendment in 1804. Designed to eliminate intrigue between the electors of the defeated party and the vice-presidential candidate of the victorious party, the amendment also made it less likely that a final decision could be made at the electoral stage by reducing the number of presidential votes of each elector from two to one while maintaining the same requirement for election. As long as the Republican party continued to coalesce behind one candidate, the tendency of the new amendment was obscured. But with the collapse of the Republican caucus in 1824, it became evident that under nonpartisan competition a House election would be the normal result. The outcome of the election of 1824 demonstrated this at the same time that it confirmed some of the worst fears about the House system—its tendency to promote confusion and intrigue and its inability to gain full public confidence.

Van Buren and his followers argued that party competition could ensure that the election was determined at the electoral stage by providing the candidates with broad national followings. If there were no continental figures in the nation, the reputations of the parties would take their place; if there were too many continental figures, the parties would limit the field. Party competition thus offered an institutional solution to a problem that the Founders had relied on chance to resolve.

The defense of parties on this ground became a major issue in the election campaign of 1836. The Whigs, hoping to defeat the Democrats by winning a different candidate in each section of the country, launched an attack against the legitimacy of partisan activity. This attack was answered by the Democratic campaign committee, which reflected the views of its candidate, Martin Van Buren. "Is it not a thousand times better," the committee asked, "that the evils of a [party] convention . . . should be borne than that we should be exposed to the calamities of an election by the House?" The committee went on to argue that since no constitutional amendment could be agreed upon, party competition thus offered the only existing means to overcome the contradiction between the Founders' intention to keep the election from the House and the actual tendency of the existing electoral process.[22]

Van Buren's second defense of party competition was that it was the best device under existing circumstances for controlling presidential ambition. In proposing party competition to solve a problem at the Founders had wanted to solve by nonpartisanship, Van Buren was not necessarily challenging the Founders' plan, for nonpartisan competition in the 1820s bore little resemblance to what the Founders had envisioned. Direct popular appeals by the candidates had become an accepted element of the campaign, a change that resulted from the precedent of the election of 1800 and from the transformation of the elector from a discretionary trustee to a bound agent. Given this new circumstance, a different solution to the problem of controlling the popular arts was required. If popular leadership was now legitimate, the challenge was somehow to distinguish its healthy from its unhealthy expressions and to devise some institutional means to admit the former and exclude the latter.

Nonpartisan competition, according to Van Buren, was no longer an answer to this problem. On the contrary, it was the very cause of personal factionalism and dangerous leadership appeals. It allowed a large number of candidates to enter the contest without doing anything to channel the direction of their ambition. In his analysis of the presidential campaign of 1824, Van Buren charged that the contenders treated questions of public policy as mere "shuttle-cocks." Issues were seized by the candidates long before the election year and kept "unsettled . . . as it was expedient to presidential aspirants that they should be."[23] The length of the campaign had no limitation, with the consequence that politics continually interfered with governing. Van Buren summed up his views of the effects of nonpartisan competition as follows:

> In the place of two great parties arrayed against each other in a fair and open contest for the establishment of principles in the administration of government [there were] personal factions . . . having few higher motives for the selection of their candidates or stronger incentives to action than individual preference or antipathies. . . . [These] moved the bitter waters of political agitation to their lowest depths.[24]

Van Buren presented his case against nonpartisanship to a large number of his contemporaries, including the influential Thomas Ritchie, editor of the *Virginia Enquirer*. In a letter to Ritchie in 1827, Van Buren identified the two leadership styles he feared from a nonpartisan campaign: a personalistic image appeal devoid of all principle—he had Jackson specifically in mind—and demagogic issue arousal, particularly as it might play on sectional prejudices. Ritchie had already become an adherent of Van Buren's pro-partisan ideas and had argued the case for restraint on political ambition in a series of editorials in 1824: "Ambitious struggles for power, with the bitter uncontrollable passions which they inevitably engender, are the most formidable evils which threaten free governments." Ritchie hoped he would never see "the spectacle of five or six candidates for the Presidency . . . traveling through the country, courting support . . . and assiduously practicing all the low arts of popularity."[25]

According to Van Buren and Ritchie, party competition would prevent candidates from devising their own appeals and compel them to adhere to the safer principles on which they planned to establish the major parties. The character of leadership appeals would be controlled by institutions rather than left subject to accident and personal candidate strategies. Nominations would be made by party leaders knowledgeable about national politics and in a position to deliberate about which candidate could best maintain a delicately balanced party coalition. Issue appeals in the name of one or another of the parties would be admitted, but appeals independent of parties would be discouraged. The system would remain formally open to challenges by new parties, as two-party competition was a doctrine founded on opinion, not law. But the bias of the electoral process was against openness in the modern sense of eliminating all institutional controls designed to discourage certain kinds of appeals. It was the task of those founding the new parties to establish their credibility and enlist public support behind them on a long-term basis. Party in this respect would be made "prior" to political leadership. Leadership would not formulate new principles or create new electoral alignments but articulate the established principles and maintain existing coalitions. If this implied a loss in the dynamic character of leadership, it also promised a greater degree of safety and moderation.

Having made the theoretical case for renewed party competition, Van Buren turned to his partisan task of creating the Democratic party. Although one should not doubt the sincerity of his frequently expressed commitment to "old republican" principles, there was nevertheless a strong element of pragmatism in his search for a partisan division. To Ritchie he wrote, "It would take longer than our lives (even if this were practicable) to create new party feelings to keep these masses together."[26] The old electoral divisions would do, and Van Buren found in John Quincy Adams' program for national improvements the perfect opportunity for rallying the old forces together against the neo-Federalism of the Administration. Van Buren sought to show his fellow partisans that the same doctrine of party competition that promoted the general good also contributed to the advantage of their own party. Disguised Federalists would be denied the luxury of being considered safe Republicans. Moreover, nonpartisan politics, though appearing fair on the surface, in fact benefited those elements in society which could more easily concert their activities without parties—the same criticism one often hears today against primaries and nonpartisan elections. Van Buren argued that it was the wealthy who derived the advantage from nonpartisan politics. The people, being easily divided, needed a recognizable label and a trusted organization around which to rally.[27]

While Van Buren wanted to retain the same basic electoral alignment that existed under the first party division, he sought to establish a different kind of partisanship. The contest over first principles of the regime would be replaced by a more moderate division over the scope of federal power. Parties dividing on this question could exist together without each feeling the need to destroy a seditious rival. To go along with this more restrained partisanship, Van Buren proposed a new ethic of tolerance. The original partisans, Jefferson once wrote, "cross the streets and turn their heads the other way, lest they should be obliged to touch their hats."[28] Van Buren offered a different model. He proclaimed his pride in not being "rancorous in my party prejudices" and in maintaining friendly personal relations with many political opponents.[29]

From Van Buren's argument about the need for party principles, one might conclude that he favored what some scholars refer to as "Burkean" parties, i.e., parties that are divided by significant differences of principle but which nevertheless share a commitment to the existing political system. But Van Buren's parties were criticized at the time as they would be again at the turn of the century—for avoiding real divisions and for promoting the self-interest of their job-seeking members. There was some basis for this criticism. Van Buren acknowledged that the principles of the parties would be very general, in part so that each party could accommodate a broad coalition of interests. Moreover, Van Buren recognized the need for patronage, no doubt in the belief that with a partisan division based on secondary issues, it was necessary, in order to sustain party organizations, to supplement the motivation of purpose with that of interest. His position seemed to be that pure Burkean parties are not viable as mass electoral institutions: the real choice is between dangerous parties of first principles and those that blend principle and interest. Although the modern "amateur" conception of party finds the slightest touch of interest unacceptable, it remains an unanswered question whether an ideal equilibrium point can be found and maintained at which the division over principle is sufficiently serious to sustain partisan organizations yet not so great as to threaten the underlying consensus in the regime.

While there is much in Van Buren's plan for party competition that is consistent with the views of the Founders, it nonetheless served to modify the regime in some very important ways. First, party competition recognized and institutionalized a more active role for the voice of the majority in determining national policy. Elections were no longer understood merely as a way of elevating a worthy individual; they were also contests between competing groups in which the victorious party could claim authority for carrying out its program.

Second, party competition implied a different conception of executive leadership. The Founders had wanted illustrious "continental figures" whose freedom from control by any electoral group would enable them to stand above the conflict of factions. By recognizing the need for parties of a broad coalitional character under an umbrella of general principle, Van Buren was required to accept a less elevated kind of leadership. His model was what we might call the "politician," one skilled at brokering among various groups. Executive leadership would have to be partisan in character, although the broad principles on which the parties stood would still leave room for considerable discretion. Many have seen a connection between Van Buren's concept of parties and the so-called "Madisonian system" of the Founders, for in both one finds encouragement for the formation of coalitional majorities. But it is also important to observe the differences. Madison intended the system of competing factions and coalitions to take place in the House and to be balanced by an executive standing above factions. Van Buren, on the other hand, extended the influence of the "Madisonian system" to the executive by introducing a coalitional concept of leadership into the choice of the president.

Finally, in emphasizing the restraint of ambition, Van Buren, in contrast to the Founders, may not have given sufficient scope to it. One finds a continual concern in Van Buren's thought with preventing the potential abuse of power, but little appreciation of its positive uses. It was the absence of a doctrine of the positive executive power, much more than the self-interested character of the parties, that troubled Woodrow Wilson.

WOODROW WILSON

The Progressives inaugurated the modern idea of presidential selection—a plebiscitary nomination race in which the candidates build their own constituencies within the electorate and in which the victorious candidate "captures" his party label. Along with this idea came a rejection of the view that the electoral process should control presidential ambition. The new purpose of the selection process was to build a base of popular support for the victorious candidate and help establish the concept of leadership as the central feature of the regime.

The Progressives are perhaps best remembered for their efforts to rid the political process of rampant self-interest. The plebiscitary selection process can in this respect be seen as a device to work around the corrupt party organizations and restore a measure of principle to political life. But one underestimates the full scope of the change sought by many Progressives if only these "negative" objectives are cited. A number of Progressive spokesmen articulated a new conception of how to attain the public good that rejected entirely the pluralist concept of adding together various interests to make a coalitional majority. The public good, in the view of these Progressives, could only be known directly and as a whole. The connection between this conception of politics and the new institutional roles for the presidency and presidential selection is most clearly formulated in the thought of Woodrow Wilson.

Wilson began with nothing less than a full-scale attack on the old basis of constitutional government. The public good, in his view, could not be realized through the operation of formal institutions working within the confines of legally delegated and separated powers. It had to be forged in a "life" relationship between a leader and the people. The task for what Wilson called a "pop-

ular leader" or a "popular statesman" was to overcome the inertia of institutional rule and "interpret" for the people the truly progressive principles of the
era.[30]

The most striking aspect of this concept of leadership is its informal or
noninstitutional character. Wilson called for the rule of those who would lead
"not by reason of legal authority, but by reason of their contact and amend-
ability to public opinion."[31] In justifying a much greater role for the presidency,
which was to be the source of leadership, Wilson claimed that the "greatest
power lies with that part of the government that is in most direct communication with the nation."[32] This kind of sanction for popular leadership contrasts
directly with the Founders' idea of executive authority. Wilson argued that this
new basis for the presidency was necessary in order to reestablish the possibility of presidential statesmanship, an objective for which be claimed the sanction of Alexander Hamilton.[33] But while Wilson sought to give great scope to
executive power—more, in many respects, than Hamilton might have counte-
nanced—he did so by draining the office of its formal constitutional authority
and by transforming the premise of statesmanship from one that was understood to require a substantial degree of freedom from public opinion to one
that operated entirely on the plane of public opinion. The seemingly contra-
dictory criticisms of the presidency that one finds in contemporary political
science—that the executive is an "imperial" institution, and that it is too closely
constrained by public opinion[34]—are understandable in light of the Wilsonian
underpinning of the modern executive: popular support, which is claimed as
the active source of presidential authority, is also the very factor that limits the
president's discretion.

With this understanding of leadership it is clear why Wilson objected to the
nineteenth-century view of the role of political parties. For Van Buren party
was designed to tie down leadership and restrict its appeals. Wilson, however,
wanted to encourage leaders to introduce new programs and ideas and to develop new electoral bases to support them. His plan for presidential selection,
which he outlined before the Congress in 1913, was to hold national party primaries, with the party conventions to meet after the nominees had been chosen. This plan was plainly designed to give the widest latitude to popular
leadership and to encourage constant "growth" or change in American politics.

Although Wilson is known today as the father of the party government
school in America, it is necessary to understand that he conceived of party in
an entirely different sense than Van Buren. A party is a body of people that
forms around and serves a particular leader. "No leaders, no principles; no
principles, no parties."[35] But as Herbert Croly pointed out, the concepts of
party and leadership are in tension, and it was only by means of rhetorical leg-
erdemain that Wilson could keep the two together.[36] Wilson makes parties ap-

pear and be strong when they can assist the leader but transforms them into empty shells where they might restrict the leader's freedom. One finds the same confusion in many treatments of party today—an insistence on the one hand on strong parties, yet an unwillingness on the other to interfere with the right of each aspirant to go to the people with his own program and appeal.

The transformation Wilson sought can best be understood by contrasting two different proposed methods for effecting major change in American politics. One is to set forth the new program and win the political power to enact it. This may be done by an extraordinary kind of leadership that brings into being a new party or reconstitutes an existing one. The other method, proposed among others by the party government school, is to change the constitutional system. Here the problem is said to be the way in which power is distributed under the Constitution. Particular political crises are but recurring manifestations of the same underlying structural inadequacy and cannot be solved until the institutional arrangement of power is altered. Wilson defined the existing problem of American politics in the latter sense, contending that the root of the national crisis was "leaderless government."[37] Wilson's objective, at least while a scholar, was not to delineate the principles of a new partisan division—indeed he was always vague about what programs the parties should adopt—but to alter the traditional relationship between party and leader in order to institutionalize dynamic leadership.

Every regime, it is clear, needs to be "renewed" at moments of crisis by extraordinary acts of political leadership. Given this fact, it might be said that the constraints that the Founders and Van Buren imposed on leadership were too severe. Yet one must bear in mind that they were speaking at the level of analysis of institutional structures, and institutions operating "as usual" may not be able to meet every situation or challenge. Seen from this perspective, they might not have wanted to prevent absolutely a recourse to popular leadership, but only to erect a bias against it, such that it would have to "prove" itself in the face of institutional deterrents. A bias of this kind would normally prevent the dangers of popular leadership yet still not prevent change and renewal when needed. Wilson took the opposite view and argued that a bias in favor of change in the electoral process was desirable and that under such a system leaders of high quality would continually emerge. Whereas Madison cautioned that statesmen could not always be at the helm, Wilson seemed to be devising a system in which they had to be, in which the people would constantly look for political and even moral regeneration from a dynamic leader who spoke to the conscience of the nation.

A fundamental question is whether in opening the selection system to continual change Wilson did not also open it to dangerous or demeaning leadership appeals. Wilson himself was aware that his concept of leadership was not easy to separate from demagoguery. Both were popular, both rested on awakening the people's feeling and building new issue constituencies, and both implied a concentration of power in the hands of the leader. How then might one distinguish between them? Wilson answered as follows:

> This function of interpretation, this careful exclusion of individual origination it is that makes it difficult for the impatient original mind to distinguish the popular statesman from the demagogue. The demagogue sees and seeks self-interest in an acquiescent reading of that part of the public thought upon which he depends for votes; the statesman, also reading the common inclination, also, when he reads aright, obtains the votes that keep him in power. But if you will justly observe the two, you will find the one trimming to the inclinations of the moment, the other obedient to the permanent purposes of the public mind. . . . The one ministers to himself, the other to the race.[38]

Wilson's reliance on the nature of the issue to distinguish between the two kinds of leaders is, to say the least, vague; and his reference to intent can hardly suffice as a practical means of identification. The earlier theorists sought to identify dangerous leadership by a clear external criterion, even if that criterion was only an approximation of the leadership they sought to prevent. For the Founders, it had been popular leadership, for Van Buren, personal leadership independent of a party. Only after such a visible standard had been devised could one begin to inculcate an effective norm against demagoguery and build institutional barriers against it.

MODERN REFORM

The Progressives' call for a plebiscitary selection system met with only partial success. The movement for universal state primaries got off to a promising start between 1911 and 1916, but then stalled with the decline of the Progressive movement after the First World War. In some states primary laws were repealed, while in others the party organizations were able to reassert control over the primary process. What resulted was a "mixed" system that contained elements deriving from the conflicting theories of Martin Van Buren and the Progressives. For the defenders of this system, each of these elements was seen as imposing a check on the potential excesses of its rival. The representation of the party organization served to thwart a demagogue, while the primaries enabled a popular candidate to challenge the insularity of the power brokers.[39] The new process was something less, however, than a system in the full sense of the word. Its two constituent elements continued to be reflected in two alternative nomination campaigns—the inside strategy of negotiation with party leaders and the outside strategy of direct appeals to the people. To the extent that the system gave rise to its own distinctive method of presidential solicitation, it was through a blending of these two strategies into what Hugh Heclo called an "entrepreneurial" leadership style.[40]

Even before the recent reform movement, a slight shift had begun occur in the direction of a greater reliance on the outside strategy. But it was the reforms, and in particular the increase in primaries which they prompted, that decisively established the plebiscitary character of the current system. Though the intention of the reformers on the question of increasing the number of primaries remains a matter of dispute, there can be no doubt that their rhetoric encouraged this development. One can see this most clearly in the report of the Democratic party's first reform commission, chaired by Governor Hughes. After accepting a widely held view of the late sixties that a movement politics of "issue-oriented individuals" had permanently replaced a politics based on organized groups, the Hughes commission went on to suggest that party organizations had lost all legitimacy: "whereas bargaining among representatives of party organizations once could be said to represent the interests and views of the mass constituency of the party, the decline of the interest groups behind the bosses had undercut that rationale." The only way in which the new kind of citizen could be represented in the selection process was through the direct expression of a national candidate preference, and ensuring that right became the chief objective of the reforms. History was claimed as an ally of this new principle: "A confluence of historical forces had made the 1968 Democratic National Convention an occasion of great moment in the inexorable movement of presidential politics in America toward direct democracy."[41]

The reform commissions rested their case on the grounds of reestablishing legitimacy. Without the reforms, it was said, not only the Democratic party but the two-party system itself would be threatened.[42] Yet one might well ask whether the reformers did not concede too much of the populist sentiments of the moment. Reforming the internal rules of a party is one thing; undermining the role of party organizations in the name of direct democracy is something quite different. The reliance on "closed" nominating procedures by parties in other democratic nations seems to belie the claim that direct democracy in candidate selection is a requisite of republican legitimacy. As long as the electoral system remains open, meaning that the right of new parties to challenge is not denied or impaired, it would seem that the legitimacy of the system could be defended. Under the modern reform impulse, however, a very different conception of legitimacy has been propagated. The idea of an "open" selection process for the two major parties has in some respects been offered not as a supplement to, but as a substitute for, the idea of an open electoral process.

Third parties have been linked by reformers with activity that is outside of the political system; and the recent campaign finance legislation, itself a product of a reform impulse, has placed a serious obstacle in the path of creating a new party.

If the plebiscitary system is not required to assure the legitimacy of the selection process, neither, it seems, can it be justified in terms of its effects on the other three functions of presidential selection. Promoting "good character," as we have seen, is a difficult function to assess, but there is no basis in theory and surely none in experience for concluding that a plebiscitary system guarantees candidates of greater competence or superior virtue. As regards the prevention of the harmful effects of the campaign, a number of serious problems have already become evident. By encouraging more candidates and an earlier start of the campaign, the new system introduces considerations of electoral politics into the process of governing at a much earlier date. Campaigns inevitably tend to drain normal legal authority and force an incumbent who is re-eligible to become absorbed, in Tocqueville's words, "in the task of defending himself [rather than] ruling in the interest of the state."[43] Moreover, the "openness" of the campaign to many contestants excites the ambitions of a large number of politicians and influences their conduct in the performance of their official duties. Observers of the Congress have already noted the effect of the new system in contributing to a decline of the Senate as a serious deliberative body. In accord with the need under the current system to build popular constituencies, senators having presidential aspirations have been more apt to emphasize "media coverage over legislative craftsmanship."[44]

Understanding how presidential aspirants now seek to build popular constituencies is one of the most important questions facing students of contemporary American politics. In seeking guidance on this question, some scholars have turned to V. O. Key's analysis of candidate-centered politics in the era of one-party dominance in the South. Key, like Van Buren, identified two basic forms of what we have called popular leadership: issue arousal and image appeals.[45] After the Democratic nomination race of 1972, it was widely believed that the issue-based campaign was the most likely result of the new system, with the attendant consequence of bitter factional rivalries within the parties.[46] The triumph of Jimmy Carter in 1976, however, has called this analysis at least partly into question and has indicated that "image" politics may also have a role to play in future politics, at least in quieter times. Carter's campaign, which deliberately played down hard issues and focused on moods and personality, was centrist in its ideological content and managed to hold the Democratic coalition together in a way that would have been the envy of any power-brokers. Yet there is no reason for believing that a system that replaces negotiation among party leaders with a popular election among a number of candidates will en-

courage moderate appeals or promote party consensus. Carter, it must be remembered, ran as an outsider attacking established institutions and traditional
party leaders. His unique accomplishment was to have been an insurgent of the
middle.[47]

The effect of the plebiscitary selection system on presidential leadership
and executive power is difficult to isolate, as so many other factors exert a si-
multaneous influence. But one should at least take seriously the charge that the
personalistic campaign tends to encourage executive "imperialism" by removing a former source of direct restraint on the president.[48] The checks on presidential power in the American system have traditionally been formal as well as
informal, deriving from the constitutional system of separated powers and
from the power brokers within the parties whose support was required by candidates and incumbent presidents seeking reelection. Under the present system, however, the successful candidate "owns" his party and need not answer to
specific persons who can hold him accountable. This ownership, it must be
added, has come at a high price, for the decline of parties has taken away from
the executive a valuable resource that could buy support from the public and
from members of Congress. The president now stands directly before the bar
of public opinion, and it therefore should not be surprising if presidents become more assertive in their claims to authority and more "popular" or demagogic in their methods of appeal, if only to compensate for their loss of
partisan support. In light of these difficulties, it may be asked whether we
should not reconsider the wisdom of the recent reforms, even if this implies re-
sisting "the inexorable movement . . . toward direct democracy."

PART II

Presidential Nominations of the Pre-Convention Era

Emmett H. Buell Jr.

B EFORE the appearance of national conventions in the 1830s, presidential nominations occurred in a variety of ways. Contrary to the Framers' intent, the party spirit figured importantly in the supposedly nonpartisan choice of presidential electors in 1789 and 1793, even though every single elector dutifully cast one of his two ballots for George Washington. As the runner-up in both contests, John Adams became the vice president. Two reasonably distinct and increasingly competitive parties had taken shape in Congress by 1796, when Adams sought to take Washington's place. Party competition obliged both parties to nominate candidates for president and vice president. The readings in this section focus on the original scheme of presidential selection set out by the Framers in 1787, the congressional caucus method of making party nominations for president that ended in 1824, and resort by local and state politicians to ad hoc endorsements of particular candidates even before the caucus collapsed.

THE FRAMERS' DESIGN

As William G. Mayer notes, the very first proposals to create a national executive raised more questions than they answered. The Virginia Resolutions hinted at a plural rather than a single executive, did not specify the length of the executive term, and did not say whether the executive(s) would be eligible to serve more such terms. On one point, however, the resolutions were quite clear. The national executive should be chosen by the national legislature. This initial offering underwent a massive transformation before the convention settled on a final plan only ten days before adjournment. A result of bargaining and compromise, this package provided for a single executive eligible to serve as many four-year terms as he could win, to be selected in a complex process that might end with a vote by the presidential electors of every state. In the event that a majority of electors failed to support one candidate, the House of Representatives would make the choice. Let us look more closely at what the original Constitution provided.

The second paragraph of Article II, Section 1, stipulated that "Each State shall appoint, in such Manner as the Legislature thereof may direct, a Number of Electors, equal to the whole number of Senators and Representatives to which the State may be entitled in the Congress; but no Senator or Representative, or Person holding an Office of Trust or Profit under the United States shall be appointed an Elector."[1] This language underscored the importance of states in what Madison called "the immediate election" of the president, while prescribing a "compound ratio" that regarded the states "partly as distinct and co-equal societies," reflecting representation in the Senate, and "partly as unequal members of the same society," reflecting representation in the House.[2]

The third paragraph of Section 1 stipulated: "The Electors shall meet in their respective States, and vote by Ballot for two Persons, of whom one at least shall not be an Inhabitant of the same state with themselves." With this provision, the Framers sought to prevent a cabal among the electors that might occur if all of the electors from all of the states assembled in one place to vote. Instead, the electors would vote in their respective state capitals, with each elector casting not one but two votes for president. Some electors might mark one of their ballots for local favorites, but a majority would probably cast at least one ballot for a candidate of continental reputation. After the vote, officials in each state were required to sign, seal, and deliver the results to the "Seat of the Government of the United States," where they would be opened and counted in a joint session of Congress presided over by the president of the Senate. The person winning a majority "of the Whole Number of Electors appointed" would be elected president; the runner-up in electoral votes would be elected vice president.

In the event that no candidate received a majority of electoral votes, or that two candidates received the same majority, the choice of president fell to the House of Representatives. The Constitution decreed that the House would choose one candidate from the "the five highest on the list" of electoral votes. Moreover, the vote would be taken not by individual representatives but by state delegation, with each delegation casting one vote regardless of the number of representatives comprising it. The quorum for this special procedure required that two-thirds of the delegations be present. This balloting "by States" would continue until a majority of delegations settled on a president. It was not inconceivable that the candidate who ran fifth in electoral votes could be elected with a majority of delegations that represented less than half of the nation's inhabitants.

Mayer notes that the initial version Article II proposed by the Committee of Eleven located the contingent election in the Senate. But this provision stirred up considerable opposition among Framers already worried about the Senate's power over executive appointments, treaties, and removal of impeached officials (including the president). The debate raged for the better part of two days before Roger Sherman of Connecticut moved that the contingent election be shifted to the House, where each state delegation would cast one vote. Easy passage of Sherman's compromise allowed swift resolution of the remaining issues pertaining to presidential selection, such as clarification of quorum requirements and voting majorities in the House contingent election.[3]

Some scholars have concluded that the Framers understood that the vote of the electors would become the functional equivalent of a nomination. Specifically, the House would choose among the top five candidates nominated by the electors. Max Farrand, for example, embraced this thesis when describing the Framers' reactions to the proposal for holding a contingent election in the Senate:

> And each elector was expected to vote independently according to his own best judgment. Under those circumstances, it was conceded that Washington would be chosen in the first election, but in subsequent elections it was expected that that the vote would be so scattered as not to give a majority to any one person. This would throw the election into the senate. In other words, and it was so explained again and again, and by such men as Madison, Sherman, King, and Gouverneur Morris, under this system the large states would nominate the candidates and the eventual election would be controlled by the small states. The convention acted on the assumption that this would happen in the great majority of cases.[4]

Similarly, according to Calvin C. Jillson, most of the Framers expected that the electoral vote would eventually nominate five finalists rather than elect a president. Anticipating that the Senate would decide such contests on a fairly frequent basis, delegates representing northern and small states at the Philadelphia convention coalesced to make sure that they would cast a majority of the votes.[5] Nor did perceptions change, according to Paul Schumaker, when the Convention transferred the contingent election from the Senate to the House: "In short, the founders expected that the Electoral College would nominate various candidates for the presidency to the House."[6]

Even if most Framers expected the electors only to nominate rather than make a final selection, they resolved to inoculate this initial process against the bacillus of party. But party spirit infected presidential politics all the same, even as it supplied the antidote to contingent elections. In addition to the emergence of competitive parties, the chances of a contingent election diminished with ratification of the Twelfth Amendment, popular election of presidential electors, and adoption of the unit rule by most states whereby all of a state's electoral votes went to the winner of the popular vote.

THE RISE OF COMPETITIVE PARTIES

Alexander Hamilton defended the Framers' plan in *Federalist* 68, where he assured readers that every practicable arrangement had been made to prevent "cabal, intrigue, and corruption" in the selection of a chief executive. Not only would presidential electors set aside partisan predilections when exercising their judgment, they would also assemble in their respective state capitals rather than all in one place.

Ironically, no person pursued partisan advantage more quickly or avidly than Hamilton himself. Mindful of Washington's refusal to accept the office unless he got the vote of every elector, Hamilton implored every elector to cast one of his votes for Washington. The general accordingly won election in 1789 by a unanimous vote. Hamilton also helped persuade some electors not to cast their second ballot for John Adams, even though Adams sought the vice presidency. Ostensibly, Hamilton waged this campaign to avoid a tie between Washington and Adams—a prudent precaution at a time when ballots made no distinction between presidential and vice-presidential choices. Yet it is also true that Hamilton despised Adams and took pleasure in his humiliation.[7] Adams won the vice presidency, but with less than a majority of electoral votes.

Hamilton was hardly alone in partisan efforts to manipulate the votes of electors. The seeds of Federalist-Republican rivalry had been sown during state debates over ratification of the Constitution in 1787–1788, and they sprouted in the presidential campaign of 1789. In Pennsylvania, where the voters elected presidential electors directly, Federalists endeavored to reduce the chances of an Antifederalist victory by uniting their popular support behind a single slate of electors. Federalist delegates from Philadelphia and eighteen counties accordingly met in Lancaster to nominate that slate, as well as to endorse candidates for the House of Representatives. Antifederalists convened in Harrisburg for the same purposes. In a classic case of fear arousal, Federalist newspapers published rumors that the Antifederalists meant to elect Patrick Henry and George Clinton.[8]

In a remarkably short time, then, two parties took shape, one led by Hamilton, now secretary of the treasury in Washington's administration, and the other by Secretary of State Jefferson and Congressman James Madison. For all of his admonitions against party spirit, Washington became the first Federalist president, siding with Hamilton on such key disputes as assumption of revolutionary war debts, establishment of a national bank, strict neutrality during a war between Britain and France, and approval of the Jay Treaty. Both sides forged party unity among their congressional supporters. Both relied extensively on committees of correspondence, pamphlets, and newspapers to make their case to the people, but Jefferson's Republican party proved far more adept at organizing a popular following.[9] Indeed, as early as 1791, Jefferson and Madison forged an alliance between Virginia planters and the professional politicians of New York. One indication of their success showed up in the 1792 election, when electors in several southern states cast their second ballot for George Clinton, New York's leading Antifederalist and Jefferson's ally.[10]

THE CONGRESSIONAL CAUCUS

Although the etymology of the congressional caucus is uncertain, caucuses (relatively small groups meeting in private) had been used to slate candidates for local office since colonial times. As William G. Morgan observes, newly formed parties needed a method of making presidential nominations, and since a substantial number of elites in both parties held positions in the new government, the ease of communication and assembly in one place overcame reservations about possible violation of the separation of powers.

Ostensibly, the congressional caucus procedure was simplicity itself. James Sterling Young summarizes its workings up to 1812:

> In effect a nominating convention, the caucus was a group of legislators, more or less united behind one presidential and vice-presidential aspirant, organized for the principal purpose of capturing the Presidency, by legitimating and promoting their candidacies. After agreeing upon a slate, the participants customarily made their recommendations public in a formal circular drawn up and signed in "their individual characters as citizens." A committee of correspondence, composed ordinarily of one legislator from each state represented in the caucus, was designated to communicate the caucus recommendations to the various states, their duties presumably including the job of rounding up support for their slate in their respective constituencies and state legislatures.[11]

Like every subsequent method of making party nominations, the congressional caucus had to contend with party splits. This problem afflicted the Federalists in 1800 no less than the Republicans after 1804. The Federalist caucus humiliated President Adams by refusing to stipulate that he was the presidential choice rather than his ostensible running mate, Charles Cotesworth Pinckney. This snub signaled a plot by Hamilton and his southern allies to garner more electoral votes for Pinckney than for Adams, so that Pinckney would win the presidency while consigning Adams once again to the vice presidency. Upon learning of these machinations, Adams excoriated Hamilton as an unprincipled "bastard" and "intriguant."[12]

Some important particulars have been lost to history. When, for example, did the first congressional caucus take place? In 1796, as Morgan relates, it is not clear whether one or both parties formally caucused, although it is hard to imagine notables in both parties not meeting informally. James C. Chase maintains that Jefferson had received the undivided support of his party *before* the caucus existed.[13] Other scholars have written that Jefferson received some sort of nomination in 1796. It seems likely that a caucus of *senators* did meet to fill out the ticket already headed by Jefferson but could not break a deadlock between supporters of Aaron Burr of New York and Pierce Butler of South Carolina.[14] As best can be determined, the Federalists held only one congressional caucus, a divisive affair in 1800, before resorting to an early version of a national convention. Jefferson's party used the caucus method of making presidential nominations for nearly a quarter century.

Disputes over who had the authority to summon the members also roiled caucus proceedings. The 1804 caucus met publicly, adopted formal rules of procedure, and elected a chairman. Still, on whose authority it was summoned remains unknown. When the chairman of the 1804 caucus, Sen. Stephen R. Bradley of Vermont, took it upon himself to call the next one, seventeen congressmen challenged his authority to do so. This flap had more to do with opposition to Madison than anger over Bradley's presumption. In any case, no one signed the call for the first of two caucuses in 1812. The inability to resolve so simple and yet so basic an issue spoke volumes about the institutional weakness of the caucus:

> No one thought in terms of continuing party organization. The committee of correspondence was for the campaign only, and even it was abandoned in 1812. Investing the chairman of the previous caucus with the status of a national committee was obviously unsatisfactory since there would always be a fair chance that he would not be around four years later, but at least it had been a start towards a solution. Seemingly the caucus was simply not worth working out procedures for.[15]

Similarly, the scheduling of caucus meetings followed no apparent logic, with some held as early as January and others as late as June. Proxy voting was allowed in 1808 and discontinued in 1812. In short, the process of institutionalization by which a primitive organization becomes more complex through a division of labor, fixed rules, and universal norms did not get very far in the case of the congressional caucus.

The actual number of members participating in congressional caucuses is unclear. Records are incomplete and often inconsistent. Morgan and Chase report a turnout of ninety-four members for the 1808 caucus, whereas Richard P. McCormick puts the number at "about eighty-nine."[16] Reportedly, eighty-three members of Congress showed up in the 1812 caucus that renominated Madison. Fifty-eight are said to have turned out for the first of two caucuses in 1816, 119 for the second. The 1820 caucus drew so few participants that it adjourned without making a nomination. Reports of an exceptionally low turnout for 1820 must be weighed against Wilfred E. Binkley's claim that all members of Congress were invited to participate in the caucus, regardless of party.[17] All accounts agree that only sixty-six members of Congress took part in the final caucus of 1824.[18]

Adoption of the Twelfth Amendment also helped depress caucus turnout after 1804 by immediately diminishing interest in the vice-presidential nomination. Dictated by the Republicans' concern never again to risk a deadlock like that of 1800, this amendment transformed the rules of presidential selection by stipulating separate votes for president and vice president. Future presidents and vice presidents almost certainly would be of the same party. Before its adoption, the Federalists could harbor hopes of garnering enough electoral votes to make one of their own vice president, or, at the very least, to determine the order of election for Republican candidates. Now their only alternative to being excluded from office in the executive branch was to win presidential elections, and that they could not do. As the realization of Federalist impotence set in, Republican members had even less reason to attend their caucus.[19]

Much of the poor attendance that undermined the legitimacy of caucuses after 1804 can be attributed to deliberate boycotting. "Every time the caucus met," Chase notes, "a considerable number of congressmen stayed away. Some of these frankly expressed their dislike of caucuses as improper assemblies, but most, one suspects, did not bother to go because their presence would not have affected the outcome." [20] Still others meant to cast doubt on the legitimacy of nominations they could not defeat. Owing to the absence of Monroe supporters, the 1808 caucus has been described as "less a party caucus than a mobilization of Madison's adherents."[21] Clear portents of disaster for the 1824 caucus showed up in two items printed the *National Intelligencer* of February 7. The first, signed by eleven supporters of William G. Crawford, summoned all 261 members to meet one week later for the purpose of making a presidential nomination. The second, signed by 24 congressmen representing Crawford's rivals, served notice that 181 members "deem[ed] it inexpedient, under existing circumstances, to meet in Caucus." [22] A rump caucus met anyway on February 14. Taunts, groans, and cries of "Adjourn! Adjourn!" cascaded from the gallery as each member announced his vote. Forty-eight of those present and voting hailed from only four states, while ten states had no representation whatever. Five others had only one representative each. The sixty-four votes counted for Crawford added up to most Pyrrhic of victories.[23] (It is unclear how many of the participants in this vote knew that Crawford had recently been incapacitated by a massive stroke.)

Seemingly, the constitutional objection to nomination by congressional caucus should have been greatest after the Federalist collapse ended the first era of party competition. Hezekiah Niles, one of the most prominent pundits of the day, appears to have been converted to this view after years of defending the caucus. The congressional caucus, he editorialized at this late date, possessed no constitutional power to "elect, or direct the election of, a president of the United States."[24]

The core of the constitutional argument against the caucus was that it made presidents subservient to Congress, and this clearly was not what the Framers had intended. Seemingly this threat should have loomed largest when a sitting president sought to be renominated. A president who had offended members of his own party in Congress might have to pay a heavy price for renomination. The humiliation of Adams in 1800 has already been mentioned, and while it is clear that his enemies exercised considerable power over the federalist caucus, constitutional scruples appear to have had little or no bearing on this unhappy affair. Three Republican presidents also pursued second terms during the caucus era: Jefferson in 1804, Madison in 1812, and Monroe in 1820. Unquestionably the head of his party, Jefferson encountered little difficulty in securing approval for another term; Monroe hardly needed caucus support in 1820. Only Madison's renomination appears to have aroused constitutional concerns when opponents accused him of selling out to Henry Clay's War Hawks in return for their votes in the caucus. Morgan notes the scarcity of evidence to support such a claim but does not dismiss it altogether.

In sum, the costs of caucus nomination eventually outweighed the benefits. Indeed, it never developed a way to make the outcome of a zero-sum game acceptable to the losers. By the time of its collapse, candidates unlikely to win its approval had already sought nomination from local and state assemblies, and by 1824 the caucus had become obsolete as well as irrelevant, plagued by absenteeism, factional strife, and questions about its constitutionality. Comprised of party elites who sometimes spoke for a minority of the party following, it exhibited a fatal incapacity to adapt to changing times, especially the growing pressure for more popular participation in presidential selection.

STATE NOMINATIONS

Even before the caucus's death rattle, presidential aspirants had cast about for an alternate means of obtaining presidential nominations. Monroe's disappointed supporters surveyed this ground as early as 1808. "Running for the presidency in the fluid environment of the 1820s," Merrill D. Peterson writes, "was largely a matter of arousing the zeal of political friends and opinion makes in key states, and through this network creating a favorable image of the candidate in the public mind."[25] All of Crawford's opponents in 1824 realized that he probably had a lock on the caucus and accordingly sought endorsements from supporters in important states to offset its nomination. Jackson accordingly launched his campaign two years early by eliciting a show of support from the Tennessee legislature. Lawmakers in Kentucky and Missouri soon responded by placing Henry Clay's name in contention. Maine and Massachusetts followed with endorsements of John Quincy Adams in January 1823. (John C. Calhoun also looked for endorsements from South Carolina and Pennsylvania but shifted his ambition to the vice presidency after suffering rebuffs in both states.) But this practical resolution of an immediate problem was not without limitations. In particular, it heightened attention to sectional differences, already a problem in a party that had become a congeries of factions.

Careful readers of the state resolutions will note their attempts to balance regional interests with professed intent to choose a man of national stature with a national vision. The Kentucky resolution bluntly asserted that it was high time to choose a westerner before extolling the exceptionally qualified Clay as second to none "in liberal and enlarged views of national policy." In their declaration of support for Adams, Massachusetts "republicans" acknowledged that a plethora of state nominations for different aspirants increased the risk of a House contingent election. (Ironically, this was precisely what happened after none of the 1824 candidates won an electoral majority.) Nonetheless, the Bay Staters put forth one of their own with the reminder that Massachusetts had stood behind three sons of Virginia: Jefferson, Madison, and Monroe. And, of course, Adams deserved consideration for his extraordinary record, exemplary character, and national vision. Hardly able to claim Jackson as a Pennsylvanian, the Philadelphians declaring for Old Hickory extolled him as a national hero and outstanding patriot, valorous in war and true to the Constitution.

In 1828, when Jackson unseated Adams, no method of making national party nominations for president remained. Accordingly, both Jackson and Adams sought endorsements from supporters in key states. When Jackson's party held the first Democratic convention in 1832, it met to nominate Martin Van Buren as Jackson's running mate. Jackson had already lined up endorsements from state legislatures. Very soon, however, supporters of different candidates and from different states would convene in one place. And they would bargain in ways impossible during the caucus era. The convention era had begun.

Evolution of the Presidential Selection Process During the Constitutional Convention

William G. Mayer

OF all the major issues that were discussed and debated at the Constitutional Convention, none proved as difficult to resolve as the question of how to choose the country's new chief executive.[1] To be sure, the debate over presidential selection was never as bitter and divisive as the dispute over how to apportion votes in the national legislature. No one threatened to walk out of the Convention or to seek assistance from some foreign government. But the controversy over legislative apportionment at least had the virtue of having two clearly defined alternatives with a clear set of interests behind them. What made the search for a presidential selection mechanism so frustrating was that most of the delegates seem to have been genuinely uncertain about what they wanted.

Part of the problem was simply that the Framers had so little previous experience in choosing an executive. By 1787, Americans had a remarkable amount of experience in electing legislatures, particularly by the standards of the late eighteenth century. Every colony except Georgia had been electing the lower house of its legislature for at least fifty years prior to the Revolution; the Constitution writers could also draw on what they knew (or thought they knew) about parliamentary elections in Britain. By contrast, up until 1776, almost all of the executives Americans were familiar with had acquired their powers either by inheritance (the British king) or by appointment (the colonial governors). In short, when the delegates to the Constitutional Convention gathered in Philadelphia they had, in general, only about ten years' experience in electing executives—and while that experience did have some influence on their deliberations, it was simply not enough to provide many clear or firm lessons.

This is not to say that the Framers were entirely devoid of ideas on the subject of executive selection. Most delegates had some relatively well-established opinions about what the selection process should promote or guard against. Unfortunately, none of the major alternatives seemed to meet all of these goals. "There are objections agst. every mode [of electing the president] that has been, or perhaps can be proposed," James Madison observed at one point. This subject, said James Wilson, "is in truth the most difficult of all on which we have had to decide." Indeed, he added that "he had never made up an opinion on it entirely to his own satisfaction."[2]

The story begins shortly after the Convention was called to order. After several days spent in examining credentials and formulating the rules of procedure, what Madison called the "main business" of the Convention began on May 29, 1787, with a lengthy speech by Gov. Edmund Randolph of Virginia. After describing the major defects of the Articles of Confederation and the dangers confronting the new nation, Randolph offered fifteen resolutions—referred to as the Virginia Resolutions—that were to serve as the takeoff point for almost all subsequent discussion. The seventh of these resolutions called for the creation of "a National Executive . . . to be chosen by the National Legislature for the term of _____ years . . . and to be ineligible a second time."[3] The next day, the Convention resolved itself into a "Committee of the Whole House" in order to debate, vote upon, and if necessary, amend the resolutions one by one.

The Committee of the Whole first took up the seventh resolution on June 1, and by the end of the next day had essentially ratified the Virginians' original proposal. The national executive would be chosen by the national legislature and would be ineligible for reelection; his term of office was set at seven years. Yet there were dissenting voices. James Wilson of Pennsylvania opened the debate by declaring that he "was for an election by the people," though he admitted that his proposal "might appear chimerical."[4] On June 2, he offered a compromise proposal, which called for dividing the states into districts, each of which would elect, by popular vote, a certain number of "Electors," who would then meet and elect the national executive. Wilson's plan was rejected by an 8–2 vote.[5] On June 9, Elbridge Gerry of Massachusetts threw another alternative into the mix, proposing that the "National Executive should be elected by the Executives of the States." This, too, was turned down, 9–0.

On June 20, having gone through the entire set of Virginia Resolutions as a Committee of the Whole, the delegates met as a formal convention in order to reconsider the committee's handiwork. Six days later, the Convention became embroiled in the celebrated controversy over the apportionment of seats within the national legislature, a debate that would occupy the Convention—and bring all other discussion to a standstill—for the next three weeks. Thus it was not until July 17 that the Convention finally got back to the subject of how to choose the national executive.

A number of delegates, it soon became apparent, were not satisfied with the selection mechanism the Convention had adopted back in early June, though at first the opposition seemed to be confined to a small, if quite vocal, minority. The first alternative considered by the Convention was a straightforward proposal to have the executive elected by "the Citizens of the United States." It was rejected, 9–1. Next up was a plan to have the executive "chosen by Electors to be appointed" by the state legislatures. This, too, was decisively voted down, 8–2. The Convention then went back to the original Virginia proposal, in which the executive would be chosen by the national legislature, and readopted it by a 10–0 vote.

Shortly thereafter, however, the proceedings took a new and unexpected turn. Acting on a motion by William Houstoun of Georgia, the Convention voted 6–4 to delete the clause making the national executive ineligible for a second term. This apparently prompted many delegates to rethink the entire subject. The very next day, July 18, the Convention voted 8–0 to reconsider the eligibility clause, and by July 19, the delegates had decided, in the words of the official journal, to "reconsider the several clauses . . . which respect the appointment, duration, and eligibility of the National Executive."[6]

Gouverneur Morris, one of the Convention's most zealous advocates of executive power, gave the first major speech following the vote to reconsider. In a lengthy and detailed address, he vigorously defended the need for a strong executive and argued that this officer should be made eligible to stand for reelection. Morris also spoke to a belief evidently shared by the other delegates that the independence and effectiveness of the executive would be fatally compromised if reeligibility were coupled with election by the legislature. In that event, the executive would continually court the legislature's favor in order to get reelected. Since there was strong support for making the executive eligible for reelection—a motion to restore the ineligibility provision was defeated 8–2—the delegates now took the logical next step and sought out a new way to elect the national executive. The proposal they fastened on was one that had been rejected just two days earlier: to have the executive "chosen by Electors appointed for that purpose by the legislatures of the states." This time, however, the elector system was adopted by a comfortable margin.[7]

For the next four days, it appeared that the elector proposal had firmly taken root. On July 20, the Convention adopted a formula for apportioning electors among the states, giving three electors each to Massachusetts, Pennsylvania, and Virginia, two electors to six other states, and one each to New Hampshire, Rhode Island, Delaware, and Georgia. On July 21, the delegates voted to pay the electors "out of the national Treasury for the devotion of their time to the public service." On July 23, however, two delegates, William Houstoun of Georgia and Richard Dobbs Spaight of North Carolina, moved that the whole subject once again be reconsidered. Their objection, as Madison recorded it in his journal, concerned "the extreme inconveniency and the considerable expense, of drawing together men from all the States for the simple purpose of electing the Chief Magistrate." As Houstoun further explained the next day, it was improbable "that capable men would undertake the service of Electors from the more distant States."[8] After a brief debate, the Convention finally voted once again to have the executive appointed by the national legislature.

Time and fatigue now started to affect the Convention's deliberations. The delegates' original plan of action called for the Convention as a whole to frame and vote on a series of resolutions that would outline the major features of the new government. These resolutions would then be turned over to a five-person Committee of Detail, which would transform them into a first draft of the actual Constitution while the other delegates enjoyed a week or two of respite from their labors. By July 24, the committee had been appointed and every significant feature of the new government had been at least preliminarily resolved—except for the question of how to select the national executive. From July 24 to 26, the delegates continued to debate the issue. The result was a number of thoughtful speeches on the general subject of executive selection, along with a series of increasingly inventive, if not bizarre, proposals for resolving the matter. Wilson of Pennsylvania at one point moved that the executive be elected by a "small number, not more than 15" members of the national legislature, who would be chosen by lot. Other delegates argued that the best way to guarantee the independence of an executive chosen by the legislature was to lengthen the executive's term of office to ten, fifteen, or even twenty years.[9] Finally, on July 26, the Convention came back to the system it had adopted in early June: an executive chosen by the national legislature, for a term of seven years, ineligible for a second term.

The Committee of Detail reported its finished product to the rest of the delegates on August 6. The Convention then began the task of debating and revising all twenty-three articles in this draft constitution. Not until August 24 did the delegates get to Article X, which contained the provisions dealing with presidential selection. (Among its other contributions, it was the Committee of Detail that first decided to call the new national executive the "President of the United States." The title appears nowhere in the Convention's deliberations up to that point.)

The debates of August 24 showed that the delegates had made little progress in resolving their difficulties. Once again, the Convention entertained and rejected a proposal to have the president popularly elected, along with a second motion to have the president "chosen by electors to be chosen by the People of the several States." In both cases, however, the opponents of legislative selection seemed to be gaining ground. The proposal for popularly chosen electors, in particular, was narrowly defeated, 6–5. Beyond that, the delegates made just two small changes to the committee's draft, specifying that the legislature would choose the president by *joint* ballot and requiring a president to win the support of a majority of the members present in order to be elected.

With many members anxious to wrap up their work and return home, on August 31 the Convention created another committee—referred to as the Committee of Eleven because it included one member from each state then in attendance—to deal with those parts of the Constitution that had been postponed or not acted upon. And it was this committee, reporting back to the full Convention on September 4, that was primarily responsible for devising the presidential election process finally adopted.

The system the committee settled on was, to say the least, highly complicated. The initial choice was to be made by a group of electors, to be appointed in whatever manner a state legislature might choose, with each elector casting a vote for two different persons. The electors would meet in their own states, thereby obviating the problem raised back in July by Houstoun and Spaight. If no candidate received a vote from a majority of the electors, the choice would then devolve upon the Senate, which would choose from among the top five finishers in the electors' balloting. (The Senate would also decide the issue if two or more candidates received a vote from a majority of the electors but were tied for the lead.) Finally, the person with the second largest number of votes would become vice president, an office that had never been mentioned at all during the Convention until it appeared in the committee's report.

Between September 4 and 6, the Convention tweaked and revised the committee's report in a number of small ways but made only one significant change. A considerable number of delegates objected to the fact that, if the electors failed to settle upon a candidate, the decision would be referred to the Senate, a body that had already been assigned an important role in making treaties and appointments. Hence, on September 6, the contingent election was transferred to the House of Representatives, with each state having one vote.

This issue aside, the new selection plan seems, after an initial period of skepticism, to have received widespread support. As Abraham Baldwin of Georgia remembered some years later, "The mode was perfectly novel, and therefore occasioned a pause; but when explained and fully considered was universally admired, and viewed as the most pleasing feature in the Constitution."[10] In particular, a motion to scrap the committee's plan and go back to legislative election was decisively defeated, 8–2. Most major provisions in the plan were approved on September 6 by substantial margins. The role of the vice president received some brief discussion on September 7, and then the delegates moved on to other topics.

The settlement of the presidential selection question was an important turning point in the evolution of the presidency. As the text of the Constitution stood in early September, many of what are today regarded as distinctively presidential powers—the power to negotiate treaties and to appoint judges and ambassadors—were actually entrusted to the Senate. It was only after the delegates had concluded that there was a viable way to choose the president that they were willing to transfer these responsibilities to the executive.[11]

AN ATHEORETICAL COMPROMISE?

What are we to make of this convoluted story—and of the even more convoluted plan the Convention finally adopted? What do they tell us about the Framers' intentions with regard to presidential selection? According to some observers, the answer is: not much. Perhaps the most influential statement of this position appears in a 1960 article by John Roche. For Roche, the complicated set of procedures set forth in Article II, Section 1, is best understood as a political compromise, not as an attempt to institutionalize a particular theory of presidential selection. As Roche puts it,

> The Brearley Committee on Postponed Matters [the Committee of Eleven] was a superb aggregation of talent and its compromise on the Executive was a masterpiece of political improvisation. . . . The vital aspect of the Electoral College was that it got the Convention over the hurdle and protected everybody's interests. The future was left to cope with the problem of what to do with this Rube Goldberg mechanism. In short, the Framers did not in their wisdom endow the United States with a College of Cardinals—the Electoral College was neither an exercise in applied Platonism nor an experiment in indirect government based on elitist distrust of the masses. It was merely a jerry-rigged improvisation which has subsequently been endowed with a high theoretical content.[12]

In my opinion, Roche's argument is greatly overstated. He is of course correct to claim that the presidential selection process finally incorporated in the Constitution was a compromise. But to say that a particular outcome is a compromise is very different from saying that it is meaningless or random. In fact, compromises are almost never random. Compromise becomes necessary when two or more sides to a dispute care enough about an issue to refuse to accept someone else's preferred solution. That sets definite limits on what will work as an acceptable compromise. For example, if an employer wants to pay his workers $5 an hour and the workers want $10 an hour, the standoff can be settled in various ways. Which solution is adopted depends on circumstances that are difficult to predict, but the most likely settlement will fall somewhere between $5 and $10.[13]

The claim that the Convention's compromise on presidential selection was meaningful is also supported by a second important point. While Roche is right when he credits the Committee of Eleven with political shrewdness, most of the major features in the final package they proposed were not of the Committee's invention. Actually, most of the key elements had already been debated and discussed by the full Convention over the preceding three months.

This is particularly true of the most distinctive feature of the presidential election process: its use of an intermediate body of presidential electors, later called the electoral college. Indirect election was a common way of filling top positions in government at the time the Constitution was written. In ten of the thirteen states, the chief executive—called governor in some states, president in others—was elected by the state legislature, which was, in turn, elected directly by the people. State legislatures also selected each state's representatives to the Confederation Congress and would soon be used to elect U.S. Senators. But state legislators performed a variety of other functions besides choosing governors and congressmen. What was distinctive about the electoral college was that its members were to be chosen for the *sole* purpose of selecting the president. Once they had performed that task, their job was finished.

The only apparent precedent for this sort of arrangement was the Maryland Senate. Under the constitution that Maryland had adopted in 1776, every five years the voters in each county elected two electors, who then met two weeks later in the state capitol to elect fifteen senators, nine from the western shore, six from the eastern.[14] To what extent the members of the Constitutional Convention had the Maryland example in mind when they adopted an elector-based system for choosing the president is unclear. There are scattered references to the Maryland Senate during the Constitutional Convention, clearly indicating that many delegates were aware of how that body functioned, but none occurred during the debates about presidential selection. So far as I can determine, the only contemporary account that draws an explicit link between the electoral college and the Maryland Senate is that of former governor James Bowdoin of Massachusetts, who told the state's ratifying convention, "This method of choosing [the executive] was probably taken from the manner of choosing senators under the constitution of Maryland."[15] But Bowdoin himself was not a delegate to the Constitutional Convention, and his claim that this is what had "probably" occurred suggests that he had no direct knowledge of what actually motivated the Convention.

Whatever the origin of the idea, it was definitely not newly hatched by the Committee of Eleven and then sprung on an unsuspecting convention, which then approved it with little time to think about it. To the contrary, the use of presidential electors had been discussed, off and on, for three months before the committee decided to make it the core of its presidential selection package. The idea of having the president chosen by a body of intermediate electors had first been proposed by James Wilson on June 2, just four days after Edmund Randolph opened the main business of the Convention. By mid-July, as we have seen, the use of presidential electors had clearly emerged as the major alternative to legislative election. On July 19, the Convention approved a proposal to have the president "chosen by Electors appointed for that purpose by the legislatures of the states"—though several days later it voted to reconsider that decision and return to a legislative selection process. On August 24, a motion providing for choice of electors "by the people of the several states" lost by only one vote. There was, then, nothing particularly innovative or creative about the Committee of Eleven's decision to refer the choice of president to a body of intermediate electors.

The same point can be made about several other key features of the final constitutional provisions concerning presidential election. The Convention considered two types of elector proposals between early June and early August: one in which voters directly chose the electors, and another in which state legislatures made the selection. The mechanism finally adopted by the Convention, in which states would appoint the electors "in such Manner as the Legislature thereof may direct," was an obvious way to split the difference. The dual vote plan, under which electors would cast two votes rather than one, had been suggested by several speakers on July 25.[16] The idea of having a contingent election in the legislature if a majority of the people or electors could not concur on a single candidate was advanced by James Wilson on July 17.[17] (It was also, of course, a sop to those who still thought that the legislature was the best place to select the president.)

WHAT THE FRAMERS INTENDED

Against that background, it is reasonable to ask whether most, if not all, the Framers of the Constitution subscribed to certain core concepts. As can best be determined from the record of Convention debates and deliberations, most delegates embraced four concepts. First, they wanted to preserve and enhance executive independence. Second, they feared the ill effects of cabal, intrigue, and corruption. Third, they shared a heightened concern for the interests of small states. And fourth, they entertained a cautious respect for popular participation. Agreement on these fundamentals helps to explain why the final compromise on presidential selection took the form it did.

EXECUTIVE INDEPENDENCE

If the Framers wanted anything out of the presidential selection process, it was to preserve, if not enhance, the independence of the executive. This theme came up repeatedly at the Convention and was expressed by speakers who otherwise disagreed about the best method of executive selection. I found only one delegate, Roger Sherman of Connecticut, who spoke in favor of executive dependence.[18]

This concern to uphold executive independence reflected a remarkably high level of agreement among opponents as well as supporters of the Constitution that the powers of government should be separated, not consolidated in the same hands. Separation of powers had become a key doctrine in Anglo-American political thought, and, as several contemporary scholars have argued, it is best thought of as a family of related theories in which opinions differ regarding the precise meaning of separation as well as why separation was desirable.[19] Yet few contested the basic point made most emphatically (and influentially) by Montesquieu: that separation of powers was essential to avoid tyranny and preserve liberty.[20] The Framers also recalled the common experience of state governments that had been established shortly after the Declaration of Independence. With few exceptions, the new state constitutions of these states had created very strong legislatures and very weak executives. In practice, moreover, their legislatures had eroded what little actual power executives had been granted. Often these legislatures acted in apparent violation of their constitutions.

When it came to creating the national executive, the delegates to the Constitutional Convention were determined to chart a different course. For this reason, above all others, the Convention finally decided not to have the executive chosen by the national legislature. Under such an arrangement, most delegates feared, the executive would be tempted to curry favor with the legislature by surrendering his constitutional powers. As James Madison put it, "If it be essential to the preservation of liberty that the Legisl: Execut: & Judiciary powers be separate, it is essential to a maintenance of the separation, that they should be independent of each other. The Executive could not be independent of the Legislature, if dependent on the pleasure of that branch for a reappointment." George Mason, who disagreed with Madison on many other issues, agreed on this point. Mason "opposed decidedly the making of the Executive the mere creature of the Legislature as a violation of the fundamental principle of good Government."

If so many delegates worried about maintaining the independence of the executive, why then, on three occasions, did they opt for selection by the legislature? For some, the answer lay in adding a clause that rendered the executive ineligible for reelection. With no prospect of another term, the executive would feel no temptation to give up his powers to the legislature. Accordingly, the Convention sooner or later supplemented every vote to vest the national legislature with executive power with a ban on reeligibility. Still, even delegates who went along with this coupling expressed misgivings about denying reeligibility. Some sought to resolve the tension by focusing on legislative selection, maintaining that it remained the best option even though "liable to objections." Others hoped that some practicable system could be devised that would provide for reeligibility as well as executive independence.

FEAR OF CABAL, INTRIGUE, AND CORRUPTION

At the heart of the revolutionary ideology, as Bernard Bailyn has shown, was a set of beliefs about power. Americans believed that the "ultimate explanation of every political controversy" came down to the "disposition of power." Power's most essential characteristic was aggressiveness. "The love of power," said theorist James Burgh, "is natural; it is insatiable; it is whetted, not cloyed, by possession." "Mankind in general" simply could not withstand its temptations. Such beliefs fed a general and deep-seated fear of conspiracies, for power assaulted liberty not directly or frontally but indirectly and subtly, whittling away the rights of the people while corrupting their morals.[21]

Eleven years after declaring independence, America's political leaders better appreciated the positive uses of power, as well as the dangers that arose when a regime lacked sufficient power to enforce its laws and treaties. Yet as the Convention debates, particularly those connected with executive selection, make clear, the fear of power that had helped spark the Revolution was still very much part of the new nation's ideology and political culture.

Repeatedly during the debates over executive selection, delegates attacked one proposal after another as unduly conducive to intrigue and corruption, while advocating others on grounds that they worked against such evils. The Framers not only feared domestic attempts to manipulate the process for some illicit purpose, they also worried about foreign efforts to corrupt the choice of a chief executive. Not generally given to flights of fancy, Madison warned that foreign attempts to influence the process were especially likely if the national legislature made the choice:

> The Ministers of foreign powers would have and make use of, the opportunity to mix their intrigues & influence with the Election. Limited as the powers of the Executive are, it will be an object of great moment with the great rival powers of Europe who have American possessions, to have at the head of our Governmt. a man attached to their respective politics & interests. No pains, nor perhaps expence, will be spared, to gain from the

Legislature an appointmt. favorable to their wishes. Germany & Poland are witnesses of this danger. In the former, the election of the Head of the Empire, till it became in a manner hereditary, interested all Europe, and was much influenced by foreign interference—In the latter, altho' the elective Magistrate has very little real power, his election has at all times produced the most eager interference of foreign princes, and has in fact at length slid entirely into foreign hands.[22]

The effect of such concerns can be seen in otherwise puzzling details included in the version of presidential selection finally agreed to by the Convention. For example, the Constitution explicitly forbids anyone "holding an Office of Trust or Profit" in the national government from serving as a presidential elector. With this provision, the Framers sought to prevent the president from packing the electoral college with his "pensioners" and "placemen."

In the same vein, Article II required electors to meet "in their respective States" rather than assemble as one body in the national capital. While this provision was probably included to satisfy concerns about the distances that some electors would have to travel if all assembled in one place, it had the additional appeal of erecting yet another barrier to corruption. Now the intriguing party would have to subvert thirteen assemblies of electors instead of one. Moreover, the Constitution required all electors to vote on the same day, so that early voting in some states would not influence electors in other states. This vote would be by written ballot rather than viva voce, the latter a common practice whereby voters openly declared their preferences in public.[23] By requiring ballots, the Framers hoped to make the vote a secret, thereby lessening the possibility that electors would seek favors from the president or that the president would reward electors who voted for him. It is also worth noting that while the Constitution required each state to list "the Persons voted for" as well as "the Number of Votes for each," it did not ask for the names or voting preferences of individual electors.

Though the national legislature was given a role in the election process if no candidate received a majority vote, the Constitution's authors added two provisions designed to make the contingency election safe from intrigue and corruption. The electoral vote tallies in each state were to be transmitted "sealed" to the seat of government; and if no candidate had a majority, the House was required to choose a president "immediately." The apparent assumption was that the voting within each state would not be known until the ballots were counted by the president of the Senate, so that no one would know whether a contingent election would be needed or who the five highest vote-getters would be. Since the House would then hold an immediate election, potential conspirators simply would not have time to implement their nefarious schemes.

However contrived and ineffective these provisions might appear to twenty-first-century eyes, they constituted the plan's principal selling points when the Committee of Eleven presented its plan on September 4. James Wilson, for example, called the plan "on the whole a valuable improvement [over legislative election]. It gets rid of one great evil, that of cabal & corruption." George Mason, who was at the opposite pole from Wilson on most matters involving presidential election, nevertheless "confessed that the plan of the Committee had removed some capital objections, particularly the danger of cabal and corruption."

CONCERN FOR THE INTERESTS OF SMALL STATES

Although the Framers took longer to settle on a scheme of presidential selection, they had an even more difficult time with the apportionment of representatives to the national legislature. Large states wanted both houses apportioned on the basis of population; small states wanted an equal voice in at least one house. The standoff brought the Convention to an impasse for three weeks and seemed for a time to threaten it with dissolution.

Once that issue had finally been settled, no one was in a mood to revisit it. So when the Convention took up the presidential selection process one day later, the delegates seem to have been especially anxious to accommodate small states' interests and concerns. Over the next two months, every new proposal for electing the national executive was evaluated, at least in part, on whether it gave small states an adequate voice in the process.

Again, numerous provisions in the final text of the Constitution clearly reflect this concern. Giving each state a number of electoral votes equal to the number of its senators and representatives in Congress meant that small states had a greater voice in presidential selection than they would have had under a purely popular vote system. This formula simply replicated the compromise over legislative apportionment.

In mid-July, when proposals for choosing the executive by popular vote first received extended discussion at the Convention, a principal objection made by small-state delegates was that election by the people would effectively guarantee that only residents of a few large states could become president, since most people would vote for a candidate from their own state, thus excluding small-state contenders. (Given the notorious parochialism of the time, and the absence of such nationalizing agencies as political parties, this was not an irrational fear.) On July 25, however, several delegates came up with an interesting solution: to have each person vote for two different candidates, at least one of whom could not be a resident of the voter's own state.[24] This proposal, originally made with respect to ordinary voters, was applied by the Committee of Eleven to presidential electors and thus incorporated into the Constitution.

The dual vote system did not entirely alleviate the fears of small-state delegates. The problem, as Madison noted, was that a voter might cast one meaningful vote for a resident of his own state, and then "throw away his second [vote] on some obscure Citizen of another state, in order to ensure the object of his first choice." The best way to prevent this, the Committee of Eleven decided, was to make the second vote meaningful: to have the presidential electors select two public officials instead of one. Before September 4, the vice presidency had never even been hinted at in the Convention's deliberations, and the office hardly seemed justified by the duties assigned to it. When the utility of the vice presidency was debated on September 7, Hugh Williamson, a member of the Committee of Eleven, was particularly blunt. "Such an officer as vice-President was not wanted," he declared. "He was introduced only for the sake of a valuable mode of election which required two to be chosen at the same time."

If no candidate received a majority of electoral votes, the final decision would be made by the legislature. But where in Congress to lodge this important responsibility? Originally, as we have seen, the choice was to have been made by the Senate. When a number of delegates felt that this entrusted too much power to a body that already had a somewhat aristocratic aura, the Convention amended the committee's proposal by transferring the final choice to the House of Representatives, with each state having one vote. In either case, the contingent election was conducted in a way that gave every state an equal vote; population was irrelevant.

When the decision did fall to the House of Representatives, it was to choose among the top five finishers in the electoral vote. This, too, was a concession to small states, one more way to give small-state residents a reasonable chance to be elected president. When an attempt was made to reduce the number of candidates in the contingent election from five to three, Roger Sherman of Connecticut, a vociferous defender of small-state interests, declared that he "would sooner give up the plan" than accept this change.

In normal circumstances, according to Article I, Section 5, a quorum in the House of Representatives was a majority of the members. When deciding contingent elections, however, a quorum was defined as "a Member or members from two thirds of the States," and the winning candidate had to receive "a majority of all the states." Both provisions were added to the committee's report in order to prevent a handful of large states from conducting the election by themselves. There is, by contrast, no provision in the Constitution requiring that any particular percentage of the total membership be present when the House is choosing the president. (A motion to add such a provision was rejected, 6–5.)

A CAUTIOUS RESPECT FOR POPULAR PARTICIPATION

A common criticism of the Constitution's provisions on presidential selection, particularly the electoral college, is that they meant to stifle democracy and protect the power and property of the upper class. Along with other academics of a progressive bent, J. Allen Smith and Charles Beard popularized this charge in the early 1900s. Smith laid out the basic case as follows:

> The desire of the [Constitutional] Convention to secure to the President and United States Senators more freedom from popular control than was enjoyed by the corresponding state officials is most clearly seen in the mode of election prescribed. . . . They provided that the President should be chosen by an electoral college, the members of which were not required to be elected by the people. This, it was thought, would guard against the choice of a mere popular favorite and ensure the election of a President acceptable to the conservative and well-to-do classes. It was taken for granted that the indirect method would enable the minority to control the choice.[25]

Like nearly every other charge in the Progressive School indictment, this one does not withstand close analysis. The Framers took a more complicated and nuanced view of popular participation than the likes of Smith and Beard allowed. True, some Framers complained about an "excess of democracy," but others exhibited just as much fervor when insisting that the new government build on a broad and popular foundation. The final structure of the Constitution embodied both elements, but this compromise did not simply split the difference. Throughout the Convention, the Framers attempted to view people as they are, not what they might become; they also endeavored not to be distracted by simple slogans or maxims.

Whatever else one might say about the Framers' president, he would sit as the head of a republican government, not as king. A few delegates expressed mild support for a limited monarchy, but most rejected the idea, however virtuous in theory, as unsuited to the peculiar genius of the American people. Perhaps the closest any delegate came to proposing a monarchy was Alexander Hamilton, in his famous speech of June 18, in which he recommended that the "supreme Executive authority of the United States" be vested in a "Governour," who would be elected by popularly chosen "Electors" to serve effectively for life (or during "good behaviour").[26] But Hamilton's proposal attracted almost no support, and when the delegates returned to William Paterson's New Jersey Plan on the following day, they proceeded as if Hamilton had never spoken. Perhaps realizing that he had gone too far, Hamilton soon left Philadelphia and absented himself from much of the remaining Convention.

The Framers did not agree on what role the people should play in electing a republican executive. Elbridge Gerry and George Mason were outspoken in opposing popular election. Mason offered a particularly blunt assessment, declaring, "It would be as unnatural to refer the choice of a proper character for chief Magistrate to the people, as it would, to refer a trial of colours to a blind man." Gerry expressed a similar view: "The people are uninformed, and would be misled by a few designing men." Although often quoted, these declarations probably did not represent the sentiment of most of the Framers. Indeed, I count only four delegates who expressly took this stand during the Convention, whereas six spoke positively about the public's capacity to choose the nation's chief executive.[27] Even though this tally consists only of delegates who spoke to the issue, it hardly suggests a Convention filled with raging antidemocrats.

How the typical delegate felt about these matters is better understood by looking at the vote on the issue. On the surface, the outcome of the vote supports the Progressives' criticism. On the two occasions when the question of popular election came up for a vote, it lost, 9–1 on July 17, and 9–2 on August 24.

Why was it defeated? The major objection was not that the public was unfit to take part in such an election or that it had no right to be involved, but that a popular election was simply impractical. Even the supporters of popular election sometimes conceded this point. Wilson, for example, was one of the two most fervent advocates of direct election in the entire Convention (the other was Gouverneur Morris). Yet when Wilson first introduced the idea on June 1, Madison quotes him as saying that "he was almost unwilling to declare the mode [of presidential election] which he wished to take place, being apprehensive that it might appear chimerical. He would say however at least that in theory he was for an election by the people."

Though Wilson did not say in that speech what exactly was "chimerical" about popular election, in subsequent discussion of the subject, two points were most often made. First, given the extent of the new nation, and the absence of a national communications network, most Americans were ill equipped to render judgments about political leaders from any state except their own. The problem was not an inherent lack of capacity, but a lack of information essential to the choice. This factor seems to explain much of Mason's opposition to a popular election system. Immediately after his celebrated comment likening the people's knowledge to a blind man's, Mason said, "The extent of the Country renders it impossible that the people can have the requisite capacity to judge of the respective pretensions of the Candidates."[28] Indeed, on June 1, Madison quotes Mason as saying that he favored the idea of having the people appoint the executive, but thought it impracticable."

Given this lack of information, and the general perception that most Americans had considerably stronger ties to their states than to their union, a popular election system had one other severe liability in many delegates' eyes: it would give a huge advantage to candidates from large states and make it all but impossible that a small-state candidate could ever get elected president. This was perhaps the single most common objection raised to having the people elect the president directly. The people, said Roger Sherman, "will generally vote for some man in their own State, and the largest State will have the best chance for the appointment." Hugh Williamson was more emphatic: "The people will be sure to vote for some man in their own State, and the largest State will be sure to succede." "The objection drawn from the different sizes of the States," Oliver Ellsworth insisted, "is unanswerable. The Citizens of the largest States would invariably prefer the Candidate within the State; and the largest States wd. invariably have the man." In short, the Convention's rejection of a popular election system was not necessarily an indication that they were uneasy or uncertain about democracy.

Perhaps the strongest argument against characterizing the Convention members as adamantly opposed to any popular role in the election of the president lies in the provision they finally adopted for choosing members of the electoral college. The elector-based proposals that were offered to the Convention between early June and late August were of two types: direct choice by the voters, or selection by state legislatures. If the Framers had been so concerned about insulating presidential elections from popular participation, they could have required that electors be chosen by the state legislatures, as they had already done for U.S. senators. In fact, they left it up to the voters. While not mandating that the electors be chosen by popular vote, they at least allowed the states that option, by saying that each state could appoint its electors "in such Manner as the Legislature thereof may direct." This, of course, was a compromise, but one not easily styled as either pro- or antidemocratic.

CHAPTER 2

Federalist 68: The Mode of Electing the President

Alexander Hamilton

To the People of New York: The mode of appointment of the chief magistrate of the United States is almost the only part of the system of any consequence, which has escaped without severe censure, or which has received the slightest mark of approbation from its opponents. The most plausible of these, who has appeared in print, has even deigned to admit that the election of the president is pretty well guarded. I venture somewhat further, and hesitate not to affirm that if the manner of it be not perfect, it is at least excellent. It unites in an eminent degree all the advantages the union of which was to be wished for.

It was desirable that the sense of the people should operate in the choice of the person to whom so important a trust was to be confided. This end will be answered by committing the right of making it, not to any pre-established body, but to men chosen by the people for the special purpose, and at the particular conjuncture.

It was equally desirable, that the immediate election should be made by men most capable of analyzing the qualities adapted to the station, and acting under circumstances favorable to deliberation, and to a judicious combination of all the reasons and inducements which were proper to govern their choice.

Alexander Hamilton served in the American army during the Revolution, participated in the Annapolis and Philadelphia conventions, coauthored *The Federalist* with James Madison and John Jay, became the new nation's first secretary of the treasury, and otherwise figured prominently in partisan politics of the early republic. His date of birth has never been precisely fixed, but he came to a relatively early end, killed in a duel by Vice President Aaron Burr in 1804.

A small number of persons, selected by their fellow-citizens from the general mass, will be most likely to possess the information and discernment requisite to such complicated investigations.

It was also peculiarly desirable to afford as little opportunity as possible to tumult and disorder. This evil was not least to be dreaded in the election of a magistrate, who was to have so important an agency in the administration of the government as the President of the United States. But the precautions which have been so happily concerted in the system under consideration, promise an effectual security against this mischief. The choice of *several*, to form an intermediate body of electors, will be much less apt to convulse the community with any extraordinary or violent movements, than the choice of *one* who was himself to be the final object of the public wishes. And as the electors, chosen in each state, are to assemble and vote in the state in which they are chosen, this detached and divided situation will expose them much less to heats and ferments, which might be communicated from them to the people, than if they were all to be convened at one time, in one place.

Nothing was more to be desired than that every practicable obstacle should be opposed to cabal, intrigue, and corruption. These most deadly adversaries of republican government might naturally have been expected to make their approaches from more than one quarter, but chiefly from the desire in foreign powers to gain an improper ascendant in our councils. How could they better gratify this, than by raising a creature of their own to the chief magistracy of the Union? But the convention have guarded against all danger of this sort, with the most provident and judicious attention. They have not made the appointment of the president to depend on any pre-existing bodies of men, who might be tampered with beforehand to prostitute their votes; but they have referred it in the first instance to an immediate act of the people of America, to be exerted in the choice of persons for the temporary and sole purpose of making the appointment. And they have excluded from eligibility to this trust, all those who from situation might be suspected of too great devotion to the president in office. No senator, representative, or other person holding a place of trust or profit under the United States, can be of the numbers of the electors. Thus without corrupting the body of the people, the immediate agents in the election will at least enter upon the task free from any sinister bias. Their transient existence, and their detached situation, already taken notice of, afford a satisfactory prospect of their continuing so, to the conclusion of it. The business of corruption, when it is to embrace so considerable a number of men, requires time as well as means. Nor would it be found easy suddenly to embark them, dispersed as they would be over thirteen States, in any combinations founded upon motives, which though they could not properly be denominated corrupt, might yet be of a nature to mislead them from their duty.

Another and no less important desideratum was, that the executive should be independent for his continuance in the office on all but the people themselves. He might otherwise be tempted to sacrifice his duty to his complaisance for those whose favor was necessary to the duration of his official consequence. This advantage will also be secured, by making his reflection to depend on a special body of representatives, deputed by the society for the single purpose of making the important choice.

All these advantages will happily combine in the plan devised by the convention; which is, that the people of each state shall choose a number of persons as electors, equal to the number of senators and representatives of such state in the national government, who shall assemble within the state, and vote for some fit person as president. Their votes, thus given, are to be transmitted to the seat of the national government, and the person who may happen to have a majority of the whole number of votes will be the president. But as a majority of the votes might not always happen to center in one man, and as it might be unsafe to permit less than a majority to be conclusive, it is provided that, in such a contingency, the House of Representatives shall select out of the candidates who shall have the five highest number of votes, the man who in their opinion may be best qualified for the office.

The process of election affords a moral certainty, that the office of president will never fall to the lot of any man who is not in an eminent degree endowed with the requisite qualifications. Talents for low intrigue, and the little arts of popularity, may alone suffice to elevate a man to the first honors in a single state; but it will require other talents, and a different kind of merit, to establish him in the esteem and confidence of the whole Union, or of so considerable a portion of it as would be necessary to make him a successful candidate for the distinguished office of President of the United States. It will not be too strong to say, that there will be a constant probability of seeing the station filled by characters preeminent for ability and virtue. And this will be thought no inconsiderable recommendation of the Constitution, by those who are able to estimate the share which the executive in every government must necessarily have in its good or ill administration. Though we cannot acquiesce in the political heresy of the poet who says: "For forms of government let fools contest—That which is best administered is best,"—yet we may safely pronounce, that the true test of a good government is its aptitude and tendency to produce a good administration.

The vice president is to be chosen in the same manner with the president; with this difference, that the Senate is to do, in respect to the former, what is to be done by the House of Representatives, in respect to the latter.

The appointment of an extraordinary person, as vice president, has been objected to as superfluous, if not mischievous. It has been alleged, that it would have been preferable to have authorized the Senate to elect out of their own body an officer answering that description. But two considerations seem to justify the ideas of the convention in this respect. One is, that to secure at all times the possibility of a definite resolution of the body, it is necessary that the president should have only a casting vote. And to take the senator of any state from his seat as senator, to place him in that of president of the Senate, would be to exchange, in regard to the state from which he came, a constant for a contingent vote. The other consideration is, that as the vice president may occasionally become a substitute for the president, in the supreme executive magistracy, all the reasons which recommend the mode of election prescribed for the one, apply with great if not with equal force to the manner of appointing the other. It is remarkable that in this, as in most other instances, the objection which is made would lie against the constitution of this state. We have a lieutenant governor, chosen by the people at large, who presides in the Senate, and is the constitutional substitute for the governor, in casualties similar to those which would authorize the vice president to exercise the authorities and discharge the duties of the president.

CHAPTER 3

The Origin and Development of the Congressional Caucus

William G. Morgan

The debates at the constitutional convention, the writings of the Founding Fathers, and the Constitution itself make it clear that the political party system was scarcely envisioned by those who laid the foundations of the American governmental structure. To their surprise, however, rather substantial parties had been built within a decade of the inception of the federal government.[1] But the rise of the party system brought a multitude of new problems to be resolved, not the least of which concerned the question of nominations for president and vice president. How, indeed, could the newly formed parties concentrate their strength behind two specific candidates, thus avoiding a dissipation of political support upon other individuals whose chances for victory on a national basis were slim at best? The solution to this weighty problem proved to be the congressional nominating caucus, a political institution which for nearly a quarter-century dominated the selection of aspirants for the nation's two highest offices. The rather unstructured state of party organization (which was to persist throughout the Federal Era) and the lack of speedy transportation and communication would not permit a complicated method for choosing party nominees, and it was perhaps only natural that the members of Congress, who were al-

From the *Proceedings of the American Philosophical Society* 113 (April 1969): 184–96, with permission from the American Philosophical Society. See original source for full footnote citations. William G. Morgan taught history from 1965 to 1974 at Oral Roberts University in Tulsa, Oklahoma. He now works as a financial consultant in Tulsa.

ready in the capital [. . .] should represent their respective states in this important function. Since congressional elections were sometimes decided in terms of the presidential question, the relationship to nominations appeared even more logical.

The caucus system, then, arose as a practical device to meet a practical need in a practical political arena. That a congressional nomination was a flagrant violation of Baron de Montesquieu's principle of the separation of powers seemed to present no problem to the caucus participants. Whatever might be said of acting in a different—and non-legislative—capacity in choosing candidates in the caucus, the congressmen were *still* members of the legislative branch. Thus, their control over the selection of candidates for the nation's top two executive offices inevitably controverted the separation principle. So, at least, observed John Quincy Adams, who as secretary of state wrote in 1819 that the nominating caucus was "a practice which places the president in a state of undue subserviency to the members of the legislature."[2]

Adams' statement suggests another—and doubtless originally unintended —potential use to which the caucus might be put: a weapon in the arsenal of Congress in its struggle with the president. Jefferson, one of the master builders of the Democratic-Republican party, had no difficulty with the caucus, to be sure, but subsequent chief executives throughout the caucus era were surely aware of the necessity to be on reasonably good terms with congressional leaders if they expected to be renominated. In a sense, these presidents were the creatures of the Democratic-Republican congresses which controlled the selection of candidates, and the power relationship between the two branches was certainly altered, at least potentially so, by the role played by the legislature in deciding who would be the party standard-bearers in the race for the country's highest political prizes.

It should be noted that nomination by caucus had significant roots in earlier years. In February of 1763, John Adams mentioned in his diary that a "Caucus Club" gathered periodically to choose "selectmen, assessors, collectors, wardens, fire-wards, and representatives . . . before they are chosen in the town."[3] This practice apparently dated back [. . .] to the first quarter of the eighteenth century, when the senior Sam Adams and a group of men met to devise a plan for presenting candidates for public office.[4] In the Middle Atlantic and New England areas, such meetings for the purpose of making nominations became commonplace during the latter half of the eighteenth century.[5] These precedents doubtless influenced the thinking and the activities of political leaders who desired to ensure party solidarity; the caucus having been employed previously on a relatively small scale, it was not illogical to utilize this method for selecting the two officials elected by the entire country.

The term "caucus" has an undetermined etymology, however; some writers have suggested that the word probably came from the name "Caulkers' Club," a politically oriented association of shipbuilding mechanics in Boston. Others have postulated that its origin may be traced to the Latin word *caucus* or the Greek *kaukos*, a drinking vessel, since the early Caucus Club seems to have been characterized by secrecy and conviviality. Another possibility is that "caucus" was derived from the Algonquin word *caucauasu*, one who promotes or advises, since Indian terminology was often adopted in naming New England political associations. Whatever its origin, all three possibilities possess implications illustrative of the early caucus; the latter two appear to be more plausible, since the word seems to have been in use before the Caulkers' Club existed.[6]

Earlier analysts have failed to agree upon the year in which the congressional nomination machinery began. In his multi-volume history of the United States, Richard Hildreth asserted that no formal nominations were made in 1796.[7] Two political scientists, James A. Woodburn and Thomas H. McKee, have agreed with this position. Other writers, however, have suggested that there was a caucus—perhaps even two—in 1796.[8] John B. McMaster, for example, concluded that the first nominating caucus was held by Republican members of Congress in the summer of election year; Thomas Jefferson and Aaron Burr were supposedly selected at this meeting. Stuart Lewis has indicated that Oliver Wolcott claimed the first caucus was a gathering of Federalist congressmen, also in the summer of 1796, which agreed to support John Adams and Thomas Pinckney. Wilfred E. Binkley, a capable observer of the presidency, indicates that both Federalists and Republicans probably held informal congressional caucus meetings to select candidates. W. N. Chambers, a contemporary analyst, suggests that the Federalists met in a "quasi-caucus" to accept these candidates. While admitting that the Republicans held a caucus, both Chambers and Noble E. Cunningham, Jr., who mentions no Federalist meeting, insist that the group, having already accepted Jefferson, were unable to agree concerning the party's candidate for vice president.[9]

This more recent interpretation concerning the Republicans appears to be correct. In any case, various Federalists reportedly knew about a Republican meeting which unsuccessfully sought to designate the second member of a ticket headed, through common consent by Jefferson.[10] It is doubtful whether any specific congressional caucus was held, however; the scanty evidence would suggest an informal gathering of Republican notables who collaborated on the question. Whatever agreement [. . .] was reached, the electoral vote demonstrated a startling lack of Republican unity: Burr received only thirty votes, less than half of Jefferson's sixty-eight. Evidence that the Federalists carried on some kind of consultation about their nominations is seen in a letter from Oliver Wolcott, Jr., to his father in which he mentioned that Thomas Pinckney was the party's contender for vice president. His rather general statement is something less than conclusive evidence that a *caucus* of congressmen was held, however; Federalist letters indicate communication and agreement on John Adams and Pinckney as the party's candidates, but it is very unlikely that there was any congressional caucus or even a specific summit meeting of party leaders to make the decision. The Federalists achieved a reasonable, though not complete, unity in casting their electoral votes; despite Alexander Hamilton's maneuvering designed to bring in Pinckney ahead of Adams, the South Carolinian received fifty-nine votes to Adams' seventy-one.[11]

The increasingly partisan character of the election of 1800 prompted both parties to hold congressional caucuses in an effort to gird themselves more effectively for the struggle. Though these meetings were "unofficial," they nevertheless proved to be invaluable in coordinating party strength. In early May, many of the Federalist congressmen in Washington gathered secretly to determine to support John Adams and Charles C. Pinckney equally; their action was later disclosed publicly in hopes of obtaining wider support for the chosen ticket.[12] Adams was ultimately faced, however, with opposition from Alexander Hamilton and such other Federalists as Timothy Pickering, Oliver Wolcott, Robert Goodloe Harper, and John Rutledge, Jr., in the vigorous, but unsuccessful, attempt led by Hamilton to contrive a coup in which Pinckney would receive more electoral votes. This group attempted to gain the support of the Essex men in this effort to overthrow Adams but was turned away. Though criticizing Adams in their letters, they refused to forsake him as a candidate. In losing to Jefferson and Burr, the New Englander's electoral count totaled sixty-five, while a single vote was thrown away from Pinckney to preserve the order of finish intended by most Federalists.[13]

The Republicans held a similar meeting. It was understood, of course, that Jefferson would be the party's leader; the primary candidates for second place were two New Yorkers, George Clinton and Aaron Burr, since the Republicans had fared well in the recent elections in that state. James Nicholson, a prominent party leader from New York was sent to each of these men to probe their feelings about the nomination. Both were reticent, but Burr was consulted after Clinton, and two of his Republican friends, arriving during the interview, persuaded him to consent to the nomination. Nicholson then converted Clinton's hesitance to a strictly negative response and reported favorably concerning Burr.[14]

Forsaking the Senate chamber, the site of the Federalist nomination, a group of important Democratic-Republican leaders convoked a *sub rosa* caucus in May to name Burr as Jefferson's running mate.[15] Interestingly enough, this group of about forty-five Republican congressional stalwarts, which convened at Marache's boarding house in Philadelphia reportedly was attended by several who were not members of Congress. The fateful decision to pledge equal support to Jefferson and Burr was no doubt the result of the "lesson" of 1796. Neither presidential contender wanted the other for his vice president, a rather awkward situation which the American political system permitted until 1804. Though some expected one vote to be thrown away from Burr in South Carolina, so intent were the Republicans on unity that their candidates both received seventy-three total electoral votes, thereby relegating the final decision to the House of Representatives and paving the way for the Twelfth Amendment.[16]

In 1804 the congressional caucus achieved "regular" status as a system of nomination. Starting from their defeat in 1800, the Federalists never again held a congressional nominating caucus, but an announced meeting of 110 Republican members of Congress convened on February 25, selecting Senator Stephen R. Bradley to act as chairman. The primary task of this group, of course, was to name a candidate for vice president; for a variety of reasons, Burr was dropped in favor of George Clinton, another notable New York politician. The decision on this question [. . .] was reached only after opposition to Clinton from an unexpected quarter: the Westerners wanted "something more than the free navigation of the Mississippi. . . . They aspire to give a vice president to the United States." John Breckinridge of Kentucky was their man. To settle the point and avoid unpleasant discussions, a ballot was taken, and Clinton outdistanced Breckinridge by sixty-seven to twenty. Attorney General Levi Lincoln received nine votes; John Langdon got seven; and even Gideon Granger, the postmaster general, was named by four delegates. Jefferson, of course, was accepted without dissent. Though some Republicans objected to the method of congressional nominations, comparatively little unhappiness was aroused by the "official" beginning of the reign of King Caucus.[17]

By 1808, however, strenuous opposition had begun to develop against this newly established nominating system. Particular displeasure was displayed by the Clintonian faction, which supported their chief, Vice President George Clinton, rather than the administration heir-apparent, James Madison. Clinton himself was suspicious of political machinations in Washington as the time for the caucus approached and indicated that the politicians in the capital should be employed in more useful pursuits.[18]

The Old Republican faction in Virginia provided another active cell of opposition, urging that James Monroe be the Republican standard-bearer; despite a previous lack of interest, Monroe's attitude changed as the campaign neared.[19] But before Monroe returned from his diplomatic endeavors in England, Wilson C. Nicholas and William Branch Giles had labored effectively in both Washington and Richmond to ensure Madison's nomination by Congress and by the Virginia legislative caucus. The Madisonians planned to hold an early caucus in Washington in hopes the choice of Madison there would clinch the Virginia nomination. Samuel R. Bradley issued a notice on January 19, 1808, calling a Republican caucus for the evening of January 23. Of the Republicans in Congress, ninety-four met according to plan.[20] There was considerable question among congressmen concerning Bradley's authority to convoke a caucus. Though claiming that the power had been given him at the previous nominating gathering and stating the reasons for calling the caucus, he declared his jurisdiction at an end. At the suggestion of William Branch Giles, however, Bradley was named to chair the meeting, and voting began soon after Richard M. Johnson had been selected as clerk. For president, Madison received eighty-three ballots, while Monroe and Clinton each had three (five abstained). Thinking that Monroe would accept this turn of events and hoping to conciliate the Clintonians, the meeting designated the New Yorker for second place on the ticket by giving him seventy-nine votes, compared to five for John Langdon, three for Henry Dearborn, and one for John Quincy Adams. This result drastically dispelled a rumor by a Clintonian that his chief would be chosen.[21] After Madison and Clinton were declared duly nominated, a committee of correspondence was chosen and a public resolution justifying the caucus was composed. The resolution said the members were acting as private citizens and the caucus method was adopted "from the necessity of the case; from a deep conviction of the importance of union to the Republicans . . . and as being the most practicable mode of consulting."[22] A more exemplary statement on the practicality of the caucus would be difficult to find.

The Virginia caucus was scheduled for January 28, but Madison's lieutenants decided it would be best to surprise the Monroe forces by acting before the news of the congressional nomination arrived. They sent invitations to Madison partisans in the legislature to meet at the Bell Tavern on January 21. The Monroe forces were blocked in their effort to counteract this move by calling a general caucus on the same day. As a result, two caucuses were held on January 21; 124 Madisonian legislators unanimously nominated their man and drew up an electoral ticket at the Bell Tavern, while a group more friendly to Monroe met at the capitol, where their candidate was nominated by a vote of fifty-seven to ten. The Monroe group met again on January 23 and 25 to complete their arrangements and name an electoral slate.[23]

The dissident candidates refused to accept the verdict. The New Yorker thought the caucus group appeared reticent and somewhat embarrassed about the whole subject—at least as far he was concerned—for they failed to ask, either individually or corporately, whether he would accept their nomination for vice president.[24] Clinton felt the caucus had "produced all the evil consequences that might be expected from that ill-timed . . . measure. It has created jealousies and divisions that never can be healed and has had a dangerous and pernicious effect on our public deliberations at a moment when our country . . . called upon us for union." The Vice President also noted that the nomination had caused a division in Virginia and suggested that Monroe had a larger following among the people of that state despite Madison's large majority in the legislature, which was elected while his opponent was out of the country.[25] Indicating that intrigue and management were resorted to in order to assure the success of the caucus nomination, Clinton succinctly expressed his opposition: "They will, however, have difficulties to contend with." He disavowed any complicity in the caucus and denounced it as an "off-spring of Quiddism," which rather picturesquely illustrates his firm belief that the administration and the "regular" nomination were strongly tainted with Quid implications.[26]

There was talk among Clintonians that victory in the state elections in 1808 would naturally lead to New York's electoral votes being cast for their chief. Moreover, if necessary to promote success elsewhere, they felt a nomination of Clinton for the presidency could be effected in his home state, though this attempt failed.[27] One confidant wrote to Madison that the Clinton party in New York was playing a game of intrigue and slander: "His hired libellers are again set upon the scent, to defame; and you are the victim."[28] In addition, there appears to have been some thought of cooperation between Clinton and Monroe against Madison, in which Clinton would ostensibly run for the presidency and Monroe for the second office—though the supposed plans may have involved a switch in positions later in the race. It is doubtful, indeed, whether any such coalition was ever actually concluded, but there were efforts toward this end in the Clintonian ranks, and the *American Citizen* of New York, a supporter of the vice president, in May openly discussed a Clinton-Monroe ticket as if it were already settled. Some of Monroe's advisers were decidedly cool to the idea of this New York–Virginia alliance.[29]

As the campaign progressed, a brief flash of hope appeared from an unexpected source—the Federalists. The Federalists in Rhode Island were apparently working to see electors chosen who would cast the electoral vote for Clinton for president and Monroe for vice president, according to the rumored agreement of this nature between the two men. Though the two groups had actively fought each other in the New York elections the previous spring, Clinton's opposition to the embargo and favorable outlook toward other of their policies caused twenty-five to thirty Federalist leaders from eight states to hold an embryonic national convention in New York City in August to consider the possibility of effecting a coalition with his forces. Such a course of action was rejected, and the group nominated Charles C. Pinckney and Rufus King.[30] Despite definite indications that Clinton could scarcely win, some of his supporters, even late in the campaign, urged fighting for the cause until the race was over. Clinton, in effect, found himself with both his presidential and vice-presidential hats in the ring—causing considerable irritation among Madison's lieutenants. In fact, some Republicans insisted that they would support Clinton according to the caucus agreement only if he withdrew as a presidential contender, and a movement in Virginia to deprive the New Yorker of that state's vice-presidential votes had to be squelched by party leaders. On another front, Monroe expressed hope as late as October that the Federalists might turn to him when they realized their own candidates had no chance, and the Old Republicans in Virginia backed Monroe to the last.[31]

Indeed, many factious Republicans voiced their opposition. Realizing that neither Clinton nor Monroe had any chance of being chosen at the caucus, most of Madison's opponents boycotted the meeting, thus enabling them to denounce the system. Matthew Lyon, for example, wrote to Bradley expressing disapproval of a congressional nomination for three reasons: the Constitution prohibits any congressman from being an elector; no specific authority for a caucus is listed in that document; and the meeting would nominate Madison instead of Clinton.[32] Such criticism is typical. A joint anti-caucus manifesto issued by some from the Randolph and Clinton factions was along the same line. They specifically objected to the mechanics of the caucus and the potential dangers of intrigue and improper governmental relationships when the separation of powers was broken down. The declaration contained additional, and less tangible, objections as well: the caucus was a "gross assumption of power not delegated by the people," directly hostile to the principles of the Constitution, and an attempt to transfer the selection of president and vice president to Congress. But the crucial motive is revealed when Madison is opposed as the nominee.[33] The practical, rather than altruistic and theoretical, opposition to the caucus is aptly demonstrated by John Randolph; in 1804 he favored the nominees and the caucus, while in 1808 he opposed both.

Various newspapers took up the cudgel. *The Northern Post* (Salem, N.Y.) condemned the caucus as an attempt of Congress "to dictate to their constituents for whom they shall vote" and as representing "a combination of principle and practice, the most odious and destructive, that ever actuated the mind of man." The article also insisted that the Constitution was in danger of being nullified should the system become established.[34] Taking a diametrically opposed point of view, *Colvin's Weekly Register* came out strongly in favor of the congressional nomination. Terming the caucus "a good old custom which has prevented intrigue and distractions among Republicans," Colvin denounced those opposed to Madison's nomination as being motivated by "the foul monster Ambition," suggesting that they might well be more amenable to a caucus had their favorite been chosen.[35] In subsequent issues, the *Register* continued the battle; one article attempted to refute at length the declaration of the Randolph group. Among other things, Colvin pointed out that those opposed to the caucus in 1808 had supported it in 1804 and asserted that they actually disliked the person nominated rather than the mode of selection.[36]

The editor's observations are indeed penetrating. Doubtless, many of the Republicans who opposed the caucus did so because their candidate failed to receive the nomination. As in times past and in years to come, American politics proved to be an essentially *practical* struggle. Of course, caucus opponents *sounded* considerably more altruistic and idealistic by couching their arguments in constitutional terms. Whatever the cause of opposition, the system successfully withstood the attack. The caucus exercised a powerful influence even among New York Republicans. Though there was considerable division among those in the northwest part of the state, many of Madison's adherents declared their personal preference for George Clinton and indicated they would cheerfully support their favorite son if they thought he could obtain a "republican majority." While thinking well of Madison, they were primarily induced to back him "on account of his having been nominated in the ordinary way, and from fear of a fatal division of the republican party."[37] The caucus system had thus become sufficiently entrenched by 1808 for many to consider its nominations as the "ordinary way." By election time Republicans had closed their ranks considerably and brought their influence to bear for the caucus ticket. The nation approved the nomination by sweeping Madison into office.

The year 1812 provides an outstanding example of the possible influence of the caucus over the president. The nation hovered on the brink of war, but some of the more belligerent congressmen thought Madison seemed reticent to pursue a course leading to hostilities. Though feeling in December of 1811 that Madison was ready for war if American complaints were not rectified by May, William Lowndes of South Carolina later observed that "one of the most curious anecdotes with the declaration of war in 1812 is that of the effort of the executive to prevent a declaration of war."[38] John C. Calhoun also commented on what he felt was a lack of zeal toward the war question on the part of Madison.[39] A contrasting view is presented by Madison's most capable biographer, Irving Brant, who insists that the president was more willing to have war than has been assumed.[40] In any case, Madison was doubtless aware of the relationship between the caucus, the War Hawks, and his need for renomination. Some commentators insist that Henry Clay, John C. Calhoun, and the other war men *did* use the congressional nomination as a tool to goad Madison into a war policy, but no letters or other documents appear to exist which incontrovertibly verify the assertion. One unnamed politician did apparently tell Augustus Foster, the British minister, that the caucus had not been held on time because the war congressmen were suspicious of Madison's intentions.[41] The very nature of the role of the caucus in the president's relationship with Congress makes it seem plausible that the War Hawks might intimate to Madison that they would fail to support him [. . .] should his timidity continue; any communications on the question were probably verbal or implied, and this may well account for the seeming scarcity of direct documentary evidence one way or the other. But it is unlikely that any *overt* threat was made to Madison on this question, because as recent research by Irving Brant and others suggests—the policy gap between the Hawks and the president was much less than previously supposed. Whatever the case, Madison had many enemies in Congress among his own party. The dissident John Randolph of Roanoke remarked that while he was unable to provide any side information on "kingmaking,"

> There is in the majority, as that motley group in Congress is called, a very considerable party averse to the present Palinarus. Whether their hostility will develop itself at the ensuing election, it is not yet determined even among themselves. Certain it is, that very little deference to the reigning monarch is shewn by the leaders, in the two halves of Congress, or even by their humble followers.[42]

Such was the opposition Madison faced in the house of his friends. In the case of what might be termed "non-majority Republicans," the dislike for the president became obvious rather soon in the campaign. A number of people worked for Clinton over Madison. "Intrigues are going on in every hole and corner, the object of which is to make either DeWitt Clinton or Armstrong the next President or Vice President. You are hemmed in on every side."[43]

In any event, the caucus was not held until after Madison had determined to pursue a war policy. In response to a notice, eighty-three of 133 Republican members of Congress gathered in the Senate chamber on May 18; J. B. Varnum and R. M. Johnson were selected as chairman and secretary. Madison received unanimous support, and John Langdon was chosen as his running mate by defeating Elbridge Gerry, sixty-four to sixteen, with two scattered votes. When Langdon declined the nomination, Gerry was chosen to fill the vacant place by another caucus held on June 8, receiving seventy-four of seventy-seven votes.[44]

Despite the exigencies of war, there was concerted opposition to this caucus. Several congressmen favored Madison, but honestly opposed nominations by the legislature; such men refused to attend the meeting, but generally refrained from instigating vehement opposition to the system. The Clintonians, however, now led by the late vice president's nephew, DeWitt Clinton, opposed both Madison and the war. Congressmen of this persuasion generally stood against the regular nomination, of course. One friend wrote to Madison that the Federalists were openly expressing their support of Clinton and that there was an organization of sorts from Maine to Georgia which had existed since 1809 to oppose the Virginian's reelection. To make things worse, many of the opposition had used federal patronage to strengthen their position. A meeting of ninety-one of the ninety-five Republicans in the New York legislature proceeded to nominate the new junto chief by a unanimous vote, subsequently appointing a committee to promote his election.[45]

The New York committee of correspondence charged with working for the Clinton cause addressed a printed circular letter to many Republicans. After beginning the missive with a frank evaluation that DeWitt Clinton was an abler and more suitable candidate for the nation's problems, the committee concentrated on opposition to the caucus[:]

> But another cause urges us more strongly than any other to appeal to you—it is one of principle—it involves a great constitutional question, which is now for the first time brought fairly to the test. The members of congress have nominated Madison as the next President. *This interference in the nomination of a President by a congressional caucus at the seat of government, we conceive to be unwarranted by the constitution— a violation of its spirit, and dangerous to the Republic.* The state of New York has openly resisted this usurpation, and by the nomination of DeWitt Clinton has brought the question directly before the American people.[46]

Thus was anti-caucus a cornerstone of Clinton's campaign structure.

Shortly after, in an open letter addressed to the American people, the legislature's committee expressed its displeasure with the congressional nomination, insisting that "the nomination of a candidate for the presidency . . . by an association of members of Congress . . . is hostile to the spirit of the federal Constitution, dangerous to the rights of the people, and to the freedom of election." The proper method of nomination, they suggested, was by "the states which enjoy the constitutional right to elect." Moreover, the letter expressed the fear that the caucus would become so firmly established as to be tantamount to the electoral college: "The Congress will appoint the President, and the constitutional electors will be mere officers to register its edicts." Under such circumstances, a foreign nation might well be able to secure the choice of a man friendly to their interests by bribing Congress. Of course, the letter could scarcely conclude without vilifying James Madison and glorifying DeWitt Clinton.[47] Though some of these men were no doubt sincere, a more realistic interpretation of the above arguments must be expressed in terms of personal interest. The caucus had failed to choose Clinton, so any attempt to justify his candidacy would logically be based in part on an assertion of the impropriety of a congressional nomination. New York's attitude toward the caucus at this time is interesting in view of her legislature's resolutions in 1823 favoring the use of the system for the campaign of 1824.

As in 1808, there were important voices raised in favor of the caucus. Hezekiah Niles supported it as the most practicable mode of selecting nominees; how else could candidates be put forward in such a large nation without considerable confusion? Niles showed insight when he bluntly remarked that "those who condemn the *manner* in which the nomination was made, are rather dissatisfied with the persons nominated, without having candor enough to confess it."[48] While this attitude contrasts with Niles's vehement opposition to the caucus after 1820 and doubtless was not universally applicable, it demonstrates perception of the motives of many politicians of the time. Politics was a real game with real stakes, and issues were fully exploited as political weapons—though frequently couched in terms representing somewhat more altruism on the part of the contesting sides than actually existed.

Meanwhile, other political machinations were afoot. Realizing the utter impossibility of electing a ticket of their own, the Federalists began to consider DeWitt Clinton as a possible fusion candidate; at least his election would lead, they felt, to measures calculated to conclude the war. In Massachusetts, for example, Clintonians were making no secret of their cooperation with the Federalists. To decide the question, a *sub rosa* convention of about seventy important Federalist leaders from eleven states met in New York in September of 1812. Though Rufus King, one of the party stalwarts, strongly urged that no such cooperation be extended to dissident Republicans, the meeting determined, in effect, to support Clinton as the only candidate who might defeat Madison. That the president was reelected by an electoral vote of only 128–89 attests to the effectiveness of this quasi-union between Federalists and Clintonians.[49] King Caucus, however, had successfully weathered another challenge to his legitimacy.

The political stage had experienced substantial changes by 1816. According to precedent, Madison was preparing for retirement after two terms in office. For various reasons—especially their opposition to the war in general and the Hartford Convention in particular—the Federalists were extremely weak nationally, and the presidential chair would obviously be awarded to the consolidated Republican nominee. Monroe had long since been reconciled with the administration, and, having served for several years as secretary of state, he was the front-running contender. But this electoral struggle was to witness a significant degree of opposition to continuing the Virginia Dynasty. Various New York Republican leaders were in the vanguard of the anti-Virginia forces; urgently desiring to elect a man from the Empire State, they looked to Governor Daniel D. Tompkins as the man to carry the banner. There was insufficient support for Tompkins in the other states, however, and the majority of the New York congressional delegates opposed to Monroe, as well as other anti-Virginia congressmen, turned to William H. Crawford, despite the uncertainty of whether he wished to run.[50] The contenders for caucus honors had been narrowed to two. Unlike other years, the caucus would be a true battleground. But some of Monroe's friends, fearing Crawford's strength, hoped to prevent a congressional nomination. Indeed, certain observers thought no caucus would be held.[51]

On March 10, however, an anonymous and somewhat unexpected notice calling the caucus for two days later was sent to Republican members of Congress. Some thought this to be an attempted coup by the Crawford partisans, and only fifty-eight attended this meeting; the group passed a resolution, signed by Senator Jeremiah Morrow, chairman of the caucus, and Representative Lewis Condict, secretary, postponing the decision until March 16. In the meantime, a more authoritative announcement of the meeting was to be made in order to stimulate a larger attendance. This effort achieved considerable success; 119 of the approximately 140 Republican congressmen gathered at the later assembly. It was said by some that Monroe's friends feared the worst, and while various ones thought of not participating in the caucus, a gathering of the Virginian's friends apparently decided the evening before the caucus reconvened to attend the meeting in order to prevent a nomination. Accordingly, perhaps, as soon as Samuel Smith had been named chairman and Richard M. Johnson secretary, Henry Clay offered a resolution that it was inexpedient for the caucus to make a nomination. After this proposal was negatived, another abortive motion, submitted by John W. Taylor of New York, declared that the practice of congressional nomination should be discontinued entirely. Having silenced opposition within its ranks, the meeting proceeded to vote; apparently, some members who favored Crawford defected, and Monroe won by a narrow margin, sixty-five to fifty-four. Daniel Tompkins, the erstwhile presidential hopeful, won the decision for second place on the ticket over Simon Snyder by a tally of eighty-five to thirty. Apparently quite willing to go along with his colleagues, Clay reversed his earlier position and proposed the resolution which officially declared the candidates nominated, later mentioning the caucus and his votes for Monroe and Tompkins in matter-of-fact fashion.[52]

The decision was accepted with relatively few hard feelings within the party, particularly in view of the closeness of the contest. Deciding to bide his time until after Monroe's tenure in the executive chair, Crawford readily deferred to the choice.[53] Because of the nature of the situation, opposition to the caucus by disgruntled candidates and their friends was substantially reduced in 1816. The controversy about the election which had appeared in the *National Intelligencer*, for example, virtually vanished within a short time after the caucus. But disapproval of the system had by no means vanished. Speaking in the House some two years before, for example, William Gaston, a North Carolina Federalist who would naturally oppose a *Republican* caucus, referred to the institution as a method "which appears to be monstrous," going on to say that "it might be corrected or the character of this government will be fundamentally changed." In a House debate in 1816, Jabez D. Hammond of New York also cast some doubts on the value of the congressional nomination.[54] Considerable opposition to the caucus was voiced in Pennsylvania, where an anti-caucus electoral ticket was nominated. The noise was more fearsome than the practical political effects, however: though party regulars accused the anti-caucus insurgents of courting Federalist support and seeking to advance DeWitt Clinton, the "opposition" ticket formed was neither pledged to any candidates nor opposed to Monroe.[55]

Other voices of dissent were also raised. The *Examiner* of New York, a Federalist paper, lashed out with vigor at the system of corrupt and profligate *"caucussing."* The article goes on to characterize the caucus as a means of nomination to which "the people of this country have so soon become so servile." The editor's true feelings are revealed, however, when he insisted that any caucus should include Federalists.[56] Even a politically impotent group scarcely enjoys being left out.

A subsequent issue of *The Examiner* urged the people to unite against the regular nominee as the best means to defeat the congressional nomination. Another condemned the caucus as trespassing on the people's right to elect a president: "It is the *Caucussers* who nominate, and the people who are called upon to go through the drudgery of conforming to their edicts. [...] From the many, the power has been usurped by a few." But *The Examiner* was a New York as well as a Federalist paper and anti–Virginia Dynasty was part of its bill of fare; cooperation was even suggested between the Federalists and Crawford to beat Monroe.[57] As a supporter of John Quincy Adams in 1824, Hezekiah Niles termed this caucus the first attempt "to dictate to the people, instead of following their lead," but he showed no such hostility to the system at this time.[58] The congressional method of nomination had survived another campaign. Some, indeed, lauded the caucus as essential to perform its usual task of unifying the various segments of the party behind a common candidate.[59]

But the caucus was to wane rapidly in succeeding years. The Era of Good Feeling saw the Federalists fade into virtual extinction—at least on a national scale—and the original need for a congressional nomination, fading commensurately with the Federalists, virtually disappeared. In fact, a group of forty-six Republican congressmen met to consider making nominations in 1820, only to adjourn without action because of lack of support. In the words of one observer, the caucus had "evaporated in smoke."[60]

The election of 1824 proved to be the *coup de grace* of the congressional nominating system. The multiplicity of candidates helped to ensure its downfall, especially since the opponents of William H. Crawford, the caucus favorite, stood against such a nomination. Andrew Jackson was in the vanguard of these forces, followed by John C. Calhoun, John Quincy Adams, and somewhat less vigorously, by Henry Clay. Old Hickory was especially vehement in his denunciations, insisting that the caucus would "politically put down the individual they may hold forth" and hoping that the people would "put intrigue and caucus forever down."[61] The system suffered additional harm when Crawford attracted comparatively scant support in the caucus and among the electorate. Though Crawford's chances were no doubt seriously impaired by his severe paralytic stroke in September of 1823, the increasing feeling against the congressional nomination helped to reduce his chances even further. This abortive nomination served to signal the end of the reign of King Caucus. Nominations by state legislatures and local groups were used in 1828, and the election of 1832 witnessed the inauguration of the convention system.[62]

The caucus arose to answer the need of the rather unexpectedly burgeoning parties to direct their support behind candidates chosen by a reasonable consensus. Since the newly formed political groups had no elaborate organizational structure, the members of Congress naturally provided the highest level of party cooperation and collaboration. This was particularly important in view of the comparatively rudimentary status of transportation and communication at the beginning of the nineteenth century; it would have been extremely inconvenient for an independent nominating group to have met, even had party development progressed sufficiently to have permitted such action. The use of local caucuses during the eighteenth century also made the transition to a congressional nomination somewhat easier. From an irregular and secret device, the caucus became both regular and public.

Nomination by Congress was primarily a practical political tool. Though some sincerely opposed the system on constitutional grounds, personal interest played the larger part—regardless of how theoretical the arguments were. Thomas Hart Benton, the long-time senator from Missouri, observed that the system's demise came when many people were against it, not so much on principle as on realistic grounds: the caucus would select a candidate to whom they were opposed.[63] But the caucus system doubtless served a useful function during its existence. It helped to reduce considerably the confusion which the Constitution allowed in the election of the nation's highest executive officials, despite the fact that congressional nominations controverted the basic principle of the separation of powers. The system was unable to withstand the drive toward more democratic institutions, however. As more people gained the suffrage and a larger number of states conceded the right of their inhabitants to choose electors for president, greater was the demand that a popular voice be granted in the choice of party nominees. This irrepressible force, plus opposition by political hopefuls not chosen by the system, assured the speedy decline of the congressional caucus.

CHAPTER 4

State Nominations of 1824 Candidates

KENTUCKY LEGISLATORS ENDORSE HENRY CLAY

Resolved, That Henry Clay, late speaker of the house of representatives of the United States, be recommended as a suitable person to succeed James Monroe as president thereof.

In respectfully inviting the attention of the people of the United States to a citizen of Kentucky, as a fit person to fill the highest office in their gift, that portion of the citizens of Kentucky now assembled, will not conceal that they entertain a warm affection for, and a strong confidence in, their distinguished fellow citizen whom they have ventured to propose; nor deny that they think the time has arrived, when the people of the west may, with some confidence, appeal to the magnanimity of the whole union, for a favorable consideration of their equal and just claim to a fair participation in the executive government of these states. Sectional motives they are ready freely to admit, ought not to have a predominant influence in the choice of a chief magistrate: But it cannot be disguised that they ever must have some weight, until that sentiment shall be eradicated from the human breast, which attaches man most to those whom he knows best, and to the objects which are nearest and dearest to him. It is not,

The endorsement for Henry Clay is excerpted from a proclamation of the Kentucky legislative caucus meeting held in Frankfort on November 18, 1822. See *History of American Presidential Elections 1789–1968,* ed. Arthur M. Schlesinger Jr., Fred L. Israel, and William P. Hansen (New York: Chelsea House, 1971), 1:392–93. Support for John Quincy Adams is excerpted from a declaration by Massachusetts Republican legislators and town delegates issued in Boston on January 23, 1823 (ibid., 1:394–95). Support for Andrew Jackson is excerpted from a statement issued in October 1823 (ibid., 1:399).

however, alone, nor principally, upon considerations merely local or personal, but on those of a much more liberal and elevated character, that they rest the pretensions of the individual whom they now recommend: For they believe, without disparaging, in the smallest degree, the very great and acknowledged merits of the other illustrious men, to whom public attention has lately been directed, that, throughout his whole public career, no American statesman has been less actuated by narrow or selfish impulses, and that he yields to none in eminent services, in distinguished ability, in political rectitude and virtue, nor in liberal and enlarged views of national policy.

In presenting him, therefore, to the consideration of their fellow citizens, they think they are authorized to believe, that they have consulted the best interests of the whole union, as well as the feelings and interests of the west, and that they may be allowed to hope that his strong claims to the confidence and approbation of his country, will be properly appreciated, and his talents and public services justly rewarded. And, on the question being put thereon, the said resolution and address were unanimously adopted.

MASSACHUSETTS REPUBLICANS SUPPORT JOHN QUINCY ADAMS

That the time for electing a successor to the present illustrious chief magistrate of the United States is so far distant that it cannot now be ascertained what then will be the condition of the country, or who among its citizens can be most usefully called to that arduous and responsible station. But the great importance of the office then to be filled, and the momentous consequences of deciding who shall be the person to fill it, have commanded attention in every part of the Union, and in various forms and by various authority, eminent men are holden forth for the approbation and suffrage of the people.

Your committee are not inclined to favor the practice of nominating a candidate for the presidency by assemblies in the states, for this, among other obvious reasons, that the tendency of such nomination is to throw the election into the house of representatives, where, as experience has proved, it is liable to manifold abuse. In their view it is desirable that the attention of our fellow citizens should be drawn to a candidate, rather by the commanding influence of his character than by any local or sectional feelings arrayed in his support.

But as unanimity, to a good degree, is most desirable on this great occasion, and as the opinion of one section of the country must be made known to others that a common sentiment and feeling may, in the end, be produced, the committee see great propriety in the public expression of such opinion as prevails among their fellow citizens, with a view, not as partisans, to contend for the election of a favorite, but to disseminate information that may be necessary for an intelligent decision by the people.

The republicans of Massachusetts, actuated by a national spirit, have always avoided, as the greatest national evil, any measures which would bear a local or sectional construction. They have, with pleasure, given their undivided support to elevate to office those illustrious citizens of the south, who have, for the last twenty-two years, so ably conducted the destinies of the nation, convinced that they were worthy to sustain, and justly entitled to receive, the highest honors and utmost confidence of the people.

Among the candidates, now before the public, is a citizen of this commonwealth, and the committee believe it is not only due to his high character, but that it is respectful to their republican brethren throughout the United States, to declare the opinion which our political friends in this commonwealth entertain of his qualifications for the high office of president of the United States. By making such declaration, no determination is expressed to support the individual in question, at all events and under all possible circumstances. Such inflexibility of opinion might destroy that common principle of action from which is to be expected an harmonious and useful result.

By declaring to our friends, in other parts of the United States, our opinion and feelings, at the present time, we mean to convey information which may influence their deliberations, and are not precluded from receiving and examining, with candor, their sentiments and wishes, in the hope that, by the interchange of opinion, the minds of the whole people may be eventually fixed on that man, who, in all his official relations, will most worthily sustain the character of an American patriot.

The committee, therefore, recommend the following resolution to be adopted:

Resolved, That we have unlimited confidence in the republican principles of *John Quincy Adams*: That we hold in the highest respect the uniform integrity of his public and private character: That we consider his exalted talents, his various and eminent services, his political experience, and his profound knowledge of the great interests of the nation, as pledges of the ability with which, as the chief magistrate of the American people, he would promote their prosperity and honor.

PHILADELPHIA SUPPORTERS DECLARE FOR JACKSON

Resolved, That we hold it to be the imperative duty of the people, as well as a sacred right secured to us by the constitution, to select our own candidate for the presidency of the United States, independent of all interference, and aloof from all dictation.

Resolved, That, as democrats, we maintain the right to think and act for ourselves, and never will surrender to a self-constituted aristocracy, that freedom of opinion, which is, at once, the source of our greatness and the preserver of our liberties.

Resolved, That, in accordance with these principles, we will support General Andrew Jackson as the next president of the United States.

Because, he has always been a uniform and consistent democrat.

Because, he is eminently qualified, both as a statesman and a warrior, to govern the nation wisely, in peace, and to conduct her triumphantly through war.

Because, as a patriot, we have full confidence in his moderation, his virtue and his firmness; being a friend to the rights of man and universal suffrage.

Resolved, That we consider Andrew Jackson as having claims to the gratitude of this republic, for this distinguished station which no other candidate can prefer, and which we are bound to grant, by our love of country, our devotion to liberty, and our admiration of patriotism.

Resolved, That this meeting pledge themselves solemnly to one another, to devote all their exertions to promote the election of general Andrew Jackson to the presidency of the United States. [. . .]

Resolved, That this meeting do, earnestly, recommend to the friends of Jackson throughout the state, to hold meetings and organize their strength in their several districts, thus taking a firm stand in defense of their country, the constitution, and the glorious principles of *seventy six.*

PART III
The National Nominating Convention

Emmett H. Buell Jr.

NO other institution in the history of presidential nominations matches the longevity of the national convention. Its history divides into three reasonably distinct eras: the heyday of conventions from 1836 to 1908, the mixed system that began with the first presidential primaries in 1912 and ended with a bang in 1968, and the present system starting in 1972.

Until 1912 national conventions exercised all of the power to pick the presidential nominees of major parties. Delegates, alternates, cynical reporters, and hundreds if not thousands of onlookers filled cavernous halls to take part in a spectacle unsurpassed in American politics. For the better part of a week, the typical convention featured torchlight parades, marching bands, florid speech-making, fights over credentials and platforms, frantic caucusing of delegations, boisterous floor demonstrations, a dramatic roll call of the states frequently requiring many ballots, and sometimes a "stampede" to decide the presidential choice. This spectacle continued well into the twentieth century, even as conventions gradually lost the essence of their power over nominations.

From 1912 to 1968, the number of delegates owing their election to primary voters ranged from one-third to half of the total, even though the number of primaries declined after a surge in 1916.[1] Many delegates chosen in primaries nonetheless attended as formally unbound to any candidate. Even when the ballot permitted voting for supporters of particular candidates, primary voters in some states routinely elected entire slates of uncommitted delegates. In Massachusetts, for example, only uncommitted delegates were chosen in the Republican primaries of 1916, 1920, 1932, 1940, 1944, and 1948. The same held for the state's Democratic primaries in 1920, 1924, 1940, 1944, and 1948. Still other delegates won seats at conventions as ostensible supporters of "favorite sons" given little or no chance of nomination. As late as 1968, all of Ohio's primary votes went to the likes of Stephen M. Young and James A. Rhodes.[2] Primaries, in short, frequently made no connection between presidential preference and delegate selection. Nor did they seriously impinge upon the power of conventions to reject candidates leading in the primary preference vote.

The GOP first demonstrated this power in 1912 by renominating President William Howard Taft, even though former president Theodore Roosevelt had won most of the primaries and dominated in the total vote. Other Republican nominees who trailed in the overall preference vote included Associate Justice Charles Evans Hughes in 1916, Sen. Warren G. Harding in 1920, President Herbert Hoover in 1932, New York governor Thomas E. Dewey in 1948, and Gen. Dwight D. Eisenhower in 1952. Similarly, the 1920 Democratic convention chose Ohio governor James Cox, hardly a big winner in the primaries. Democrats rejected William G. McAdoo in 1924, even though he swept the primaries with nearly 60 percent of the total vote. Sen. Estes Kefauver likewise dominated the primary struggle in 1952 but lost out to Gov. Adlai Stevenson. Stevenson did not want the nomination but finally yielded to pressure from President Truman and other party leaders. Vice President Humphrey secured his party's nomination in 1968 without officially contesting a single primary.[3]

Hubert Humphrey became the Democratic nominee at a most inopportune moment. Deep differences over Vietnam, race, and poverty—punctuated by the murders of Dr. Martin Luther King Jr. and Sen. Robert F. Kennedy—cast a pall over the nominating process. The convention had been scheduled to coincide with President Johnson's birthday, but now, no longer seeking renomination and concerned about security, LBJ stayed away. One week before the convention got under way in Chicago, McCarthy strategists on the Rules, Credentials, and Platform committees served notice that they would show the convention and its larger audience "just how mechanically, how wickedly, how ruthlessly a small band of machine bosses controlled the party at home and forced it forward in war abroad."[4] Rancor spilled onto the floor during debates over the plank on the war in Vietnam. Rules and credentials fights focused on the disparity between the preference vote in key primary states and the allocation of delegates. McCarthy supporters issued a report listing primaries where Humphrey got most of the delegates despite winning only a trace of the primary vote. Outside the hall, Chicago police used clubs and tear gas against demonstrators seeking to distract if not disrupt the convention. Network news programs frequently cut away from convention speeches to showcase this violence. Images of youthful McCarthy volunteers bloodied by police billy clubs enraged McCarthy delegates and lent momentum to their minority resolution calling for a commission to reform the rules of delegate selection. Party regulars allowed the motion to carry, thereby opening the door to national party control of their party's nominating process.[5] One consequence of reform—as supplemented by previous changes in American politics—was loss of the convention's power to pick nominees independently of primary outcomes.

ORIGINS AND INSTITUTIONAL DEVELOPMENT

Scholars differ when tracing the roots of the national nominating convention. James S. Chase contends that the nominating convention originated from a lengthy process dating back to the eighteenth century "in which the local and state convention became the prevailing method of nominating candidates for public office." Indeed, by his account, state and local nominating conventions had become so familiar to politicians in the 1830s that few regarded the idea of a national convention as new.[6]

Samuel Eliot Morison points to an 1808 gathering of Federalist leaders in New York City as the first time that a national gathering of party leaders nominated a presidential candidate. Attended by upwards of thirty delegates representing seven states in the North, this conclave seriously considered supporting Vice President George Clinton, a less objectionable Republican than James Madison. Four years later, the Federalist convention actually did endorse a Republican, DeWitt Clinton.

Unquestionably the rebirth of party competition proved critical to the rise (or reappearance) of the national convention. Parties needed to nominate tickets in a way that would be seen as legitimate and representative, that would unite rather than divide. Properly organized and skillfully conducted, a national convention would also attract party workers from a variety of states while providing a setting conducive to deliberation, bargaining, and reconciliation.[7]

At least some of these hopes appear to have influenced an 1830 gathering of Antimasonic leaders in Philadelphia. Recognized by some as the first national nominating convention in the modern sense, this meeting convened to consider the best way to nominate presidential and vice-presidential candidates. Not enough Antimasons held seats in Congress to make a congressional caucus feasible, so the conferees hit upon a national convention in which "adherents who had no representation whatever in public office" would participate.[8] They accordingly called upon delegates to assemble in Baltimore one year later for the purpose of making presidential and vice-presidential nominations. Altogether, 116 delegates representing thirteen states north of Maryland answered the call and nominated a former Mason, the understandably reluctant William Wirt, for president.[9]

Noteworthy differences distinguished this convention from the Federalist meetings of 1808–1812. The Antimasonic convention opened its proceedings to public view and attracted many more participants. Antimasons adopted formal rules of procedure, the most important of which stipulated that a presidential nomination required the approval of three-fourths of the delegates. The purpose of this supermajority provision was to build party unity, always a problem for the conflicted Federalists. The Antimasons also ended with an address to the people extolling the virtues of their ticket.

The National Republican party also settled on the national convention as the method most suited to its electoral circumstances. Its only convention met in Baltimore on December 12, 1831, with 156 delegates in attendance. After opening their proceedings to the press, delegates nominated Henry Clay of Kentucky for president and Rep. John Sergeant of Pennsylvania for vice president. They also issued an address to the people lavishing praise on Clay while excoriating Andrew Jackson. "Young" National Republicans later drafted a statement of party principles.[10]

Baltimore hosted yet another national convention in May 1832, when the Democrats met to pick a vice-presidential nominee more to Jackson's liking than John C. Calhoun. Approximately 320 delegates representing every state except Missouri showed up. They had been chosen by various caucuses and conventions at the state and local level. Some but not all states adhered to an informal rule that the number of delegate votes should be equal to the number of a state's electoral votes.[11]

Once gaveled to order, the delegates adopted rules that would shape Democratic party proceedings for a century or more, starting with one that pegged delegate votes to electoral votes. The convention also agreed that a spokesman would announce the vote of each delegation rather than allowing members of the delegation to report individually. This provision laid the foundation for what became known as the unit rule, whereby a majority of delegates bound the minority to support its candidate. The unit rule took some time to catch on at Democratic conventions. Once accepted, as Carl Becker related in 1899, the rule greatly enhanced the power of party leaders over delegates. Critics understandingly assailed the rule as inimical to the independence of delegates. Supporters successfully wrapped the rule in the rhetoric of states' rights.[12] It remained a staple of Democratic conventions until suspended in 1968 and formally abolished in 1972.[13]

The first Democratic convention also adopted a supermajority rule whereby nominations required two-thirds of all delegate votes allocated. In 1840 and again in 1848, Democratic conventions resolved that the rule should apply only to delegates present and voting rather than total delegate votes. In 1860, however, a badly divided Democratic convention in Charleston approved a return to total delegate votes. After several days of bitter sectional strife over the platform, most southern delegates bolted the convention. Their departure certainly thinned out the opposition to the favorite, Sen. Stephen A. Douglas of Illinois, but it also meant that Douglas had to win 202 of roughly 250 votes remaining. The task proved too much for the "Little Giant," and, after fifty-seven ballots, the convention adjourned without making a nomination. A second Democratic convention dominated by Douglas supporters met in Baltimore, but the two-thirds rule adopted in Charleston still held. Douglas led his closest rival by more than two to one on the first two ballots but still fell short of 202 delegate votes. At this point, the convention unanimously declared Douglas its nominee for having won two-thirds the votes of all delegates present and voting.[14]

The two-thirds rule also helped protract the 1924 Democratic convention, which required 103 ballots to end a standoff between William G. McAdoo and Gov. Al Smith. Again, deep party divisions greatly supplemented the normal difficulty of achieving a supermajority. The 1924 debacle remained fresh in Democratic memory eight years later, when Sen. Huey Long of Louisiana and other supporters of Franklin D. Roosevelt called for nomination by simple majority. Irate southerners cried foul, forcing FDR to disavow any intent of meddling with tradition. Once settled in the White House, however, Roosevelt worked successfully to abolish the rule in 1936.

While it remained on the books, the two-thirds rule worked in tandem with the unit rule. Clearly, two-thirds would have been even more difficult to obtain without the unit rule. Taken together, these rules encouraged bargaining at Democratic conventions even as they complicated the calculations of delegates, party leaders, and candidates. Moreover, as Carl Becker noted in 1899, defenders of the two-thirds rule worked out a clever response to critics. When the two-thirds rule came under attack, they argued that the unit rule must also go; otherwise, a minimum and artificially unified coalition of big and almost evenly divided delegations might force a minority nominee upon the convention.[15] Sufficient resolve to abolish both rules simultaneously never materialized. Yet it also bears noting that no nomination resulted from minority exploitation of the unit rule at the eight conventions still employing the unit rule after the two-thirds rule had been abolished.

Although Republicans never required a supermajority for nomination, they did make occasional use of the unit rule. In 1860, for example, the Illinois delegation showed up at the Chicago convention pledged to vote for Lincoln as a unit. The rule figured importantly at the 1876 convention, when three Pennsylvania delegates challenged the rule because it prevented them from exercising their independent judgment. (The rule had been imposed on the delegation by the state's Republican convention.) After much debate, the national convention upheld the authority of its chairman to overturn the decision of the state convention. This did not prevent Sen. Roscoe Conkling of New York, Sen. Don Cameron of Pennsylvania, and Illinois party leader John Logan from relying on the unit rule in an effort to renominate former president Ulysses S. Grant in 1880. To win (thereby infringing on the sacred tradition of no third term set by George Washington), Grant needed every delegate vote from New York, Pennsylvania, and Illinois. Since he faced opposition in each of these key delegations, only the unit rule could secure their full support. Conkling, Cameron, and Logan accordingly railroaded the unit rule through their respective state conventions, and Cameron—in his capacity as national party chairman—intended to uphold the unit rule by fiat, since he presided over the convention prior to its election of a temporary chairman. As news of this cabal leaked, however, supporters of the other candidates resolved to abolish the unit rule. They prevailed in a vote of the whole convention that ultimately cost Grant the nomination.[16]

Once firmly established, the national nominating convention assumed all of the responsibility for deciding presidential and vice-presidential nominations. Through a committee system it became the sovereign voice of the party with respect to platforms, rules, delegate credentials, and apportionment of delegates. In 1832 and 1836, Democrats elected the same individual as both permanent as well as temporary chairman. Thereafter, those two posts went to different individuals until the 1968 convention did away with the temporary chairmanship altogether.[17] The first Democratic convention to adopt a platform met in 1840. The Whigs followed suit in 1844. An early version of the Democratic National Committee (DNC) surfaced in 1844. Whistling past the graveyard, the Whigs established their own national committee in 1852.

TYPES OF CONVENTIONS

Gerald M. Pomper classifies conventions according to the amount of discretion that delegates enjoy in choosing presidential nominees and by the show of support for candidates. Delegates enjoyed more discretion in multi-ballot than in single-ballot conventions. To date, most single-ballot conventions have been of the "ratifying" type, so called because delegates have no alternative to the nominee-apparent. Accordingly, the nominee wins on the first ballot with at least two-thirds of all delegate votes. Delegates enjoy greater discretion at "limited-choice" conventions where (1) two or more candidates compete for the nomination, (2) the winner prevails on the first and only ballot, and (3) the winner receives less than two-thirds of the vote. Two Democratic nominations of the limited-choice type (those of 1904 and 1928) occurred during the period when the two-thirds rule was in effect. In both cases, a shift occurred immediately after the first ballot, thus negating the need for a second. Conventions requiring two or more ballots nominate "major" candidates (who receive at least 20 percent on the first ballot) or "minor" candidates (less than 20 percent on the first ballot).[18]

Table 1 applies Pomper's classification to all Democratic and Republican nominations, grouped according to convention eras. In every period and for both parties, "ratifying" conventions show up most frequently. Overall, Republicans have held more of these conventions than Democrats, a pattern especially apparent after the Democrats abandoned the two-thirds rule. Three of eight Democratic nominations between 1972 and 2000 were of the "limited-choice" type, compared with only one for the GOP. As for multi-ballot conventions, "minor" candidates won most of their nominations during the 1832–1908 period, although the last of these nominations (Harding and Davis) occurred in the 1920s. No Republican has needed more than one ballot to win nomination since 1948, no Democrat since 1952.

A ratifying convention need not be an occasion for celebration. Astonish-

Table 1

Democratic and Republican Presidential Nominations, Grouped by Convention Eras

	Democrats							
	1836–1908		1912–1968		1972–2000		1836–2000	
	N	%	N	%	N	%	N	%
Convention type								
Ratifying	8	42	7	47	5	62	20	48
Limited choice	1	5	3	20	3	37	7	17
Major candidate	6	32	3	20	—	—	9	21
Minor candidate	4	21	2	13	—	—	6	14
Total	19	100	15	100	8	99	42	100

	Republicans							
	1856–1908		1912–1968		1972–2000		1852–2000	
	N	%	N	%	N	%	N	%
Convention type								
Ratifying	7	50	8	53	7	87	22	59
Limited choice	2	14	3	20	1	12	6	16
Major candidate	1	7	2	13	—	—	3	8
Minor candidate	4	29	2	13	—	—	6	16
Total	14	100	15	99	8	99	37	99

Source: Gerald M. Pomper, *Nominating the President: The Politics of Convention Choice* (New York: Norton, 1966); *National Party Conventions 1831–1996* (Washington, D.C.: Congressional Quarterly Press, 1997); *New York Times* coverage of 2000 conventions.

Note: Some columns do not total to 100 percent due to rounding. Ratifying and limited choice conventions required only one ballot; multiple ballots were needed to nominate major and minor candidates.

ing as it may seem, the 1968 Democratic convention qualifies as a ratifying event (Humphrey won 1,759.25 delegate votes out of 2,574.25 cast). Republicans faced an even grimmer choice in 1932: renominate Hoover and almost certainly lose, dump him and lose for certain.[19]

That said, the value of being nominated by a ratifying convention must be assessed against nominations made by the opposition. Table 2 compares every Democratic and Republican convention since 1856. The record shows that almost every nominee chosen by a ratifying convention has won when matched against an opponent nominated under different circumstances. In instances where both conventions nominated by ratifying majorities, Republicans went on to win six of eleven elections. When neither party tendered a ratifying nomination, Republicans won four of seven elections.

Table 2
Convention Type and Success of Nominees in Presidential Elections, 1856–2000

	Democratic ratifying	Republican ratifying
Nominees winning election	5	6
Incumbents seeking renomination	4	4
Incumbents winning reelection	4	3

	Democratic ratifying	Republican other
Nominees winning election	5	2
Incumbents seeking renomination	4	2

	Democratic other	Republican ratifying
Nominees winning election	2	9
Incumbents seeking renomination	1	7
Incumbents winning reelection	0	6

	Democratic other	Republican other
Nominees winning election	3	4
Incumbents seeking renomination	0	1
Incumbents winning reelection	0	0

Source: Gerald M. Pomper, *Nominating the President: The Politics of Convention Choice* (New York: Norton, 1996), 182–93; *National Party Conventions, 1831–2000* (Washington, D.C.: Congressional Quarterly Press, 2001).

Note: The "other" categories combine major candidate, minor candidate, and limited choice types. Both parties held ratifying conventions in 1864, 1872, 1900, 1908, 1936, 1944, 1964, 1988, 1992, 1996, and 2000. Democratic ratifying conventions were matched against other types of Republican conventions in 1888, 1892, 1916, 1940, 1948, 1968, and 1976. Other types of Democratic conventions contrasted with ratifying Republican conventions in 1868, 1896, 1904, 1924, 1928, 1932, 1956, 1960, 1972, 1980, and 1984. Neither party held a ratifying convention in 1856, 1860, 1876, 1880, 1884, 1912, 1920, and 1952. Owing to the uncertainty of the 1876 outcome, Tilden and Hayes have been omitted from the "other/other" comparison.

Convention type also appears to influence an incumbent's chances of getting reelected. Except for Cleveland in 1888, Hoover in 1932, and George H. W. Bush in 1992, every sitting president renominated by a ratifying convention has been reelected. Thus far, every president renominated under limited-choice conditions has gone down to defeat: Harrison in 1892, Taft in 1912, Ford in 1976, and Carter in 1980. In every case, the president faced serious opposition from leaders of his own party.

"AVAILABILITY" OF PRESIDENTIAL NOMINEES

It was once axiomatic that presidential aspirants had to demonstrate their "availability" to merit serious consideration at the nominating convention. Presumably this applied not only to front-runners but also to "favorite sons" (nominated by their home state), long shots (named on the first ballot but given little chance), and "dark horses" (late entrants in the presidential balloting), since aspirants of the last three descriptions had rarely won nomination.

Availability may be defined in many ways, but according to James Bryce, electoral considerations trumped all others. Except in extraordinary circumstances, he wrote in 1888, voter appeal in selected states supposedly counted a great deal more than the candidate's integrity, intelligence, or experience. To paraphrase Bryce's argument, it is better to choose an "inferior" candidate from a large state with many electoral votes than to select a "somewhat superior" candidate from a smaller state. Better also to choose someone from a competitive rather than a dependable state. Bryce's maxim persisted well into the next century. Sidney Hyman wrote in 1959, "a candidate is preferred who comes from a pivotal state which has a large electoral vote and which does not have a one-party voting pattern."[20] In 1964, Paul David and associates likewise cited the conventional wisdom of choosing nominees from "large" and "politically doubtful" states rather than small and safe ones.[21]

We can assess the accuracy of these claims precisely, first, by classifying each state's size according to the difference between its electoral vote total and the average electoral vote for all of the states in any given election. (In 1836, for example, New York had forty-two electoral votes, nearly quadrupling the 11.1 average for all twenty-six states.) "Big" states exceed the national average by two times or more, while "medium" states also exceed the national average, but by less than a factor of two. "Small" states cast fewer than average electoral votes. As for competitiveness, we may categorize "dependable" states as those voting for the nominee's party in all three of the previous presidential elections, and "doubtful" states as those voting against the nominee's party at least once in the last three elections. The most doubtful state for Democrats is one that is dependably Republican, just as a dependably Democratic state is most doubtful for Republicans. Thus defined, both measures allow for relative changes in a state's size and competitiveness over time.

Remarkably few states show up as "big" over the entire span of electoral history since 1836. New York has easily topped the list in size as well as in competitiveness for nearly all of this period. Consistently the biggest until California surpassed it in 1972, the Empire State has voted Democratic twenty times, Whig two times, and Republican twenty times. A slender margin of victory in New York has sometimes decided presidential outcomes—as in 1884—when Grover Cleveland carried the state by a mere 1,047 votes out of nearly 1.7 million cast. (James G. Blaine probably lost New York and the election by not promptly disavowing a supporter's infamous "Rum, Romanism, and Rebellion" remark.)[22] Pennsylvania first qualified as a big state in 1836. Ohio has been an electoral powerhouse since 1844. Illinois achieved this status in 1872, as did Texas in 1932, California in 1944, and Florida in 1992. Virginia briefly enjoyed big-state status in 1836 and 1840.

The number of "medium" states has ranged from five to fifteen over the same span of electoral history. Kentucky, for example, enjoyed this distinction from 1836 through 1928. Hardier perennials include Massachusetts and Tennessee (in every election since 1836), Virginia (since 1844), Indiana (since 1852), and Missouri (since 1864). The range is deceptive, however, because it takes in Georgia, North Carolina, Tennessee, Texas, and Virginia—all medium states that broke with the Union during the Civil War.

As Bryce observed in 1888, no son of a formerly Confederate state would enjoy any prospect of getting nominated for president for the foreseeable future. Only Woodrow Wilson succeeded before Lyndon Johnson won the prize in 1964, and Wilson achieved this feat while governor of New Jersey.[23] Johnson, moreover, almost certainly would not have won the nomination had he not been John Kennedy's vice president.

In sum, the Democrats have conferred 59 percent of all their presidential nominations on residents of big or medium states of the doubtful type, and the same holds true for 42 percent of all Republican nominations. Consistent with Bryce's claim about the value of coming from a large state, New York has dominated the lists of candidates from both parties (thirteen of forty-two nominations on the Democratic side and nine of thirty-eight on the Republican side). Ohio, Illinois, California, Texas, New Jersey, Pennsylvania, Massachusetts, and Indiana have also figured importantly as big if not always doubtful states in the nominating politics of at least one party. Both parties have broken Bryce's rule on occasion and picked sons of small states. Among Democrats matching this description, only Pierce of New Hampshire represented a small and safe state. Cass, McClellan, Bryan, Davis, Humphrey, McGovern, Mondale, and Clinton all hailed from more competitive states. All four Republicans in this category—

Blaine, Landon, Goldwater, and Dole—came from small and dependably Republican states.

Clearly, "availability" in the halcyon days of the national convention meant more than residence in a large and competitive state outside of the South. Except for recent immigrants, most Americans of Bryce's day had lived through the Civil War. For the rest of the nineteenth century, every presidential candidate nominated by the GOP except James G. Blaine had served in the Union army, and in Blaine's case the Republicans balanced the ticket with John A. Logan, a "political general" who had performed heroically in battle. Badly split by the war, the Democrats understandably put less of a premium on Union army service, as the nominations of Horatio Seymour, Samuel Tilden, and Grover Cleveland attest.

Like Bryce, Sidney Hyman in 1959 noted the importance of religious and ethnic background to presidential nominations. Hyman also held that experienced officeholders, governors, candidates who "come from" small towns, men acceptable to leading economic interests, and exemplars of "all that is virtuous in home and family life" had a much better chance of nomination than men who did not answer to these descriptions.[24] Moreover, the process of "natural selection" excluded women, "colored peoples," and the foreign-born (already barred by the Constitution). Similarly, it supposedly ruled out as men with serious health problems, histories of "spectacular marital difficulties," big-city identities, and little government experience.[25]

Readers should have little difficulty in finding exceptions to these generalizations. Fremont was born illegitimate, Buchanan never married, and Lincoln exhibited symptoms of acute depression. Wilson had a long history of hypertension, Harding showed early signs of heart disease, and polio afflicted FDR, who stood erect only with leg braces and "walked" with the help of others. Party leaders knew about these physical limitations even if the general public did not. Moreover, Harding and Franklin D. Roosevelt hardly stood out as paragons of marital fidelity, while Stevenson won nomination despite a messy divorce. No nominee personified big-city habits more than Al Smith. A recent convert to the GOP, Willkie won nomination without having served a day as an elected official. McClellan, Grant, Hancock, and Eisenhower had no prior experience in elected office, although none was a stranger to national politics.

Table 3 compares Democratic and Republican presidential nominees according to ethnicity, childhood spent in small towns, church affiliation, and the last government post held prior to nomination. It shows that all of the Republicans and all but one of the Democrats traced their ancestry to Western Europe, mostly to the British Isles. Michael Dukakis stands out as the lone exception as the offspring of Greek immigrants. History has also upheld Hyman on the preponderance of nominees raised in small towns—77 percent of Democrats and 80 percent of Republicans.[26] His claim of an inordinate advantage for Protestants still holds true. Except for Smith, Kennedy, and Dukakis, every convention nominee (Whigs included) has been a Protestant of some sort, including several who belonged to no one church but worshipped at several. Presbyterians stand out as the largest Protestant denomination among Democrats, followed by Baptists and Episcopalians. Among Republicans, Episcopalians and Methodists top the list.

Table 3
Backgrounds of Democratic and Republican Presidential Nominees

	Democrats, 1836–2000		Republicans, 1852–2000		Combined party totals	
Ethnicity	N	%	N	%	N	%
British	25	83	18	72	43	78
Other Western European	4	13	7	28	11	20
Other	1	3	—	—	1	2
Raised in small town	23	77	20	80	43	78
Church affiliation						
Baptist	5	17	2	8	7	13
Episcopal	5	17	7	28	12	22
Methodist	1	3	6	24	7	13
Presbyterian	9	30	2	8	11	20
Other Protestant	5	17	7	28	12	22
Catholic	2	7	—	—	2	4
Other	1	3	—	—	1	2
None	2	7	1	4	3	5
Last office before nomination						
Governor of a state	12	40	6	24	18	33
Vice president	6	20	5	20	11	20
U.S. senator	5	17	5	20	10	18
U.S. representative	2	3	2	8	4	7
Cabinet secretary	—	—	3	12	3	5
Ambassador	2	7	—	—	2	4
Supreme Court justice	—	—	1	4	1	2
Army general	2	7	2	8	4	7
Other	1	3	—	—	1	2
None	—	—	1	4	1	2

Source: Joseph N. Kane, *Presidential Fact Book* (New York: Random House, 1998); William A. DeGregorio, *The Complete Book of U.S. Presidents*, 5th ed. (New York: Gramercy Books, 2001); Leslie H. Southwick, *Presidential Also-Rans and Running Mates, 1788 Through 1996* (Jefferson, N.C.: McFarland, 1988); correspondence with Southwick regarding ethnicity of Stevenson, McGovern, and Dole; Bob Zelnick, *Gore: A Political Life* (New York: Regnery, 1990).

Note: "British" ethnicity includes English, Scottish, Irish, Welsh, or some combination thereof. The most common combinations were Anglo-Irish and Scotch-Irish.

This table also lists the last offices held by candidates prior to winning the presidential nomination. On the one hand, the combined figures uphold Hyman's conclusion that governors win more nominations than anybody else. On the other hand, the Democrats have nominated twice as many serving governors as the GOP, including five from New York (Seymour, Tilden, Cleveland, Smith, and Franklin Roosevelt).[27] Little by way of party difference surfaces in the nomination of vice presidents and senators, but only the Republicans have plucked nominees from the Cabinet (Blaine, Taft, and Hoover) and the Supreme Court (Hughes).

ARE GREAT MEN NOMINATED?

Bryce famously answered no: too many factors in U.S. politics work to keep potentially great presidents from getting nominated. Since the passing of Jefferson, Madison, and Adams, he wrote in 1888, "no person except General Grant has reached the chair whose name would have been remembered had he not been president, and no president except Abraham Lincoln has displayed rare or striking qualities in the chair." Given a choice between a luminary and a mediocrity, Bryce argued, party leaders prefer the dimmer but more electable candidate. Brilliant men cast a harsh light on lesser sorts as they build their careers in politics; they also make enemies and unsettle key constituencies.

Greatness defies easy measurement, of course, and Bryce's comparison of American presidents with British prime ministers hardly qualifies as objective.[28] Harold J. Laski took issue with Bryce's listing of Daniel Webster and John C. Calhoun as examples of great men spurned by the convention system. The answer to that argument, Laski wrote in 1940, was that conventions did nominate first-rate men like Abraham Lincoln, Woodrow Wilson, and Franklin D. Roosevelt. Moreover, he argued, "The reasons which stopped others would have been powerful reasons against their elevation in any representative democracy."[29] Subsequent defenders of convention choices have listed Charles Evans Hughes, Wendell Willkie, Thomas Dewey, Harry Truman, Adlai Stevenson, Dwight Eisenhower, Richard Nixon, John Kennedy, and Hubert Humphrey as noteworthy exceptions to the Bryce rule.[30]

Bryce's bias clearly shows up in his denigration of Van Buren, Polk, and Buchanan as "mere politicians," unworthy to follow in Washington's footsteps. Conversely, Jefferson, Madison, Monroe, and John Q. Adams stand out as "men of education, of administrative experience, of a certain largeness of view and dignity of character." Moreover, all had served "in the great office of secretary of state." Although no one disputes that Buchanan ranks near the bottom of American presidents, few would count Madison, Monroe, or John Q. Adams among our most accomplished presidents. Since Bryce placed so much stock in resumes, let us take a closer look at Buchanan's record: he won election to the Pennsylvania legislature and to both houses of Congress; he represented the United States as minister to Russia and Great Britain; and, yes, he also held the great office of secretary of state. Similarly, Van Buren served in the New York legislature and the U.S. Senate before becoming governor of New York, secretary of state, and vice president. Polk won his nomination after a term as governor of Tennessee and seven terms in the U.S. House, including two terms as Speaker. As for grand visions, did Monroe or Adams offer any as big as Polk's "Manifest Destiny" or Van Buren's competitive party system?

Although recognition of Polk's accomplishments have since boosted his standing, many of Bryce's assessments still resonate with presidential experts. Table 4 shows that preconvention presidents fared quite well in a recent poll of scholars, pundits, and practitioners of politics. But so did a dozen nominees of powerful conventions, including Lincoln, both Roosevelts, Wilson, Truman, and Eisenhower. As for presidents chosen in the current primary-dominated system, all except Carter were assessed in this survey as mediocre or worse. But, writes Murray Edelman, "ascription of leadership is profoundly a function of the passing of time. The leader as an historical figure is not the same symbol as he was to his contemporaries. Always, however, he is made to be what will serve the interests of those who follow him or write about him or remember him."[31]

TICKET BALANCING

After choosing a presidential nominee, the delegates turn next to the choice of a running mate. Contrary to M. Ostrogorski's suggestion in chapter 7, the delegates frequently attached great importance to the vice-presidential choice, even when motivated by parochial concerns or smitten by oratory. For much of convention history, presidential nominees ostensibly left the choice of a running mate to party leaders and the delegates. Not every choice went down well with the top of the ticket, as in 1912, when Wilson's managers accepted Gov. Thomas Marshall of Indiana as a running mate in return for desperately needed votes. Wilson objected to Marshall when informed of the deal, but to no avail.[32]

Franklin D. Roosevelt broke with tradition in 1940 by demanding that the Democratic convention nominate Secretary of Agriculture Henry Wallace, an ardent left-winger, as his running mate. News of FDR's ultimatum outraged delegates already upset by the direction taken by the New Deal. Only after a concerted effort by party leaders and Eleanor Roosevelt did the delegates pick Wallace over twelve other names placed in nomination.[33] In 1944, however, party leaders forced Wallace off the ticket. The 1940 precedent proved to be more important than the rebuff of a dying FDR four years later. Presidential nominees now had the power to pick their own running mates. Only one has since surrendered this responsibility to the convention, and when Adlai Stevenson took this "bold" step in 1956, House Speaker Sam Rayburn called it "the damnedest fool idea I ever heard of."[34] (Owing to vote shifts after the sec-

Table 4
Nominating Systems and Perceived Presidential Greatness

Quartile ranking	Presidential nominating system			
	Electoral College, Cong. Caucus, States, 1789–1828	*Conventions alone decide the nomination, 1832–1908*	*Conventions supplemented by primaries, 1912–1968*	*Primaries decide the nomination, not conventions, 1972–1996*
First	Washington (3), Jefferson (4), Jackson (8), Madison (10)	Lincoln (1), T. Roosevelt (5)	F. Roosevelt (2), Wilson (6), Truman (7), Eisenhower (9)	
Second	Monroe (13), J. Adams (14), J. Q. Adams (18)	Polk (11) Cleveland (16), McKinley (17), Taft (20)	L. Johnson (12), Kennedy (15)	Carter (19)
Third		Van Buren (21), Hayes (25), Arthur (28), Taylor (29), Garfield (30)	Hoover (24)	Bush (22), Clinton (23), Reagan (26), Ford (27)
Fourth		B. Harrison (31), Tyler (34), W. H. Harrison (35), Fillmore (36), Pierce (37), Grant (38), A. Johnson (39), Buchanan (40)	Nixon (32), Coolidge (33), Harding (41)	

Source: Derived from William J. Ridings Jr. and Stuart B. McIver, *Rating the Presidents*, rev. ed. (New York: Citadel Press, 2000), xi.

Note: This table reports rankings (in parentheses) obtained from 719 historians, political scientists, and other political analysts. The summary scores reported above were based on respondents' judgments of each president's leadership qualities, accomplishments, crisis management skills, political skills, appointments, character, and integrity. The Bush entry is for George H. W. Bush, the forty-first president. Nixon's location is arbitrary because it spans the mixed and contemporary systems. W. H. Harrison's rating is especially suspect owing to his brief time in office.

ond ballot, Sen. Estes Kefauver prevailed over a youthful John F. Kennedy. This marked the last time that either party needed more than one ballot to choose a vice-presidential nominee.)

Running mates have always been chosen with the idea of balancing the ticket. If a westerner wins the grand prize, Ostrogorski avows, then the consolation prize must go to an easterner. Paul T. David and associates attach similar importance to geographical balance, even to the point of concluding that a lack of regional balance spells defeat in the fall.[35] Indeed, region figured importantly as a factor in choosing vice-presidential running mates. All but five of forty-one Democratic tickets paired candidates from different regions, as did thirty-three of thirty-six Republican tickets.[36] Clearly, some regions figured more importantly than others in striking these bargains. Table 5 shows that north-easterners headed 52 percent of all the Democratic tickets and that men from what today we call the Midwest headed an additional 27 percent. Whether as presidential or vice-presidential nominees, northeasterners and midwesterners shared the honors on nearly one-third of all Democratic tickets. Similarly, men from the Northeast and Midwest received top billing on 72 percent of all Republican tickets. Only Republican tickets made room for westerners, while southerners fared much better among Democrats.

What looks like regional balance, however, might also be a match-up of states of varying electoral clout, or states with different voting histories. If state size and partisanship matter in the choice of presidential nominees, why not in the selection of a running mate? From this perspective, the pairing of two big states need not constitute an imbalance—unless both have histories of dependably voting for the nominee's party. But a ticket consisting of two candidates from small states is unbalanced, regardless of how competitive these states might be.

Table 5 indicates that state size figures importantly in the match-up of presidential and vice-presidential nominees. Big-state representatives have headed 49 percent of all Democratic tickets, compared with 61 percent on the Republican side. Medium-state representatives have topped another 22 percent of the Democratic tickets, compared with 25 percent of those nominated by the GOP.

Consistent with Bryce's argument, both parties have been reluctant to pair one small state with another. Five Democratic tickets violate this norm: Franklin Pierce (New Hampshire) and William R. King (Alabama) in 1852, William J. Bryan (Nebraska) and Arthur Sewall (Maine) in 1896, John W. Davis (West Virginia) and Charles W. Bryan (Nebraska) in 1924, as well as Hubert Humphrey (Minnesota) and Edmund Muskie (Maine) in 1968. Only once did the Republicans approve such a combination, in 1856, when they hitched John C. Fremont of California to William L. Dayton of New Jersey. (All but the Pierce-King ticket lost.)

Table 5
State Factors in Balancing of Democratic and Republican Tickets, 1836–2000
(in percentages)

Vice-presidential nominee's state	Presidential nominee's state		
Democrats	*Northeast*	*Midwest*	*Other regions*
Northeast	—	10	5
Midwest	22	5	9
Other	30	12	7
Total	52	27	21
Republicans			
Northeast	—	33	8
Midwest	14	8	12
Other	17	—	9
Total	31	41	29
Democrats	*Big*	*Medium*	*Small*
Big	12	7	7
Medium	22	5	12
Small	15	10	10
Total	49	22	29
Republicans			
Big	31	8	11
Medium	19	6	—
Small	11	11	3
Total	61	25	14
	Dependably Democratic	*Doubtful*	*Republican*
Democrats			
Dependably Democratic	7	2	2
Doubtful	5	54	12
Dependably Republican	—	15	2
Total	12	71	17
Republicans			
Dependably Democratic	6	6	3
Doubtful	6	36	19
Dependably Republican	—	6	19
Total	12	48	41

Note: The second Republican row totals to 101 due to rounding. Ns are 41 for the Democrats and 36 for the Republicans, owing to deletion of the 1840 Democratic and 1864 Republican conventions. In 1840 the Democrats refused to renominate Richard Johnson as Van Buren's vice president; in 1864 the Republican ticket of National Union included Andrew Johnson of Tennessee, a state that had seceded and accordingly had no vote in the election.

Source: *Presidential Elections, 1789–1996* (Washington, D.C.: Congressional Quarterly Press, 1997) and *Presidential Elections, 1789–2000* (Washington, D.C.: Congressional Quarterly Press, 2002).

Table 5 also addresses the issue of state voting records. Because a doubtful state is intended to contest electoral votes otherwise taken for granted by the opposition, it follows that at least one resident of a doubtful state would show up on 93 percent of all Democratic tickets. The Republican figure is 81 percent. Other things being equal, it inefficient to take both nominees from dependable states and even more so when both states are small.

Table 6 shows that region, electoral votes, and state voting history all figure in the politics of ticket balancing. Competitiveness—measured by a state's voting record in the three preceding presidential elections—is the most common variable in Democratic ticket balancing overall, as well as the most common for Democratic conventions from 1832 to 1908. State size stands out as the most frequent factor in balancing Republican tickets. Largely because of Ohio's importance, competitiveness has mattered less to Republicans than size or region.

The near universal appearance of state indicators hardly tells us all we need to know about ticket balancing. Consider the Republicans' 1940 nomination of Wendell Willkie, ostensibly of New York, and Sen. Charles W. McNary of Ore-

Table 6
Comparison of State Factors in Ticket Balancing

	Democrats		Republicans		Total	
	N	%	N	%	N	%
1836–1908						
Regional	16	89	12	92	28	90
State size	16	89	12	92	28	90
Competitiveness	17	94	10	77	27	87
1912–1968						
Regional	14	93	14	93	28	93
State size	13	87	15	100	28	93
Competitiveness	13	87	13	87	26	87
1972–2000						
Regional	6	75	7	87	13	81
State size	8	100	8	100	16	100
Competitiveness	8	100	6	75	14	87
1836–2000						
Regional	36	88	33	92	69	90
State size	37	90	35	97	72	93
Competitiveness	38	93	29	80	67	87

Source: *Presidential Elections, 1789–1996* (Washington, D.C.: Congressional Quarterly Press, 1997) and *Presidential Elections, 1789–2000* (Washington, D.C.: Congressional Quarterly Press, 2002).

gon. Herbert Eaton's account makes clear that neither state size nor regional balance had much to do with placing McNary on the ticket:

> Willkie was an internationalist pledged to the cause of all possible aid to the Allies; McNary was a leading isolationist who had even voted against repeal of the arms embargo. Willkie endorsed reciprocal trade agreements and lower tariffs; McNary was a high-tariff man. Willkie came to national fame fighting public ownership of utilities and TVA; McNary favored the New Deal power program. Willkie was supremely confident of his ability to win the election; McNary was on record as predicting certain defeat if Willkie were the nominee. McNary, as a life-long Republican and party leader in the Senate, did, at least, help to offset Willkie's johnny-come-lately Republicanism.[37]

Yet another reason to put McNary on the ticket is that he had just lost the nomination to Willkie. Ostrogorski mentions compensating a rival as a factor in ticket balancing, but one should not make too much of this, as Jesse Jackson discovered in 1988. Having finished second in the overall primary vote, Jackson demanded that Dukakis accept him as running mate. In fact, less than one-fourth of all Democratic tickets have been balanced in this way, and Dukakis's choice of Sen. Lloyd Bentsen is a case in point. The Republican figure is slightly higher at 28 percent.[39] Yet when an erstwhile rival offers something the nominee-apparent lacks, the logic of the situation may call for an exception to general practice. By putting Lyndon Johnson on the ticket, Kennedy greatly helped his chances in the South. Similarly, Reagan overcame his disdain for George H. W. Bush in 1980 because Bush had demonstrated strength during the primaries in industrial states where Carter appeared weak.[40]

Another frequently mentioned motivation behind the choice of vice-presidential nominees is to appease a disappointed faction, perhaps by seeking its approval or even allowing it to make the selection. One should hesitate before quantifying the frequency of this variable, however, because faction overlaps so much with region. Clearly, factions representing ideological or policy differences frequently have figured in the choice of a vice-presidential running mate. This happened in 1880, when the "half-breeds" backing James Garfield appeased the GOP "stalwarts" by giving the vice-presidential nod to Chester A. Arthur.[41] A similar arrangement led to slating John A. Logan as Blaine's running mate in 1884. Logan's selection also had the virtue of compensating a defeated rival. Gerald Ford's surprise choice of Bob Dole went down well with Reagan's disappointed supporters at the 1976 Republican convention.[42]

On notable occasions, however, such differences were simply too bitter to paper over, as was evident in 1952 when Eisenhower refused to accept not only

Sen. Robert Taft, his main rival for the nomination, but also Taft's recommendation, Sen. Everett Dirksen.[43] George W. Bush likewise refused to embrace John McCain in 2000, despite McCain's demonstrated appeal to independent voters.

Several other criteria of occasional importance to ticket balancing should be noted. Governors nominated for president often choose Washington insiders to offset their inexperience in foreign affairs and national policymaking. Recent examples include Carter, Dukakis, and George W. Bush.[44] Summing up Bush's choice of running mate, a capital source noted, "Bush didn't choose Dick Cheney because he would deliver Wyoming."[45]

Ostrogorski mentions personal wealth as an important factor in filling the second spot, and history casts up at least two examples of Democrats who were chosen mainly for their personal fortunes: William H. English (Hancock's running mate in 1880) and Henry Gassaway Davis (on the ticket with Alton B. Parker in 1904).[46] Although not the principal concern, wealth also figured importantly in at least two vice-presidential nominations by the GOP: Levi P. Morton (paired with Harrison in 1888) and James S. Sherman (on the ticket with Taft in 1908).[47]

Religion has also played a part in ticket balancing, albeit infrequently. New York's Al Smith, the first Catholic ever nominated by a major party for president, shared the 1928 ticket with Joseph T. Robinson of Arkansas, a Methodist. (Robinson was also the Senate Democratic leader, a southerner, and a "dry" on the Prohibition issue). John Kennedy, the next Catholic nominated by the Democrats for president, likewise chose a Protestant southerner, Lyndon Johnson, as his running mate. George McGovern, a Methodist, picked Sen. Thomas Eagleton, a Catholic, but soon replaced him with another Catholic, Sargent Shriver, after an embarrassing search precipitated by revelations that Eagleton had undergone psychiatric therapy, including electric shock treatments. Also a Catholic, Rep. Geraldine Ferraro stands out chiefly as the first woman ever put on the ticket by a major party. Sen. Joseph Lieberman gained similar prominence as the first Jew nominated by a major party for vice president.

One presidential slate of recent vintage—Bill Clinton and Al Gore in 1992—has often been described as having thrown out the rulebook of ticket balancing. Clearly Clinton and Gore had much in common. Both were white, Baptist, southern, from neighboring states, and relatively young. Both had been active on the Democratic Leadership Council. Both happily steeped themselves in the details of public policy. Clinton's camp hyped this putative break with tradition by proclaiming: "This ticket is different."[48] Still, Gore's strengths offset Clinton's weaknesses in traditional if unheralded ways: Gore's congressional experience balanced Clinton's inexperience in national government, just as Mondale had done for Carter. Tennessee commanded nearly twice as many electoral votes as Arkansas, and neither state had voted Democratic in a presidential election since 1976.

In sum, the concern to represent different elements of the party has always played some part in the choice of running mates. A choice seemingly balanced along regional lines may actually have more to do with a state's size or competitiveness, factional considerations, adding experience to the ticket, or some other factor. The importance attached to these criteria may change over time, but a perceived need to balance the ticket in one or more ways remains relatively constant.

SIZE, DELIBERATION, AND COLLECTIVE BEHAVIOR

No aspect of the nominating convention has attracted more criticism than its huge size. A mass meeting of such gigantic proportions, critics tirelessly argued during the convention's heyday, is incapable of deliberation. Knowingly or not, such critics took their case directly from Madison's elegant statement of the "size principle" in the *Federalist*:

> In the first place, the more numerous any assembly may be, of whatever characters composed, the greater is known to be the ascendancy of passion over reason. In the next place, the larger the number, the greater will be the proportion of members of limited information and of weak capacities. Now it is precisely on characters of this description, that the eloquence and address of the few are known to act with all their force. . . . Ignorance will be the dupe of cunning; and passion the slave of sophistry and declamation.[49]

Deliberation can be defined as a process based on the exchange of logical and factual information for the purpose of persuading opponents to accept a solution that best serves the greater good.[50] In this vein, Bryce denounced conventions as "monster meetings," concluding, "such a meeting is capable neither of discussing political questions and settling a political programme, nor of deliberately weighing the merits of rival aspirants for the nomination."[51]

Ostrogorski took an even harsher view of the convention's capacity for deliberation, disparaging almost every proceeding he witnessed. This disdain surfaces in his excoriation of platforms as cynical and disingenuous. It also shows up in his contempt for convention oratory, in slaps at the "wire-pullers," and in the characterization of the convention as a "a colossal travesty on popular institutions." But his heaviest blows fell on the delegates, whom he likened to puppets, lunatics, and stampeded cattle.

Similar references to collective irrationality abound in popular writings on the convention. William Allen White, a respected journalist and 1920 delegate, recounted how his fellow Kansans swung to Harding in an hour of "heat and confusion and insanity."[52] After observing a spirited demonstration in support of Al Smith in 1924, Will Rogers joshed: "Why, if they ever took a sanity test at a political convention, 98 percent would be removed to an asylum."[53]

No one disputes that the presidential nominating convention had become a massive affair by the 1880s. The number of delegates attending Republican conventions began at 567 in 1856, exceeded 700 by 1872, and surpassed 1,000 by 1912. It peaked at 2,277 in 1988 and dipped to 2,066 in 2000. Similarly, the number of Democratic delegates jumped from 1,154 in 1932 to 4,339 in 2000.[54] Delegates, of course, did not have the convention all to themselves. Alternate delegates joined the throng on the floor, while reporters, spectators, and supporters filled the galleries. A better idea of convention crowds can be gleaned from estimates of attendance at the six Republican conventions held in Philadelphia: "several thousand" in 1856; 3,000 in 1872; 20,000 in 1900; 17,000 in 1940; 16,500 in 1948; and 22,350 in 2000.[55]

Whether these enormous gatherings gave rise to collective insanity is a different matter. Numerous scholars rose to the convention's defense. Writing in 1940—at a time when totalitarianism cast a gigantic shadow over democracy's future—Pendleton Herring pointedly took issue with Ostrogorski and other critics who viewed convention proceedings through the "thick lenses of moralistic and rational values."[56] Those steeped in the ways of democracy, he argued, appreciated the value of allowing the party's rank and file to participate physically and emotionally in the common enterprise, even when their exuberance got out of hand: "Here are the men who must carry the brunt of the campaign. Here they have their chance to meet, to shoulder together, to act together, to feel together. The relationship of follower and leader is seldom an intellectual bond."[57] Clinton Rossiter hit the same note in a classic book on the American presidency: "Most criticisms of this noisy, plebeian, commercial institution are really criticisms of the noisy, plebeian, commercial civilization within which it operates." Moreover, Rossiter observed, "it is yet to be proved that men who act like deacons can make a better choice of candidates for the presidency than men who act like clowns."[58] Likewise, Herbert McClosky observed that the stereotype of "Babbitts who wear funny hats and engage in juvenile hijinks" is hardly fair to most delegates who "are above average in education, have participated in politics for many years, have usually held public or party office, are active in their local communities, and associate with the men who lead and manage affairs in almost every segment of society."[59]

As for lack of deliberation, Herring saw such criticism as misguided. Conceding that the force of intellect seldom triumphed on the convention floor, he countered that a mass meeting should not be judged for failing to function like a small committee. Rather, the convention's primary task was to settle on an electable nominee, one that would help the ticket back home and unite the party nationwide. These were its principal responsibilities and, to make good on them, party leaders had to bargain and compromise. Interestingly, Herring made no mention of the potential for deliberation in small group settings, most notably when state delegations caucused.

Much ink has been spilled in debates over the purpose, substance, and integrity of party platforms. Ostrogorski and other critics of his day called attention to ambiguity and circumlocution in the wording of key planks. Herring and other defenders of the convention process maintained that platforms helped unite the party. Moreover, most pointed up leading differences with the opposition party. Some even included solemn pledges to deliver on specific promises. In 1932, for example, Democrats characterized their platform as "a covenant with the people," and promised to implement "the principles, policies, and reforms herein advocated." Republicans expressed similar sentiments in 1936, 1940, and 1944: "The acceptance of the nominations tendered by this Convention carries with it, as a matter of private honor and public faith, an undertaking by each candidate to be true to the principles and program herein set forth."[60] Studies of platform content have found that both parties provide voters with enough information to make informed choices, and, further, that presidents have tried to make good on these promises upon winning election.[61]

Whatever their normative perspectives, most observers acknowledge that uncertainty was far more important in the decision making of old-fashioned conventions than deliberation. Ostrogorski maintained that uncertainty typically characterized balloting at the convention, owing to intrigues not yet consummated. The first ballot in such circumstances did not even reveal the full strength of rival forces, in part because convention managers often held some votes back for the second round. Bryce rendered a similar account of strategic balloting:

> The second ballot . . . sometimes reveals even more than the first. . . . The gain of even twenty or thirty votes for one of the leading candidates . . . so much inspirits his friends, and is so likely to bring fresh recruits to his standard, that a wily manager will often, on the first ballot, throw away some of his votes on a harmless antagonist that he may by rallying them increase the total of his candidate on the second, and so convey the impression of growing strength.[62]

In 1963 Nelson Polsby and Aaron Wildavsky addressed how delegates coped with rumor, disinformation, and competing claims of electability in making decisions, a problem greatly exacerbated by the great size of the convention, the difficulty of monitoring the activities of opposing camps, multiple ballots, and the absence of a titular leader. Much depended on the degree to which participants shared a common ranking of candidate strength, as interpolated from preconvention polls, primary outcomes, procedural votes at the convention, the presidential balloting, and reports of shifting support in key delegations.[63]

Building on the work of Polsby and Wildavsky, Eugene McGregor searches for indicators that might have helped delegates and party leaders cope with uncertainty at seventeen multiballot conventions from 1872 to 1948. Decision makers in McGregor's analysis genuinely wanted to side with the winner but had difficulty in divining just who that might be. Delegates frequently had little inkling of deals made in their name by party leaders, and party leaders could not be certain that promised coalitions would actually form. How, then, to obtain reliable information? McGregor argues that during this period both delegates and leaders alike looked closely at the results of the first two ballots and paid particular attention to gainers on the second ballot. McGregor's decision rule corresponds to the conclusions of Bryce and Ostrogorski: "The candidate who gains the largest share of the votes from the first to the second ballot will be the eventual winner no matter how many ballots are needed for nomination." Yet, as McGregor concedes, Republican conventions did not adhere to this rule when nominating Hayes, Garfield, Harrison, and Harding, none of whom posted the biggest gain on the second ballot. Party leaders in each case resolved the deadlock in ways contrary to the hypothesis.

Democratic conventions operating under the two-thirds rule cast up another sign that eventually proved misleading. As Herbert Eaton notes, sixty-eight years of experience had taught Democrats that the first candidate to win a simple majority of the delegate votes was destined to win the supermajority needed for nomination. When Champ Clark crossed the threshold on the tenth ballot in 1912, his supporters wasted a critical hour in premature celebration. Meanwhile, Wilson's handlers formed a blocking coalition with supporters of Rep. Oscar Underwood. Clark lost the nomination to Wilson.[64]

In sum, the old-fashioned nominating convention was no place for purists irked by political circus. Compromise often characterized the choice of presidential nominees; it figured even more frequently in the choice of running mates and writing of platforms. The size of the convention unquestionably limited opportunities for deliberation and affected the collective behavior of delegates in important ways. Although hardly ideal, deliberation did go on at the convention, but it occurred at the level of small groups, when a state delegation or a handful of party leaders caucused to review their options. Despite myriad distractions, party leaders and delegates were able to identify signs of a candidate's strength. In addition to indicators already mentioned, the failure of a favorite to clinch the nomination early betrayed clear signs of weakness to delegates eager to side with a winner. Most if not all participants settled for a second or third choice if the sacrifice meant getting on the bandwagon before it rolled to victory. Even the rush to judgment so castigated by Ostrogorski exhibited a certain order: breaks always preceded stampedes and stampedes came just before the final ballot.

PURISTS VERSUS PROFESSIONALS AT THE CONVENTION

Critics of the convention in its heyday typically wrote delegates off as venal, parochial, and mediocre at best. Ostrogorski asserted that the vast majority of delegates sought only personal gain, while Bryce saw delegates as no more qualified to make presidential nominations than ordinary citizens. In the same vein, Paul David and associates described the delegates of the late nineteenth and early twentieth centuries as "boss-ridden, ill-educated, and preoccupied with the hope of political spoils."[65]

Studies since the 1940s have painted a rather different picture of convention delegates, and we can only wonder whether earlier accounts accurately described the delegates or unfairly caricatured them. It seems unlikely that delegates of the late nineteenth and early twentieth centuries did not divide along the political fault lines of their day, such as "stalwarts" versus "half-breeds" or progressive reformers against party regulars. Indeed, reform-minded activists of the Gilded Age—disparaged as "morning glories" and "goo goos"—bear more than a passing resemblance to "amateurs" and "purists" of the late twentieth century. In any case, James Q. Wilson introduced a new generation of political scientists to these distinctions in a book on 1950s political clubs in big-city politics in which he defined the amateur politician as an activist dedicated to a politics that will result in good public policy. Wilson argued that good public policy does not spring accidentally from the usual struggle for personal and party advantage. Rather it results from a steadfast commitment to merit, an approach that makes compromise unwelcome even when necessary.[66] In contrast, Wilson's "professional" politician cares about winning elections rather than holding to abstract ideals. To the professional, compromise lubricates the wheels of politics and makes it possible to form winning coalitions. If there is a greater good, it is a by-product of winning elections.[67]

Aaron Wildavsky applied a similar classification to delegates attending the 1964 Republican convention. He found that virtually all of the "purists" agreed with Goldwater on the issues and admired the strength and honesty of his convictions, as shown in the following fragment of an interview:

INTERVIEWER: What qualities should a presidential candidate have?

DELEGATE: Moral integrity.

INTERVIEWER: Should he be able to win the election?

DELEGATE: No, principles are more important. I would rather be one against 20,000 and believe I was right. That's what I admire about Goldwater. He's like that.

INTERVIEWER: Are most politicians like that?

DELEGATE: No, unfortunately. . . . But, now, for the first time in my life, we have a candidate who acts as he believes. He doesn't change his position when it is expedient.

INTERVIEWER: Do you think if the party loses badly in November it ought to change its principles?

DELEGATE: No. I'm willing to fight for these principles for ten years if we don't win.

INTERVIEWER: For fifty years?

DELEGATE: Even fifty years.

Some professionals sided with Goldwater but did so out of loyalty to the GOP. Asked to compare his views with those of more ardent Goldwater supporters, a conservative delegate from California described himself as "more practical" and more aware of the need to live together. "We are a minority party in California and we can't afford to squabble amongst ourselves. The art of politics is the art of compromise. If I can get a whole loaf, I'll take it. If not, I'll take half rather than lose it all."[68]

Purists or amateurs turned up at the 1968 and 1972 Democratic conventions as supporters of Eugene McCarthy and George McGovern. Wildavsky and Polsby drew parallels between Goldwater and McCarthy supporters, and, by another account, amateurs constituted 51 percent of all of the Democratic delegates in 1972, a 30 percent increase from 1968.[69] Subsequent research has softened the distinction between purists and professionals—at least when applied to caucus-convention activists in later years—so that purists appear more concerned with winning elections than has previously been acknowledged.[70]

REPRESENTATIVENESS OF CONVENTION DELEGATES

When asked to grapple with the many meanings of representation, political scientists readily adopt Hannah Pitkin's distinction between *standing for* and *acting for,* as well as her categories of *formalistic, symbolic,* and *descriptive* representation. Each has obvious application to presidential nominating conventions.[71]

In the convention context, *formalistic* representation pertains chiefly to the selection of individuals to play the role of delegates rather than to how the role is played. Still, selection criteria have consequences for the other dimensions of representation. For example, parties have always struggled with the question of how best to allocate delegate positions. As previously noted, the early solution was to apportion delegates in accordance with each state's electoral votes, also an indirect measure of state population. Eventually the failure of this method to provide fair representation of party followers—as opposed to all state inhabitants—became apparent. In 1950 a committee of prominent political scientists pointed up leading inequities: "Theoretically . . . the delegates represent simply population—Republican voters and nonvoters as well as Democratic voters. Because the rural population is greatly overrepresented in Congress, the urban centers, though virtually the party's backbone, are strongly discriminated against." To underscore their point, these experts cited enormous variations in the ratio of Democratic delegates to Democratic voters in 1948. The Illinois ratio was 1:33,245, whereas in Nevada it was 1:3,129. Similar disparities showed up on the Republican side: 1 delegate per 29,290 Republican voters in New York, compared with 1:894 in Nevada.[72]

The formal aspect of representation also arose when state parties selected delegates in closed and poorly publicized caucuses. This issue made its way onto the reform agenda of the McGovern-Fraser Commission in 1969–1970, with the result that state parties were required to give advance notice of all delegate selection activities and to open their proceedings to all interested persons who considered themselves Democrats.[73]

Symbolic representation speaks to efforts of the purveyors of symbolism to convince an audience.[74] If candidates are to be perceived as paragons of virtue, for example, these claims must be made credible to audiences whose support is critical to winning elections. Ostrogorski describes how the makers of nominating speeches soaked their rhetoric in such symbolism. For the most part, television has forced an end to prolix nominating speeches—with Bill Clinton's seemingly endless endorsement of Dukakis in 1988 as a notable exception—but convention rhetoric has lost none of its symbolic importance. This holds especially for nominees' acceptance speeches. Indeed, the most important function of today's conventions is to project symbols that revive party loyalty, mobilize party workers, arouse independents, and, hardly least, impress a cynical press corps. More so than in Ostrogorski's day, these messages are meant for a national audience rather than the assembled delegates.[75]

Issues of *descriptive* representation have forever been a part of American politics. John Adams captured the essence of this dimension when he avowed that an assembly empowered to act on behalf of others "should be an exact portrait in miniature, of the people at large, as it should think, feel, reason, and act like them."[76] But myriad studies have shown that convention delegates hardly constitute an exact miniature of their party's followers or of voters in general. A study of both 1944 conventions, for example, found that lawyers made up nearly one of every four delegates.[77] Lawyers outnumbered union members seventeen to one at the 1948 Democratic convention.[78] Jeane Kirkpatrick reported in 1976 that convention delegates "went to school longer, made more money, and had better jobs" than most other Americans.[79] Her words still applied in 2000, when 23 percent of all Republican convention delegates and 12 percent of their Democratic counterparts claimed a net worth of more than $1 million. More than half of all delegates in both parties reported family incomes exceeding $75,000, compared with 19 percent of all voters. Seventy-seven percent of Republican delegates and 72 percent of Democratic delegates in 2000 had earned one or more college degrees, compared with 28 percent of all voters.[80]

When one compares delegates to party adherents, the resulting differences are not always so big. Race is a case in point. African Americans routinely constitute a fifth of all Democratic delegates, as well as roughly a quarter of all Democratic voters. Likewise, the mere trace of a black vote in Republican primaries and for Republican candidates in the general election squares with the typically tiny presence of African Americans at Republican conventions, a figure rarely higher than 3 percent.[81]

Since publication of a seminal study by Herbert McClosky et al. in 1960, scholars have examined differences and similarities in attitudes between delegates and followers of the same party.[82] Working with surveys of delegates to the 1956 conventions, McClosky and associates found that most Democratic and Republican delegates clustered at opposing ends of the liberal-conservative spectrum, while most Democratic and Republican loyalists occupied the center. Republican delegates appeared especially isolated from the mainstream, so that the Republican rank and file often held views more closely to those of Democratic followers and convention delegates.

This view of Republican elites out in right field dominated conventional wisdom about convention delegates until reforms of the late sixties and early seventies inclined researchers to revisit the issue. In 1972, Jeane Kirkpatrick found that it was the Democratic delegates who stood ideologically apart from the mainstream as well as from rank-and-file Democrats. Several studies disagreed as to whether the Democratic delegates in 1976 remained as ideologically isolated as they were in 1972.[83] Research in the 1980s revealed the emergence of a vast ideological gulf between Democratic and Republican elites.[84] This gap had increased to such a point in the mid-eighties that "liberal" and "conservative" no longer meant the same thing to Democrats and Republican.[85]

Pollsters now routinely ask delegates to identify themselves as "conservative," "very conservative," "liberal," or "very liberal." In 2000, 57 percent of Republican delegates described themselves as conservative or very conservative, compared with 1 percent liberal. Conversely, roughly one-third of their Democratic counterparts professed some degree of liberalism, while only 4 percent admitted to being conservative.[86] True, "moderates" showed up as the modal group in both samples, but this classification is of limited value because the middle of the Republican road lies well to the right of the Democratic center.

Responses to survey questions about specific policy issues support the generalization that delegates differ substantially from followers of the same party. In 1996 and 2000, for example, more Democratic voters sided with Republican delegates than with their own party elites in supporting a balanced budget amendment, an end to welfare payments after five years of dependency, tax-paid school vouchers, and substituting the death penalty for life imprisonment. The same surveys also showed that most Republican voters agreed with Democratic delegates on banning assault weapons, requiring safety locks on handguns, using trade restrictions to promote domestic industries, limiting the amount of campaign contributions, protecting the environment, and enhancing workplace safety through greater regulation of business. Even so, the same polls pointed up strong intraparty agreement on federal spending, affirmative action, and Social Security reform.[87]

In sum, the overwhelming preponderance of survey evidence shows that delegates constitute a socioeconomic elite when compared with their party's rank and file. But differences based on race, gender, and religion appear insignificant. Some issues bring out big differences between delegates and loyalists of the same party; other issues reflect consensus. Republican and Democratic delegates continue to view each other across a deep partisan divide.

THE REDUCED ROLE OF CONTEMPORARY CONVENTIONS

By many accounts, the contemporary convention is but a remnant of its former self. The old debate about bargaining and deliberation over presidential nominations has ended because convention nominations have become mere formalities. Except for the Republican convention of 1976, every nomination made since 1952 has been decided before the delegates actually convened. "As a practical matter," Polsby notes, "delegates pledged to candidates in each state are cleared if not actually named by the candidates and their agents. Such delegates represent nobody but the candidate to whom they are pledged. It is difficult to see in whose behalf they might presume to deliberate in the unlikely event they were to decide to do so."[88]

William G. Carleton anticipated this loss of the convention's foremost power eleven years before the Democratic debacle of 1968. He correctly forecast the end of smoke-filled rooms, multiple ballots, and dark-horse nominees, as well as their replacement by ratifying or limited-discretion conventions. His further contention that convention choice would be reduced to the best-known or most popular candidates has held up fairly well.[89] Carleton attributes this transformation largely to the rise of radio and television, the growing importance of presidential primaries, and increased involvement of "pressure groups," then mainly economic in focus. Subsequent analyses support the general thesis while putting particular emphasis on developments such as the Great Depression and World War II that nationalized American politics while undermining the power of local and state party organizations.[90]

No development has contributed more to the nationalization of presidential nominating politics than the advent of television. Sig Mickelson relates how television's coverage of the 1952 conventions proved far more transformative than anybody at the time realized. Perhaps inadvertently, choices made on the spot by CBS editors set lasting precedents for future coverage. Consider the decision to cut away from platform proceedings so that correspondents could interrupt with "breaking news" from the convention floor or other rumor mills. Then as now, networks had to deal with dreaded "dead time." Anchors and other "talking heads" thus took center stage. CBS executives also wrestled with the ethics of penetrating meetings closed to the press and public. Then as now, getting the story trumped propriety. Readers also get a whiff of network bias that has occasioned so much reaction in recent years.[91] Here, Mickelson recalls the CBS debate over airing all of Sen. Joe McCarthy's speech at the Republican convention or only snippets. In yet another hint of things to come, Eisenhower supporters exploited CBS coverage to project more youthful images than the opposition.

Today, thanks largely to influence of television, national conventions are likened to operatic performances, tightly scripted and carefully rehearsed with satisfaction of the audience utmost in mind.[92] A speaker's importance is gauged by the allotment of prime time to his appearance. Old-fashioned floor demonstrations no longer take place because they eat up precious television time. Governors, mayors, and others called to the microphone during the roll call of the states must forgo nearly all of the traditional display of state pride that added so much color to this once climactic moment. In 2000 the GOP drained what little excitement the roll call engendered by breaking it up over several days.

Parties hold conventions to put their nominees in the best possible light for the fall campaign, while networks televise conventions to attract large audiences. Unless delivered by celebrities plucked from the entertainment world, testimonials extolling the virtues of nominees strike network executives as soporific, hence bad for Nielsen ratings. A fight, however, never fails to attract a crowd. But, as Martin Wattenberg notes, conflict at the convention harms the party's chances in November. In every instance from 1964 to 1984, the party holding the more divisive convention attracted the most coverage. It also lost the election.[93]

It follows that nominees-apparent strive to minimize conflict whenever possible, and especially when allocating prime time slots to convention speakers. The GOP learned a bitter lesson in 1992 when Pat Buchanan used his time to sound the tocsin of culture war. Typically, potential troublemakers only get to speak when C-SPAN alone is covering the proceedings. The same holds for platform disputes.

The strategy of flying under the radar has become increasingly possible because all of the traditional networks no longer offer gavel-to-gavel coverage. Regardless of party in-fighting, the amount of convention exposure plunged precipitously after 1984. Today, relatively few households watch what little coverage the traditional networks still provide.[94] In 2000, one episode of *Survivor* attracted twice as many viewers as the total number watching convention coverage on other networks.[95]

It appears unlikely, however, that networks would follow the advice of ABC's Ted Koppel and simply pull the plug on convention coverage. For one thing, acceptance speeches still attract big audiences. Invariably hyped as somehow critical to deciding the outcome of the horse race, these presentations strike campaign themes and disclose likely lines of attack on the opposition. Network commentators accordingly parse the text for traces of clarity, commitment, and credibility.

Pundits also pay close attention to the "convention bounce" that usually follows adjournment. One week before the 2000 Republican convention, for example, the Gallup Poll showed Bush leading Gore by 50 to 39 percent. Immediately afterwards, Bush led by 54 to 37 percent. But Gore got a boost right after the Democratic convention that not only wiped out Bush's lead but also put him one percentage point ahead. As 2000 illustrates, some bounces soon dissipate while others, like Gore's, last well into the fall campaign.[96]

Analysis of convention gains from 1964 to 1992 reveals an average post-convention bounce of six points, exactly what Bush got out of his convention. The biggest gainers were Clinton (sixteen points in 1992), Carter (ten points in 1980 and nine in 1976), and Mondale (nine in 1984). Of the eighteen men nominated for president during this time, only one (McGovern in 1972) got no convention bounce whatever. Johnson and Humphrey picked up only two points each, while Dole improved his poll rating by only three points.

Such numbers mean little unless viewed in context. Huge gains may turn a race around, as happened in 1992, but they may also underscore a candidate's weakness, as with Carter in 1980 and Mondale in 1984. Although a negligible gain in poll ratings may indicate a nominee in serious trouble (McGovern, Humphrey, and Dole), a similarly small bounce like Johnson's in 1964 might just as well signal inelasticity in a lead already prohibitive. Equivalent gains by opposing nominees need not indicate an even division of voter preferences. Dukakis and George Bush got basically the same bounce in 1988 (seven points to six), but the net result was that Bush held the lead right up to election day.[97] Owing to back-to-back bounces of unusual magnitude for Clinton and Gore, the average Democratic gain since 1964 now exceeds that of the Republicans by roughly two points.[98]

Cities still compete for the honor and economic benefits of hosting conventions, and the parties still take account of political, economic, and symbolic factors when selecting a site. For example, Republicans chose New York City as their 2004 convention site partly to symbolize renewal after the terrorist attacks of September 11, 2001. Moreover, the economic benefits for the Big Apple's economy are substantial, such as $5 million to rent Madison Square Garden, $2.5 million to erect and equip the podium, and another $1.5 million to transport delegates and staffers to and from the hall. To entice the GOP, New York City's Host Committee promised to raise $94 million, and by late June of 2003 it had obtained pledges totaling $91 million, all this on top of a federal grant of roughly $14 million.[99] In 2000, Republicans raised more than $66 million and Democrats $31 million to host their conventions in Philadelphia and Los Angeles.[100]

In conclusion, the functionally diminished convention of today still serves a useful purpose for parties and presidential tickets. Although it merely affirms a presidential choice already decided by primary voters and a vice-presidential nomination already announced by the nominee-apparent, this ritual of approval still bears significantly on the fall campaign. The convention also puts the party stamp on the platform as well as on all proposed rules changes that get to the floor. Delegates attending future conventions probably will bear no greater resemblance to party rank and file than those of previous years. As before, their affluence, educational attainment, party commitment, and ideological fervor will distinguish them from the party's rank and file in important respects. Although generally subdued when contrasted with the exuberant spectacles that once so offended Ostrogorski, the contemporary political convention still brings together the party faithful of every state and federal territory. Delegates socialize, promote their personal agendas, build alliances, recharge their partisan batteries, and thus electrified, go forth into battle.

CHAPTER 5

The First National Nominating Convention

Samuel Eliot Morison

The national party convention as a method of nominating candidates for the presidency and vice presidency dates back in unbroken line to the election of 1832. Long before that, however, the same method was secretly employed by the Federalist Party. The Federalist convention of 1812 [. . .] has hitherto been regarded as the solitary instance of a national party convention before 1831.[1] This can no longer be maintained, for new material has recently come to light which tells the story of a secret meeting of Federalist leaders in New York in 1808 that nominated Pinckney and King for the presidency and vice-presidency, and served as a model for the convention of 1812. This was the original national nominating convention.

A peculiar problem of the Federalist Party, repeated in 1808 and in 1812, brought about this premature appearance of the keystone to modern party machinery. On each occasion the policy pursued by the Republicans—in 1808, embargo; in 1812, war with Great Britain—seemed absolutely destructive to the class and sectional interests represented by the Federalists. It was vitally necessary for them to defeat Madison at any cost. In each year an insurgent Democrat[2]—in both cases a Clinton—entered the presidential race with more or less of the Federalist policies as his platform. The question before the Feder-

From "The First National Nominating Convention, 1808," *American Historical Review* 17 (July 1912): 744–63. Morison (1887–1976) ranks among America's foremost historians. A prolific author, he spent most of his teaching career at Harvard and won many prizes for his published scholarship.

alist Party then, was whether to run their own candidates, or, with much greater chance of winning, to back the insurgent already in the field. Some method was necessary to reach a decision on this point that would be binding on the whole party. One alternative was to adopt the congressional caucus, the prevailing method of presidential nomination in the Republican Party. But to this there were many objections. The Federalists had already, in 1800, found the caucus ineffective for party harmony. In 1808, moreover, there were too few Federalists at Washington to make a Federalist caucus practicable, and the growing unpopularity of this method, even in the Republican Party, was counted on by the Federalists as part of their political capital against Madison. A convention of delegates was the only alternative.

Early in 1808 the political situation, in regard to the approaching presidential election, was as follows. For the Federalists the outlook was extremely gloomy. In looking over the list of electoral votes it was hard to see how 89, a majority, could be secured for a Federalist candidate. Since the election of 1804, in which Pinckney and King received but 14 electoral votes, the party had continued to lose ground in the states. The governments of New Hampshire in 1805, and of Vermont and Massachusetts in 1807, became for the first time in their history Democratic in every branch. In Congress, the Federalist minority was a negligible quantity. In consequence, it seemed hopeless to expect success for Federalist candidates. Timothy Pickering wrote from Washington in January: "The federalists here are in point of numbers so utterly impotent; and democracy governs in nearly all the States with such an overwhelming majority; nothing would be more remote from the contemplation of the federalists than to set up candidates of their own for President and Vice-President. They have only a choice of evils"—to support one of the insurgent movements in the Republican Party.[3] Of these there were two. The regular administration nominations—Madison for president and George Clinton for vice-president—were made by "Bradley's Caucus," consisting of 89 out of the 130 Republicans in Congress, on January 23. Two days earlier the "Quids" in the Virginia legislature, John Randolph's insurgent sect of some two years' standing, nominated James Monroe for the presidential chair. George Clinton's candidacy, caused by the disappointed ambition of his clan for the regular presidential nomination, was announced in March, and speedily supported by a number of influential Republican newspapers. Indications soon appeared that the Clintonians were bidding for Federalist backing. Rumor had it that Clinton disapproved of Jefferson's Embargo; James Cheetham and, of all persons, the *ci-devant* Citoyen Genét, vied with the Federalist editors in exposing French influence in the administration. Here was the Federalists' opportunity. Instead of going down to certain defeat with candidates of their own, why not join in supporting Clinton, who was thus endorsing their policies? Coalition with the Democrats was not unprecedented—it had already been effected in state elections in Pennsylvania, New York, and Rhode Island.

There was a certain amount of correspondence early in the year among leading Federalists in regard to the presidential nominations, but serious consideration of that topic was postponed until after the spring elections in Massachusetts and New York. These elections were in reality a part of the presidential election, for in New York it was already provided that the legislature would choose presidential electors, and in Massachusetts, as no method had yet been fixed, the decision rested with the legislature about to be chosen. Under those circumstances, it seems strange that the Federalists did not make their presidential nominations before the state elections began. They probably wished to make a test of their strength, before deciding between separate candidates and a coalition with the insurgents.

The results of the early state elections were highly encouraging to the Federalists. In Massachusetts, owing to the injudicious nomination of Christopher Gore, they failed to capture the governorship, but secured what was far more important, a working majority in both houses of the legislature. The New York Federalists failed to do so well, but managed to increase their delegation in the assembly from 21 to 45, which, out of a total number of 105, would make a Clinton-Federalist alliance irresistible. These results were brought about mainly through the skillful use by Federalist leaders of a potent electioneering weapon furnished them by Jefferson—the Embargo. They were quick to see its possibilities for stirring up the people. "The Embargo will 'touch their bone and their flesh' when they must curse its authors," wrote Timothy Pickering.[4] The first gun of the Massachusetts, and incidentally of the presidential campaign, was Pickering's violent attack on the administration's policy in his letter to Governor Sullivan.[5] It was printed in every Federalist newspaper in the country, and thousands of copies, in pamphlet form, were circulated throughout the state and the Union. Pickering's letter was the means of "arousing the people from their lethargy," of playing on the distress which commercial restriction caused a seafaring population, and shaking off the fatal apathy that had characterized the Federalist Party in the last seven years. Federalist leaders rightly calculated that popular discontent with the "Terrapin Policy" would increase in geometrical ratio to its duration. The Massachusetts and New York elections turned the tide of "corruption so, rapidly extending";[6] might not the ebb tide of reaction prove strong enough to carry a Federalist candidate to the presidential chair?

With these considerations in their minds, the leaders now began in earnest the work of deciding on the moot question of the presidential nomination. The first move came from Philadelphia. Charles Willing Hare, a prominent Federalist of that city, one of its representatives in the Pennsylvania assembly, wrote Harrison Gray Otis on June 2, 1808:

> We are desirous here to learn what steps you mean to adopt in Massachusetts, with regard to the election of President. Whether you determine to nominate a federalist, or to support General Clinton, it is equally necessary that we should hear from you. Our Electors are chosen in November by the people, in one ticket for the whole State. Hence the time has nearly arrived, at which in the event of its being determined to support a federal candidate, some previous arrangements should be made. Or if you and our friends generally are inclined to vote for Clinton it is right that we should be apprized of it, in order that we may prepare to yield an efficient support to that portion of the democrats, who advocate his election. As your Legislature is now federal and is in session it is generally expected here that the first movement will be with you. And your advice would have decisive influence with us.[7]

Details of the action of Federalist leaders in Massachusetts, on receipt of Hare's letter, are preserved in two letters of Christopher Gore to Rufus King.[8] The Federalist legislative caucus at Boston appointed a Committee of Twenty, which in turn appointed a Committee of Correspondence, "to correspond with the Federalists in other states on the business of the next Election of President and V. President," and "for the purpose of concerting our arrangements, and ascertaining, as far as could be done, the Weight of the Federalists in the next Election." The committee consisted of George Cabot, Harrison Gray Otis, president of the senate, Christopher Gore, who had been elected to the house after his defeat for the governorship, Timothy Bigelow, speaker of the house, and James Lloyd, a Boston merchant who had just been chosen Adams's successor in the United States Senate. All were Boston men, and all, except Otis, were of the Essex junto persuasion, recognizing Pickering as their leader.[9] The committee held a meeting on June 10, when "after some Conversation, it was deemed advisable to propose a meeting of Federalists, from as many States, as could be seasonably notified, at New York the last of this, or the Beginning of the next month."[10]

Here, then, is the original proposition for the original nominating convention.[11] The idea was revolutionary in party machinery, both from a Federalist and a national point of view. By 1808 the Republican Party had brought the convention system of nomination to a high degree of development in the states, but this movement was regarded by the Federalist Party with mingled suspicion and contempt. Ever since the pernicious activities of the Jacobin clubs—the "self-created societies" of 1793–1794—every type of extra-legal machinery was anathema to Federalists, especially to the New England section of the party. Nominations by conventions of delegates were illegal, revolutionary, despotic. The people were bartering away their franchise in promising to support the candidates of a set of delegates.[12] In the eyes of most Federalists in 1808, the only proper methods of nomination were by mass meetings, or by personal friends of the candidate. Hence, when as frequently happened, the leaders found the use of some proscribed method of nomination a political necessity, the fact was carefully concealed from the body of the voters. This was the case with the convention of 1808; the modern student will search the Federalist press in vain for the slightest hint of its existence. Our knowledge of it is derived exclusively from the correspondence of the Federalist leaders, and from impudent disclosures by Republican editors, who naturally took great pleasure in lifting the veil of secrecy.

The work of securing a national representation in the convention was carried on by personal communications from Boston, New York, and Philadelphia. The Massachusetts Committee of Correspondence met on June 10. [. . .] On the day following the committee meeting Otis wrote Hare in Philadelphia and received from him an answer as follows, dated June 19:

> I received yours of the 11th on the 16. I immediately took measures for convening a few of our most active firm and discreet friends. A Meeting of about a dozen was held yesterday—at which your objects and reasoning were stated—and so far as regards the propriety of the proposed convention, immediately and without hesitation acquiesced in. A Committee consisting of Messrs Fitzsimons R Waln Latimer Morgan and myself, were appointed to correspond with you—and in obedience to your suggestion to "organise for the South." We shall immediately write to some of our friends in Maryland and Delaware, and after having heard from them I shall again address you. It has appeared to us, that the second Monday in August would be a convenient time for assembling. The State of our foreign relations will then have been better ascertained, and some further Manifestations of public feeling will probably have been made. At the same time it will not be too late for a full correspondence with the Southern Federalists.

Subsequent letters from Hare to Otis inform us that a delegate was sent to Delaware, but that James A. Bayard, the Federalist "boss" of that state, threw "cold water upon the idea of holding a Meeting, and in his letters here has rather endeavored to persuade us to abandon the project."[13] Through Robert Goodloe Harper the cooperation of the Maryland Federalists was secured.

South Carolina was communicated with through the Charleston "junto," as John Rutledge jocosely called a Federalist committee in that city. The New York Federalists were informed of the convention project through Gore's letters to Rufus King; and judge Egbert Benson, after a personal interview with the Massachusetts committee, was given the task of attending to Connecticut and New Jersey. Benson reported to Otis from New York on July 13 as follows:

> On my return through Connecticut I saw Messrs. Goodrich and Daggett; and after being at Home a day or two I determined to go to New Jersey, where I saw Messrs. Ogden and Stockton; and to Philadelphia, where I saw Messrs. Rawle and Hopkinson. To all these several Gentlemen I mentioned how anxious and zealous You were in Boston as to the ensuing Presidential Election, and Your Intention to convene a number of our Friends from other States to confer and come to some general Understanding on the following Points, Whether it shall be advisable for Us to have federal Candidates for President and Vice President? If so, Who shall they be? If not, then, Shall the federal Electors, wherever they may happen to be chosen, vote for Clinton or for Madison?, and lastly, Shall the Removal of the Seat of Government, back to Philadelphia, be attempted?—that my mission to them was to suggest that they should instantly associate to themselves such Persons as should think proper to form a Committee of Correspondence through You with our friends in Boston, and You doubtless will hear from them soon. The Gentlemen in Philadelphia will send some Person on the like Errand to Delaware.

No effort seems to have been made to get into communication with the North Carolina Federalists, who proved strong enough to give Pinckney three electoral votes, or with Virginia, where Federalism still prevailed along the Potomac and the Shenandoah. The western states, where the party still existed in a moribund state, were also neglected, although some attempt was made to communicate to them the nominations. Federalism was as much out of place beyond the Alleghenies as powdered hair and silk stockings. In Georgia, the Federalist Party had been dead since 1800.

In the third week of August this embryo national convention met in New York. Its existence even could not be guessed from Federalist journals, but the coming together of so many noted Federalists did not escape the vigilant eyes of the Democratic press. Where the sessions were held can only be a matter of conjecture. Representatives were present from eight states: New Hampshire, Vermont, Massachusetts, Connecticut, New York, Pennsylvania, Maryland, and South Carolina. Rhode Island was unable to send a delegate, because no one could be spared from the state campaign that was then going on. Delaware was unrepresented on account of Bayard's opposition to the meeting; New Jersey for unexplained reasons. The number and the personnel of the members is also largely a matter of conjecture; but [. . .] the total number could not have been more than twenty-five or thirty. The great handicap to a wider representation was undoubtedly the expense and time necessary at that period for a journey to New York. [. . .] Of the method of choosing delegates we have no direct evidence, but there can be no doubt that they were selected by the exclusive committees formed in the different states as indicated by Hare's and Benson's letters.

In composition, as in objects, the resemblance of the 1808 convention to that of 1812 is striking. The latter was attended by over seventy delegates, but the sectional representation was the same as in 1808. Delegates were present from the three northern states which failed to take part in 1808, but in both conventions the West was unrepresented, and the South only by Maryland and South Carolina. In neither was any attempt made to limit the size of the delegations. Both were representative only of the party leaders, and both were intended to be kept secret from the mass of voters.

Of the proceedings of the 1808 convention, we know no more than the bare result, but the whole question between supporting Clinton and making separate nominations was so thoroughly threshed out in the correspondence preceding the convention, that we may fairly assume the line of argument that led to the rejection of the project of coalition. The question was simply one of expediency. Were the Federalists strong enough to elect their own candidates? If not, would Clinton bring the party enough votes to ensure victory? Would the election of Clinton benefit the Federalists in any case? These are the questions the pro and con of which were discussed down to the eve of the convention, and there is no reason to suppose that the final decision was reached from any different data. The Federalist correspondence is again our only source, for the Federalist press kept silence on this as on other matters connected with the nomination.

The chief support of the Clinton coalition came from Boston. Otis, whose eloquence, it is said, turned the balance in favor of DeWitt Clinton in the Federalist convention of 1812, was equally strong in favor of George Clinton in 1808. Another powerful advocate of coalition was George Cabot. Cabot since 1804 had occupied in his party a position similar to that of Jefferson in the Republican Party after 1808. From Brookline, as from Monticello, the active party leaders received letters that spoke with authority. Easily the intellectual leader of his party since the death of Hamilton, George Cabot in his study at Brookline saw what no other Federalist had the wisdom to see, that a page of democratic evolution had been turned, and the days of Federalist ascendancy had passed never to return. He writes Otis,[14] already on his way to New York, that it is useless to attempt the election of a Federalist president—the Democrats are in a majority, and:

> find from Dr. M that Mr. R and other respectable Federalists have often de-
> clared their doubts of the utility of a Federal President in the shameful
> state to which our affairs have been brought—but there is a great differ-
> ence of opinion between them and me on the final effect of Jeffn and Madn
> continuing at the head 4 years more. they believe the evils that wou'd be
> produced by protracting the period of their maladministration wou'd
> make madmen wise; we think it wou'd make wise men mad. to me it seems
> incredible that the many will ever from a sense of their own abuse of power
> voluntarily transfer it to those over whom they have been exercising it. if
> there are sufferings they will chiefly be ours, or if universal they whose vice
> and folly produce them will never ascribe those sufferings to their own
> misconduct. If however Discontent demands a change it will be made in
> favor of the most turbulent who in such times are exclusively heard. I think
> the quietude of the Community under the Embargo laws with the extraor-
> dinary Rescripts that followed, furnishes the amplest proof of Mr. Jeffer-
> son's absolute power. . . . The people will adhere to those who are the
> instruments of their passions, and will shun those who wou'd controul
> them.

Cabot believed that Clinton would reverse the policy of Jefferson, and that his election should be sought as the greatest attainable good. The correspondence indicates, however, that the decisive element in the discussion was the practical question, whether Clinton could carry Pennsylvania. Down to the middle of July it seemed probable that he could. Early in 1808 the alliance between the Federalists and Constitutional (conservative) Republicans of Pennsylvania, which had supported the administrations of McKean, broke up. The Constitutionalists, eager to anticipate the Conventionalists (radicals), in the favor of the administration, held a caucus at Lancaster, early in March, nominated Spayd for governor, and an electoral ticket pledged to vote for Madison. Shortly afterwards the Conventionalists, headed by Duane and Leib, called a mixed legislative caucus, nominated Simon Snyder for governor, and a second Republican electoral ticket—unpledged, but apparently intended to vote for Clinton.[15] As there seemed to be some doubt about this, a convention of Snyderite delegates from the towns of Northumberland County held on June 28, and controlled by two strong Clinton Democrats, Samuel Maclay and William Montgomery, tried to force the hand of their party by resolving to support the

Conventionalist electoral ticket, on the understanding that its vote would be cast for Clinton.[16] This looked as if Clinton could carry Pennsylvania with the aid of the Federalists, and the Philadelphia Federalists were almost converted to the coalition, when the real leaders of the Conventionalist party, Duane and Leib, came out for Madison in an unmistakable manner. In an *Address to the Citizens of Pennsylvania,* they rebuked the Democrats of Northumberland County for their endorsement of Clinton, asserted that the Lancaster electoral ticket would vote for Madison, and eventually patched up a truce with the conservative wing of their party. By the time that the Federalist convention met in New York, Democratic harmony in Pennsylvania was complete, and it was obvious that Clinton's independent strength outside New York was nil.

That Clinton could carry New York State, with Federalist aid, was certain. Were, however, nineteen electoral votes worth the abandonment of principle that a coalition with Clinton would imply? One of the traditional principles of the Federalist Party was that only within its ranks could be found men competent to govern the country. The nomination of Clinton would be a frank admission to the contrary. Judge Theodore Sedgwick wrote on this aspect of question to Otis on June 6:

> It is of infinite importance that the leading federalists should conduct in such manner as to convince the publick that they are actuated by principle. This, I imagine, can hardly be the case unless they act by themselves, and keep themselves separate from the differant parties into which their adversaries are divided. . . . I cannot endure the humiliating idea that those who alone from education, fortune, character and principle are entitled to command should voluntarily arrange themselves under the banners of a party in all respects inferior, and in many odious, to them.

It was distance as well as expediency that lent enchantment to the view of an alliance with Clinton. The New York Federalists would have none of him. "We have condescended twice to tamper with Democratic Candidates," writes Abraham Van Vechten to Otis,[17] "and in both instances have been subjected to severe self-reproach. Our experimental knowledge of the Clintonian System is a powerful Antidote against affording it any facility here." He and his friends saw nothing to choose between George Clinton and James Madison.

For the reasons given, then—the weakness of Clinton and the fact that his nomination, while helping the Federalists little or none, would injure their party character—the New York convention decided to place Federalist candidates in nomination. Their decision was announced to the Charleston Federalists in the following words:

After several Meetings, and after the most mature and dispassionate Consideration of the Subject, we formed a conclusive opinion, as to the Line of Conduct most proper for the Federal Party to observe. It was decided to be our Correct and dignified Policy to afford neither Aid nor Countenance, direct or indirect, to any of our political opponents, but, holding ourselves perfectly distinct, to nominate Federal Characters for the offices of President and Vice President, and to support them, with our uniform, zealous, and vigorous exertions. . . . Having decided on the Measure, no difference of opinion could exist as to the Selection of Candidates, and Charles Cotesworth Pinckney for the office of President, and Rufus King for the office of Vice President, became without the least Hesitation our Choice.[18]

This was the same ticket as in 1804. The choice of Pinckney was due to his high character and reputation of patriotism, to the hope of capturing his native state, and to the wish of avoiding the stigma of sectionalism, of which political parties in the United States have always been remarkably sensitive. He was distinctly the "most available" candidate.

The above letter shows conclusively that the convention carried out the purpose for which it was summoned, and made a definite nomination of president and vice-president. This was not done in 1812. The convention of that year broke up after registering a simple *voeu* in favor of DeWitt Clinton, leaving the real decision to a committee that was to sit in Philadelphia and continue the correspondence.

Having summoned and carried on the convention in secret, it was necessary to be extremely discreet in announcing its nomination. The original plan for the public nomination, and the reasons for making an eleventh-hour change, are given in the following letter of October 4, from Thomas Fitzsimons of Philadelphia to Gore, Otis, and Lloyd, the Massachusetts delegation:

When we separated at New York, it was understood, that the result of our Conference, should not be made public, until, the event of the Election in Pennsylva. should be known, and until the Conferees from that State, should deem a publication of it proper.

Circumstances have since Occurred, which in their oppinion rendered any publication of that Kind Inexpedient, and led them to conclude that the safer Course, would be to leave our friends in each state to Announce the Candidates to their fellow Citizens, at such time, and in such way as they should themselves think best. We were Led to this conclusion, from having observed something like a jealousy, in our friends at having a Nomination so Important decided on by so small a No. as we were, and without any Special authority for the purpose, for altho there appears to be no division of sentiment thr'out the state, as to the Candidates, yet it was deemed most prudent that it should appear rather the result of General sentiment than as the Choice of a few to bind their party. to this effect, I wrote our friends at New York, still considering ourselves bound to conform to what they and our Eastern friends should recommend. the Gent at New York appear to think as we do—and that you may be consulted, I send this unsealed to them.

Further explanation is given in a letter of the Philadelphia committee, to that of New York, quoted in a letter of the latter to the Massachusetts committee:

We were influenced to this determination by a very general disapprobation expressed by our friends of the Caucus at Washington and what we experienced in our State canvass. Considerate people are convinced that measures must be digested by the few, nevertheless among the mass each is desirous that he should be one of the number. It was therefore judged most advisable that our friends in each State should set on foot their canvass in the way they should deem most eligible.[19]

The frankness of these letters makes comment almost superfluous—but the writer cannot help pointing out how the secret methods of the Federalists are beginning to react upon themselves. When we recall the method by which the Philadelphia committee (which undoubtedly chose the delegates to New York) was formed, by convening "about a dozen" of "our active, firm, and discreet friends," the "jealousy" of the outsiders is not surprising.

After quoting the above letter, the New York committee continues:

In consequence of this we have no expectation of any public nomination in Philadelphia and considering it important to be made without delay, we think that Massachusetts is not only entitled to originate the measure, but that coming from that quarter it would produce the greatest sensibility and interest in its favor, particularly in this State. We therefore submit to the consideration of our friends in your State the propriety of immediately proceeding to make the nomination in the manner which shall appear to them the most advantageous and impressive. In this State it will instantly be repeated and supported as far as we are able, and we have no doubt it will be followed by our political friends in every other State. We are satisfied it would not produce so good an effect to commence this business here and there are also local considerations which induce us not to wish to originate the nomination. We can give no certain assurance of supporting it by the vote of this State and if we were to begin this measure it might excite ir-ritation and increase the difficulty of obtaining the aid of either section of the opposite party among us, on which our hopes as to this State at present depend. The latter consideration with us is important and we flatter our-selves you will unite in the opinion that it is most expedient for Massachu-setts to begin the nomination, the success of which alone, we think can save our Country from disastrous events.

The Massachusetts committee apparently accepted the responsibility thus thrust upon them. In the *New England Palladium and the Repertory* of October 18 appears the formal announcement:

We have the satisfaction to learn, from information collected from every part of the Union, that one common sentiment prevails among the Feder-alists, with respect to Candidates for the two first offices in the National Government, and that the men selected by the approving voice of the whole American party, to preserve the Union, and to prevent a calamitous war, are for President, the Hon. Charles Cotesworth Pinckney, of South Carolina, for Vice President, the Hon. Rufus King, of New York. In Massa-chusetts a formal nomination of these great patriots has been delayed for the sole purpose of collecting the sentiments of the great body of Federal-ist—the TRUE AMERICANS in other States. It being now ascertained, that among these their exists but one opinion; Massachusetts will obey the dic-tates of her own inclination, while she conforms to the wishes of her sister States, in supporting the above Candidates; and our friends in these States may rest assured, that the characters of the men and the dangers of the country will ensure unanimity without the aid of any Caucus, or other pre-liminary.

This deceptive statement was the official announcement of the presidential nomination—two or three weeks only before the choice of electors. The nom-ination was already generally known, however. On October 12 the New York *Evening Post*, impatient perhaps at the delay, announced it as coming from "several respectable sources," and the Charleston *Courier* had made it known at least a month before. It had been noted by the principal Republican newspa-pers, but was not copied into Federalist journals until after the publication by the *Evening Post* and the Boston papers.

A description of the campaign of 1808 is beyond the scope of this article. Until the October state elections in New Jersey and Pennsylvania went against them, the Federalists were sanguine of success, but after that their only hope was a forlorn one—of converting the hostile majority in the New York legislature, and of carrying South Carolina. In the latter state the Federalists gave Charles Pinckney the hardest struggle of his political career, but the Republicans secured an overwhelming majority in the legislature, which chose electors. Vermont and Maryland also disappointed the Federalists, and Charles Cotesworth Pinckney secured only 47 electoral votes to Madison's 122. This was a notable increase over the fourteen votes of 1804; it began a brief Federalist Renaissance which lasted until 1815.

The student of this period cannot fail to be impressed by the subordinate role which Pinckney's name played in the campaign, even in the last three weeks of it, after his nomination was formally announced. Many of the leading Federalist journals, including the Boston *Columbian Centinel,* never even published the nomination. The casual reader of these newspapers would scarcely know whom the Federalists had chosen for their leader, were it not for the frequent contrast of Pinckney's oft-quoted words, "Millions for defense and not one cent for tribute," with Madison's "France wants money and must have it." The Republican Party, on the contrary, made the record and character of Madison one of their leading issues. This extraordinary neglect of their candidate is probably due to the fact that the Federalists when nominating Pinckney at New York did not altogether give up the idea of swinging over their electoral votes at the eleventh hour if George Clinton developed any unexpected strength. Otis, apparently, threatened to bolt the convention's nomination within two weeks after it was made. Hare writes him, September 6, reiterating the arguments against supporting Clinton, and urging him "not to set things afloat, *unless you can certainly elect Clinton.*" An attempt was made by Theophilus Parsons to seduce the Connecticut legislature into the same course.[20] In Rhode Island, no public announcement of Pinckney's nomination was made; it was urged in favor of the members of the Federalist electoral ticket that they were "not pledged to vote for any candidate. Those who advocate their election confide it to their Wisdom, and integrity."[21] The significance of the Rhode Islanders' move is explained by a letter of James B. Mason of Providence,[22] written after the Federalist electors had been chosen, urging that the entire electoral vote be swung over to Clinton, in the hope of choosing him president as the "least of two evils."

Such were the objects, the composition, and the results of this first of national party conventions. Altogether it was an assembly typical of the Federalist Party. A few well-born and congenial gentlemen, who could afford the time and expense of travel, were chosen by their friends to settle in a quiet and leisurely manner the questions that agitated their party. From the body of voters neither authority nor advice was asked, and profound secrecy sheltered the convention's deliberations from vulgar scrutiny. The New York convention of 1808, like all Federalist machinery of the period, was based on the right of the leading men in the party to settle nominations and party business without the slightest cooperation of the people. The voter's advice is not asked, but his implicit obedience is required. He is to vote for candidates nominated he knows not how, because it is thought best by "those who alone from education, fortune, character and principle are entitled to command." Herein lay one of the fundamental principles of the Federalist Party, and, in the writer's opinion, the chief cause of its failure. The Federalist machinery failed for the same reason that the entire party failed: it sought to suppress and to curb public opinion rather than to guide and lead it, and the people preferred "those who are the instruments of their passions" to "those who wou'd controul them." The secret national party convention, representing only the leaders, passed out of existence with the Federalists. It remained for Democratic politicians of the thirties, with improved methods of communication, and fatter campaign chests, to discover that a national convention of delegates, chosen by the body of voters, was the most effective method of nominating a president.

CHAPTER 6

Why Great Men Are Not Chosen President

James Bryce

Europeans often ask, and Americans do not always explain, how it happens that this great office, the greatest in the world, unless we except the Papacy, to which any man can rise by his own merits, is not more frequently filled by great and striking men? In America, which is beyond all other countries the country of a "career open to talents," a country, moreover, in which political life is unusually keen and political ambition widely diffused, it might be expected that the highest place would always be won by a man of brilliant gifts. But since the heroes of the Revolution died out with Jefferson and Adams and Madison some sixty years ago, no person except General Grant has reached the chair whose name would have been remembered had he not been president, and no president except Abraham Lincoln has displayed rare or striking qualities in the chair. Who now knows or cares to know anything about the personality of James K. Polk or Franklin Pierce? The only thing remarkable about them is that being so commonplace they should have climbed so high.

Several reasons may be suggested for the fact, which Americans are themselves the first to admit.

One is that the proportion of first-rate ability drawn into politics is smaller in America than in most European countries. This is a phenomenon whose causes must be elucidated later; in the meantime it is enough to say that in France and Italy, where half-revolutionary conditions have made public life ex-

From *The American Commonwealth* (London and New York: Macmillan, 1888), 1:100–10. Given the title of viscount in 1914, Bryce (1838–1922) lived an extraordinary life as a mountain climber, jurist, member of Parliament, diplomat (including seven years as ambassador to the United States), and prolific author.

citing and accessible; in Germany, where an admirably organized civil service cultivates and develops statecraft with unusual success; in England, where many persons of wealth and leisure seek to enter the political arena, while burning questions touch the interests of all classes and make men eager observers of the combatants, the total quantity of talent devoted to parliamentary or administrative work is far larger, relatively to the population, than in America, where much of the best ability, both for thought and for action, for planning and for executing, rushes into a field which is comparatively narrow in Europe, the business of developing the material resources of the country.

Another is that the methods and habits of Congress, and indeed of political life generally, seem to give fewer opportunities for personal distinction, fewer modes in which a man may commend himself to his countrymen by eminent capacity in thought, in speech, or in administration, than is the case in the free countries of Europe.

A third reason is that eminent men make more enemies, and give those enemies more assailable points, than obscure men do. They are therefore in so far less desirable candidates. It is true that the eminent man has also made more friends, that his name is more widely known, and may be greeted with louder cheers. Other things being equal, the famous man is preferable. But other things never are equal. The famous man has probably attacked some leaders in his own party, has supplanted others, has expressed his dislike to the crotchet of some active section, has perhaps committed errors which are capable of being magnified into offenses. No man stands long before the public and bears a part in great affairs without giving openings to censorious criticism. Fiercer far than the light which beats upon a throne is the light which beats upon a presidential candidate, searching out all the recesses of his past life. Hence, when the choice lies between a brilliant man and a safe man, the safe man is preferred. Party feeling, strong enough to carry in on its back a man without conspicuous positive merits, is not always strong enough to procure forgiveness for a man with positive faults.

A European finds that this phenomenon needs in its turn to be explained, for in the free countries of Europe brilliancy, be it eloquence in speech, or some striking achievement in war or administration, or the power through whatever means of somehow impressing the popular imagination, is what makes a leader triumphant. Why should it be otherwise in America? Because in America party loyalty and party organization have been hitherto so perfect that any one put forward by the party will get the full party vote if his character is good and his "record," as they call it, unstained. The safe candidate may not draw in quite so many votes from the moderate men of the other side as the brilliant one would, but he will not lose nearly so many from his own ranks. Even those who admit his mediocrity will vote straight when the moment for voting comes. Besides, the ordinary American voter does not object to mediocrity. He has a lower conception of the qualities requisite to make a statesman than those who direct public opinion in Europe have. He likes his candidate to be sensible, vigorous, and, above all, what he calls "magnetic," and does not value, because be sees no need for, originality or profundity, a fine culture or a wide knowledge. Candidates are selected to be run for nomination by knots of persons who, however expert as party tacticians, are usually commonplace men; and the choice between those selected for nomination is made by a very large body, an assembly of over eight hundred delegates from the local party organizations over the country, who are certainly no better than ordinary citizens. [. . .]

It must also be remembered that the merits of a president are one thing and those of a candidate another thing. An eminent American is reported to have said, to friends who wished to put him forward, "Gentlemen, let there be no mistake. I should make a good president, but a very bad candidate." Now to a party it is more important that its nominee should be a good candidate than that he should be good president. As Saladin says in *The Talisman*, "a wild cat in the chamber is more dangerous than a lion in a distant desert." It will be a misfortune to the party, as well as to the country, if the candidate elected should prove a bad president. But it is a greater misfortune to the party that it should be beaten in the impending election, for the evil of losing national patronage will have come four years sooner. "B" (so reason the leaders), "who is one of our possible candidates, may be an abler man than A, who is the other. But we have a better chance of winning with A than with B, while X, the candidate of our opponents, is anyhow no better than A. We must therefore run A." This reasoning is all the more forcible because the previous career of the possible candidates has generally made it easier to say who will succeed as a candidate than who will succeed as a president; and because the wire-pullers with whom the choice rests are better judges of the former question than of the latter.

After all, too, and this is a point much less obvious to Europeans than to Americans, a president need not be a man of brilliant intellectual gifts. Englishmen, imagining him as something like their prime minister, assume that he ought to be a dazzling orator, able to sway legislatures or multitudes, possessed also of the constructive powers that can devise a great policy or frame a comprehensive piece of legislation. They forget that the president does not sit in Congress, that he ought not to address meetings, except on ornamental and (usually) nonpolitical occasions, that he cannot submit bills nor otherwise influence the action of the legislature. His main duties are to be prompt and firm in securing the due execution of the laws and maintaining the public peace, careful and upright in the choice of the executive officials of the country. Eloquence, whose value is apt to be overrated in all free countries, imagination, profundity of thought or extent of knowledge are all in so far a gain to him at they make him a bigger man, and help him to gain a greater influence over the nation, an influence which, if he be a true patriot he may use for its good. But they are not necessary for the due discharge in ordinary times of the duties of his post. A man may lack them and yet make an excellent president. Four-fifths of his work is the same in kind as that which devolves on the chairman of a commercial company or the manager of a railway, the work of choosing good subordinates, seeing that they attend to their business, and taking a sound practical view of such administrative questions as require his decision. Firmness, common sense, and most of all, honesty, an honesty above all suspicion of personal interest, are the qualities which the country chiefly needs in its chief magistrate.

So far we have been considering personal merits. But in the election of a candidate many considerations have to be regarded besides personal merits, whether they be the merits of a candidate, or of a possible president. The chief of these considerations is the amount of support which can be secured from different states or from different regions, or, as the Americans say, "sections" of the Union. State feeling and sectional feeling are powerful factors in a presidential election. The Northwest, including the states from Ohio to Dakota, is now the most populous region of the Union, and therefore counts for most in an election. It naturally conceives that its interests will be best protected by one who knows them from birth and residence. Hence *prima facie* a Northwestern man makes the best candidate. A large state casts a heavier vote in the election; and every state is of course more likely to be carried by one of its own children than by a stranger, because his fellow citizens, while they feel honored by the choice, gain also a substantial advantage, having a better prospect of such favors as the administration can bestow. Hence, *ceteris paribus,* a man from a large state is preferable as a candidate. New York casts thirty-six votes in the presidential election, Pennsylvania thirty, Ohio twenty-three, Illinois twenty-two, while Vermont and Rhode Island have but four, Delaware, Nevada, and Oregon only three votes each. It is therefore, parties being usually very evenly balanced, better worthwhile to have an inferior candidate from one of the larger states, who may carry the whole weight of his state with him, than a somewhat superior candidate from one of the smaller states, who will carry only three or four votes. The problem is further complicated by the fact that some states are already safe for one or other party, while others are doubtful. The Northwestern and New England states are most of them certain to go Republican; the Southern states are (at present) all of them certain to go Democratic. It is more important to gratify a doubtful state than one you have got already; and hence, *ceteris paribus,* a candidate from a doubtful state, such as New York or Indiana, is to be preferred.

Other minor disqualifying circumstances require less explanation. A Roman

Catholic or an avowed disbeliever in Christianity would be an undesirable candidate. Since the close of the Civil War, any one who fought, especially if he fought with distinction, in the Northern army has enjoyed great advantages, for the soldiers of that army, still numerous, rally to his name. The two elections of General Grant, who knew nothing of politics, and the fact that his influence survived the faults of his long administration are evidence of the weight of this consideration. It influenced the selection both of Garfield and of his opponent Hancock. Similarly a person who fought in the Southern army would be a bad candidate, for he might alienate the North.

On a railway journey in the Far West in 1883 I fell in with two newspapermen from the state of Indiana, who were taking their holiday. The conversation turned on the next presidential election. They spoke hopefully of the chances for nomination by their party of an Indiana man, a comparatively obscure person, whose name I had never heard. I expressed some surprise that he should be thought of. They observed that be had done well in state politics, that there was nothing against him, that Indiana would work for him. "But," I rejoined, "ought you not to have a man of more commanding character. There is Senator A. Everybody tells me that he is the shrewdest and most experienced man in your party, and that he has a perfectly clean record. Why not run him?" "Why, yes," they answered, "that is all true. But you see he comes from a small state, and we have got that state already. Besides, he wasn't in the war. Our man was. Indiana's vote is worth having, and if our man is run, we can carry Indiana."

"Surely the race is not to the swift nor the battle to the strong, neither yet bread to the wise, nor yet riches to men of understanding, nor yet favor to men of skill, but time and chance happeneth to them all."

These secondary considerations do not always prevail. Intellectual ability and force of character must influence the choice a candidate, and their influence is sometimes decisive. They count for more when times are so critical that the need for a strong man is felt. Reformers declare that their weight will go on increasing as the disgust of good citizens with the methods of professional politicians increases. But for many generations past it is not the greatest men in the Roman Church that have been chosen popes, nor the most brilliant men in the Anglican church that have been appointed archbishops of Canterbury.

Although several presidents have survived their departure from office by many years, only one, John Quincy Adams, has played a part in politics after quitting the White House. It may be that the ex-president has not been a great leader before his accession to office; it may be that he does not care to exert himself after he has held and dropped the great prize, and found (one may safely add) how little of a prize it is. Something, however, must also be ascribed to other features of the political system of the country. It is often hard to find a vacancy in the representation of a given state through which to re-enter Congress; it is disagreeable to recur to the arts by which seats are secured. Past greatness is rather an encumbrance than a help to resuming a political career. Exalted power, on which the unsleeping eye of hostile critics was fixed, has probably disclosed all a president's weaknesses, and has either forced him to make enemies by disobliging adherents, or exposed him to censure for subservience to party interests. He is regarded as having had his day; he belongs already to the past, and unless, like Grant, he is endeared to the people by the memory of some splendid service, he soon sinks into the crowd or avoids neglect by retirement. Possibly he may deserve to be forgotten; but more frequently he is a man of sufficient ability and character to make the experience he has gained valuable to the country, could it be retained in a place where he might turn it to account. They managed things better at Rome in the days of the republic, gathering into their senate all the fame and experience, all the wisdom and skill, of those who had ruled and fought as consuls and proctors at home and abroad.

"What shall we do with our ex-presidents?" is a question often put in America, but never yet answered. The position of a past chief magistrate is not a happy one. He has been a species of sovereign at home. He is received—General Grant was—with almost royal honors abroad. His private income may be insufficient to enable him to live in ease, yet he cannot without loss of dignity, the country's dignity as well as his own, go back to practice at the bar or become partner in a mercantile firm. If he tries to enter the Senate, it may happen that there is no seat vacant for his own state, or that the majority in the state legislature is against him. It has been suggested that he might be given a seat in that chamber as an extra member; but to this plan there is the objection that it would give to the state from which he comes a third senator, and thus put other states at a disadvantage. In any case [. . .] it would seem only right to bestow such a pension as would relieve him from the necessity of reentering business or a profession.

We may now answer the question from which we started. Great men are not chosen presidents, firstly, because great men are rare in politics; secondly, because the method of choice does not bring them to the top; thirdly, because they are not, in quiet times, absolutely needed. I may observe that the presidents, regarded historically, fall into three periods, the second inferior to the first, the third rather better than the second.

Down till the election of Andrew Jackson in 1828, all the presidents had been statesmen in the European sense of the word, men of education, of administrative experience, of a certain largeness of view and dignity of character. All except the first two had served in the great office of secretary of state; all were well known to the nation from the part they had played. In the second period, from Jackson till the outbreak of the Civil War in 1861, the presidents were either mere politicians, such as Van Buren, Polk, or Buchanan, or else successful soldiers, such as Harrison or Taylor, whom their party found useful as figureheads. They were intellectual pigmies beside the real leaders of that generation—Clay, Calhoun, and Webster. A new series begins with Lincoln in 1861. He and General Grant his successor, who cover sixteen years between them, belong to the history of the world. The other less distinguished presidents of this period contrast favorably with the Polks and Pierces of the days before the war, but they are not, like the early presidents, the first men of the country. If we compare the eighteen presidents who have been elected to office since 1789 with the nineteen English prime ministers of the same hundred years, there are but six of the latter, and at least eight of the former whom history calls personally insignificant, while only Washington, Jefferson, Lincoln, and Grant can claim to belong to a front rank represented in the English list by seven or possibly eight names. It would seem that the natural selection of the English parliamentary system, even as modified by the aristocratic habits of that country, has more tendency to bring the highest gifts to the highest place than the more artificial selection of America.

CHAPTER 7

The National Convention

M. Ostrogorski

The choice of candidates for the presidency and the vice presidency of the re-public is always invested with exceptional importance. The stake is enormous; it includes the highest prize to which the ambition of an American citizen can aspire; it confers for the space of four years executive powers extending over a whole continent, and among others that of patronage, which has in its hands the life and death, so to speak, of 150,000 office-holders scattered over the face of the union; it settles the destinies of the rival parties for many a year to come, perhaps. As the popular vote is confined to candidates selected in the national conventions, the attention of the whole country, excited to the highest pitch by the great periodical duel, centers on these assemblies so as to make them a unique institution, and their working under the eyes of the whole fever-stricken nation a unique spectacle. The citizen who pays no heed to the affairs of his state and of his city, fires up on the approach of the national conventions; but, by a singular piece of inconsistency, he does not on that account trouble himself more about the operations which pave the way for them, which deter-mine their character; he takes hardly any interest in [. . .] the local conventions from which the national convention will issue like a cast from a mold. This great gathering appeals rather to the American elector's naturally excitable temperament than to his public spirit. The formation of the national conven-tions is, therefore, left to the professional politicians. The latter are proportion-ally far more numerous in them than in the state conventions, which include

From "The National Convention," *Democracy and the Organization of Political Parties* (New York: Macmillan, 1902), 2:244–79. A Russian, Moisei Ostrogorski (1854–1919) was educated in law and worked in the czarist ministry of justice before sojourning in Britain and the United States, where his massive, two-volume treatise on political parties first appeared in 1902. He returned to Russia in 1906 and served briefly in the Duma before retiring from politics.

local notabilities, respectable personages, who, as a rule, stand aloof from politics. These personages are not so eager to accept the gratuitous mission of national delegate, which entails a long journey and an absence of a good many days, involving considerable loss and expense. Out of loyalty to their state they will go so far as to make some sacrifice to attend the state convention, but they are less ready to make it for the union, which does not hold exactly the same place in their affections. [...] Personal *amour-propre* has, also, something to do with the abstention of the local bigwigs, who naturally play the first fiddle in the state conventions, whereas in the national conventions they would be lost in the crowd. Moreover, the politicians are very anxious to obtain the position of delegate to the national convention for themselves, for every vote which helps to make the future president there has a high commercial value; it gives its owner claims on the gratitude of the future administration, which takes the form of places from an embassy in Europe down to a postmastership in the Far West. There are, no doubt, a certain number of delegates whose sole aspiration is to lend a hand in the great work of the party, out of devotion to its cause, or from mere vanity which courts opportunities for coming forward. But the great majority, and they may be estimated at nine-tenths, are occupied exclusively with their own interests at the convention. In the crowd of politicians who flock to the conventions all ranks are represented: senators of the United States, state governors, and so on down to aspirants to modest places; and each of them has an "axe to grind."

The representation at the national conventions is established on a fixed basis: each state sends to them [...] twice as many delegates as it has representatives and senators in the Congress. [...] Besides this, the territories, represented in Congress by delegates only without a voice, and the District of Columbia, not represented at all, are empowered to take part in the conventions. Their populations are not allowed to vote for the president, but in order to develop party life in the territories, the organizations of the parties concede to them and to the District of Columbia [...] a representation at the conventions. [...] The House of Representatives, having at the present moment 357 members, and the Senate ninety for the forty-five states, the double number of the delegates to the national conventions gives a total of 894 plus forty-two delegates for the territories of Alaska, Arizona, New Mexico, Oklahoma Indian Territory, Hawaiian Islands, and the District of Columbia. In addition an alternate is appointed for each delegate to take his place in case he is prevented from attending. The four delegates who represent the senators of the state multiplied by two are chosen by the state conventions, and are called "delegates at large"; the other delegates who correspond to the members of the House of Representatives are chosen, to the number of two for each congressional district, by the district conventions. That is the invariable mode of election followed by the

Republican party; whereas the Democrats elect in certain states such as New York [...] all the delegates in the state convention, the state being considered [...] as alone possessing a political individuality. This conception of the representation of the state, of a highly centralizing character, has received, in the Democratic party, a still more serious application in the form of the "unit rule," which restricts the right of the individual delegates to vote according to their preferences; the state convention, whether it elect only the four delegates at large or all the delegates, can order them to vote in a lump at the national convention, in accordance with the decision of the majority. [...] Republican state conventions have repeatedly tried to introduce the unit rule; but the national conventions, beginning with that of 1860, on each occasion admitted the right of the delegates to vote as they pleased. On the other hand, the state conventions of all the parties, without distinction, often give the delegates peremptory instructions to vote for a particular presidential candidate. However, these instructions leave the delegates a certain latitude; for if the candidate who has been prescribed to them does not succeed in obtaining a majority, they will have to choose one from among the other competitors, and at their own discretion, so that in reality the delegates come to the national convention with full powers.

The convention meets in the summer of the "presidential year." [...] The business preliminary to the convention is entrusted to the national committee of the party, which is appointed every four years, in the national convention, by the respective delegations of all the states and territories, each of them choosing one member. In the beginning of the year, the national committee calls on the state committees to proceed to the election of the delegates, and, at the same time, fixes the date and the place of the meeting of the convention. Before the Civil War, the national conventions almost always met in a city of the East [...] but since the extraordinary development of the West [...] the parties have been in the habit of holding their grand council in a city of the central West, at Chicago, for instance. The enormous influx of visitors caused by the sitting of the convention, and perhaps, also, local *amour-propre,* makes several cities compete for the honor of having it. [...] The applicants promise to provide, in addition to a large sum of money to defray the cost of the convention and the traveling and hotel expenses of the members of the national committee and their wives, all the elements of comfort required by visitors, including fine weather. In other cities the heat is unbearable in summer, but in their city never. [...]

A few days before the opening of the convention, the city in which it is to be held assumes a special aspect, "a convention aspect," the streets, adorned with a profusion of flags and bunting flying over the crossings, the hotels inhabited by the delegations, and other political "headquarters," are thronged by a huge crowd [. . .] from morning till evening, and even later. The whole town is swamped with [. . .] "pre-convention enthusiasm." The arrival of the delegations provokes the first outbursts of it. Each state delegation arrives in a body, accompanied by a more or less considerable number of fellow citizens of their native state, who escort their delegates. Very often the delegation comes with a band and in a special train. [. . .] At the station a solemn reception awaits the delegation. Zealous political co-religionists formed into clubs for the duration of the presidential campaign, or delegations which have already arrived, go to meet the new delegation and welcome it with harangues and applause re-echoed by the shouts of the assembled crowd. Then the whole company walks in a procession to the hotel in which the delegation has engaged rooms. To the sound of drums and fifes, in the midst of a frenzied crowd, the new arrivals march past, adorned with badges, medals, and ribbons bearing the name of their state. [. . .] The delegation is preceded by its banner, and perhaps it displays yet another emblem, such as a gilt alligator, or even a live eagle. [. . .]

Each state delegation has its official abode or [. . .] "headquarters" in a hotel, known from afar by a large sign and flags. It occupies, according to the rank of the state and the more or less active or retiring part played by it in the presidential campaign, a single room in which a hapless delegate in his shirt sleeves sits on duty, or a whole suite of apartments which are always full of crack politicians and wire-pullers. The headquarters is the meeting place not only of the members of the delegation, but of all the citizens of the state who attend the convention, either to help the different candidates in the campaign or as spectators. [. . .] The number of visitors who have come simply as sightseers is enormous. [. . .] The "headquarters" of the states are the principal points of attraction to the crowd; the streets adjoining them are blocked to such an extent that it is sometimes necessary to stop all wheeled traffic. [. . .]

The candidatures are almost always numerous. They are spoken of a very long time before the meeting of the convention. It may be said that people begin to talk about the candidates for the next election, and discuss the claims of personages considered as "presidential possibilities," almost the day after the inauguration of the new president. Aspirants to the chief magistracy start an "underground canvass" at an early stage, to prepare their candidature. If they are very rich or, what comes to the same thing, if they have attached themselves to important special interests, such as manufacturers enriched by a protectionist tariff, or powerful companies or "trusts," they conduct this underground canvass with much method—they systematically work the primaries from which issue, step by step, the national convention. In any event, during the year which precedes the meeting of the convention, in a good many states the feeling of the politicians settles down in favor of one or more of its more or less eminent citizens as candidate for the presidency of the union. This feeling stamps him as the "favorite son" of his native state and makes him a competitor. Every national convention is confronted with half a dozen or more "favorite sons" of somewhat unequal merit and reputation. Some have had a fairly long political experience either in Congress or as member of the cabinet or state governor; others, and this is not so common, have hardly had an opportunity of winning their spurs in public life, but have achieved a local position, especially through the arts of the politician. Some are not known at all outside their own state, the popularity of others extends beyond its limits, and a few have a national reputation. Side by side with these candidatures brought forward with perfect good faith, there are others which are a mere speculation— almost a form of blackmail. A powerful boss who is absolute master of the delegation of his state, since it was chosen by *his* machine, who, consequently, controls several votes at this convention, runs a candidate with the sole object of selling his withdrawal at a high figure. The candidate thus marked out for the part of pawn is, perhaps, the only person unaware of the fact; as state governor or ex-ambassador he thinks that the honor offered to him is perfectly natural. Sometimes the boss gets himself nominated as presidential candidate by the state convention, and he will remain so up to the very last moment; as soon as he has made his deal with the probable winner, has bargained for the amount of presidential patronage to which he considers himself entitled, he will go over to his side with the whole delegation of the state. Among the genuine candidatures, a good many are put forward only as a matter of form, without any chance of success, simply by way of tribute to the distinguished citizen who represents the dignity of the state for the occasion. Perhaps the good fortune of being a "dark horse," who will be chosen at the eleventh hour in preference to more distinguished aspirants, is in store for some of these "favorite sons," and they will be looked on as "dark horse possibilities"; but the "dark horse" is just as likely to be an outsider and to appear for the first time at the last moment only. The dark horse is not necessarily an obscure personage; on the contrary, he may be very well known in the country and perhaps be extremely popular (as, for instance, General Sherman, the hero of the Civil War, who ranked among the dark horses at the Republican convention of 1884); but he does not appear to command acceptance as a presidential candidate. On the other hand, some of the candidates, one or two, are brought out of the ruck from the very first (this was the case, at the same convention, with J. G. Blaine and Chester A. Arthur, at that time President of the United States). Their great national reputation, their high rank in the party, or the part played or special position occupied by them in the political conjunctures of the moment, or their character, which exercises a fascination over the masses, give them an exceptional force of attraction. They are not only "favorite sons" of their respective states, but general "favorites"; and the personality of this or that "favorite" appears to be so commanding that he becomes the "logical candidate" of the situation. But that is no proof whatever that he will be adopted by the convention; the "favorite," as we shall see, is more likely than not to be beaten.

To whatever category the aspirant belongs, the progress of his candidature must depend on the herculean efforts put forth during the few days which precede the convention, and in the course of the session itself. Each aspirant has at his disposal for this purpose not only the delegation of his state, which plunges wildly into the fray, but numerous special workers, all controlled by a head manager, an expert in this particular line, and who generally belongs to the delegation of the state and is sometimes a well known personage. Their efforts are directed not only to the delegates, whose votes are asked for, but also to the outside multitude, with a view to creating a moral atmosphere favorable to the aspirant and pressing on the delegates with the weight of public opinion. This twofold propaganda, which constitutes what is called "the boom" or "booming," in political slang, is full of dramatic and spectacular incidents. The part of the program intended for the outside public is addressed almost exclusively to the senses. True, speeches are made to the public, mass meetings are got up in front of the hotels, and speakers discuss the situation and the merit of the candidate from the balconies. But the favorite plan is to make the candidate popular by demonstrative methods—by exhibiting and shouting out his name, by spreading abroad the reproduction of his physiognomy. The headquarters of each candidate is provided with large bales of his portraits, with leaflets relating his glorious life, and, especially, with badges bearing his name and his likeness. [...] Every citizen who puts on this ribbon or button confesses thereby his belief in the candidate, and is qualified for making proselytes, who, perhaps, are converted solely by the artistic execution of the badges. On the building occupied by the headquarters, above the banner with a picture of the candidate, is displayed his name, in huge letters, and in the evening it reappears in the form of luminous globes, the varied colors of which attract the gaze of the crowd.

But the most important part of the boom of the candidate in the streets consists of concerts, serenades, parades, and processions, by day and by night. The persons figuring in these processions [...] are imported by hundreds and thousands from the candidate's own state and from elsewhere. They are formed into companies, generally wearing a special dress, and, headed by a band, they walk through the streets to show how many admirers the candidate possesses. [...] Along with these sights for the eye, the boom includes a very important vocal element [...] which consists in bellowing out the candidate's name; the aforesaid companies [...] numbering perhaps hundreds of persons, scour the streets uttering more or less articulate cries in which the candidate's name can be distinguished. They overrun the hotels, and, jostling each other in the passages, execute their repertoire, consisting of a single refrain [. . .] or at most, some lines like the following: "Ho, ha, he! Who are we? We are the Bland Club from K. C. (Kansas City). We're hot stuff! That's no bluff. Vote for silver and you'll have stuff!" Or again: "He's a runner; he's a winner. Wahoo waugh! Wahoo waugh! Billy McKinley! Billy McKinley! Wahoo waugh! Wahoo waugh!"

These gymnastic and vocal propagandists form one of the three factors of the situation, along with the delegates and the spectators. While acting on the latter, they are meant to impress the former in the long run; and, perhaps [. . .] they succeed in doing so.

But, in any event, the conversions effected by the boom in the street cannot be of importance. Not so with the boom which aims directly at the delegates. This kind of boom also tries to puff the presidential aspirant, but by more refined methods. After having discreetly reconnoitered the hostile and rival positions, the managers of each aspirant direct their attacks toward the weaker points, in order to capture as many delegates as possible. They endeavor to spread abroad the impression that their client is most likely to obtain a majority; that it is, consequently, good policy to join him instead of persisting in the support of an aspirant doomed to defeat. They quote, with some stretch of their imagination, the delegations which have "mentioned" or even "endorsed" their aspirant; they have on their office table ready-made lists, copies of which they eagerly distribute, and which show, state by state, the exact total of the votes which he will poll at the first ballot—a total which is always exaggerated. A few members of the delegation are detached as "missionaries," and visit the headquarters to make proselytes; they ask to be heard by the delegations, and, in more or less closely reasoned speeches, they plead the cause of their candidate before one delegation after another, and perhaps prove the weakness of his competitors. They are received courteously and listened to attentively; but a straightforward answer is seldom given them. Everybody is on his guard. [. . .] Everything depends on the combinations which are being formed elsewhere, and you never know exactly what to believe; [. . .] at one time you are told that the adherents of the presidential aspirant A and those of B have combined, and that creates a new situation, the surface of the electoral chessboard is radically changed thereby; at another time comes the grave news that a "break" has taken place in the delegations of this or that state; they can no longer be depended on. [. . .] In reality, it is all a matter of bargaining: they calculate, they appraise, they buy, they sell, but the bargain is rarely stated in definite terms; there is a tacit understanding that the delegate who gives his vote will have a claim on the lucky winner. Only a small number of delegates are bought straight out with cash. [. . .] Laborious negotiations proceed all along the line; it is a continuous series of conferences, of councils of war [. . .] in which the leaders expend and exhaust their energies. [. . .] On the Sunday preceding the opening of the convention the agitation reaches its height, in spite of the Anglo-Saxon Sabbath; it is the day of crisis [. . .] on which the principal actors have come to an understanding about the candidates and the program. But this does not make the final result any more of a certainty; the convention always has great surprises in store.

The sittings of the national convention are public, and generally attract from 10,000 to 15,000 spectators. The members of the convention alone number nearly 2000 persons, consisting of 930 delegates and as many alternates. The convention [. . .] always sits in a building of vast size, and generally erected for the purpose. The opening of the doors is awaited by an enormous crowd, a portion of which will be excluded for want of tickets. [. . .] At last the doors are thrown open, the crowd rushes in and occupies all the seats in a twinkling, without any disorder; [. . .] the eye can scarcely take in the amphitheater, the benches and galleries are black with people, the bright July sun plays upon the human sea through the innumerable panes of glass which form the roof of the building. All the galleries are hung with flags and bunting encircling the portraits of the great ancestors of the republic. [. . .] A muffled hum of voices fills the vast enclosure like the mutterings of the ocean gathering its waves before it lets loose the storm, while from above issues other sounds of a clearer and more melodious kind: on a gallery over the presidential platform an orchestra, completely hidden by the hangings, plays popular airs and wafts down upon the crowd the sweet and tender strains of "America."

In the meantime the chairman of the national committee ascends the platform, knocks on the desk with a gavel, and calls the convention to order, after which a clergyman offers up a prayer to invoke the blessings of Heaven upon the labors of the assembly. [. . .] After the prayer, the chairman of the national committee [. . .] submits to the convention the names of the temporary organization of the convention, which are, as a rule, adopted by the assembly without debate.[1] The temporary chairman receives the gavel from the chairman of the national committee and delivers a speech, which is hailed with applause and shouts. This is the first explosion of the enthusiasm of the crowd, which is destined to reappear only too often in the course of the session.

The convention begins by selecting its four great committees, viz. the committee on credentials, on permanent organization, on rules and order of business, and on platform or on resolutions. The roll of all the states is called, the chairman of each delegation announces the names of the members, one for each committee, whom it appoints to act on them. Thereupon the convention adjourns, and the committees set to work at once in order to submit their reports on the following morning. [. . .] The most important reports of the committees are those of the committee on credentials and of the committee on resolutions. The former decides all the cases of contested seats. These last are always numerous; sometimes individual delegates contend for the position, at others two complete delegations appear for the state, each claiming to be the duly elected one; [. . .] the delegation which is admitted will be able to aspire to favors at the hand of the government which the convention will bring into existence. [. . .] Sometimes the decisions of the committee on credentials are not ratified by the convention; but this seldom happens. After the report of the committee on credentials, the convention considers the report of the committee on permanent organization, which submits to it the names of the permanent officers of the convention. This list [. . .] is settled beforehand by the national committee [and . . .] accepted without opposition. The permanent chairman delivers a long speech on the political situation, repeatedly and frantically interrupted by cries of approval, which are a sort of installment offered by the crowd of the shouts with which it will shortly receive the platform to be submitted by the committee on resolutions.

The platform, which is supposed to be the party's profession of faith and its program of action, would appear to be the main business of the convention; in reality it is only a farce—the biggest farce of all the acts of this great parliament of the party. The platform presents a long list of statements [. . .] relating to politics, in which everybody can find something to suit him, but in which nothing is considered as of any consequence by the authors of the document, as well as by the whole convention. It is a catalogue revised and enlarged from one convention to another. If a new problem is beginning to stir the country, if any question not only of a political but of a social or humanitarian nature is interesting public opinion for the moment, the platform hastens to re-echo it, in order to show [. . .] the party's solicitude for the particular cause. It is not even necessary that American interests should be involved; it is enough if the question affects the elector's sensibility as a man. It is therefore considered good taste to insert in the platform of the party an expression of sympathy with, for instance, the persecuted Armenians in Turkey, and good policy to declare for Irish Home Rule, and to protest against the harsh treatment of the Jews in the dominions of the Tsar, the Irish and the Jews having many coreligionists [. . .] among the electors of the United States. All the more are the authors of the platform on the lookout for the special preoccupations of American citizens, which stir the public mind or disturb private interests. For instance, the scandals of the spoils system having exasperated opinion and made "civil service reform" a question of the day, the platforms of both parties hasten to add a strongly worded paragraph in favor of the reform, which all the delegates in quest of spoils of course hate like poison; and every future platform reaffirms the pious declaration. If there is an urgent problem which demands a straightforward solution, the concoctors of the platform endeavor to word it in language which can bear different constructions, to compose a "straddling" one. [. . .] Exceptionally, at times of grave crises which distracted the party, when there was no loophole, the platform has met the question of the day with a straightforward answer which, on two occasions, was the signal for a formal split in the party; to wit, at the Democratic convention in Charleston, in 1860, on the subject of slavery, and at the Democratic convention of Chicago, in 1896, about the free coinage of silver.

But, apart from cases of this kind, the sole object of the platform is [. . .] to catch votes by trading on the credulity of the electors. The declamatory form and the ambiguous statements of this document of the party both tend in this direction. As an indication, therefore, of the policy of the future administration elected on this platform, the latter is of no value. In this respect, the letter of acceptance of the candidate adopted by the convention, in which he states his aims and his views on the great questions of the day, is far more important. [. . .] The platform has just as little significance and authority for Congress. Its members consider themselves in no way bound by the program laid down in the convention, for they know perfectly well under what circumstances and with what mental reservations it has been promulgated. The promises of the platform which the party that has come into or remained in power has not redeemed, will only provide matter for violent denunciations in the next platform of the opposite party, which will arouse the indignant enthusiasm of the assembled crowd, expressed in applause and shouts loud enough to shake the walls of the building.

All the states are invited in alphabetical order to introduce their aspirants. Those who have any respond to the invitation by putting up speakers to support the claims of their "favorite sons," or, in general, of the men whom they prefer. These champions are carefully selected beforehand from among those delegates who are most conspicuous for their eloquence, as well as for their influence. The principal spokesman of each aspirant makes the nominating speech in his favor, then another delegate, or several delegates, second the nomination in less elaborate speeches; and so on until the list of the states and of the aspirants is exhausted. It is only when all these torrents of eloquence have ceased to flow that the voting begins. The nominating speeches are looked on as the aesthetic treat and the *pièce de resistance* of the entertainment. The eulogium of the aspirant is generally pompous and bombastic; it tries to be at once persuasive and affecting. It dwells on the aspirant's special chances of being elected if he is adopted as a candidate; it tells the story of his life, beginning with the days of his childhood and his youth. If they have been full of toil and hardship, so much the better: that will melt the hearts of the audience; if he has had to go barefoot for want of shoe leather, that is a real godsend; the people, "the plain people," will recognize in him "one of themselves," and the others will share this feeling out of democratic snobbery. For there is nothing so becoming in American society as the humble beginnings of a successful man. [...] Whatever the real position and the notoriety of the aspirant [...] the speaker who eulogizes him never considers himself under any restriction in the choice of terms for glorifying him; the speech teems with the most extravagant epithets and with metaphors of extraordinary boldness. The orator lays under contribution the poets, mythology, modern history, ancient history, and that of Rome in particular. [...] At the Democratic convention of 1896 a candidate was introduced in these terms: "We give you another Cicero—Cicero to meet another Catiline." Another candidate, a farmer from the West, was put forward as "that illustrious statesman and patriot, that Tiberius Gracchus"; and the speaker adjured the convention to vote for the American Gracchus "by the ashes of your ancestors; by the memories of your great and venerated dead; by the love which you bear to your children; by the duty which you owe to posterity; in the name of all that men hold sacred." In the majority of cases, the authors of these impassioned appeals know perfectly well that their clients have not the faintest chance of obtaining a majority in the convention, and all the delegates and the public are aware of it too; but the grand specimen of eloquence is none the less delivered and listened to with conviction, for, as in the theater, if the actors and the audience did not look as if they believed that it has all really happened, there could be no play at all

It is remarkable, as illustrating the psychology of the American elector, that for more than sixty years, from the date at which one finds the prototype of the nominating speech, the national convention style of eloquence has not changed, amid the incessant progress of American society. [...] Here is an address delivered at the Republican convention in favor of a candidate who obtained 13 votes out of 813. After having sketched the history of the Republican party and of its glories, the speaker narrates the life of the aspirant:

> X was born in North Carolina. He draws from southern blood and southern soil and southern skies the generous chivalry of a nature that abhors cant and hypocrisy and falsehood, and feels the stain like a wound. Thirty-four years ago he came, a poor, barefooted, penniless boy, to the rugged soil of Connecticut, where breathing its free air, listening to its free speech, and taught in its free school, he laid the foundation of a manly character and life in principles which are is enduring as Connecticut's everlasting hills. [...] The fierce light that beats against a presidential candidate will explore his record in vain, and he will come out brighter from the blaze. His life is gentle, and the elements are so mixed in him that nature might stand up and say to all the world, "This is a man." [...] If he is nominated, all elements can support him, for he is a radical conservative and a conservative

radical; a friend of Garfield and a friend of Grant. Sir, if he should be nominated, it would ensure you Connecticut by a 10,000 majority. [. . .]

The eloquence of the speakers [. . .] only produces its full effect when accompanied by the more or less noisy manifestations with which the audience
greets the speeches and the names of the presidential aspirants who form the
subject of them. Every speech is interrupted and brought to a close by more or
less frantic shouts; being looked on as a criterion of the aspirant's popularity,
these outcries impress the delegates, make the weak hesitate, and sometimes
decide the wavering. The campaign managers of each aspirant, therefore considering these manifestations as a card in their game, procure them by means
of a paid *claque*, judiciously distributed over the enormous hall. This is the last
and the most impressive act of the "boom" organized on behalf of the aspirant;
inside the convention building the boom becomes an apotheosis. As soon as
the aspirant's name is uttered, the delegates who support him and the paid ap-
plauders jump up on their seats and break into cheers or other less articulate
cries, which are immediately taken up by a more or less considerable section of
the crowd. The latter are only too ready to make a row, they have almost a phys-
iological need of this relief; it is enough for the *claque* to give the signal for
them to go into convulsions. If the aspirant is a favorite a very popular man,
whom the forecasts place in the first flight for the presidential race, the delir-
ium reaches an indescribable pitch of intensity. Hardly has the speaker pronounced his name when his portrait, which has been held in reserve, is hoisted
aloft and carried about the hall, every one is on his legs, shooting, screaming,
tossing hats and handkerchiefs into the air, waving small flags and open umbrellas. It is a sort of pandemonium or bedlam. If one could imagine a crowd
of 15,000 persons all attacked at once with St. Vitus' dance, one would obtain a
faint idea of the scene presented by the convention.[2] The chairman [. . .] is quite
helpless, it is in vain that he tells the band to play in order to tranquilize the assembly; a duel begins between the orchestra, which energetically strikes up the
"Star-Spangled Banner," and the yelling crowd; now and then a few sounds
from the instruments are audible, but they are instantaneously drowned by the
shouting. [. . .] The paroxysm is at its height. [. . .] The crowd does not stop
until compelled by fatigue, by exhaustion. Spectators who know what is coming have taken out their watches from the very beginning, like certain travelers
at the entrance of a long tunnel. The duration of the uproar, carefully noted
down, is not only of importance for the effect of the moment; it is formally
placed on record, and later on people will point out that the uproar for McKinley did not last more than twenty-two minutes, that is to say less than that with
which Blaine was honored. [. . .] At last the string of panegyrics is at an end;
wearied with oratory and overcome by the tremendous physical exertion, every

one takes breath to prepare for the new and supreme emotions to be afforded by the ballots.

The voting for the candidates is attended with the same publicity as all the proceedings which go before it: as the name of each state is called out, in alphabetical order, the chairman of the delegation announces to whom it gives its votes. In the Democratic conventions, where the "unit rule" is in force, the votes are all credited to a single candidate, that of the majority of delegates, and the chairman of the New York delegation, for instance, declares "seventy-two votes for so-and-so," although thirty-five delegates are against him. In the Republican conventions, where each delegate is entitled to vote as he pleases, the chairman of the delegation announces several candidates, if there is occasion for it, mentioning at the same time the number of votes given to each. However, even in the Democratic convention each delegate has the right to challenge the declarations of his chairman. In that case, the clerk of the convention calls the roll of all the delegates, who each state the name of their candidate. This does not alter the result, all the votes are given to the candidate chosen by the majority; but the minority gets an opportunity of making a public demonstration in favor of its candidate. [. . .] The majority which an aspirant must obtain to be proclaimed candidate is a bare majority with the Republicans, and a two-thirds one with the Democrats. The reader is aware that the two-thirds rule is of very old standing, and will recollect the way in which it was used in certain Democratic conventions to disqualify popular aspirants, such as Martin Van Buren. Repeated attempts have been made to abolish the two-thirds rule, but without success; it has become part of the Democratic patrimony. [. . .] According to one version, the rule was adopted in the interest of the southern states, which wanted to prevent the free states of the North and of the West from thrusting a president on them against their will. Another explanation is that the majority was fixed at two-thirds to ensure complete harmony between the president and the federal senate, a portion of whose members is renewed in two-thirds of the states almost at the same time as the occupant of the chief magistracy of the union. As has always been the case, the two-thirds rule somewhat facilitates intrigue, but it does not delay the gathering of a majority round some name or other more than on the Republican side, owing to the unit rule, which by automatically assimilating the minorities, quickens the coagulation of the various elements of the convention.

The maneuvers and the intrigues relating to the person of the future president, which have been carried on by managers and powerful state bosses, may be paralyzed by the force of public opinion, which sometimes imposes its candidate on the convention with inflexible persistency. The politicians, at least the big ones who are working for themselves, are in that case defeated before the battle begins. Thus, for instance, in 1892 the head politicians of the Democratic party, along with Tammany Hall, were hostile to Cleveland's candidature; but in the country at large it aroused the greatest enthusiasm; and the politicians had to yield and give him a majority at the first ballot. His Republican rival, Harrison, who then filled the presidency and was seeking renomination, was opposed by several state bosses, who combined to insure his defeat; but the bulk of the delegates did not follow them, believing in Harrison's success with the electorate, and brought him in also at the first ballot. However, such a direct pressure of opinion is of extremely rare occurrence. Generally, when the balloting begins, the situation is still very uncertain, for it depends entirely on intrigues and maneuvers which, although they have been prosecuted unremittingly, have not yet led to a result. The first ballot, therefore, is hardly ever decisive; it barely [...] approximate[s] [...] the strength of the rival forces. [...] To make an impression on the convention, the managers of the principal aspirants try to bring up all their following and to show "presidential strength," except when a smart manager holds back a few votes for the second ballot with object of proving that his aspirant is gaining votes, and of making this example contagious. Most of the delegates, who are running obscure "favorite sons," are free from all these preoccupations. They have voted for these aspirants and will vote for them again in or two ballots [...] but they are really waiting [...] for the moment when they can decently throw them over and join the winners.

But who is to win; who will be the man? This is the question which consumes all the human beings packed in the huge building; [...] each fresh ballot is expected to furnish the answer. The chiefs [...] of the various aspirants, alone keeping a cool head amid the general excitement, combine the movements on the board. All the dispositions suggested by the last ballot must be made immediately, for the ballots follow each other without a break. Hurriedly, the heads of different delegations exchange a few words, give a word of command; or a delegation of a large state withdraws for awhile to come to an agreement; these conferences are sometimes particularly passionate and uproarious. [...] To prevent an alliance between A and B, who are leading, a considerable number of votes are given to B. [...] To keep the totals of the eminent aspirants stationary, after several successive ballots, is also an important result; it is hoped to this the followers of aspirants who are doomed to failure will go on voting for them ballot after ballot. For a certain number of ballots, therefore, it is only a sparring match; votes are given to aspirants and withdrawn from them; are borrowed for one ballot and scrupulously returned on the next.

On their side, the favorites, as well as the aspirants of the second class, try to gain the votes of the humble aspirants, to "get their strength." The question is, which of the powerful aspirants succeed in detaching the most votes of this description. All the negotiations and the maneuvers which have preceded and have been carried on during the convention have tended in this direction; and it is now, under the running fire of the votes announced for the various competitors, that the supreme decision must be taken by those delegates who command a [. . .] considerable amount of "presidential strength." When they have satisfied themselves, after a few ballots, that their own candidates have no prospect of success, they go over with a quiet conscience, into the camp of a more fortunate aspirant. In so doing, they no doubt consult their own interests, that is to say, sell themselves as dear as possible and, perhaps, also let themselves be carried away by personal sympathies and antipathies. [. . .] Having given up his pet aspirant, if he had one, each delegate tries to join the ranks of a "winner," of an aspirant likely to carry the day in the country, and to procure for the party power with all its consequences. In a word, he looks out for the "available candidate" among the aspirants; [. . .] if the aspirant has a certain amount of popularity, if he is personally "magnetic," so much the better. [. . .] His physique is not immaterial either. His political position, perhaps a very poor one, is capable of being advantageously made up for by that of his state. If this latter is a doubtful state, in which the parties are evenly balanced, it may not be able to resist the temptation of having one of its sons in the presidency, and may, on this occasion, give his party a majority, which majority will, perhaps, be decisive for the victory of that party in the whole union, if the state is a large one like New York, for instance, disposing of thirty-six votes in the Electoral College. A state of this kind is, consequently, looked on as a "pivotal" state, and the aspirant who belongs to it is *ipso facto* an available candidate. New York, which has long played the part of pivotal state, has, therefore, imposed many presidential candidates on the national conventions. A state in which one of the two parties has a permanent majority, and which cannot turn the scale in favor of that party in the presidential contests, or a very small state, like Maine, for instance, is not on that account deprived of the chance of supplying a presidential candidate, but, then, the latter must be a man who holds a very leading position; this was the case with J. G. Blaine, a citizen of Maine.

It may well [. . .] happen that after several ballots none of the favorites succeeds in detaching enough votes from his rivals to obtain a majority. This is the moment for the "dark horses" to appear on the course. They must not forestall this moment; if they come forward at the first ballots to try conclusions with the favorites, they run the risk of being hopelessly beaten at once. Their merit resides precisely in the character of *makeshift* which they possess; and they can only turn it to account when a feeling of weariness comes over the assembly. The dark horses sometimes try to force the hand of the convention by combining their small groups [. . .] but it is not easy for them to come to an understanding, for the coalition can only be made for the benefit of one of them. They have to trust rather to chance to bring the right man out of the ruck. Perhaps a favorite, despairing of his own success, will, to prevent the triumph of the rival favorite, himself transfer all his "strength" [. . .] to a dark horse; perhaps the latter, by laboriously increasing his total at each successive ballot, will command success in the end.

Each ballot is followed with the utmost anxiety by the whole assembly, and it invariably gives rise to noisy manifestations. During the roll call of the states the adherents of the various aspirants applaud and utter shouts of delight as soon as a delegation announces that it votes for their man. When the result of the ballot is proclaimed, an explosion of enthusiasm, often ending in a grand uproar, greets a rise in the total of votes obtained by an aspirant. If the rise is accentuated at the following ballots, the crowd of delegates and spectators becomes delirious. More or less earthly shrieks, cries of animals, hats thrown into the air, red umbrellas opened, flags and banners frantically waved, start the pandemonium afresh. The standard of the state to which the aspirant in question belongs [. . .] is pulled up, and in a twinkling it is surrounded by the standards of the several other states, which salute it, and all form a procession, which marches several times round the hall along its unencumbered passages. The sitting is practically interrupted; it is impossible to proceed to a new ballot; in vain does the chairman cry out [. . .] "Call the roll"; the delegations do not answer. [. . .] With nerves strained to the utmost, the public awaits the dramatic moment from the second ballot onward, and says to itself on each occasion: "It will come this time." This moment sends a thrill of anticipation through the politicians of the convention and causes them a violent emotion, in which they indulge with a feeling of delight. As soon as the "break" takes place, the whole assembly has an epileptic fit, stamping on the floor, yelling, carrying round standards in a procession, etc., in the way with which we are familiar. The politician whose influence has brought about the break will, of course, be in good odor with the candidate when the latter has become president; he can count upon an embassy or some other "good thing."

Sometimes the ballot in which the "crisis" has taken place is the last, sometimes one or two more ballots are required to gather a majority round the name of the lucky winner; but his success grows more marked with each moment, and a little sooner or later he will "be landed." When his triumph appears tolerably certain, a sort of panic seizes on the delegates who had hitherto voted for other aspirants, and they rush to join the winner in a wild [. . .] "stampede." One after another they are in a hurry to retract their vote before the ballot is closed. Here is an old man who jumps on a chair as nimbly as his bulk will allow him, and cries out in a choking voice: "Mr. Chairman, Mr. Chairman!" and when [. . .] he catches the chairman's eye, he announces that his state changes its mind, and gives its [. . .] votes to so-and-so. Several other heads of delegations make a declaration to the same effect. [. . .] To prevent the stampede [...] the champion of the rival aspirants, who see the hurricane coming, have but one resource [...] adjournment of the convention; but the latter is generally too excited to consent. [...] As soon as the result of the last ballot is announced, the champion of one of the defeated aspirants proposes to the convention to make the nomination of their fortunate rival unanimous. The motion is carried, a grand uproar of the regulation kind, with the war dance of the standards, greets the happy event, the band strikes up "Hail to the Chief," and the assembly goes mad for half an hour or so.

But there remains the selection of a candidate for the vice presidency. This task does not detain the convention long; not that the aspirants to the second dignity are less numerous, but because the assembly is already exhausted, and because it is not in the habit of attaching much importance to the post of vice president, whose influence in the government of the union and the distribution of offices is *nil*. [...] The conventions make use of this candidature to gratify personal or local vanity, which it is advisable to soothe or turn to account. They bestow the honor as a consolation stakes on one of the defeated aspirants to the presidency, or on a citizen of a different part of the country to that to which the candidate adopted for the chief magistracy belongs. If the latter comes from a state in the West, the vice presidency is given to an eastern man to silence the jealousy of the populations of the East. It is desirable that this person should also be very rich [...] so that he can contribute a large sum to the expenses of the election campaign; and often the place is one for a millionaire. The procedure for the selection of the candidate for the vice presidency is just the same as for the presidency: roll call, introduction of the aspirants in high-faluting speeches in which they appear surrounded with a halo of virtue and glory; several consecutive ballots, and the shouts of the crowd; but these latter already betray a certain weakness and lassitude, the arms move mechanically, all the voices are hoarse.

At last, after a session of several days, the end is reached; the convention adjourns *sine die*. All is over. As you step out of the building you inhale with relief the gentle breeze which tempers the scorching heat of July; you come to yourself; you recover your sensibility, which has blunted by the incessant uproar, and your faculty of judgment, which has been held in abeyance amid the pandemonium in which day after day has been passed. You collect your impressions, and you realize what a colossal travesty of popular institutions you have just been witnessing. A greedy crowd of office-holders, or of office-seekers, disguised as delegates of the people, on the pretense of holding the grand council of the party, indulged in, or were the victims of, intrigues and maneuvers, the object of which was the chief magistracy of the greatest republic of the two hemispheres—the succession to the Washingtons and the Jeffersons. With an elaborate respect for the forms extending to the smallest details of procedure, they pretended to deliberate, and then passed resolutions settled by a handful of wire-pullers in the obscurity of committees and private caucuses; they proclaimed as the creed of the party appealing to its piety, a collection of hollow, vague phrases, strung together by a few experts in the art of meaningless language, and adopted still more precipitately without examination and without conviction [. . .] they adjured the assembly to support aspirants in whose success they had not the faintest belief; they voted in public for candidates whom they were scheming to defeat. Cut off from their conscience by selfish calculations and from their judgment by the tumultuous crowd [. . .] which alone made all attempt at deliberation an impossibility, they submitted without resistance to the pressure of the galleries masquerading as popular opinion, and made up of a *claque* and of a raving mob which, under ordinary circumstances, could only be formed by the inmates of all the lunatic asylums of the country who had made their escape at the same time. Here this mob discharges a great political tradition; it supplies the "enthusiasm" which is the primary element of the convention. [. . .] Produced to order of the astute managers, "enthusiasm" is served out to the delegates as a strong drink, to gain complete mastery over their will. But in the fit of intoxication they yield to the most sudden impulses, which has the last word. The name of the candidate for the presidency of the republic issues from the votes of the convention like a number from a lottery. And all the followers of the party [. . .] are bound, on point of apostasy, to vote for the product of their lottery. Yet, when you carry your thoughts back from the scene which you have just witnessed and review the line of presidents, you find that if they have not all been great men—far from it—they were all honorable men; and you cannot help repeating the American saying: "God takes care of drunkards, of little children, and of the United States!"

CHAPTER 8

Rationality and Uncertainty at National Nominating Conventions

Eugene B. McGregor Jr.

Almost all theories of coalition building make stringent assumptions about the information rational actors have at their disposal. For only when calculating politicians can be reasonably certain about the effects of their decisions on the outcome of a contest will their behavior conform to the precise patterns postulated in mathematical or spatial models. Should politicians in reality be faced with either faulty information about the moves of other actors—imperfect information—or information which does not indicate clearly their calculated impact on contest outcomes—incomplete information—then it may be difficult if not impossible for even the most "rational" politicians to make the fine calculations implied in most models.[1]

This research examines the possibility that multi-ballot national nominating conventions—a favorite source of data for many models—can in many cases be described as political contests in which the amount of uncertainty is relatively high.[2] Since the very condition—perfect and complete information—necessary for prediction according to available formal models is absent, the extent to which one can generalize about the behavior of real politicians trying to make rational decisions is still open to question. The argument here

From *Journal of Politics* 35 (May 1973): 459–78, with permission from Blackwell Publishing. Table formats have been altered slightly. Eugene B. McGregor Jr., a professor in the School of Public and Environmental Affairs at Indiana University, has published extensively on public policy and management issues.

is that uncertainty itself may produce predictable patterns of behavior which can be derived logically from a number of propositions already substantiated in previous work.

A HISTORICAL PERSPECTIVE ON MULTI-BALLOT CONVENTIONS

Multi-ballot national nominating conventions all have indecision in common. Since 1872, slightly less than 100 years of nominating conventions have witnessed seventeen multi-ballot presidential nominations and four nominations which showed all the indecision of multi-ballot conventions, but which involved only one ballot followed by a series of shifts throwing the nomination to the first ballot front-runner. These conventions are listed in table 7.

With few exceptions, these conventions have been the final scenes of factional warfare within an out-party undirected by an incumbent president who would normally seek and obtain renomination or promote the candidacy of a successor. (Not since the Republican convention of 1884 refused to nominate President Chester Arthur for a second term has an incumbent president sought and been unable to obtain his own renomination or the nomination of a candidate of his choosing). A few cases of multi-ballot conventions have occurred at the convention of the party which already held the presidency. But in each case, the incumbent president was either physically incapacitated at the time of

Table 7
Multi-Ballot and Near Multi-Ballot Conventions since 1872, by Party

Democrats			Republicans		
Year	Nominee	Ballots	Year	Nominee	Ballots
1876	Tilden	22	1876	Hayes*	7
1880	Hancock	2 + shift	1880	Garfield*	36
1884	Cleveland	2 + shift	1884	Blaine*	4
1896	Bryan*	5	1888	Harrison	8
1904	Parker	1 + shift	1916	Hughes	3
1912	Wilson	46	1920	Harding	10 + shift
1920	Cox	44	1940	Willkie	6
1924	Davis	103	1948	Dewey	3
1928	Smith	1 + shift	1952	Eisenhower	1 + shift
1932	Roosevelt	4			
1948	Truman*	1 + shift			
1952	Stevenson*	3			

Source: Richard C. Bain, *Convention Decisions and Voting Records* (Washington, D.C.: Brookings, 1960). The format of this table has been altered from the original (ed.).

Note: *Nominee of party occupying the White House.

the convention or did not choose to exert the influence necessary to the smooth and predictable transfer of power.

THE PROBLEM OF UNCERTAINTY

Some evidence indicates that these are also the conventions which generate the most confusion for the most rational of political actors. Nelson W. Polsby and Aaron B. Wildavsky cogently point out the informational difficulties faced in such contests: there is the absence of a titular leader who would arbitrate the competing claims to power; over 1,000 delegates jammed into a hall in a strange city have great problems following all the maneuverings of candidates and key delegations; and politicians variously interpret the standard indicators of candidate strength such as the polls, primaries, and balloting on procedural motions.

Under these conditions, how do politicians act? One theoretical answer is that rational "leaders" (that is, those who command the allegiance of several delegates collectively called a proto-coalition) and "followers," both of whom might otherwise use the deliberate strategies discussed above, are forced to cope with uncertainty.[3] Each leader attempts to maximize his following at the same time that he uses his proto-coalition size to bargain with other leaders for payoffs, with his bargaining power directly related to the size of his proto-coalition. Followers, however, want to maximize payoffs which are the policies a prospective party nominee feels obliged to support in return for delegate support at the convention. Should the nominee become president, this policy debt follows him into the White House.

But access to a possible future president makes it essential that each delegation contribute support to the nomination. Delegations have a tremendous stake in picking the winner before the candidate actually does become the winner, since greater payoffs flow from an earlier, rather than a later commitment to the eventual winner.[4] Thus, the convention itself produces the dilemma of uncertainty affecting leaders and followers alike: discovering who everyone else thinks the winner will be and either becoming important in supporting the candidacy—a problem for followers—or striking a profitable bargain—a problem for leaders—with the candidate who seems likely to be nominated. Even if the likely nominee is ideologically antagonistic to one's view, it would appear to be rational political behavior to pursue such a strategy since there is precious little public policy utility which can come from vigorously opposing the candidacy of the man who will go on to win the nomination and, perhaps, the presidency.

Political scientists have long noted that multi-ballot conventions do not wait to stampede until after a candidate has acquired a winning majority.[5] Rather, opposition collapses when the eventual winner is somewhat short of the coalition size needed to clinch a nomination. In simple-majority (50 percent-plus-one) conventions, the opposition has held firm when a candidate has had as much as 41 percent of the vote (for example, Ulysses S. Grant, who lost, in 1880) but never for a coalition larger than that in a convention held since 1876. In two-thirds rule conventions, candidates have acquired as much as 59 percent of the delegates (for example, Franklin D. Roosevelt, who won, in 1932) before the opposition collapsed.

One explanation for this phenomenon is the obvious pressure which mounts on delegations to cast their lot with the near winner, beginning an avalanche in that direction and thereby claiming credit for the nomination. Part of the motivation for this action must be uncertainty. Delegates are simply ignorant of the deals being made both on and off the convention floor and can only assume that when a coalition creeps over the 41 percent mark it is dangerous to count on the rest of the opposition holding together against the front-runner. Since most delegations find it necessary to make the same assumptions about the convention process, a stampede of delegates to the perceived winner is symptomatic of the uncertainty inherent in such a political event.

But if delegates have their problems with uncertainty, so do the leaders at the convention. Leaders lack perfect and complete information about minimum winning coalition size and blocking coalitions because their followerships are subject to constant change. Much of this uncertainty undoubtedly stems from the fact that followings are built—like most followings—upon informal deals and understandings—upon the willingness of the followership to follow, rather than upon legally binding commitments.

This delegate freedom is partly seen in the method of delegate selection. Prior to 1968, of the thirteen states and the District of Columbia which selected delegates by primary, only primaries in the District of Columbia and Oregon legally bound delegates to a presidential candidate. Of the twenty-eight states which selected delegates at the state convention, since 1956 only Indiana legally tied her delegates to a candidate on the basis of a preferential primary. The rest of the states chose delegates either by state committee, or by a combination of state convention, district convention, and primary where different methods were used for selecting district delegates and delegates-at-large. In none of these cases were delegates bound to candidates under the sanction of state law, except in Arkansas when the delegates were bound to the winner of an optional, preferential primary.[6]

But if most delegate votes are committed through political deals, the accounting problem does not get more simple after the first ballot. As table 8 shows, each additional ballot at the convention usually brings substantial shifts of delegate votes. These are votes in search of access to a winning candidate, and they create problems for both leaders and followers. Leaders find it diffi-

Table 8

Delegate Vote Shifts for the Democratic Conventions of 1932 and 1952 and the Republican Conventions of 1940 and 1952

Year and party	Total ballots	Total votes	Vote shifts on convention ballots								
			First to second		Second to third		Third to fourth		Fourth to fifth	
			Votes shifted	% shift	Votes shifted	% shift	Votes shifted	% shift	Votes shifted	% shift
1932 D	4	1,154	11	0.1	5.5	0.4	262.5	22.7	—	—
1940 R	6	1,000	85	8.5	108.5	10.5	90	9.0	249.5	24.9
1948 R	3	1,094	66	6.0	—	—	—	—	—	—
1952 D	3	1,230	146.75	11.9	252	20.5	—	—	—	—

Source: Official Proceedings of each convention. The format of this table has been altered from the original [ed.].

Note: McGregor calculated the number of votes shifted by adding the vote changes for all candidates and dividing by two; the sixth ballot of the 1940 Republican convention was unanimous for Wilkie; the third ballot of the 1948 Republican convention was unanimous for Dewey; the switch to Stevenson followed the third Democratic ballot in 1952. Vote totals are for the forty-eight states that constituted the union in the years observed.

cult to count on a proto-coalition holding firm as a basis for concluding further deals. Followers are not always sure of the nature of the coalition they leave, join, or continue to support.

In table 8 the percentage of voting switch has been computed between each roll call for the most recent multi-ballot conventions: Democratic conventions, 1932 and 1952; Republican conventions, 1940 and 1948. While the range varies from a low of 0.04 percent to a high of 25 percent, even an 8.5 percent shift involving eighty-five votes, as in the Republican convention of 1940, can cause real uncertainty if only because such a shift counts twice: someone loses eighty-five votes and someone gains eighty-five votes. Most shifts involve even larger numbers of delegates.

Even more important is that these voting shifts do not appear to be random exchanges. As table 9 shows, the movement in the direction of the eventual winner begins early. With one exception, the eventual winner of the last four multi-ballot nominations gained many more votes and lost many fewer between each ballot than his closest rival. The one exception occurred in the 1940 Republican convention between the third and the fourth ballot. At this point Sen. Robert A. Taft gained two more votes than Wendell L. Willkie, but lost seven votes while Willkie lost none!

In the cases of the Republican convention of 1948 and the Democratic convention of 1932, it can be argued that the eventual winners—Thomas E. Dewey and Franklin D. Roosevelt—were not surprising since they were obvious leaders from the beginning. But such predisposition was decidedly not the case with the Democratic convention of 1952 and the Republican convention of 1940, in which these the initial front-runners were overtaken and defeated by Adlai E. Stevenson and Wendell Willkie, respectively. Delegates who switched could not have known as early as the second ballot how many votes would be won and lost by each candidate or that the coalition to which they were switching would go on to win. Yet a consistent pattern of decisions by seemingly rational political actors emerges. Very early in the convention a few switches presage what later proves, with an accelerating volume of switches, to be the choice of the whole convention.

Since, theoretically, rational decision-makers switch from one coalition to another only when they think they are joining the proto-coalition that will eventually win control of the party—with greater rewards for those who commit themselves earliest—one is led to ponder what produces such unmistakable trends so early in these nominating conventions. Are there recurring patterns of political behavior which result from the attempts of politicians to deal with ignorance? Polsby and Wildavsky suggest that the answer to this question may have something to do with a candidate's ability "to gain acceptance of a specific interpretation of the signs and portents which will be favor-

Table 9

Voting Shifts for Major Candidates in Democratic Conventions of 1932 and 1952 and Republican Conventions of 1940 and 1952

	1932 Democratic		1952 Democratic		1940 Republican		1948 Republican	
	Winner	Runner-up	Winner	Runner-up	Winner	Runner-up	Winner	Runner-up
	Roosevelt	Smith	Stevenson	Kefauver	Willkie	Taft	Dewey	Taft
First to second ballot								
Votes lost	0	7.5	0	11.5	1	6	1	21
% of total	0	0.6	0	9.3	0.1	0.6	0.1	1.9
Votes gained	11.5	0	59.5	34	67	20	82	71
% of total	1	0	4.8	2.8	6.7	2.0	7.5	6.5
Second to third ballot								
Votes lost	2	4	0	92.5	1	12	0	274
% of total	0.1	0.3	0	7.5	0.1	1.2	0	25.0
Votes gained	7.5	0	293	5.5	89	21	579	0
% of total	0.5	0	23.8	0.4	8.9	2.1	52.9	0
Third to fourth ballot								
Votes lost	0	16.75	—	—	0	7	—	—
% of total	0	1.4	—	—	0	0.7	—	—
Votes gained	263	17	—	—	47	49	—	—
% of total	22.8	1.5	—	—	4.7	4.9	—	—
Fourth to fifth ballot								
Votes lost	—	—	—	—	2	4	—	—
% of total	—	—	—	—	0.2	0.4	—	—
Votes gained	—	—	—	—	125	127	—	—
% of total	—	—	—	—	12.5	12.7	—	—

Source: Official Proceedings of each convention. The format of this table has been altered from the original (ed.).

able to him."[7] What is important about contested conventions, then, may not be the "realities" of deals, polls, and primary results, but what politicians think these events mean in terms of a candidate's chances for capturing the nomination.

Put differently, the hypothesis is ventured that candidates can be influential in contested conventions only when they significantly affect the notions of events held by the delegates. Delegates and candidates alike are forced, consistent with the motives discussed earlier, to cope with uncertainty by using what information they have to make inferences about the nomination chances of the candidates. People move from what they know to what they do not know, and successful candidacies must have an impact on those things viewed by politicians as establishing a certainty from which inferences are drawn.

In multi-ballot conventions, and perhaps at single-ballot conventions as well, the most reliable information about probable winners is actual balloting—or other contests which are publicly decided. Votes do not lie, and they are recorded for all to see. In multi-ballot conventions they become particularly important because more than one round of balloting must occur before a winner is chosen. Votes are one of the few reliable indicators of relative candidate strength. They are available to all the delegates on an equal basis, and each round of balloting reveals more information about candidate strength and the probable nominee.

From the first ballot, for instance, delegates can form some opinion about how close the lead candidate is to stampeding the convention. In many instances, failure of the lead candidate to capture the nomination by the first ballot shows the real weakness in his coalition, for if he were such a strong candidate, he would have attained the nomination on the first ballot. By the second ballot, the delegates know which of the candidates has added the greatest number of votes to his coalition. Very early in the convention, then, delegates begin to accumulate knowledge about the probable winners in the only way uncertain calculators can—they study publicly available evidence of the relative strengths of the candidates. Under these conditions the voting itself affects future voting decisions.

Thus, one plausible hypothesis about convention behavior is suggested by this discussion: under conditions of uncertainty, delegates who are anxiously trying to pick a winner find it easier to cast their lot on the third ballot with the candidate who has made the largest gain from the first to the second ballot. If this hypothesis is true, then a corollary is also true: the candidate who gains the largest share of the votes from the first to the second ballot will be the eventual winner no matter how many ballots are needed for nomination.

From the standpoint of the delegates such a forecast would appear to be logical because the ability to add delegates to a coalition is a sign that stalking horses, favorite sons, and various deals are manifesting themselves in the form of a steadily growing coalition. Since the delegates are uncertain about what crucial shifts are likely to occur on the next ballot, they use what they do know as a guide for their next voting decision.

These hypotheses would also be logical from the standpoint of the leaders of proto-coalitions. The candidate with the largest gain between the first and second ballots has an appealing argument which he can present to those uncommitted to him: "Join me now and share in the proportionate rewards or get stuck voting for a loser." The leaders of other proto-coalitions must also be uncertain about the delegate shifts likely to occur with each succeeding ballot, and they too have a great incentive to throw their support behind the eventual winner since they can share in the payoffs divided among the winning coalition.

At the same time, several conditions limit the applicability of the two hypotheses. One is that intense ideological cleavages can produce behavior unexplained by this model. Ideologically committed delegates are not so much concerned about supporting the candidate who everyone else thinks will be the winner as they are in making sure that their political views prevail. Thus, losing an opportunity to join the eventual winner can be a more desirable outcome than joining forces with a candidate who is an ideological enemy.[8]

Second, for delegates concerned primarily with capturing state or local office, the problem is not only to maximize access to the national party nominee but to support the candidacy which promises the greatest electoral success in the home state. Thus, many delegates may find it rational to oppose a "winning" contender for the nomination who is likely to be unpopular at home.[9] Such motivations often explain sectional dimensions of American politics, for the question many delegates ask is whether, say, a governor of New York will, as a presidential nominee, help the state party capture a gubernatorial or senatorial race in California or Alabama.[10]

Third, conventions "controlled" by only a few political bosses can produce unexpected results because great uncertainty is not an appropriate assumption to apply to the bargaining process. Uncertainty is created at national nominating conventions largely because of the numbers of independent political actors; in such cases, the various followings are not "bossed" to accept the decisions of an oligarchy but exercise a judgment of their own. Only an oligarchy is not influenced very much by early shifts of delegates from one candidate to another since it is a small group of leaders—not the followership—which guides the shifts. In such conventions, it would not be unusual to expect that true dark horses could emerge from obscurity in the earlier ballots as compromise candidates who consummate bargains struck between warring factions of party leadership. Dark horses can emerge in this manner because the convention is not conducted under the conditions of extreme uncertainty discussed above.

The voting data presented in tables 10 and 11 show that, for the most part, the two hypotheses advanced earlier describe precisely what has happened at multi-ballot conventions over the past 100 years. The exceptions will be accounted for below, but for the seventeen cases of multi-ballot conventions since 1872, eleven winners can be predicted by this method.[11] The candidate making the largest gain from the first to the second ballot went on to win the nomination, and this result even obtains in the 1912 Democratic convention which nominated Woodrow Wilson after 46 ballots! Perhaps even more important is the fact that eight out of the ten most recent multi-ballot conventions—held since 1892—show this pattern of events.

It should also be pointed out that many of the correct predictions are not at all obvious if we consider either the rank among the contenders or the percentage of the total vote held by the eventual winners at the end of the second ballot. In three recent cases—Thomas E. Dewey in 1948, Franklin D. Roosevelt in 1932, and Charles Evans Hughes in 1916—we find instances of front-runners merely adding the few necessary votes in order to clinch the nomination in four votes or less. But in five of the most difficult cases—Adlai E. Stevenson in 1952, Wendell L. Willkie in 1940, James M. Cox in 1920, Woodrow Wilson in 1912, and William Jennings Bryan in 1896—we are able to predict the outcome even though each candidate moved from an initial second and third running in the lists and a small percentage of the first ballot vote to become a winner. It seems very unlikely in all of these cases that the candidates attained the nomination because of a momentous speech, such as the one made by Bryan in 1896, or an unusually noisy demonstration, such as the one for Willkie in 1940, but rather because leaders and followers alike made the kinds of calculations indicated above.

The Democratic conventions are of interest because our hypothesis obtains in seven of the nine cases with only the convention of 1884 and the marathon meeting of 1924 as the exceptions. Even the existence of a two-thirds-majority-decision rule at the conventions prior to 1936 did not change the pattern. The reason for this, perhaps, is that while a two-thirds rule probably encouraged the formation of blocking coalitions, the rule did not obviate the need of delegates to decide who the eventual winner would be and join the winning coalition as early as possible.

What the two-thirds rule really did was to give ideological and sectional enemies the means for protecting themselves in conventions likely to run out of control as uncertain delegates joined the bandwagons of perceived winners. For instance, the 103 ballot Democratic convention of 1924 found wet, Catholic, and urban Alfred E. Smith from New York City opposing an obvious rival in dry, Protestant, and rural Sen. William Gibbs McAdoo from California. These opposing camps were not only as antagonistic as party factions have gotten at national nominating conventions, but both factions knew they possessed

Table 10

Predicted Winners of Democratic Multi-Ballot Conventions, 1876 to 1952

	1876	1880	1884	1896	1912	1920	1924	1932	1952
Ballots needed to nominate	2	2+ shift	2+ shift	5	46	44	103	4	3
Biggest gainer from first to second ballot (vote gain)	Tilden (134.5)	Hancock (149)	Hendricks (122.5)	Bryan (60)	Wilson (15)	Cox (25)	Smith (10.5)	Roosevelt (11)	Stevenson (51.5)
First ballot ranking of biggest gainer	1	1	1	2	2	3	2	1	2
Eventual winner	Tilden	Hancock	Cleveland	Bryan	Wilson	Cox	Davis	Roosevelt	Stevenson
Vote % after second ballot for eventual winner	72.5	43.4	57.9	21.2	31.0	14.5	2.9	58.8	26.3

Source: Richard C. Bain, *Convention Decisions and Voting Records* (Washington, D.C.: Brookings, 1960).

Note: Every convention except the one in 1952 operated under the two-thirds rule.

Table 11
Predicted Winners of Republican Multi-Ballot Conventions, 1876 to 1948

	1876	1880	1884	1888	1916	1920	1940	1948
Ballots needed to nominate	7	36	4	8	3	10	6	3
Biggest gainer from first to second ballot (vote gain)	Blaine (11)	Washburn (7)	Blaine (14.5)	Alger (32)	Hughes (75)	Lowden (48)	Willkie (66)	Dewey (81)
First ballot ranking of biggest gainer	1	5	1	3	1	6	3	1
Eventual winner	Hayes	Garfield	Blaine	Harrison	Hughes	Harding	Willkie	Dewey
Vote % after second ballot for eventual winner	8.5	1.3	42.6	10.9	30.4	6.0	17.1	47.1

Source: Richard C. Bain, *Convention Decisions and Voting Records* (Washington, D.C.: Brookings, 1960).

firm blocking coalitions of at least 367 votes, one-third-plus-one of the delegate votes. The certainty of a blocking coalition left each rival unsusceptible to the other's bandwagon because each had prior knowledge that the bandwagon was doomed to failure. Thus, neither candidate won the nomination. We cannot say to what extent other conditions—such as bossism—contributed to the deadlock. But the 103 ballots are testimony to the intensity of the cleavages at that convention.

The Republican conventions show a different pattern involving several exceptions to the hypotheses. These exceptions are alike in that they were all "deadlocked" conventions which turned to dark horse candidates moving from the comparative obscurity of earlier ballots (that is, less than 11 percent of the vote) to capture the nomination after a last minute stampede by delegates to join the bandwagon. These conditions were true in four Republican conventions: 1920, which nominated Warren G. Harding; 1888, which chose Benjamin Harrison; 1880, which nominated James A. Garfield; and 1876, which chose Rutherford B. Hayes over James G. Blaine. Since each of the cases involved a 50 percent-plus-one majority as the decision rule, it is not possible to argue that in each case a single ideological or sectional blocking coalition anchored to one candidate existed. Any blocking coalition of that size would also have been sufficient to claim the nomination.

Yet, prior to 1920 delegate behavior does not seem affected by voting shifts. Delegates voted in the end for politicians whose chances for the nomination at the beginning of the balloting could only have been thought improbable by our test. Four candidates—Hayes in 1876, Garfield in 1880, Harrison in 1888, and Harding in 1920—captured the nomination in the same way by moving from a first ballot strength of 8.5 percent, 1.3 percent, 10.9 percent and 6.0 percent, respectively, failing to make the largest gain on the second ballot, and winning each contest only after protracted balloting. Such a pattern is indicative not only of generous accounts of ideological and sectional conflict within a party which won most of the presidential elections of that era but of some degree of oligarchical control as well. The precipitous manner in which convention stalemates were converted to victories for obscure candidates in the late hours of seven- to thirty-six-ballot conventions suggests that reasonably certain arrangements were made among party leaders about the switches of crucial blocks of delegate votes.

Certainly the mechanism for converting leaders' decisions into delegate votes can be found in the delegate selection process. Delegates in both political parties were, and are, often handpicked by the party leaderships at state committee meetings and state conventions, rather than through primaries, as a reward for loyal party service. Republican party history prior to 1920 is particularly rife with the deals contracted by party elders such as Boies Penrose, Mark Hanna, and Henry Cabot Lodge.[12] It is no surprise, perhaps that

Progressive Republican Robert M. LaFollette's championship of primaries as a means of rank-and-file participation in decision-making was aimed at eradication of one of the leading political practices of the day.[13] Thus, it would seem that the fabled "smoke-filled room" reflects a bygone era of American politics. The effect of the smoke-filled room is to prevent the use of the same assumptions permitting the prediction of more recent convention outcomes.

CONCLUSIONS

The basic conclusion of this research is that Polsby and Wildavsky are correct in emphasizing the importance of uncertainty in decision-making at national nominating conventions. Political behavior is affected, it would seem, by the information generally available to rational decision-makers. That uncertain delegates are affected by such public information is seen in our ability to predict correctly from among several contenders the winners of most of the recent multi-ballot conventions. Deviations from predicted outcomes have been only partly explained with the three basic kinds of limitations of the uncertainty principle, including extreme ideological division, patterns of sectional politics, and oligarchical control of the delegations.

Second, this research suggests that even single-ballot conventions can be better understood as dynamic processes in which uncertain politicians pay close attention to indicators of candidate strength as a basis for their decisions. To pay more research attention to single-ballot conventions seems particularly desirable in light of the infrequency of multi-ballot conventions in recent times. One possible research approach would be to examine other major convention conflicts, like party-platform or credentials fights, which would produce information about the relative standings of opposing coalitions prior to actual balloting. The hypothesis suggested here is that winners of "tests of strength" would be predicted as winners on the first ballot for reasons already suggested.[14] The Republican conventions of 1952, 1964, and 1968 and the Democratic conventions of 1956, 1960, and 1972 would be obvious candidates for such analysis.

Finally, what is further indicated in these findings is that those who eventually come to hold power and influence often are those who successfully transmit the impression that the flow of events favors their cause. The vehicle for this transmission consists of the generally available indicators of power to which all political actors must turn if they are uncertain about where power really does lie. Whether bureaucratic power, power among nations, or community power is also established in the manner described here remains to be seen. But if bureaucrats, nations, and community leaders do, in fact, act as though these indicators are measures of power, then predictable patterns of behavior should be discovered under such an assumption.

CHAPTER 9

The Revolution in the Presidential
Nominating Convention

William G. Carleton

During the past three decades, the presidential nominating convention has been undergoing a major transformation. Party methods of nominating presidential and vice-presidential candidates are yielding, without much formal or structural change, to twentieth-century mass democracy. Delegates to national conventions, even the biggest of the "big shots," are in the process of being reduced to popular rubber stamps, very much as presidential electors were reduced to nullities during the first decade of our present federal Constitution. Increasingly a national nominating convention is merely choosing its nominee from among popular national favorites; increasingly it is being forced to pick the national favorite. The days of the favorite son, the dark horse, the stalking horse, the smoke-filled conference room, the senatorial and congressional cabal, and the decisive trading of votes by local bigwigs are numbered, if indeed they are not already finished. "Insiders" and members of the political "club" are being cut down to size and forced to accept the leadership of those who have made successful national pre-convention campaigns and of those who have become national "names" and mass celebrities.

More time will elapse before this trend is commonly recognized. Even when it is more firmly established than it is, the temptation of the journalists and magazine writers to play up the color and suspense of the old-fashioned convention, to anticipate the maneuvers of the behind-the-scenes manipula-

From *Political Science Quarterly* 72 (June 1957): 224–40, reprinted with permission. William G. Carleton (1901–1982) taught political science at the University of Florida.

tors and the alleged kingmakers, of the Thurlow Weeds, the Mark Hannas and the Jim Farleys, will be strong. Undoubtedly the prospective strategic and "decisive" moves of the Lyndon Johnsons, the Frank Lausches, the Stuart Symingtons and the Carmine De Sapios of the day (which in fact will not materialize) will be widely trumpeted to the public. Especially will this be true of the next Democratic national convention, for Democratic leadership during the next four years will be in Congress, and Democratic congressional leaders will be blown up to balloon size, only to be rudely deflated at the next convention.

The sooner we realize the altered nature of the nominating convention the better off we shall be, for some of the problems already produced by the trend of the past three decades demand thoughtful consideration now.

In 1956, the conventions of both parties again strongly verified the trend of the past thirty years. Eisenhower, of course, was the undeniable national favorite of the Republicans. By way of the long grueling primary route, Stevenson, by the time of the Democratic convention, had emerged as the undoubted national favorite of the Democrats. Moreover, the conventions of 1956 revealed that the trend is also becoming applicable to the vice-presidential nominees. Even had Harold Stassen begun his "Stop Nixon" campaign six months earlier and enlisted the support of many of the most powerful of the politicians of the international wing of the Republican party, it is doubtful that Nixon, who had become a national "name," could have been stopped, short of direct and vigorous intervention by President Eisenhower himself. But the most telling illustration of the trend to nominate only national "celebrities" is afforded by the dramatic convention conflict over the Democratic vice-presidential nomination.

There is no doubt that Estes Kefauver, by the time of the opening of the Democratic National Convention of 1956, had become a national "name." His television performances as senatorial "crime buster," his national run for the presidential nomination in 1952, and his arduous primary fights in all parts of the country in 1956 had made his name and personality well known to the country. At the Chicago convention of 1956 he was forced to organize a sudden and spontaneous drive for the vice-presidential nomination against the forces which in the past have been "kingmakers" in national conventions. Kefauver faced the bitterest kind of opposition from these traditionally powerful forces. He was opposed by the big city bosses, who remembered all too well his exposure of the alliance of the underworld and the city politicos. He was opposed by the Southern delegations, who usually follow local and personal leadership to a greater extent than do delegations outside the South and who regarded Kefauver as too liberal and as a renegade to white Southern sentiments on racial questions. He was overwhelmingly opposed by congressional Democrats, by congressional cronies and "insiders," who felt that Kefauver did not belong to their "club." Any acute observer who watched the convention proceedings soon became aware of a congressional cabal, more particularly of a senatorial cabal, bent on defeating Kefauver. The maneuverings of senators Kennedy, Gore, Johnson, Smathers, Fulbright, Monroney, Symington, Long and even Humphrey, and of Speaker Rayburn, Representative McCormack and "Les" Biffle were quite obvious.

Now it is important to note that even powerful members of the Congress are not, by today's standards, national "names." They may head important committees, now and then get their names in the headlines of the inside pages of the *New York Times,* and occasionally "make" the national press associations; but today all of this is a far, far cry from becoming a national "celebrity," from becoming a familiar name and personality among the mass of people. To become a national celebrity, it takes more, too, than a human-interest story in a national mass-circulation magazine, a story predicting how such and such a governor or senator is maneuvering himself into a position of "kingmaker" in a forthcoming old-fashioned national convention. All of this seems to come as a surprise to congressional leaders, who are accustomed to being very big men in congressional chambers and lobbies, and who collectively, as the Congress, can on occasion still be very potent indeed. But increasingly presidential politics involve popular group and mass activities in the country at large. Presidential politics are being divorced from local and congressional politics. Hence the growing separation of presidential Republicans from congressional Republicans, of presidential Democrats from congressional Democrats. When congressional leaders at national conventions throw bouquets at one another, as they do so profusely, they do not seem to be aware that the country does not know and appreciate them in the way they know and appreciate one another.

Powerful, then, as the city bosses, the southern leaders, and the congressional bigwigs would have been in a Democratic national convention of the nineteenth century and of the early twentieth century, they were no match, even in a *vice-presidential* contest, when pitted against a national "name" with a grass-roots national following and the backing of national farm and labor organizations. Undoubtedly, too, Senator Kennedy, the convention runner-up against Kefauver did better than otherwise he would have because of his Catholicism. Many a New Deal delegate (particularly from Massachusetts and New York), many a delegate who ordinarily looks at politics from the national or presidential angle, deserted his normal political allegiances to seize this unusual opportunity to vote for a fellow Catholic. However, the failure to nominate for vice-president Kefauver, the runner-up in the popular primaries, would have been followed by a keen sense of frustration by rank-and-file Democrats the country over.

What is most important about the results of the Democratic and Republican conventions of 1956 is that they confirmed a presidential nominating trend which has been well in evidence in all presidential nominating conventions following 1924. For after 1924 the convention of each party has picked a national favorite—usually *the* national favorite—as the presidential nominee. The last time a Republican nominating convention chose a favorite son (after national favorites had deadlocked the convention) was in 1920, when Harding was nominated. The last time a Democratic nominating convention chose a favorite son (after national favorites had deadlocked the convention) was in 1924, when John W. Davis was nominated.

The trend of the past thirty years is unmistakable. Let us trace it.

In 1928, Herbert Hoover, opposed for the Republican presidential nomination by a miscellany of unimpressive favorite sons, was the overwhelming choice of the rank-and-file Republicans of the nation. He was easily nominated. Likewise, for months prior to their Houston convention, the nomination of Al Smith by the Democrats was a foregone conclusion. Indeed, the choice of Houston, a Southern and Protestant city, as the place for holding the Democratic convention was a pre-calculated attempt to make Smith's almost certain nomination palatable to Southerners and Protestants. Smith was clearly the logical candidate. In a strongly Republican era, he had been elected governor of New York four times, when other northern Democrats had gone down like ninepins. Two of Smith's triumphant elections had taken place since the Madison Square Garden convention of 1924 [when Smith failed to win the nomination]. Under these conditions, most Democrats throughout the country felt that to turn down Smith would be a rank injustice and a positive insult to the Irish-Catholics, who long had been a bulwark of Democratic strength, and to other "non-nativist" Americans of the large cities.

In 1932, Hoover was obviously the choice of the Republicans; and Franklin D. Roosevelt, the popular governor of New York, was the outstanding national favorite among the Democrats, as evidenced by primaries, national opinion polls, local straw votes, and other barometers of public opinion.

In 1936, Roosevelt was the inevitable Democratic nominee. By the time the Republican convention opened, Governor Alf Landon [of Kansas], one of the few Republican survivors in high office, was far in the lead for the Republican nomination.

In 1940, mass pressures had been built up for Roosevelt's third nomination, and those parochial forces formerly so important in national conventions (in this case represented by old-fashioned politicos like "Jim" Farley and "Jack" Garner) were powerless to stay the mass trend. The Republican convention of 1940 revealed even more dramatically than the Democratic convention the enormous strength of the new mass forces over the old parochial ones.

Mass pressures were responsible for the nomination of Wendell Willkie.

The average Republican delegate did not want Willkie. The average Republican politician, guided by the old rules of the game, had every reason to be suspicious of him. The old rules demanded a professional, a proved vote-getter, and Willkie was a rank outsider, an amateur who had never tested his mettle with the voters. Moreover, he was a big-business man, a Wall Street businessman, a businessman identified with the most unpopular of big businesses, public utilities. And, most unholy of unholies, Willkie was not even a good Republican, if indeed he was a Republican at all. He had been a life-long Democrat; only as late as 1938 had he formally renounced the Democrats and become a Republican. The nomination of Willkie defied all of the old rules; he was nominated solely because of mass pressures and the historical logic of the situation. (The historical logic of the situation is looming larger and larger in all of our political decisions as we attempt to wrestle with the increasingly remote, impersonal and global problems of our time, and it will bulk even larger in the future.) It so happened that Willkie's three chief contenders for the nomination—Taft, Dewey and Vandenberg—represented more or less isolationist records. Willkie had no isolationist record and he tended to be an "interventionist." Willkie's position, in contrast to that of his opponents, had by the time of the Republican convention become a decisive advantage, for France had fallen and the whole country was watching with breathless anxiety the battle of Britain. Americans were frightened, and American opinion with respect to the foreign situation was moving rapidly away from isolationism. Moreover, many of the nation's magazines of mass circulation, most conspicuously the Luce publications, had been beating a steady drumfire for Willkie for weeks before the convention opened. His nomination, then, represents a striking victory for mass historical forces, the techniques of Madison Avenue advertising experts, and the agencies of mass opinion—polls, radio and big-time journalism—over the traditional, leisurely paced rules of American politics.

In 1944, the logic of the historical situation made Roosevelt, America's wartime leader and world spokesman, the Democratic nominee. The national favorite among the Republicans was Thomas E. Dewey, who had progressively modified his old isolationism and who, because he was governor of New York, the most populous state in the Union and a microcosm of the nation's racial, religious, national and economic groups which bulk so large in contemporary national welfare politics, was by all odds the most "available" Republican in high elective office.

In 1948, Truman, a sitting President and world leader in a time of crisis, was in a position to dictate his own nomination. Dewey, in spite of his defeat in 1944, was the logical Republican choice. Since that time he had been reelected governor of New York, and in a series of hard-fought primary contests with

Stassen and others, he had emerged as the undoubted national favorite among the Republicans.

In 1952, the victory of Eisenhower over Taft for the Republican nomination was a spectacular victory of an attractive national and world celebrity, supported, too, by the most effective advertising techniques afforded by Madison Avenue. Eisenhower, the biggest of "names," won over a lesser "name." Eisenhower represented all of the new mass forces in politics; Taft represented all of the old and orthodox methods of the traditional American political game, even to the rounding up of delegates from the rotten-borough Republicans of the South in the gamey way sanctioned by age. On the Democratic side, Stevenson appeared to be the reluctant candidate seeking to avoid becoming the national favorite, but actually by the time of the Democratic convention he had been the subject of such a terrific national publicity build-up that the polls showed him running ahead of those who had engaged in the primary contests.

In 1956, as we have seen, Eisenhower was still the same glamorous celebrity he had been for many years, and in addition he was backed by the enormous power and prestige of the presidency, and aided by the smooth television techniques of Robert Montgomery and the shrewd showmanship of James E. Hagerty. Stevenson, in many a slugging primary, had pushed his way into first place among the Democrats. And, most significant of all, the trend in both parties toward nominating for president the national favorite appeared for the first time to be extending itself to the vice-presidential candidates as well.

The true significance of what has been happening to our nominating conventions beginning with 1928 can be seen only when contrasted with the situation before 1928. Throughout most of American history, the nomination of a "dark horse" was not infrequent, and the nomination of a favorite son (a politician prominent in his home state, but not nationally) or of a national favorite who was not the national favorite was the common practice. Indeed, it has been only in the past thirty years that we have developed the amorphous but nonetheless fairly accurate methods of determining the national favorite in each party and the mass pressures which are now applied to produce his nomination.

In the past, we could speak accurately of the national favorite only when a popular sitting president was seeking renomination; or when there arose a magnetic personality with a passionately devoted personal following among the rank and file—a Thomas Jefferson, an Andrew Jackson, a Henry Clay, a Stephen A. Douglas, a William Jennings Bryan, or a Theodore Roosevelt; or, more rarely, in the case of a genuinely popular military figure like Ulysses S. Grant. Most military heroes nominated for the presidency have been synthetic political figures manufactured for the occasion by behind-the-scenes professional politicians—as in the nominations of William Henry Harrison, Zachary Taylor, Winfield Scott, John C. Fremont and Winfield S. Hancock. At the time of their first nominations, Lincoln, Cleveland, Bryan and Wilson were only national favorites among many national favorites; none of these was *the* national favorite. Theodore Roosevelt did not become *the* national favorite among the rank and file of Republicans until after he had succeeded to the presidency. The traditional pattern was clear: most conventions had before them a number of national favorites and favorite sons, and by a process of attrition a national favorite (usually not *the* national favorite, for *the* national favorite rarely existed) finally emerged victorious, or the contest between national favorites became so bitter that the convention was deadlocked and out of stalemate a favorite son or, more rarely, a "dark horse" emerged. (I put the term "dark horse" in quotation marks because actually a "dark horse" was usually a favorite son primed for entry at the strategic moment.)

The traditional way of nominating presidential candidates very frequently led to a miscarriage of the hopes and expectations of the rank and file of party members. Clay's loss of the nomination to Harrison saddened most Whigs, and Scott's nomination in 1852 left most Whigs cold. Among Democrats for the same period, Polk in 1844 was a dark horse, Cass in 1848 was a lesser national favorite, and Pierce in 1852 was another dark horse. In 1856, the Republican Fremont was a more or less synthetic figure, and the Democrat Buchanan represented the triumph of the professional politicians over Stephen A. Douglas, the favorite of the rank and file.

In the decades following the Civil War, the situation was much the same. The Democratic nominee of 1868, Horatio Seymour, was a favorite son. In 1872, the Democrats reluctantly endorsed the Liberal Republican nominee, Horace Greeley, whose nomination by the Liberal Republicans had occasioned amazement bordering on consternation. The Democratic nominee in 1880, General Hancock, was a somewhat ridiculous figure without popular appeal. On the Republican side, the nomination of favorite-son Hayes in 1876 gravely disappointed the idolatrous followers of James G. Blaine, who was the national favorite with the rank and file. Garfield, the Republican nominee in 1880, was a dark horse; and Benjamin Harrison, the Republican nominee in 1888, was a favorite son.

During the first decades of the twentieth century, the nominating conventions began responding more to national and democratic forces outside the conventions, and these decades may be considered transition decades to the period which began in 1928. Nevertheless, many conventions of the first two decades of this century disappointed the democratic expectations of the country. The nomination of Alton B. Parker by the Democrats in 1904 was a "dud." The nomination of James M. Cox in 1920 represented the victory of a favorite son, or at best of a lesser national favorite. The nomination of favorite son John W. Davis in 1924 was the result of the prolonged deadlock in the Democratic convention and was distinctly anti-climactic. It came after a locked convention had taken 103 ballots and could not produce a more satisfactory candidate. On the Republican side, the nomination of President Taft over Theodore Roosevelt in 1912 clearly represented a victory of maneuver-by-politicians over the newer democratic methods; and in 1920 the nomination of Harding over three national favorites represented the triumph of local politicians and congressional cabal over the verdict of the primaries, the triumph of the old methods at their very worst.

Why have our nominating conventions been going through a process of revolutionary transformation during the past thirty years? Basically, the transformation is a response to the more integrated, mass society in which we live. Increasingly we are dealing with problems that are remote and beyond personal experience, that appear in the guise of historical necessity or inevitability or crisis. The professional politician steeped in localism (and this includes the average congressional politician) now is less sure of himself, often feels his inadequacy, and turns to celebrities on the national and world stage for leadership. Hoover, Willkie and Eisenhower became national celebrities outside politics before they became political leaders. Franklin Roosevelt's third and fourth nominations were made possible (indeed, "necessitated") by world crisis. (In the future, situations like these will increase, not decrease, and they likely will lead to an alteration of the constitutional amendment prohibiting more than two presidential terms.)

Increasingly, national leaders are being made in this way: The ambitious person seizes and exploits his "chance" on the national or international stage (as Kefauver did as Senate "crime buster"), the mass media of publicity make him a "name," and, having become a "name," he is made a bigger "name" by the same mass media of publicity. We are approaching a condition where celebrities outside of politics—Hollywood, television and radio stars, sports heroes, and fiction writers—or even the wives of celebrities (they bear the "name," do they not?) carry greater weight in political campaigns than do long-time congressional leaders or state governors.

The pre-convention primaries and campaigning have done much to alter the nature of the nominating convention. True, the number of states having presidential primaries of one kind or another (to elect delegates to the national condition, or show a popular preference, or both) has not increased in the past thirty years, but these primaries are coming to have a significance in the nominating process they did not have in 1912 or 1920 or 1924. Today, when a politician enters the primaries and makes good showings, he becomes the subject of concentrated national publicity. His activities are carried every day by the national press services, and his name regularly appears in all the daily papers of the country. Human-interest stories about him are featured in the magazines of mass circulation. He appears on national radio and television programs. On a Sunday afternoon he "meets the press" for millions to see and hear. National public-opinion polls carry his name and periodically rate his popularity. He becomes a "name," a celebrity. Even his wife or near relative becomes a "name"—Pat, Nancy, and "Buffie" become almost as well known as Nixon, Kefauver, and Stevenson. If put to the test, does anyone doubt that during the campaign of 1956 a Pat Nixon or a Nancy Kefauver could have drawn larger audiences than a Sam Rayburn or a Joe Martin?

The primaries allow the politician an opportunity to become a "name." They allow the unknown and the semi-known to become really known. They allow him the chance to become a celebrity along with the celebrities in other fields of activity and achievement. The time is fast approaching, if indeed it has not already arrived, when a politician cannot hope to be president or even vice president without first becoming a celebrity. The days when the political lightning in a nominating convention would strike an unknown or a comparative unknown are over. *If politicians do not find the ways to make themselves household names, real national celebrities, presidential nominations will go to celebrities in other fields.* The art of being an effective national political leader is compounded of many ingredients, but today the first ingredient is to know how to become a national celebrity, for without this the other ingredients cannot be put to use. For this reason, even if all the state presidential primaries were abolished, the skillful politician in search of the presidency, the politician not yet a national "name," would still have to go to the country, line up the mass pressure groups, beat the bushes, and corral delegates in a popular way. Only by these methods could he get the concentrated national publicity that makes him a celebrity. Without the primaries, his road to national fame would be still harder, but he would have to find it. That day is now passed when an astute politician can reach the presidency merely by the quiet search for delegates and the lining up of congressmen, local leaders and bosses; merely by using the methods of closet conference, maneuver, manipulation and bargaining.

Another reason for the transformation of the nominating convention is the increasing importance of mass pressure groups. Today, the candidate must not only deal with the leaders of the mass pressure groups, but he must also go to the members of these groups and convince them of his sincerity and ability to perform. Truman got the Democratic vice-presidential nomination in 1944 when he was found to satisfactory to the big labor organizations. That year, Byrnes failed in his quest for the same nomination when national labor, Catholic and Negro groups turned him down. Barkley's 1952 "boom" for the presidential nomination collapsed when it was punctured by the national labor leaders. Kefauver owed his 1956 vice-presidential nomination in no small part to the support of national farm and labor organizations.

It is curious that the transformation of the nominating conventions has not been more generally recognized. After all, the nomination of presidential candidates is as important the election itself. The effects of an increasingly integrated and mass society have been recognized in almost all other areas of our life. We even recognize these in our presidential *elections.* It is pretty well understood that presidential elections are no longer won by patching together local and state disaffections and interests and thereby eking out a national victory, as Garfield did in 1880, Cleveland in 1884, Harrison in 1888, and Cleveland again in 1892. (There is increasing group politics—and our parties are federations of many group interests—but it is more and more national and less and less local, state and sectional politics). There have been fourteen presidential elections during the twentieth century, and all of these except those of 1916 and 1948 have been national landslides, expressions of national waves of opinion. However, we still persist in thinking of the presidential nominating machinery in terms of local bosses and kingmakers, in terms of the parochial and provincial politics of the nineteenth century. Such thinking, while picturesque, is no longer realistic.

The activities that surround a nominating convention are deceptive. The proceedings and ritual on the floor of the convention itself are very much as they were in 1868 or 1880 or 1900. Outside, in the lobbies and hotel rooms, there are still the button-holing of delegates, the anxious bargaining, the exciting secret conferences. But all of this is now subordinate in decision-making to the group and mass pressures, developed or enormously expanded and intensified during the past thirty years, which now beat upon the delegates and conferees from all sides.

Most Americans, even American political scientists, think in terms of form and structure. It is the heritage of our living under a written constitution. Because the forms and structure of the national nominating convention are little changed, we have been slow to recognize the revolution that has already been worked in our national nominating machinery. The vast changes in the nominating machinery of the localities and states are recognized because those changes were accompanied by changes in the machinery, in the abolition or drastic alteration of the old convention system and the adoption of complete or mixed primary systems. It was thought that similar changes in machinery would be applied to the national nominating conventions, that more states would adopt presidential primaries or that a national presidential primary would be adopted. However, few structural and formal changes have taken place on the national level. There has been no increase in the number of presidential primary states in the past thirty years. The national primary has not been adopted and it is not likely to be adopted. A few states have clarified their presidential primary laws. One of these is Florida, which now requires party voters to select from slates of delegates pledged to particular candidates, just as presidential electors are now pledged to vote for the national nominees of their party. Hidden from national view, but significant, is the fact that in many of the states the delegates to the state conventions, which in turn select the delegates to the national conventions, are now chosen in local primaries.

The trend to nominating the leading national favorite, then, is the result of many factors: the crisis world in which we live; the rapidity with which events that affect the increasingly interrelated lives of all of us occur; the phenomenal growth of the mass media of communications; the increasing activities of mass pressure groups; the pervasiveness, accuracy and notoriety of the public opinion polls; the democratization of the methods of selecting delegates to the national conventions; and the ways all of these in turn intensify the importance of the presidential primaries. However, today, the democratic process is coming to depend less and less upon the formal and periodic nominating and electoral machinery and more and more upon the ever-multiplying means for informally and pervasively ascertaining public opinion from day to day. In short, the revolution has been wrought not so much by changes in machinery and structure as by the vast chances in social forces outside of machinery and structure, new and altered forces which operate on and permeate machinery and structure.

It is probable that by 1976 or 1980 all that a nominating convention will do will be to meet to ratify the nomination for president of *the* national favorite already determined by the agencies, formal and informal, of mass democracy; to ratify the nomination for vice-president of the second leading national favorite; to endorse a platform already written by leaders responding to national and group pressures; and to stage a rally for the benefit of the national television audience. Delegates and "leaders" in national conventions, like presidential electors, will have become rubber stamps.

Conservatives, who deplore the social trends leading us from the local and the personal and toward the centralized and the impersonal, will hesitate to accept these conclusions, and if they accept them they will want to do something to halt the trends. Twentieth-century "liberals," less concerned with personal liberty and with more faith in mass democracy, will welcome these trends. Pragmatists will accept the trends, realize that nothing can be done basically to change them, and attempt to find solutions to the specific problems they raise. For these trends raise many specific problems in government and politics. I shall suggest merely few of these.

For one thing, since the forces of national mass democracy are affecting the presidency much more and at a faster pace than they are affecting the Congress, we are now more and more faced with a widening gap between the president and Congress, between presidential politics and congressional politics, between presidential Republicans and congressional Republicans, between presidential Democrats and congressional Democrats. The implications of this for a frightening prolongation and intensification of the stalemate between the legislative and executive branches and for continued inability to enact needed legislation are obvious. What can be done about this is another story, and a complicated one. Primarily we must rely on the substantive realignment of parties now gradually taking place, on progressive Republicans in the prairie states and in the Northwest becoming Democrats, and on the conservatives in the South becoming Republicans. Premature attempts to hasten this trend by centralized national party machinery over congressional nominations and elections might actually retard the trend and aggravate the situation.

For another thing, are we not in danger of prematurely killing the chances of genuinely first-class national leaders and depriving ourselves of their services by over-reacting nationally to parochial situations in individual and often provincial states? Why should international-minded Wendell Willkie have been broken on a single throw of loaded dice in an isolationist state like Wisconsin? Why should a Stevenson or a Kefauver be "made" or "lost" by the results of a primary in a state as atypical as Florida, where the political divisions normal to most states mean so little that its two United States senators, representing the overwhelming middle-class consensus of its *rentier* classes, tourists, and comfortable civic-club and chambers-of-commerce communities, are returned to Washington with no opposition? (Fortunately for the survival of both Stevenson and Kefauver, in the 1956 Florida primary they ran neck-and-neck among the small number of voters who bothered to vote.)

Of most immediate concern, it seems to me, is the rescuing of our politicians from the intolerable wear and tear on their bodies and nervous systems which the requirements of mass democracy increasingly are imposing upon them. This is coming to be a question of their sheer physical survival, and a nation we are running greater and greater risks in allowing our parties to be led during an entire election year—during the long months of pre-convention campaigning and then during the three months of the campaign itself—by harassed and exhausted leaders with little time to analyze for themselves the enormous problems with which they must cope.

How can our presidential candidates be rescued from the increasing brutalities and tortures of the system? Mass democracy will have to find ways to use pervasively and effectively the mass media of communication—television, radio and motion pictures. These mass media are partly responsible for the fact that a candidate for president must now become a national celebrity in order to get a nomination. These mass media now make it possible for the candidate to reach the voters without going directly to them in person. Yet up to now the uses of these mass media have not been within adequate reach of the candidates, so they have enormously expanded their personal contacts and appearances, expanded them to the near-breaking point. This constitutes a cruel and preposterous paradox.

To meet the expanded costs of the pre-convention contests and the campaign itself, the federal government may have to step in to underwrite the expenses of radio and television campaigning and of a reasonable amount of newspaper and magazine advertising. Earlier in our history, governments did not even defray the expenses of preparing the ballots. These expenses and some other election costs were home by the candidates and the parties. Now all of these things are regarded as the legitimate government costs of an election and are borne by the local and state governments. However, the costs of campaigning are as necessary as the costs of the election itself, and the public may have to come to accept public financing of reasonable campaign costs as legitimate, just as legitimate as the public financing of ballots, voting machines, polling places, and clerks.

After this hurdle has been cleared, there will be all sorts of specific and technical difficulties. How are the bona fide candidates to be distinguished from the frivolous ones? Is a candidate who does not file in any of the state presidential primaries to be considered a candidate? Is the candidate who files in the state primaries to be considered a federal or a state candidate, and if he is to be considered a federal candidate for purposes of certain campaign costs, in how many states must he file? These are just a few of the questions that will arise.

During the first two decades of the twentieth century, the presidential election was subjected to the ways of modern mass democracy. We have not yet solved many of the problems involved in this transformation, particularly those involving campaign finances and adequate use of radio and television time. During the past three decades, the presidential nominating process likewise has been subjected to the ways of mass democracy. This constitutes a more decisive break with the past, for it involves a revolutionary transformation of the nominating conventions, a substitution of mass choices for the deliberations and decisions of political leaders, the subversion of the only effective institution that has stood between the presidency and mass pressures. This revolution is already pretty much of an accomplished fact, although that fact has hardly come to be recognized. It is high time that we recognize it; more, that we begin to tackle the problems which have been raised by this revolution.

CHAPTER 10

Television's Great Leap Forward

Sig Mickelson

The nation's attention was riveted so intently on television in the summer of 1952 that it surprised even the experts. The reason: the two national political conventions that dominated most of the month of July. All four networks covered the conventions from gavel to gavel, some 150 hours in all. More than 55 million persons, in excess of 61 percent of the nation's population, watched some part of the two meetings. At peak periods, more than 60 percent of American homes with televisions tuned in.

Only a few were fully prepared for the phenomenal response to television's first full effort at covering national politics. Political leaders, while giving lip service, were totally unprepared for the public's mass fascination with the new medium. They had only grudgingly acceded to network demands for suitable camera locations adjacent to the floor. They were fearful that giving up the space would deprive loyal party members of choice seats. The Republicans even refused permission to build a camera platform on the arena floor for head-on shots of the rostrum, a decision that was reversed in subsequent years after party leaders had an opportunity to note how much better Democrats looked when photographed from the camera platform they had refused to sanction.

From *Whistle Stop to Sound Bite: Four Decades of Politics and Television* (New York: Praeger, 1989), 33–48, reprinted with permission of Greenwood Publishing Group, Westport, Conn. Sig Mickelson (1914–2000) was the first president of CBS News, capping a career that began with CBS radio in 1943.

Even those of us who had been preparing for more than eighteen months for the biggest enterprise television had ever undertaken did not fully believe our confident boasts that we were on the threshold of a revolution in communications and politics. We knew the conventions would be big and exciting, but not many of us fully anticipated the enormity of the public response. Part of the surprising response rose out of the fact that most of the nation would have its first chance to look in on the quadrennial extravaganza. In 1948, the last time that the parties had met to select presidential and vice-presidential candidates, only a handful of viewers in the Northeast had been able to tune in any part. Only 400,000 homes in the entire country then had receivers, and only nine cities could receive signals on existing network lines. When the gavel fell to open the Republican convention on July 7, 1952, 18 million homes in sixty-two interconnected cities across the country would be able to receive the network broadcasts.

Campaign managers for the principal candidates were certain that television was a force they could not overlook, but only the Eisenhower staff came near to fully estimating the power the medium would demonstrate. The Eisenhower campaign leadership realized that it would take an uphill battle to wrest the presidential nomination away from the more solidly entrenched Senator Taft from Ohio. They concluded that if they played it right, television would give them the magic weapon that would enable them to mobilize public opinion sufficiently to override the control of the political machinery maintained by the Taft forces.

The Taft campaign management was aware of the potential power of television. It had mounted an aggressive television campaign in the 1950 Ohio Senate race, which the senator had won handily. Television liaison personnel were on the job, but they did not show the imagination or enthusiasm of the Eisenhower forces. They were anxious to get their story on the air, but there was no evidence that we could detect of any television-based overall strategy.

Newspapers, news magazines, and radio and television had been haranguing the public for months about the impending spectacle. Those of us directly involved in planning had made scores of speeches and answered countless questions from media reporters. The public was well aware that hundreds of reporters and technicians, and thousands of pounds of electronic hardware were being shipped to Chicago for an unprecedented spectacle. But we were so preoccupied with preparations that we had no notion how massive the reaction would be.

Jack Gould, the broadcast critic of the *New York Times*, had a hunch that, in retrospect, makes him seem positively clairvoyant. On June 22, two weeks before the Republican convention opened, Gould wrote, "Television is going to wield a major and perhaps determining influence this year over both the conventions and the campaign to follow. This year, the 18 million receivers installed in homes will turn the nation into a gigantic town meeting."[1]

There was a vague feeling that Gould was right. All available evidence pointed to a phenomenal escalation of interest in both television and the conventions. But it was almost impossible to visualize just how explosive that new attention to the video screen would be. Those of us in the front lines were too busy preparing for an event for which there were no guidelines to contemplate more than what the next task on our checklists might be.

President Harry Truman removed the last doubt that both the conventions would be no-holds-barred donnybrooks when he withdrew his name from the list of Democratic contenders. At the conclusion of a televised address on March 30, he startled everyone by adding a line to his prepared script announcing that he would not be a candidate. For the first time since 1928, there would be no incumbent in the race. The winners would be decided on the convention floor.

There were no odds-on favorites in either party. Senator Taft of Ohio had an edge over other Republican contenders, but some of his support depended on winning a number of critical contests to be fought out in the party's credentials committee. General Eisenhower was coming on fast, but as the convention date approached, he still lagged behind the Ohio senator. Governor Earl Warren of California and Harold Stassen were still in the running. General Douglas MacArthur was scheduled to deliver the keynote address. There was speculation that he might ignite the convention with his dramatic oratory and run off with the nomination.

On June 22, two weeks before the GOP's opening date and one week before the credentials committee was scheduled to meet, Senator Taft was easily the front-runner, with 454 of the 604 votes needed to nominate, but a number of these, notably some of the thirty-eight in Texas, were shaky. They were being contested by the Eisenhower forces. If some could be dislodged from the Taft column and moved to Ike, the Taft margin would be razor thin. The count of committed Eisenhower delegates on June 22 stood at 390. Governor Warren at that stage could count on seventy-six, Stassen on twenty-six, and Governor Theodore McKeldin of Maryland on twenty-four. Only three were formally committed to General MacArthur, but 147 were still uncommitted and thirteen were still to be chosen. There was also believed to be considerable underlying support for MacArthur among delegates already committed to other candidates.

The critical question was whose delegates would be seated as a result of the sparring over credentials, particularly in the delegations from Texas and Georgia. If Taft were to hold his strength, he still would not be assured the 604 votes necessary to nominate but would be close. If he were to lose some to Eisenhower, a deadlocked convention was a distinct possibility. In that event, a dedicated band of MacArthur supporters was counting on an emotional and melodramatic burst of patriotic oratory in the keynote speech to swing the convention, in a frenzied patriotic orgy, to the general.

The credentials committee was scheduled to begin its deliberations on Monday, June 30. The all-network pool committee begged party officials to open the hearing room to microphones and cameras. The answer was a resounding negative. The Taft forces, in command of the national party machinery, wanted to fight the battle in private. Cameras and microphones would be an intrusion, and they might show a dark side of the party that the Taft leaders preferred to keep undercover. Those of us representing television suspected that there was little enthusiasm for revealing how Republican delegates were selected in a state that had been overwhelmingly Democratic since the Civil War.

Business scheduled for Monday would be largely organizational. Hearings were to start on Tuesday, July 1. I had been under so much pressure from management to hold down costs that I had decided to gamble that we could arrive Tuesday morning without losing anything. Even then, we would bring only a skeleton production and broadcasting crew. The main force would not arrive until Friday and Saturday. CBS technical operations, however, had been on the scene for several weeks, installing facilities so that cameras and microphones were in position and ready to go as soon as broadcast personnel appeared.

When Walter Cronkite and I stepped off the Twentieth Century Limited on Tuesday morning at 9:30, the decisive battle had already started. Worse than that, NBC, anticipating that the credentials committee would get off to a fast start, had a full staff in place and had actually been on the air from Chicago on Monday. We needed to get on the air to establish a competitive position, but we had no director. I had foolishly decided to let Don Hewitt remain in New York to direct the *Douglas Edwards Early Evening News* for another couple of days before reporting to Chicago. This left us with an anchorman, Cronkite, and full physical facilities but no director to call the shots. I asked the technical operations crew whether, if I could get television network headquarters in New York to release airtime for a broadcast, they would take directions from me. This was a touchy point, since I was not a member of the directors' union. There were no objections, so our first broadcast from Chicago found me sitting in the director's chair. Our maiden effort was followed by an urgent call to Hewitt to come to Chicago immediately, to take over.

By Wednesday morning it was evident that the battle in the credentials committee was heating up. We begged once more for the right to bring in our cameras but again were rebuffed. The only alternative was to set up in the corridor just outside the door to the committee room. Eisenhower supporters who had resisted the ban on coverage were quick to note that we were giving them a channel for releasing their version of the proceedings. Whenever the tally lights on the cameras of one of the three networks flashed on, signifying that a picture was on the air, a steady procession of delegates supporting the general made their way to microphones to furnish their version of the debate inside. It was clear that the Eisenhower delegates had been carefully selected to represent a new breed of political leader: young, attractive, and telegenic, in contrast with the traditional old-line politicians who represented Taft. The contrast could not have been missed by television viewers. It was a credit to Eisenhower planners, who had anticipated that the fresh, young look would create an image that would rub off on their candidate. They were looking not only to jaded delegates in Chicago but also to television in the expectation that delegates could be influenced by pressure from home.

Except for our slow start, we thought we were doing relatively well with our cameras stationed outside the committee room door. We were, however, missing the essence of the debate. We missed the give and take, the clash between opposing viewpoints, the personalities of the combatants, the atmosphere in the meeting room. We petitioned again for access and again were rebuffed.

That night I was sound asleep when the telephone rang. It was Paul Levitan, our director of planning and facilities. Levitan had asked me during the afternoon whether I would object if he could find some way of planting a microphone in the room where the committee was meeting. Since it didn't seem a very reasonable possibility, I rather absentmindedly gave consent. When Levitan told me he had accomplished his mission, I quickly awoke. He described how he and the deputy director of technical operations had slipped into the committee room after the corridors were clear, with the intention of hiding a microphone behind a drape. They were astonished to discover that there was already a mike there, and assumed it belonged to NBC. Further examination revealed that it would be easy to tie into the committee's own sound system, thus delivering a far superior signal. They quickly completed a simple wire-splicing maneuver, bridged into a line that would carry the signal to our studios on the fifth floor, and for double protection arranged to have a duplicate signal delivered to network headquarters in New York. At that early period in television's history, ethical considerations did not deeply disturb us.

When Cronkite arrived at the fifth-floor headquarters the next morning, he was able to put on a headset and overhear the proceedings directly from the committee room. The signal was never used on the air, but it enriched the CBS coverage by permitting Cronkite to sense the tension and bitterness that characterized the debate on the floor. It thus added a new dimension to the reports received from Eisenhower supporters as they left the meeting room to give interviews in the corridors.[2]

The contest in the credentials committee was only a prelude to the main event, but it served to whet even more interest than had already been generated. By Saturday, July 5, Chicago's Loop area was swarming with boisterous Republicans, outfitted in hats, blazers, and buttons carrying the names of their favorite candidates and their campaign slogans.

We were still concerned—needlessly, as it turned out—with the Westinghouse requirement that we program twenty hours from each convention. We decided that we ought to stockpile as many hours as we could before the convention opened on Monday morning. Finding program material was no problem. Impromptu rallies were springing up in hotel lobbies and on Michigan Avenue. "I Like Ike" banners were everywhere.

We arranged with network headquarters to assign us an hour from 8 to 9 on Saturday night. Levitan promised to find exciting material to fill the time. He had discovered that public relations representatives of the various candidates had acquired such a voracious appetite for television time that they would deliver rallies, demonstrations, and parades to order. We had some reservations about broadcasting staged events, but in the interest of filling the time with exciting material, we stifled our reservations and went on to book demonstrations and rallies to fill the hour. It is obvious now that if we had had a little more concern about journalistic ethics, we would neither have bugged the credentials committee nor have encouraged staged news. But that was 1952. Television was still boisterous, immature, and competitive.

If television can be charged with immaturity, many delegates could be found guilty of the same charge. The stunts performed by normally dignified national leaders for the benefit of the television camera were ludicrous. For our purposes, though, they served to further whet the public appetite for the main event on Monday morning. Whether they did any good for the candidate they were supporting is open to question. The most memorable performance involved Senator George Bender of Ohio, one of the dominant Taft leaders, vigorously swinging a cowbell in the lobby of the Conrad Hilton Hotel and leading a boisterous rally in singing the Taft campaign song, "I'm Looking over a Four-Leaf Clover." Wherever a television camera appeared, a crowd was sure to gather, waving pennants and banners, and pushing and shoving to dominate the scene, sometimes to the point where police had to intervene.

When Republican Party Chairman Gabrielson rapped the gavel on Monday morning, July 7, to open officially the twenty-fifth Republican National Convention, the only noticeable difference from previous conventions was the presence of television cameras that displaced some seats in the front rows of the balcony. Otherwise, television at this stage was still relatively unobtrusive. Its operating personnel were mostly working from studios, control rooms, newsrooms, and offices in one of the wings of the International Amphitheater, where they occupied 35,000 square feet of space. It was not long, however, before the convention was fully aware of television's presence.

There were no concessions to television in the opening ceremony. There were the usual presentation of the colors, pledge of allegiance, national anthem, invocation, and official photograph of the convention. Then came the welcoming speeches by the mayor of Chicago and the Republican candidate for governor of Illinois, most of it dutifully covered by television.

What was happening on the rostrum at the convention hall obviously was purely ceremonial. The story was with the milling delegates on the floor and downtown in the Loop, at the Conrad Hilton and Blackstone hotels. There the committees, even though the convention was in session, were struggling to complete the business that was essential to beginning the real decision-making. The critical impasse was caused by the credentials committee. No business could be conducted before delegates were certified and cleared to vote. That would require a report from the committee and its acceptance or modification by the full convention. Delegates whose names were on the official roll were entitled to vote on the credentials report, but only on that. So until that matter was disposed of, the convention would mark time.

We at CBS had decided months earlier that we would approach the conventions as a very large and complex news story. It was our intention that the ringmaster for our coverage, the "anchorman," should be the best-informed person in the city of Chicago, and that he should be able to interpret for the viewer the scenes portrayed on the screen. Pictures were to be used to supplement and explain the story, not stand alone for pictorial value.

An elaborate communications structure was designed to keep constant contact with reporter/correspondents. It included both strategically placed telephones and hand-held portable radio transmitters called walkie-talkies. Reports from correspondents were either to be accepted as background material for Cronkite's use or, sometimes, to go directly on the air. We were concerned with the background and interpretative information our correspondents could pick up on the convention floor, in the fringes of the hall, and in the downtown hotels. We expected the proceedings to be sufficiently complex, and many actions taken so obscure, that they would need explanation. The respected sociologists Kurt and Gladys Lang reflected the theory behind our planning when they wrote in a detailed study of the 1952 conventions, "CBS sought to cover the convention as a news service would."[3]

It became increasingly clear during the opening session that not much news was being made on the rostrum. The story, as we had expected, was on the floor or in the Loop. While speakers droned on from the platform, we interrupted with increasing frequency to report from both locations. Only by doing so could we make any sense out of what might have appeared to be inconsequential parliamentary maneuvering. The expectation of the leaders of the parties had been that television would be much more attentive to the formal program on the rostrum. Instead, a precedent was being set in which television executives made the decisions. They decided whether the speaker at the podium or the ceremony in progress should be interrupted or preempted for breaking news. In so doing, they were creating a pattern that would dominate in subsequent years.

The opening session passed quickly enough, without any fireworks. There was one disturbing note, however. NBC had appeared on the floor with hand-held portable cameras. We had heard rumors that this might happen and had looked into the possibility of obtaining one or more for ourselves, but abandoned the project because of uncertainty regarding the signal quality. The quality demonstrated by NBC was passable if not superior. It posed enough of a threat to make it imperative that we institute some countermeasure. In order to add any real meaning to the running story, we recognized that we must talk to delegates on the floor. Interviews would be immeasurably more effective if they were done on camera. We tried placing cameras on tripods on the periphery of the floor so they could be wheeled out on signal. The process, however, was too cumbersome. We needed a better solution.

Don Hewitt found the answer. He negotiated with the CBS radio network to place a camera in the CBS booth, high up against the wall behind the rostrum. From our control room we could direct our floor correspondents, who were equipped with portable transmitters, to potential sources of information or accept their offers of interviews or commentaries. The cameraman in the booth could overhear the instructions and keep a lens trained on the correspondent. Each reporter was given a flashlight to signal his position to the cameraman in the radio booth. The improvised system worked. The flashlight beams were easily visible, and a long lens on the camera enabled a tight focus on the reporter and his interviewee.

There had been no intention as the convention opened to do this much reporting from the floor, but it was evident that the infighting would be so intense and the issues dividing the forces so complicated that they could be unraveled only by constant personal contact and interviews with participants who were plotting strategy or had a major stake in the outcome of the debate.

The result could have been expected. There was chaos on the floor as broadcast reporters elbowed their way through inattentive delegates, print reporters, political handymen, and sergeants at arms in pursuit of the story. To the home viewer, though, the end justified the turmoil. There was an important story to be told, and the floor reporting in this instance added an important dimension. In subsequent conventions, when there was either no story at all or only the thread of one, the search for morsels of information turned into a mad celebrity chase as reporters and cameramen churned about in pursuit of movie stars, daughters and wives of candidates, or anybody with a name and recognizable face. That was the unfortunate legacy we left from 1952.

Just prior to the Monday night session, which was to feature the keynote speech, I had my first (and last) unpleasant confrontation with Walter Cronkite. I had been under considerable pressure from senior management to give some significant exposure to Douglas Edwards, who was our principal news broadcaster and the occupant of the chair on our 7:30 evening news. I was very fond of Doug and regarded him highly for his work on his regular news broadcast, but I was convinced that for the strenuous and challenging task of making a complex political convention understandable to our viewers, Cronkite was a better choice. The Monday evening session seemed a likely spot to give Doug his chance. It was evident there would be very little business conducted from the rostrum. The only newsworthy item on the evening agenda was the keynote speech to be delivered by General MacArthur. If the general turned out to be so eloquent that he was able to start a stampede leading to his nomination, I saw an advantage in having my best and most politically knowledgeable reporter on the floor with a microphone. In short, this seemed the best opportunity we would have to give Doug the exposure, thus keeping the network sales department and his sponsors happy.

I have never seen Walter as angry as when I told him I wanted to put Doug in his chair for the evening session. He started to storm out of the studio. I stopped him by grabbing him by the coattails. I handed him a walkie-talkie and a flashlight, and told him to get down to the floor, where we badly needed him. He stomped off, obviously still burning with resentment, but there has probably never been as effective a job done by a television reporter in as turbulent a situation as Walter did that night.

The MacArthur speech was a typical MacArthurian spellbinder, charged with emotion and characterized by the rising and falling cadences that had become the General's trademark. The audience stomped, whistled, and cheered, but the speech failed to ignite the spark that would stampede delegates into handing the presidential nomination to the General, certainly a disappointing result for his loyal supporters and probably for the General himself.

Cronkite's goal on the floor was not only to assess the response to the keynote speech and the prospects for a MacArthur boom but also to learn what was holding up the credentials committee. There was still no definitive word when its deliberations might be finished. The committee's report would not necessarily decide the final outcome of the presidential nomination race, but it surely would bear heavily on it. And the convention was dead in the water until it reported. No business except voting on the credentials report could be conducted until delegates were formally seated by vote of the convention. Except during the keynote, Walter roamed the floor unceasingly, powering his way through knots of inattentive delegates, pouncing on key leaders who could help bring some understanding to the tangled affairs, waylaying others who might have something to add. It was a virtuoso performance. But the next morning he would be back in his anchor position. His competence there was too important to waste.

There was little the convention could do while it waited for the credentials committee other than bring a parade of loyal Republicans to the rostrum to address the convention and with it, even though bored stiff by the partisan oratory, a national television audience. It was a method of rewarding faithful party workers while simultaneously killing time.

One of the party faithful scheduled for airtime was Senator Joseph McCarthy of Wisconsin. The timing could not have been worse for the networks. McCarthyism was at its crest across the nation. Fear was rampant in network corridors, where blacklists had abruptly ended the careers of widely known stars and were threatening the careers of some prominent television journalists and producers.

We had to answer several questions: Do we carry the Senator's speech or disregard it? If we start, do we dare interrupt it for news from the floor or downtown? If we don't carry it or if we interrupt it, what outrageous charge will the Senator make against us? And what damage would the charges do? None of three networks was courageous enough to incur the Senator's wrath. McCarthy's reign of terror and the bullying tactics he had so successfully demonstrated brought the proud networks to their knees. He had his time to talk to the nation, and was virtually the only one of a long procession of speakers who did. It was not a proud day for television news.

As the Tuesday night session opened, there was still no indication from the credentials committee as to when its report would be ready. Former president Herbert Hoover, symbol of Republicanism and the last member of the party to hold the presidency, was to deliver the featured address. It was unlikely, in view of the prestige of the speaker, that television would interrupt for anything less than a cataclysm.

Something else happened, however, that left me distinctly uneasy. Lack of a camera platform on the center of the floor directly in front of the rostrum was severely interfering with efforts to deliver effective pictures. The only camera angles available were profiles from side positions in the balcony. The enterprising Don Hewitt found that he could deliver a striking picture by using the camera in the radio broadcast booth directly behind the rostrum and high above it. The shot of the former president from the rear, with his audience spread out before him, was a dramatic one. There was one aspect, though, that concerned me. While watching the back of the speaker's head, it was also possible to follow the text on the Teleprompter directly in front of him. Hewitt was so fascinated by this unusual shot of a former president reading from a Teleprompter that he was reluctant to abandon it. We finally decided that it was demeaning and reluctantly gave it up.

Late Wednesday afternoon the credentials committee finally informed the chairman that it was ready to report. The majority, as expected, favored the Taft delegations, but Eisenhower supporters submitted a minority report. The ensuing debate that continued until the early hours on Thursday demonstrated how carefully the Eisenhower strategists had planned for catering to the television audience. Their speakers were younger, relatively new to national politics, and virtually unknown nationally. They were the new wave, carefully recruited to build an image not only in the hall but also on television screens across the nation. This was in clear contrast with the Taft defenders, whose image was "old guard."

The delegates apparently noted the contrast. They were also under pressure from faithful party members at home who, impressed by what they saw on the screen, urged them to support the new wave.

Tensions ran high as the debate raged on. Donald Eastvold, the Washington state attorney general and floor leader for the Eisenhower forces, conceded all states except Georgia and Texas. For those two he offered substitute motions to seat the Eisenhower delegates. Georgia was the first to come to a vote. It was close, but the Eisenhower slate won by a vote of 607 to 531. Once the Eisenhower strength had been demonstrated, Texas fell into line. The General was now virtually certain of fourteen of the seventeen Georgia delegates and thirty-three of the thirty-eight in Texas, not enough to assure him the nomination but sufficient to prevent a Taft runaway. It is clearly impossible to identify the number of delegates the skillfully crafted play for the television audience netted the Eisenhower effort, but in view of the closeness of the final vote, it was obvious that television and the Eisenhower team's use of it were decisive factors.

Once the delegates were seated, the business of the convention could proceed. By now Eisenhower was the favorite. At the end of the roll call of the states, he was only a handful of votes short of nomination. Minnesota asked to shift its votes from Harold Stassen to Ike, and the General was over the top, the Republican presidential candidate, nominated on the first ballot.

For television, the convention season was only half over. The Democrats were due to open at the International Amphitheater on July 21. Democratic officials had been painstakingly watching the Republican proceedings with particular reference to television. They were quick to approve a center platform for television cameras and redid the rostrum area to make it more attractive on the home screen. There was not much more that could be done at that late date, except to hope that they could adhere closely enough to schedule to assure that the party would look its best during prime television time.

While Dwight Eisenhower and Richard Nixon left Chicago as heroes of the Republican Party, the convention had been instrumental in elevating one other individual to star status—Walter Cronkite. Previously virtually unknown, Cronkite was now a familiar figure to millions. I became aware of just how great was his newly found fame as I walked along South Michigan Avenue with him en route to dinner one night between the two conventions. He told me he had been approached by a team of talent agents who were anxious to sign him to a contract. He wanted to know how I felt. I advised him to go ahead and sign. He was now an established television personality who would attract many high-paying assignments. I would be much more comfortable if we could negotiate through our respective representatives, his agent and my talent negotiator, rather than face to face. He subsequently signed with Stix and Gude, and as this is written, is still represented by the same firm.

The Democrats had no significant credentials contest to solve, but they had an equally sticky problem. The party had been rocked on its heels in 1948 when a number of southern delegations walked out of the convention to protest a civil rights plank in the platform. The walkout almost cost the party the election. In 1952 the party leadership wanted delegations to sign a loyalty oath pledging to support the party and its nominees, no matter what action was taken by the convention. A number of southern states bitterly resented this intrusion into their affairs. Some compromise would have to be reached before presidential and vice-presidential candidates were nominated. The alternative could be the loss of the election.

In contrast with the Republican convention, where there were two clear front-runners, there were at least five Democrats who came to Chicago with measurable support. The leader was Senator Estes Kefauver of Tennessee, who had made his reputation on television as chairman of a Senate committee investigating organized crime. But Kefauver arrived in Chicago with only about half the 604 delegates needed to nominate. Senator Richard Russell of Georgia, Senator Robert Kerr of Oklahoma, Averell Harriman of New York, and Senator G. Mennen Williams of Michigan all had sufficient strength to be considered in the running. Governor Adlai Stevenson of Illinois had no pledged delegates, but a number of dedicated workers, some of them influential in party affairs, were quietly building a sold base for a last-minute drive for his nomination. President Truman had carefully avoided committing himself, but his name was listed on the Missouri delegate roster and he was expected to attend. Unless he chose to announce his intentions earlier, he would have to reveal his choice when the Missouri delegation was polled. If he did not attend, his place would be taken by his alternate, Thomas Gavin. It was assumed that Gavin would reflect his position.

The convention started about as the Republicans' had. There were the usual opening ceremonies, but there was one noticeable difference. Adlai Stevenson electrified both the convention and the television audience with what normally would have been a purely ceremonial welcoming speech on behalf of the state of Illinois. Almost instantly he became a viable candidate. Enthusiastic endorsements from members of the television audience who had been impressed by the performance reinforced the reaction of delegates who witnessed the performance from the floor. The real battle for the nomination, however, was still four days away. Before calling for nominations, the convention had to settle the vexing loyalty oath problem and to find a way for loyal Democrats to parade to the rostrum to share some of the coveted television exposure. This led to a full quota of largely extraneous speeches. Some of the invited speakers took the trouble to gear themselves specifically to television.

One of the party faithful invited to address a daytime session while the convention was marking time was Georgia Neese Clark, treasurer of the United States. Prior to making the trip to Chicago, Mrs. Clark attended a short course CBS Television conducted in Washington for convention participants. A CBS Television press release dated July 17 reports, "As a result of her tutoring, Mrs. Clark has decided to wear a gray shantung dress with pastel collars and cuffs for her speech next Tuesday. She made her selection after trying on several dresses before the school's television cameras." Mrs. Clark also was the first to take full advantage of television's capability of transmitting illustrative material. Prior to her speech she had arranged for delivery to television control rooms of visual aids that had been designed to illustrate her message.

The Speaker of the House of Representatives, Sam Rayburn, who was to serve as permanent chairman, also went to school. The press release reports that he decided to "experiment with pancake and theatrical powder make-up (to reduce the reflection from his bald head) and was offered the services of a CBS make-up expert before he stepped up to the podium as permanent chairman." It would have been unthinkable before television to conceive of the dour speaker using the services of a theatrical makeup artist before assuming his duties in the chair.

Delegates, too, were making concessions to the new medium. "Already television has made one large contribution to the nation's taste," wrote John Crosby in his broadcast column in the *New York Herald Tribune* on July 7. "The ladies are being asked to abandon, for God's sake, those large floral print dresses which have been the tribal costume of the political committeewoman since forever. They look even worse on television."

The presence of television was largely forgotten on Thursday as the convention attacked the divisive issue of the loyalty oath. All intentions of maintaining reasonable decorum before the cameras were forgotten in the heat of the battle that did not end until after four o'clock Friday morning. Sandwich wrappers, paper coffee cups, and discarded newspapers were piled high on the floor as the angry debate went on. At one point a discarded match ignited a pile of debris. Flames shot high enough to be clearly visible on television cameras. Panic was avoided when a delegate took to a microphone near the swiftly spreading flames and shouted for calm. Other delegates stamped out the fire, and the debate proceeded.

Except for interviewing key floor leaders in an effort to interpret the ongoing debate for its viewers, television was an onlooker, not a participant. Its role was to report, not to influence. As time went on, it became more and more difficult to remain in this role. The medium soon became the message. It was too prominent, too obtrusive, too influential to remain wholly on the sidelines.

As the convention approached the call for nominations for the presidency, there was still no favorite. The nominating process would begin on Friday morning. Adlai Stevenson had been picking up support during the week following his welcoming speech, but Estes Kefauver was still in the lead in delegates committed. Attention now was focused on what President Truman would do. It was anticipated that even though he had not so far expressed support for any of the candidates, his opinion would carry substantial weight. It was now known that the President was definitely coming to Chicago. As a delegate he was eligible to vote, but he probably would not arrive until after the first ballot had been completed. His alternate, Thomas Gavin, was expected to be in the delegation when the first roll call began, and it was assumed that Gavin's vote would reflect the President's preference. It was still common practice in 1952 to call for a poll of a delegation in which each delegate would have to declare himself publicly. That meant he would have to announce his preference on television with the cameras focused tightly on him. It seemed inevitable that someone would call for such a poll to smoke Gavin out.

The President was booked to leave Washington National Airport about the time the polling would begin. We had scheduled a mobile unit to be at the airport for the departure, but I was not sure how we were to communicate with the Washington crew. Hewitt was so busy following action on the floor that I picked up the private-line phone to ask broadcast operations in New York how we were planning to coordinate the Washington cut-in. I was told that no cue line would be available to permit us to see what was happening in Washington. Broadcast operations personnel, though, would give us a play-by-play report by telephone. From the phoned descriptions we could decide when to call for the Washington picture. But I would have to keep the line open. Then there occurred a miraculous coincidence that was made to order for television.

When I placed the call to New York, the poll of the delegations was already under way. Within seconds Missouri would be called, so I asked whether the President had arrived at the airport. He had, I was told, and should be approaching the ramp in a few minutes. A camera would pick him up as soon as he came into view. I asked that I be warned as soon as he could be seen in a tight shot. The polling of the Missouri delegates had begun and by this time was nearing Gavin's name. New York told me that they had the tight shot I wanted. I said, "Take it. "

Hewitt was baffled when he saw the picture of the smiling President come up on the screen. I had not had time to tell him what I was doing, so the picture was totally unexpected. As the President stepped out of his car, I shouted, "Take Chicago." Gavin's name was the next to be called. The President's alternate got to his feet, reached into a pocket, extracted a letter, and began to read an endorsement of Adlai Stevenson for the Democratic presidential nomination. The letter was signed "Harry S Truman."

As I heard the President's name, I almost screamed into the telephone, "Take Washington." In a fraction of a second, there on the screen was President Truman on the plane's ramp, smiling broadly and waving his hat. He turned, entered the aircraft, the door closed, and we returned to Chicago. The timing was so perfect it could never have been planned. For television at that stage in its technological development, it was a case of outrageous good fortune. Only a few years later, it all could have been accomplished effortlessly, but only if the extraordinary coincidences in timing could be repeated.

The President's endorsement did not clinch the nomination for Stevenson, but it furnished a powerful boost. Coupled with the favorable impression that had been created by his welcoming speech, it moved him well into contention. The first ballot was indecisive. On the second, Stevenson moved within striking distance. By the third, the opposition was beginning to crumble, and before it was finished, Governor Adlai Stevenson of Illinois was officially declared the candidate of the Democratic Party for election to the presidency of the United States.

Would it have happened without television? That question obviously is impossible to answer. Some importance, however, has to be attached to the enthusiasm that Stevenson created with his brilliant speech at the opening session and to the spirited response from the television audience.

From television's point of view, the marriage of politics and television had been a smashing success. The medium had suddenly advanced from an intriguing curiosity to a virtual necessity. Politics would never be the same again. Doubters had been converted. Future conventions and campaigns, it was certain, would be built around television.

Some reservations, though, were voiced. Jack Gould of the *New York Times* raised one of the more pertinent ones: "It may be wise to temper some of the excitement over the role of television in politics and recognize that as the novelty of the marriage between the two fields wears off there will be a greater sense of perspective by both the broadcaster and the politician. A good rule of thumb for both would be that television's job is to report the show, not to produce it."[4]

Gould's advice would have been well taken if politicians in future convention years had not gotten so greedy that they began to look on the convention as the opportunity of a lifetime to "produce a show" that had more to do with selling the party than with selecting candidates—and if the television networks had not been so greedy for ratings that besting the competition became more important than reporting the story.

PART IV

The Rise of a Primary-Dominated Process

Emmett H. Buell Jr.

JUST as the antecedents of the presidential nominating convention go back to state practice, so, too, do the origins of the presidential primary. Although the primary concept dates back at least to 1842,[1] it was the dissatisfaction of progressives with state party nominating committees of the 1890s that inspired direct primaries.[2] The direct primary, "Fighting Bob" LaFollette thundered, would end the "menace of the machine." No longer would "a complicated system of caucuses and conventions," manipulated by party bosses, thwart the will of the voter.[3]

Once introduced, the idea of presidential primaries quickly took hold. Florida enacted the first presidential primary statute in 1901. At LaFollette's urging, Wisconsin enacted a 1905 law providing for direct election of all delegates. (Nothing was said about delegate preference for presidential candidates.) Pennsylvania followed with a 1906 law mandating direct election of national convention delegates at the district level. This statute also gave delegates the option of declaring support for specific candidates. In 1908, however, no delegate expressed such an affiliation. Alabama Democrats may have been the first to propose a primary in which voters expressed their candidate preferences, but Oregon in 1910 was the first to write this provision into law. The "Oregon idea" provided for separate votes, one to express presidential preference and the other to elect delegates. Nine other states adopted similar laws in time for the first round of presidential primaries in 1912.[4]

The 1912 primaries proved exciting but hardly decisive. As Louise Overacker explained in 1926, neither party's primaries elected enough delegates to offset the votes of those chosen by other methods: "In 1912, if Roosevelt had carried every primary and every delegate elected therein had been pledged to him, he would still have been eighty-one short of a majority, while the Democrats chosen in primaries that year made up less than one-third of the total."[5] Therefore, although Theodore Roosevelt trounced William Howard Taft in the preference vote and claimed twice as many delegates, Taft won the nomination anyway. Roosevelt promptly formed the "Bull Moose" Progressive party, got himself nominated as its presidential candidate, and ran on a platform that advocated a presidential preference primary for every state. Woodrow Wilson emerged from a tough primary battle with a slight lead in the overall vote. At the Democratic convention, he finally prevailed on the forty-sixth ballot. Wilson campaigned on a platform urging primary election of national convention delegates in every state.[6]

Once elected, Wilson wasted no time in avowing that "there ought never to be another presidential nominating convention, and there need never be another." Rather, he maintained, "the nominations should be made directly by the people at the polls."[7] Wilson followed up by asking Congress to enact a national primary system that would choose nominees "without the intervention of nominating conventions."[8]

George W. Norris makes the progressive case for direct primaries. Although his argument pertains to state politics, it also parallels the progressive stance on presidential primaries. Well aware that party nominations determine the choices available to voters, Norris maintains that voters have as much right in a democracy to choose a party's nominee as they have to cast ballots in a general election.

Labeled "wire pullers" and worse by progressive "muckrakers," party regulars correctly perceived the direct primary as one of several proposals meant to strip them of power over nominations, "boodle," and patronage. The purpose of a political party from their perspective was to gain control of government (i.e., its perquisites and resources) through the electoral process. To win, the party needed to nominate electable candidates. In full agreement with their critics regarding the crucial nature of nominations, they naturally sought exclusive rights to this power. Who, after all, had a better claim to this responsibility than those who made a career of managing and maintaining the party organization?[9]

E. E. Schattschneider takes the side of the old-fashioned party. Here he strikes at the core of the progressive premise that voters are entitled to choose a party's nominees. In his view, voters have no more right to choose nominees than fans have to decide who will quarterback for their favorite team. Voters are no more "members" of a party than fans are of sports teams. Membership confers obligations and responsibilities as well as privileges, yet the vast majority of voters have no legal responsibility or obligation to support "their" party. They pay no party dues, attend no party meetings, and need not support party candidates at the polls. This remains true today. In 1996, for example, only 9 percent of the electorate gave money to a party or candidate, a mere 6 percent attended a campaign rally or meeting, and only 3 percent worked for a party or candidate.[10] True, the proportion of party identifiers (including so-called independent leaners) voting for their party's nominee in presidential elections normally exceeds 80 percent. But more than 20 percent of all party identifiers who voted in 1968, 1972, 1980, and 1992 marked their ballots for opposition candidates.[11]

The open primary is particularly disagreeable to those who share Schattschneider's view. Most presidential primaries today are open or semi-open. Any voter may participate in a party's primary if it is open. Indeed, states holding open primaries typically dispense with registration by party. Wisconsin stands out as one of the earliest exemplars of this approach. Roughly one-fifth of all Wisconsin Republicans voting in the 1968 primary marked their ballots for Senator Eugene McCarthy, a Democrat. Austin Ranney later calculated that their support increased McCarthy's victory over President Lyndon Johnson by fourteen percentage points.[12] In 1972 and again in 1980, such crossover voters cast 11 percent of all ballots in the Wisconsin primary.[13]

Once enacted, an open primary is not easily discontinued. Encouraged by the 1975 Supreme Court ruling in *Cousins v. Wigoda*, the Democratic National Committee (DNC) forced Wisconsin Democrats to hold an advisory primary in 1984.[14] The selection of convention delegates took place in local caucuses. The DNC relented in time for Wisconsin to reprise its open primary in 1988.[15]

The open primary held by Michigan Republicans in 2000 illustrates how crossover voters can negate the choice of most party loyalists. Primary voters do not register by party in Michigan, and so Democrats as well as independents were free to help Republicans choose between George W. Bush and John McCain. According to exit polls, two-thirds of Republican voters marked their ballots for Bush. Unfortunately for Bush, they made up less than half of the turnout. McCain upset Bush, with the help of 82 percent of Democratic voters and two-thirds of independents.[16]

California moved to create the most open of open presidential primaries in time for the 2000 nominating races. Under its "blanket primary" plan, all candidates of all parties for all offices would appear on the ballot. Voters would pick one candidate per office regardless of the candidate's party affiliation or their own. That is, a Democrat could mark the presidential part of the ballot for a Republican while backing a Democratic nominee for the U.S. House.[17] Challenged by both parties in federal court, the California blanket primary was struck down by the Supreme Court as a violation of the associational rights of party members. Moreover, some justices argued, a blanket primary could result in a choice of nominees unacceptable to most of a party's followers.[18]

Still, open primaries endure, usually because state leaders view them as important to party building. Moreover, an open primary can be used to steal away discontented members of the opposition. The Georgia Republican primary is a case in point. When Georgia began holding an open presidential primary in 1976, the Republican version attracted only 188,472 voters, compared with a Democratic turnout of 614,389. By 1988, however, the gap had narrowed considerably, and, in 2000, Republican turnout topped the Democratic figure by nearly 360,000 voters.[19]

While the progressive view of primary voting and party membership clearly has prevailed, some of Norris's claims must have struck readers as fatuous or false even in his day. Consider his argument that the press would exert an influence on primaries only by full and objective reporting. Walter Lippmann had already undermined this claim in a 1922 assessment of how news reporting differs from reality.[20] Subsequent research has upheld Lippmann's analysis of coverage as selective and ineluctably biased. Images relayed in selective reporting of primary campaigns frame voter perceptions in important ways.[21] The potential to cripple a candidacy increases with the volume, intensity, and negativity of these images.[22] Selective coverage also influences races, for news organizations lavish attention on some candidates while scarcely noting others. Studies have repeatedly shown that poll standings dictate the amount of coverage most candidates receive.[23] Thomas E. Patterson even maintains that news organizations have wrested the nominating function from political parties.[24]

Norris also maintains that conventions cost more to hold than primaries, a claim that might have held true in state politics of the 1920s. But, as Alexander Heard discovered, the cost of campaigning actually increased as the primary idea caught on.[25] Norris's claim fails utterly when extrapolated to presidential nominating politics. Although parties now raise and spend huge sums on national conventions, these outlays pale in comparison with the expense of conducting thirty or more state primaries.[26]

Similarly, experience with presidential primaries has not supported Norris's assurance that legislation will really limit the amounts candidates raise and spend on political campaigns. The history of campaign finance reform teaches that limits on contributions and spending began to erode as soon as they are put in place.[27] The reform structure erected in the 1970s, for example, eventually collapsed under the contradictions of "soft money," "issue-advocacy" advertising, "bundling" of so-called hard money, and independent expenditures. Attempts to circumvent soft-money limitations included in the recently enacted McCain-Feingold bill have already begun.[28]

Perhaps the most fanciful of Norris's claims is that primaries will imbue citizens with a sense of civic obligation by informing them about issues and candidates. To the contrary, myriad studies show that likely voters learn relatively little about public policy from primary campaigns.[29] This is not to deny that news organizations lavish attention on selected candidates, particularly with respect to scandals and the "horse race." Still, despite quantum increases in news sources and in the proportion of college-educated Americans, one doubts that today's average citizen knows more about presidential nominating politics today than a century ago.

TRANSFORMATION OF THE PRIMARY PROCESS

Until 1972, the primary process revolved around thirteen states where both parties held contests on the same day. Ten states (California, Illinois, Massachusetts, Nebraska, New Jersey, Ohio, Oregon, Pennsylvania, South Dakota, and Wisconsin) started holding primaries in 1912 and continued them without interruption through 1968. New Hampshire and West Virginia joined this group in 1916. By default, New Hampshire kicked the primary season off in 1920 and has maintained this tradition ever since. Aside from New Hampshire, most of these contests took place in mid- or late spring. Those held in May or June had as much or more influence on convention choice as earlier ones. Of course, this was a time when state parties wrote the rules of delegate selection; only a few states linked the preference vote directly to delegate selection; primary voters frequently approved whole slates of uncommitted delegates; and favorite sons either stood in for serious candidates or won delegates in their own right.[30]

As previously related, this system ended with the 1968 Democratic convention. Out of this tumult came the Commission on Party Structure and Delegate Selection, soon dubbed "McGovern-Fraser" in recognition of its chairmen. Prior to the convention, McCarthy supporters had anticipated the McGovern-Fraser Commission with an unofficial body of their own headed by Governor Harold Hughes of Iowa. Its principal purpose was to issue a report decrying disparities between primary preference voting and delegate allocation in key primary states. The report called for "fair representation" of each candidate's supporters at every stage of the delegate selection process.[31] These ideas became key parts of the McGovern-Fraser agenda.

Table 12 summarizes leading reforms recommended by this and subsequent bodies commissioned to review Democratic rules. In retrospect, McGovern-Fraser laid a foundation for future changes that pretty much upheld its reforms. Its basic demands for procedural fairness won surprisingly quick acceptance from state parties and remain in effect. Direct linkage of candidate preference to delegate selection has also become standard operating practice in both parties. There are limits on bonding delegates to candidates, however, as the Winograd Commission discovered when it endorsed the so-called yank rule. Fearing defections to Ted Kennedy at the 1980 convention, the White House pushed for a rule allowing candidates to replace disloyal delegates. The convention went along, but vociferous protests convinced the Hunt Commission to propose a less binding commitment in time for the next convention. Democratic delegates now are obligated to represent the "sentiments" of those who elected them.[32] For all practical purposes, this means that delegates are obligated to support the candidates to whom they are pledged on the first (and, in all probability, the last) ballot

One break with the thrust of McGovern-Fraser reforms are set-asides for elected and appointed officeholders in government and party organizations—the so-called superdelegates. Responding to complaints that grassroots ideologues had replaced mayors, party committeemen, and even members of Congress, the Hunt Commission created this category in time for the 1984 Democratic convention, where superdelegates cast about 14 percent of all delegate votes.[33]

Ken Bode and Carol Casey offer a spirited defense of changes wrought. Interestingly, they note that the McGovern-Fraser Commission did intend to set off a trend of abandoning state committees and conventions for primary methods of delegate selection. Rather, commissioners sought to open the nominating process to party followers, assure descriptive representation of minority groups, and impose national standards on state party proceedings. Austin Ranney, a member of McGovern-Fraser, took the same line when recalling that he and most other commissioners expected that the reforms would be implanted by party leaders who retained their committees and conventions. "So here was a case in which we had a clear objective in mind," he later wrote. "We designed our new rules to achieve it; we got them fully accepted and enforced; and we accomplished the opposite of what we intended."[34]

What the reformers did not intend was an immediate, significant, and sustained increase in the number of presidential primaries held by both parties (see figure 1). Only fifteen states held Democratic primaries in 1968, compared with twenty in 1972 and forty-one in 2000. The Republican number rose from fifteen in 1968 to twenty in 1972, eventually reaching forty-three in 2000. Before 1972 the number of Democratic primaries averaged out at 15.3; afterward the average more than doubled to 32.8. The Republican average rose even higher, from 15.1 to 33.5 primaries per election year.

Those states preferring to select delegates in a nonprimary process also had to comply with reforms. No longer could old-fashioned committees meet behind closed doors to slate the delegates preferred by local and state party leaders. To comply with changes in the rules of delegate selection, these parties had to establish a process that began with local caucuses (usually at the precinct

Table 12
Major Rule Changes in Delegate Selection Promulgated by Democratic Reform Commissions

	McGovern-Fraser (1969–70)	Milkulski (1972–73)	Winograd (1974–78)	Hunt (1980–82)	Fowler (1985–86)
Selection of delegates to the national convention	All state parties adopt written rules of delegate selection; hold meetings on uniform dates, at uniform times, in accessible places with advance notice; formalize procedures by which delegates are chosen and challenged	Abolish primaries awarding all of a state's delegates on winner-take-all basis; allocate delegates according to rule of proportionality with 10 percent threshold (raised to 15 percent by DNC)	Abolish "loophole" primaries awarding district delegates on winner-take-all basis; raise threshold to 20 percent for caucuses, up to 25 percent for primaries; closed primaries only	Allow state parties to reinstate loophole primaries, award bonus delegates in proportional primaries, 20 percent threshold	Abolish loophole primaries, abolish bonus delegates, lower threshold to 15 percent in primaries and caucuses
Linkage to presidential preference	Give delegates option of listing candidate preference or running as uncommitted	Individuals running for delegate slots in caucuses and primaries designate their candidate preference	"Yank rule" adopted requiring delegates to support the candidate to whom they are pledged on first ballot	Abolish yank rule, delegates obligated to uphold their pledge on the first ballot	No change
Ex officio delegates, party leaders and elected officials	Abolished except for DNC members attending 1972 convention	Floor privileges but no vote for Democratic governors and members of Congress at 1976 convention	10 percent add-on of party leaders to be chosen by delegates, must mirror delegate preferences	Establish quota for "Superdelegates," or party leaders, to make up 14 percent of all delegates	Increase Superdelegate quota to 15.5 percent of all delegates
Affirmative action in delegate selection	Race, gender, and youth quotas	Quotas replaced by "goals" to enlist women and racial minorities	No change	Women must constitute half of all delegates at 1984 convention	Gender quota retained
Time frame for delegate selection	Calendar year of convention	No change	Shorten process with window, allow a few exemptions	Window with few exemptions	Window with few exemptions

Source: David E. Price, *Bringing Back the Parties* (Washington, D.C.: Congressional Quarterly Press, 1984); Robert E. DiClerico, "Evolution of the Presidential Nominating Process," in *Choosing Our Choices: Debating the Presidential Nominating Process*, ed. DiClerico and James W. Davis (Lanham, Md.: Rowman and Littlefield, 2000), 3–25.

level), moved next to county and/or district conventions, and ended with a statewide assembly. The final stage resulted in the choice of delegates attending the national convention. Party leaders had to publicize each gathering in advance, open the doors to all interested Democrats, make sure that minority viewpoints were represented, and scrupulously adhere to published rules. Evidently, state party leaders perceived that the burden of compliance would be less for a primary than a caucus-convention process. In 1972, Democrats in twenty-eight states selected one-third of their delegates under these rules; twenty years later, the number state parties still employing caucus-convention methods had dropped to eleven, accounting for only 9 percent of all Democratic delegates. Similarly, the number of Republican caucuses dropped from twenty-nine to twelve, with a corresponding decline in proportion of delegates from 41 to 15 percent.[35]

IOWA, NEW HAMPSHIRE, AND THE ADVENT OF FRONT-LOADING

No discussion of presidential primaries can overlook the extraordinary role of tiny New Hampshire. Well before the proliferation of primaries began, its first-in-the-nation primary had gained notoriety for roiling the waters of presidential selection. This tradition of derailing front-runners began in 1952, when Senator Kefauver upset President Truman after tirelessly campaigning in New Hampshire. Accounts differ on how much this setback influenced Truman's decision not to seek another term, but he pulled out all the same. In 1968, Senator McCarthy relied largely on student volunteers to challenge Pres-

Figure 1: Increase in Presidential Primaries after 1968

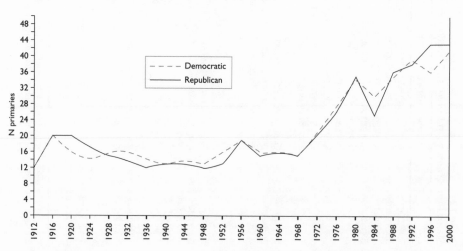

ident Johnson in New Hampshire. Johnson won the primary, but by a smaller percentage than pundits had deemed appropriate for a sitting president. Ill omens from Wisconsin also contributed to Johnson's decision not to seek renomination. Senator Edmund Muskie of neighboring Maine entered the 1972 primary as the overwhelming favorite. However, Muskie lost control of his emotions while reacting to personal attacks published in the Manchester *Union Leader*, New Hampshire's only statewide newspaper. This episode reinforced growing doubts about Muskie's emotional stability among reporters assigned to cover his campaign. Muskie won the primary, but not by the outright majority deemed necessary by the national news media. His statistical victory discredited, Muskie limped out of New Hampshire to suffer real defeats before quitting the race.

Iowa's precinct caucuses attracted virtually no national press notice prior to 1972. Confronted with the rules changes decreed by McGovern-Fraser, Iowa Democrats decided that compliance necessitated selecting a very early date in 1972 for the first of four stages in their caucus-convention process. This change unintentionally put Iowa ahead of New Hampshire in the schedule of delegate-selection events.[36] As would happen again in New Hampshire, pundits held Muskie to high expectations and then discounted his victory when it fell short of their expectations. Iowa and New Hampshire eventually worked out an arrangement whereby the nation's first caucuses would precede the nation's first primary by eight days.

In 1976, the little-known former governor of Georgia, Jimmy Carter, realized that upsets in Iowa and New Hampshire could lift him from obscurity to front-runner in short order. Local observers recall that Carter virtually took up residence in both states while most of his rivals invested their resources elsewhere. The caucuses gave Carter more delegates to county conventions than any rival; and, owing partly to Iowa, he won the New Hampshire primary. Four years later, President Carter faced a stiff primary challenge from Senator Ted Kennedy. Carter's advisors implored Democratic leaders in the South to create a regional primary that would propel the president into an early lead. Eventually, Alabama, Florida, and Georgia agreed to hold their primaries on the same March date, thereby setting the precedent for future Super Tuesdays. Helped by wins in Iowa and New Hampshire, Carter pulled away from Kennedy in mid-March as planned and wrapped up the nomination sooner than he had in 1976.[37]

No case better illustrates the payoff for long shots in Iowa and New Hampshire than Gary Hart's experience in 1984. With only a trace of support in early polls, Colorado's junior senator hardly looked like the man to knock Walter Mondale down and almost out. Like Kefauver, McGovern, and Carter before him, Hart realized that his candidacy depended on a stronger-than-expected showing in New Hampshire. Accordingly, he visited the Granite State more than any other candidate, with the possible exception of the even less well known Reuben Askew. These efforts paid off in the recruitment of volunteers in almost every town and hamlet. Their organization positioned Hart to exploit the sudden momentum that began as soon as he finished second in the Iowa caucuses. (No one was more surprised by the Iowa outcome than Hart, who had expected to finish fourth.)[38] Mondale's own polling showed Hart gaining daily on the former vice president in New Hampshire. Hart won a solid victory over Mondale, 37 to 27 percent. Overnight Hart soared twenty-seven points in the Gallup Poll. Moreover, polls in states where he had little or no organization also showed him running even with Mondale or slightly ahead. Askew, Alan Cranston, and Ernest Hollings all dropped out only hours after hearing the final returns. John Glenn, once deemed Mondale's only serious opponent, never recovered from back-to-back humiliations inflicted by Iowa and New Hampshire. More defeats on Super Tuesday finished him off. Now the field narrowed to Hart, Mondale, and Jesse Jackson. Jackson proved only a minor distraction, but Mondale had to fight for his nomination right up the final primaries in June.[39]

Mondale could not have been surprised by the New Hampshire outcome. As noted just above, his own polls showing a Hart surge during the final week of the primary campaign. But Mondale had long been wary about his chances in the Granite State. Previously on record as opposed to letting small and unrepresentative states like New Hampshire initiate the primary season,[40] he had encouraged 1983 efforts by Democratic National Committee members and organized labor to end the exemption of Iowa and New Hampshire from the party's "window." This effort collapsed in the face of determined resistance, however, and both states ended up voting even earlier than originally scheduled.[41] Mondale expected to win handily in Iowa but worried about New Hampshire. A top Mondale aide summarized his candidate's concern about New Hampshire voters: "This is not a state tailor-made for Walter Mondale. It's a very conservative state."[42]

Ironically, southern Democrats perceived New Hampshire as a springboard for maverick liberals like McCarthy, McGovern, and Hart. In the same vein, they resented New Hampshire's capacity to knock conservatives like Askew and Hollings out of contention before voters below the Mason-Dixon line got to the polls. Hoping to attract a more conservative field the next time around, as well as counteract the clout of Iowa and New Hampshire, southern Democrats put together a mega-regional primary for 1988. Resentment of Iowa and New Hampshire also figured in the decision by Democrats in other regions to hold early primaries as well. Republicans joined in this rush to front-load.

The impact of front-loading, of course, depends not only on the timing of primaries but also the number of delegates at stake. Until 1988, Florida held the biggest primary before the ides of March. Thereafter Texas, New York, Ohio, and California rescheduled their primaries for March. By 2000 a "Titanic Tuesday" had been created whereby California, New York, Ohio, Georgia, Maryland, Missouri, and all of New England except New Hampshire voted on March 7. In 1980, only eleven states, representing less than one-fifth of the nation's population, held presidential primaries before April 1. Two decades later, twenty-seven states, representing roughly two-thirds of the population, held primaries before April 1. A process that once required ten or eleven weeks to select a majority of delegates had come down to only seven weeks.[43] One consequence of this massive compression of the calendar of delegate selection events was to enhance the importance of the "invisible primary."

THE IMPACT OF FRONT-LOADING ON THE INVISIBLE PRIMARY

Arthur T. Hadley introduced a new concept in an erratic but insightful book about 1976 nominating campaigns entitled *The Invisible Primary*. Until Hadley's work, this important run-up to the first delegate selection events had remained nameless as well as unappreciated by election analysts. Not given to understatement, Hadley avowed, "the invisible primary is where the winning candidate is actually selected." The rest of the process, he concluded, is a foregone conclusion.[44] Incredibly, Hadley submitted his manuscript for publication before a single vote had been cast in the 1976 primaries. Much of what he predicted about the 1976 outcome turned out to be wrong, but if anything his assertion of the importance of the invisible primary has gained credibility over time.

This is largely because of front-loading, a development that Hadley did not anticipate. For example, front-loading and related issues of campaign finances have made the late-entry strategy infeasible. In 1976 presidential candidates still thought they jump into the race after the actual primaries had begun. Hubert Humphrey gave the matter much thought before backing off, but Gov. Jerry Brown and Sen. Frank Church actually followed through to win some western primaries. No candidate today can afford to skip the invisible primary. This is the time when aspirants raise money (indeed, qualify for matching funds), build organizations, recruit activist supporters, test campaign themes, and otherwise prepare for the frenzy to follow. This is also a time of elaborate gamesmanship between campaign organizations and campaign journalists. Candidates try to sell scenarios of impending success to media handicappers, while the great mentioners of the press take the measure of each candidate. These judgments predictably correspond to how well the candidates show up on the following indicators.

POLL STANDINGS

History since 1972 reveals that Republican front-runners emerge much sooner than their Democratic counterparts in the invisible primary. Gerald Ford topped Ronald Reagan in six of the nine polls taken from January 1974 through January 1976; Reagan led all others in eight of ten polls taken during the invisible primary of 1980; Vice President George H. W. Bush emerged as the undisputed front-runner in 1985 and never lost that advantage right up to the Iowa caucuses of 1988; he likewise eclipsed Pat Buchanan in every national sampling of voter preference during the 1992 invisible primary; Bob Dole led the pack during the 1996 invisible primary; and George W. Bush dominated in every poll of likely Republican primary voters taken in 1998, 1999, and early 2000. Of the six Democrats nominated through 2000, only Mondale and Gore established an early lead and managed to hold onto it. McGovern and Carter in 1976 never surfaced as front-runners; Carter trailed Kennedy for most of the 1980 invisible primary; Dukakis and Clinton in 1992 emerged only at the very end of their respective invisible primaries.[45]

MONEY

No phase in candidate fund-raising matches the importance of the invisible primary period. The combined effects of campaign finance legislation and front-loading have forced aspirants to raise relatively small sums, mostly from individual contributors. This takes time and, in a front-loaded process, candidates must raise most of the money they need during the invisible primary. Campaign consultant Ed Rollins succinctly summarized the challenge facing candidates for the 1996 Republican nomination: "From Super Bowl 1995 through Super Bowl 1996, a candidate has to raise between $20 million and $30 million in bites of $1,000 maximum. That takes a lot of time and organization."[46]

Up to the mid-1970s, candidates typically raised most of their war chests from relatively few very rich contributors. To finance his bid for the 1968 Democratic nomination, for example, McCarthy obtained $2.5 million of the approximately $11 million from a mere fifty contributors; at least five members of this select group gave $100,000 or more.[47] With fewer and mostly backloaded primaries to contest, candidates at this time could solicit funds later in the process and at a more leisurely pace.

The whole process changed once Congress applied the Federal Election Campaign Act (FECA) to presidential nominations in time for the 1976 primaries. Most candidates had little choice other than to abide by the law and raise most of their money from individual donations of $1,000 or less. The law also set limits on total fund raising and likewise capped the totals that a candidate could spend on each primary and on the entire race. Campaign organizations also had to disclose all sources of contributions of any consequence. Candidates willing to meet all of these conditions became eligible for matching funds if they could raise a total of $100,000 from small contributors in twenty states. Although the Federal Election Commission (FEC) has periodically adjusted spending limits to keep up with inflation, the maximum amount for individual contributions remained fixed at $1,000 through the 2000 primaries. This inflexibility only increased the importance of fund-raising during the invisible primary.

Although matching funds provided lesser candidates with a floor, it did not level the playing field. Prominent aspirants usually outstripped lesser ones by a substantial margin, and accordingly they reaped a bigger harvest in matching funds. During the 1984 invisible primary, for example, Mondale raised nearly two dollars to Glenn's one and took in more money than the combined total for the other six Democrats.[48] Indeed, since 1984 the candidate who has raised the most money during the invisible primary has won every nominating race.[49]

The FECA permitted presidential candidates to decline matching funds, in which case they could spend as much money as they could raise. But the $1,000 cap on individual contributions remained in effect until passage of the Bipartisan Campaign Reform Act (BCRA) in 2002 doubled this amount. Until Democrats Howard Dean and John Kerry declined matching funds in 2003, only Republicans had exercised this option. John Connally, former governor of Texas and a former Democrat, led they way in 1980, followed by Maurice Taylor in 1996, Malcolm ("Steve") Forbes in 1996 and 2000, and George W. Bush in 2000. Bush became the first candidate of a major party to pass up federal money and go on to win his party's nomination.[50]

MEDIA EXPOSURE

News coverage of candidates during the invisible primary closely follows the polls. The higher a candidate rates in the Gallup Poll, the greater the exposure in the news media. Republican races typically feature one clear favorite, two or three plausible alternatives, and several others given little or no chance of scoring an upset. In such instances, candidate coverage correlates strongly with poll standings. The front-runner gets the lion's share of publicity, while the least likely aspirants are almost ignored. Conversely, no candidate enjoys a consistent advantage in media exposure when the field lacks a clear hierarchy. In 1988, for example, the Democratic field lacked an obvious front-runner after a sex scandal forced Gary Hart out of the race; accordingly, none of the remaining contestants enjoyed a consistent advantage in media exposure.[51]

ENDORSEMENTS

Front-runners usually get significantly more endorsements than their rivals during the invisible primary, and 2000 was no exception. Both Gore and Bush picked up support from party elites and important groups during the invisible primary. Some testimonials turn more heads than others, of course, but, as Ceaser and Busch note, campaign observers regard the lack of endorsements as a sign of weakness.[52] Judged by this standard, as table 13 shows, both front-runners eclipsed their chief rivals. By the start of 2000, 500 superdelegates out of 716 had jumped on the Gore bandwagon. Gore also picked up a crucial endorsement from the AFL-CIO, while Bush won over Christian conservative leaders even though some of his rivals took positions more consistent with their agenda.[53]

STRAW POLLS

Whatever a straw poll represents, it is not a random sample of a party's following or a state's electorate. Participation in such events is limited to ticket holders only, with the usual price of admission typically set at $25. Candidates have expended huge sums on buying votes in hopes of humiliating their rivals and impressing the news media. State party organizations typically see the straw poll as a premier opportunity for filling their coffers and gaining national attention.

Democratic straw polls caught on after Carter surprised everyone in 1975 by winning a big straw poll at the Iowa State University campus in Ames. Three more straw votes took place in 1980 despite Carter's incumbency, as did seven more events involving at least a thousand participants in 1984. The 1984 expe-

Table 13
Front-Runner Advantage in Endorsements, 2000 Invisible Primary

	Gore	Bradley	Bush	McCain
U.S. senators	33	3	36	4
U.S. representatives	170	6	165	8
Governors	17	1	27	0

Source: James W. Ceaser and Andrew E. Busch, *The Perfect Tie: The True Story of the 2000 Presidential Election* (Lanham, Md.: Rowan and Littlefield, 2001), 68; Gore 2000 press office; Bradley campaign Web site (www.billbradley.com); McCain campaign press office; Bush Web site (www.georgewbush.com).

rience convinced national party officials that straw polls cost too much and inflicted needless damage on favorites. Democrats have held only one straw poll of note since that time, a 1992 showdown in Florida won by Clinton. In 2003, Florida Democrats clamored for a straw poll, but, after intense negotiations, settled for candidate appearances at their state party convention.

Republicans have a history of not holding straw votes in a year when an incumbent president seeks renomination. Local Republicans reportedly raised $350,000 in ticket sales for the 1995 Iowa Straw Poll in Ames.[54] They collected still more in rent for campaign tent sites near the Iowa State arena, where the candidates spoke and the vote took place. In 1999, Forbes shelled out at least $1 million to contest the Ames poll, while George W. Bush reportedly spent $750,000 on the same event. These expenditures included the costs of transporting, feeding, and entertaining their supporters.[55]

At least for Republicans, the Ames Straw Poll has taken on the carnival air of an old-fashioned convention. The smell of barbecue, the sound of music, vendors hawking T-shirts and other memorabilia, and the clash of candidate ambitions make for a spectacle seldom matched in the course of a nominating race. The 1999 showdown in Ames featured every Republican aspirant except McCain. Bush won handily with 31 percent of 23,668 votes cast.[56] This single event chopped down more presidential timber than the Iowa caucuses and the New Hampshire primary combined. Lamar Alexander and former vice president Dan Quayle fell out immediately; Elizabeth Dole and Pat Buchanan soon followed.

Despite the 1999 outcome, no omen of who will win the nomination is more misleading than a straw poll. From 1975 to 1999, eventual Republican nominees won only thirteen of thirty straw votes (in which at least one thousand activists participated). Except for George W. Bush, every Republican nominee since 1980 has lost more straw polls than he won.[57]

OTHER TESTS

The invisible primary has also gained in importance as the period when aspirants formulate and hone their campaign themes. Voters hear these messages articulated at rallies, in campaign advertisements, and, especially in televised debates. Debates provide a real test of a front-runner's abilities, especially in open races when numerous challengers gang up on the favorite, as happened during the invisible primaries of 1980, 1988, 1996, and 2000. A count of debates held during invisible primaries since 1972 would likely reveal that the number has increased with the advent of front-loading. This proposition is plausible because front-loading has lengthened the invisible primary and thereby created more opportunities for debate. Moreover, candidate debates have become obligatory, and there is some evidence that they matter in New Hampshire.[58]

FRONT-LOADING AND PRIMARY TURNOUT

Much ado has been made of declining voter turnout for presidential primaries. Elections analyst Curtis Gans estimates that only 18 percent of the voting-age population cast ballots in the 2000 presidential primaries, said to be
the second-worst showing since 1960. (The low point was 1996, when President Clinton faced no primary opposition to his renomination.) Gans largely
attributes this slide to front-loading, noting that turnout for primaries held on
or before March 7, 2000, averaged 23 percent, compared with 14 percent for
later primaries.[59] Thomas E. Patterson agreed with Gans on both counts when
summarizing the results of his Vanishing Voter Study in 2002.[60]

Some scholars writing on this subject define turnout as the percentage of
inhabitants age eighteen or older that actually go to the polls and vote. But
there is a problem with this approach because the voting-age population includes many people who, for various reasons, cannot vote.[61] For example, millions of documented aliens as well as an untold number of undocumented
aliens are not eligible to vote, but they are nonetheless counted in the census as
inhabitants. In 1994, Gans estimated that 13 million aliens of one type or another had been wrongly counted as nonvoters, whereas Everett C. Ladd put this
figure as closer to 18 million.[62] The problem extends beyond noncitizens to in-
corporate a very large number of imprisoned felons and former convicts who
have lost the right to vote, as well as a growing number of elderly and disabled
citizens who are no longer capable of voting.

In short, there is ample reason to doubt the accuracy of turnout rates based
on the entire voting-age population. If turnout has sunk to such depths, then a
different measure should point up the same trend. Though imperfect, raw vote
totals provide a direct indicator of whether turnout has actually risen or fallen.
They also make it easier to compare the turnout for Democratic and Republican primaries held on the same dates and in the same states. This is important
because, as will soon become clear, the recent pattern of turnout for Democratic primaries differs dramatically from that of the Republicans. Contrary to
conventional wisdom, the vanishing voter is much more of a problem for Democrats than Republicans.

Based on the raw vote totals going back to 1912, figure 2 shows that patterns that had once been similar diverged greatly after 1968. From 1972 to
1988, Democratic primary voting soared. In 1992, however, it plunged. Although the further decline in 1996 makes sense, given Clinton's lack of primary
opposition, the feeble rebound in 2000 fell more than 6 million votes short of
the 1992 total. A rather different picture emerges for Republican primaries. Except for 1984, when President Reagan faced no primary opposition, voting in
Republican primaries has increased in each election year, albeit usually at a

modest pace. When compared with the total vote in all of the 1988 Republican primaries, the 2000 figure represents an improvement of roughly 5 million. The net change for Democrats from 1988 to 2000 was 9 million fewer voters.

The 2000 primaries were noteworthy for differences between the parties in primary scheduling. Before 2000, most states held their Democratic and Republican presidential primaries on the same date. Seldom has one party held three more state primaries than the other in any given year. In 2000, however, the parties differed not only in the number but also in the timing of their presidential primaries.[63] "Not since the nomination race of 1936," Ceaser and Busch affirm, "has the difference in selection methods between the parties been as great."[64] New Hampshire highlighted this disparity by moving its primary date from February 20 to February 1. This opened a five-week hole in a Democratic calendar that permitted no delegate selection event prior to March 7. (Democrats held beauty contests in Delaware, Michigan, and Washington State, but only Washington drew many voters, once Bradley decided to transform the event into a showdown with Gore.) Operating under more flexible rules, Republicans scheduled February primaries in South Carolina, Arizona, Michigan, Virginia, and Washington State.

That said, one must not lose sight of the enormous disparity between Democratic and Republican turnout. Differences of this magnitude suggest that front-loading does not have the same impact on both parties. To get at this issue we must track state voting returns from one contested nominating year to the next. This permits examination of how primary voting in the same states changed in back-to-back races. For Democrats the sequence for comparison is from 1988 to 1992; similarly, the Republican sequences are 1988 to 1992, 1992

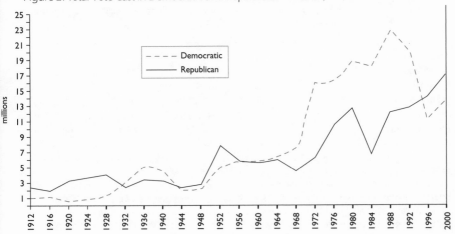

Figure 2: Total Vote Cast in Democratic and Republican Primaries, 1912–2000

to 1996, and 1996 to 2000. I also offer a comparative overview of how state turnout changed between 1988 and 2000, the two most recent years in which *both* presidential nominations came open. This overview is limited to states that held primaries in 1988 as well as in 2000 and applies only to states where both parties held comparable primaries on the same day.[65] For purposes of this analysis, front-loaded primaries occurred no later than the final week of March.

The results of the Democratic analysis appear in table 14. One can see at a glance that turnout fell off in 1992 pretty much regardless of when the Democrats held their primaries. Contrary to conventional wisdom, it increased in four contests that had been back-loaded in time for the 1992 race. (One suspects that local races of local interest accounted for these increases.) On balance, voting declined in twenty out of thirty Democratic primaries held in 1992, a net loss of 3.2 million voters compared with 1988 figures. An almost unbroken pattern of decline shows up in this table, in which voting in only one of thirty primaries in 2000 (New Hampshire) attracted greater turnout than in 1988. All told, 8.4 million fewer Democratic voters cast ballots in 2000 than in 1988, an astounding loss in excess of 40 percent.

Table 14
Relationship of Scheduling to Democratic Primary Vote Totals

	Front-loaded both years	Back-loaded/ front-loaded	Front-loaded/ back-loaded	Back-loaded both years	Total
1988–1992					
N primaries	14	0	4	12	30
N with vote increase	6	—	4	0	10
1992 vote	7,687,236	—	2,015,969	8,931,935	18,635,140
1992–1988	−1,160,021	—	114,104	−2,196,557	−3,242,474
Percent change	−13.1	—	6.0	−24.7	−14.8
1988–2000					
N primaries	14	2	3	11	30
N with vote increase	1	0	0	0	1
2000 vote	4,750,979	3,632,626	745,706	3,260,722	12,390,033
2000–1988	−4,552,477	−889,680	−476,201	−2,501,606	−8,419,964
Percent change	−48.9	−19.7	−39.0	−43.4	−40.5

Source: Derived from tables in *America Votes*, vols. 22 and 24; *The Elections of 1988* and subsequent editions, ed. Michael Nelson (Washington, D.C.: Congressional Quarterly Press).

Note: The 1988–2000 overview is limited to states in which both parties held comparable primaries on the same dates: Alabama, Arkansas, California, Connecticut, Florida, Georgia, Idaho, Illinois, Indiana, Kentucky, Louisiana, Maryland, Massachusetts, Missouri, Mississippi, Montana, Nebraska, New Hampshire, New Jersey, New Mexico, North Carolina, Ohio, Oklahoma, Oregon, Pennsylvania, Rhode Island, Tennessee, Texas, West Virginia, and Wisconsin.

Table 15 paints a very different picture of Republican primary turnout, especially after 1992. The changes from 1992 to 1996 are as follows: (1) increased
voting in twelve of seventeen primaries that were front-loaded for both races,
(2) increased voting in five of six primaries that moved to front-loaded dates in
1996, (3) a drop-off in most primaries back-loaded for races, and (4) and a net
gain of nearly 867,000 votes for all thirty-five contests. As happened in 2000,
turnout for primaries that were also front-loaded in 1996 increased by 2.3 million. Moreover, the 2000 vote total for primaries that were also back-loaded in

Table 15
Relationship of Scheduling to Republican Primary Vote Totals

	Front-loaded both years	Back-loaded/ front-loaded	Front-loaded/ back-loaded	Back-loaded both years	Total
1988–1992					
N primaries	15	0	4	12	31
N with vote increase	5	—	1	8	14
1992 vote	4,736,269	—	601,952	6,084,219	11,422,440
1992–1988	–214,453	—	–75,207	343,598	101,165
Percent change	–4.3	—	–11.1	6.0	0.9
1992–1996					
N primaries	17	6	0	12	35
N with vote increase	12	5	—	5	22
1996 vote	6,089,936	4,575,836	—	2,561,312	13,227,084
1996–1992	708,844	595,013	—	–437,001	866,856
Percent change	13.2	14.9	—	–14.6	7.0
1996–2000					
N primaries	20	0	3	12	35
N with vote increase	13	—	0	7	20
2000 vote	12,220,884	—	890,879	2,594,560	15,706,323
2000–1996	2,324,623	—	–162,380	33,248	2,195,491
Percent change	23.5	—	–15.4	1.3	16.2
1988–2000					
N primaries	14	2	3	11	30
N with vote increase	8	2	0	5	15
2000 vote	5,606,455	4,245,449	338,975	3,101185	13,292,064
2000–1988	544,130	1,210,158	–64,383	53,779	1,743,684
Percent change	10.7	39.9	–16.0	1.8	15.1

Source: Derived from tables in *America Votes*, vols. 22 and 24; *The Elections of 1988* and subsequent
editions, ed. Michael Nelson (Washington, D.C.: Congressional Quarterly Press).
Note: The 1988–2000 overview covers the same states as table 14.

1996 actually went up by a percentage point. Overall, Republican vote totals shot up by 2.2 million in 2000, a 16 percent increase over 1996.

At this point, we should recognize that front-loading need not increase a state's influence in the choice of presidential nominees. That is, a state can front-load its primary and still schedule a primary too late to make a difference. Every nominating race has a break point, after which the obvious winner wraps up the nomination. Increasingly, it appears that front-loading has shortened the interval between the break point and the acquisition of delegate majorities. Expert opinion varies on when the 1992 Democratic break point occurred. As good a claim as any is April 7, when Bill Clinton won big in New York, Wisconsin, Minnesota, and Kansas. At this juncture Clinton had acquired 1,265 delegates of 2,142 needed for nomination.[66] Published accounts more or less agree that for the Republicans the 1992 break point was March 17, the day President Bush trounced Pat Buchanan in Illinois and Michigan. Three days later Buchanan conceded that only "celestial intervention" could prevent Bush's renomination.[67] Even so, Bush did not acquire an actual majority of the delegates until May.[68] In 1996, Republicans probably crossed the Rubicon on March 12 (certainly no later than March 19), when Bob Dole won every primary on this Super Tuesday as well as 96 percent of the delegates at stake.[69] He obtained his delegate majority no later than March 26. No one disputes that March 7 marked the 2000 break point for Al Gore as well as for George W. Bush, or that both men garnered enough delegates on the following Tuesday to wrap up their nominations.

Table 16 shows that voting increased for some front-loaded primaries but not for others in the Republican races of 1996 and 2000. Classifying these contests as "early" or "late" helps explain why turnout rose in most but not in all cases. Early primaries take place on or before the break point; all others are late. In 1996, turnout improved in all twelve of the early primaries (also front-loaded in 1992) over turnout in 1992. Similarly, eleven of the thirteen primaries that had higher turnout in 2000 were early. It is also noteworthy that many of the increases in 2000 were spectacular: Washington State (where turnout was 307 percent more than in 1996), Michigan (144 percent), Rhode Island (141 percent), South Carolina (107 percent), Massachusetts (76 percent), and Maryland (48 percent). Conversely, turnout dropped in eight out of ten late contests. (The late-early distinction mattered less for six 1996 primaries that had been back-loaded in 1992. Although turnout rose for the two early contests, it likewise increased for three of four late races.)

The distinction between early and late front-loaded primaries holds up fairly well when tested by whether the contest was open or closed. Other things being equal, one expects a primary open to all voters to attract a higher turnout than one closed to all but registered party "members." (Because this generalization should also hold for semi-open primaries that are open to independents, I have grouped the two open types together.) Table 16 reveals that twelve early primaries in 1996 drew higher turnouts than in 1992. Seven of these contests were of the open variety (out of nine early and open), and five were closed (out of six early and closed). Of eleven early primaries exhibiting vote increases in 2000, nine were open (out of nine early and open) and two were closed (out of three early and closed).

To sum up, reports of declining turnout based on percentages of the voting-age population frequently ignore a simple fact noted as early as 1926: the presidential primary vote varies from party to party.[70] Recently, at least, Democrats have had much more of a vanishing voter problem than Republicans. The conventional approach possibly understates the degree of Democratic decline while paying little or no heed to Republican gains. It makes no sense to conflate these divergent trends. It does make sense to divide front-loaded pri-

Table 16
Votes Cast in Front-Loaded Primaries Before and After Republican "Break Points"

	Front-loaded for 1996	Front-loaded for 2000
Break point in race	March 12	March 7
Front-loaded for previous race	17	20
"Early" primaries	15	12
Vote increased	12	11
Early vote total	4,747,411	8,883,621
Percent change	15.8	44.9
"Late" primaries	2	8
Vote increased	1	2
Late vote total	1,342,525	3,337,263
Percent change	4.9	−11.4
Back-loaded for previous race	6	0
"Early" primaries	2	—
Vote increased	2	—
Early vote total	471,248	—
Percent change	33.9	—
"Late" primaries	4	—
Vote increased	3	—
Late vote total	4,104,588	—
Percent change	13.1	—

Source: Data for this table was derived from the sources listed in notes 66–69 to Part IV.
Note: "Early" primaries were held on or before the break point date; the previous race for 1996 was 1992; for 2000, it was 1996.

maries into early and late categories. It matters little whether the contest is open or closed for Republicans as long as it occurs before the break point. Democratic turnout has plunged in every kind of primary, whether front- or back-loaded, early or late, open or closed. Admittedly, these conclusions are derived from relatively few contests, and one must be cautious in using them to forecast the future.

Still, if the pattern persists, scholars will have additional reason to look beyond front-loading for explanations of declining turnout in Democratic primaries. A distinct possibility is that the party's primary vote has fallen off because its electoral base has eroded. Whether due to realignment or to more prosaic factors, the number of white identifiers (weak as well as strong) and so-called independents expressing some affinity for the Democratic party has dropped substantially since the 1960s.[71] Indeed, as figure 3 shows, not since 1968 has a clear majority of whites preferred the Democratic party. Moreover, since their setbacks in the 1980s, Democrats have struggled to retain a slender lead in the competition for white loyalists.[72]

A white exodus from the Democratic party has been particularly noteworthy in the South.[73] In Texas, for example, a gradual partisan realignment is said to have merged extreme right-wingers with moderates and conservatives into a new Republican majority, while the white and blue-collar base of Texas Democrats has crumbled.[74] Big changes can be seen at the elite and activist level as well. The 1990s saw a shift of party allegiances among elected officials at all levels of government, including the Congress. Still more signs of white flight surfaced in Charles Prysby's 1992 study of grassroots activists in the South. A

Figure 3: Party Identification of Voting-Age Whites, 1960–2000

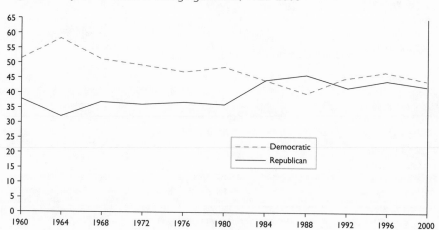

substantial number of Republican workers in his sample had defected from the Democratic party: 65 percent in Louisiana, 36 percent in Florida, 36 percent in North Carolina, and 28 percent of the Republican total for all eleven states of the former Confederacy. Conversely, former Republicans constituted only 5 percent of all Democratic activists.[75]

White disaffection with Democratic candidates and policies likely extends to the rank and file of organized labor. National Election Study (NES) data also disclose a significant drop in the number of union members identifying with the Democratic party since 1960. Similarly, surveys of Ohio unions in the 1990s revealed that on average more members claimed to be conservative rather than moderate or liberal, that a mere 16 percent felt the government should do more to help blacks, and that only 36 percent favored a government health plan in 1996.[76] While unions remain essential to the conduct of Democratic campaigns, it is also likely that a substantial number of white members vote in Republican primaries.

FRONT-LOADING AND THE PRESIDENTIAL ELECTION CAMPAIGN

Front-loading has transformed the presidential selection process by forcing such an early end to the nominating races that the fall campaign now starts no later than mid-March and, in any event, well before the official end of the primary season. First noted in 1996, this early beginning of the fall campaign that causes it to overlap with the primary process has been variously identified as the "interregnum," the "hidden campaign," and the "pre-convention phase of the general election campaign."[77]

However labeled, this interval between the de facto and the formal nomination can undermine a candidacy. It proved disastrous for Dole in 1996. First, the Clinton campaign unleashed a thunderous barrage of negative ads: 7,765 airings in twenty-four states over a four-week period ending April 19.[78] A depleted treasury and FECA limits on raising more money left Dole unable to put up much of a defense. Dole tried to counter the attacks by showcasing his Senate leadership, but Democratic colleagues effectively frustrated him at every turn. Then Dole resigned his Senate seat to campaign full time, only to stumble several times as his aides struggled to schedule events. As the San Diego convention approached, many in the party had already written Dole off. Asked to evaluate his performance thus far, nearly half of the Republican delegates sampled replied "not so good" or "poor" (compared with 99 percent of Democratic delegates who rated Clinton's campaign up to that point as "excellent" or "good.")[79]

After wrapping up his nomination on March 14, Bush used the remainder of the 2000 primary season to reprise his message of compassionate conservatism. While Bush appeared consistent, Gore tried out several versions of a fall campaign that renewed doubts about his integrity and veracity. Bush regained his lead in the polls and kept it right up to the Democratic convention.[80]

In sum, nominating races that end early give the nominee-apparent opportunities to bind up the wounds inflicted by primary battles. While these intervals were hardly unknown before front-loading, they have become more important now that front-loading has made them part of the general election campaign.

REPRESENTATIVENESS OF PRIMARY ELECTORATES

No issue relating to presidential primaries is as complex as whether primary voters are representative of all likely voters. Although nearly all who vote in presidential primaries also turn out for the presidential election, most who vote in the presidential election do not turn out for presidential primaries.[81] Moreover, some who vote in open primaries do not regard themselves as supporters of the party hosting the primary.

V. O. Key planted the seeds of research on the representativeness of primary voters by commenting that the "working electorate" was almost invariably a caricature of the "potential electorate" in southern elections.[82] Later, in a book about state politics, he observed that a primary electorate might well consist of "people of certain sections of a state, of persons especially responsive to certain styles of political leadership or shades of ideology, or of other groups markedly unrepresentative in one way or another."[83] Key thus designated two groups for study, the *primary electorate* and the *entire party following*; he also pointed up demographics, ideology, and candidate preference as points for comparison. He also warned readers that a "minuscule and unrepresentative" primary electorate might distort a party's message and unravel its coalition.[84]

Many political scientists have followed Key's lead, only to arrive at different conclusions. To answer the question of whether the primary electorate is representative of the party following, one first must define party following. Because different authors define it differently, findings vary from one operational meaning of party following to the next. The following studies illustrate the point.

Austin Ranney compared 1968 primary electorates and party followings in New Hampshire and Wisconsin.[85] Unfortunately, Ranney had to cobble a research design out of polls that had sampled rather different groups and that asked rather different questions. Accordingly, Ranney defined the primary electorate and party following differently in the two states. The New Hampshire primary electorate consisted of registered voters interviewed before the event who said they planned to turn out. In Wisconsin the sample was made up of party identifiers of voting age interviewed just after the primary and who claimed to have voted. Similarly, the New Hampshire party following consisted of registered voters who said they probably would not go to the polls, while the Wisconsin party following was comprised of party identifiers who said they had not voted. Ranney concluded that the primary electorate was somewhat older and more likely to hold white-collar jobs than the average voter.

Unlike Ranney, James I. Lengle drew his data from two surveys conducted by the same polling organization in the same state using similarly derived samples and asking pretty much the same questions.[86] This continuity enabled him to measure the presence, direction, and degree of representativeness of voters in California's 1968 and 1972 Democratic primaries. Lengle also rejected Ranney's method of comparing mutually exclusive groups, e.g., voters versus nonvoters. To keep faith with Key, Lengle maintained, one should define all *registered Democrats who turned out* as the primary electorate, and all *Democratic identifiers* as the party's following. Accordingly Lengle found that primary voters, when compared with party followers, (1) had received more formal schooling; (2) more often held professional, managerial, or other white-collar jobs; (3) identified more frequently with the upper middle class; (4) more often called themselves liberals and opponents of the Vietnam war; and (5) preferred McCarthy to Humphrey in 1968 and McGovern to Humphrey in 1972. Comparatively few primary voters were nonwhite. If a more representative vote had been cast in the 1972 primary, Lengle concluded, Humphrey would have won.

John G. Geer looked at primary exit polls for more than one nominating cycle, comparing turnout for eighteen Democratic and five Republican contests in 1976, 1980, and 1984.[87] Trading on Key's 1966 classification of voters as "standpatters," "switchers," or "new voters," he defined the primary electorate as all voters who turned out for a party's primary, *including partisans of an opposing party.*[88] He defined the party following as *all voters who supported the party's ticket on election day:* "Specifically, the following should be made up of those who usually vote for the party's candidates, those who lean toward the party yet do not always vote for its candidates, and those independents and *opposing partisans* [emphasis added] who occasionally support the party in the general election." Applying this unconventional approach, Geer discovered that primary voters generally were not better off in terms of formal education, wealth, or occupational status. Largely this was so because so many of them were elderly, living on fixed incomes, and of a generation whose formal education generally ended with high school. Geer also concluded that primary voters leaned or inclined slightly more toward the ideological center than party followers.

Herbert Kritzer focused on Democrats interviewed for the 1972 NES. Accordingly, his primary electorate consisted of all respondents claiming to have voted in a Democratic presidential primary. Rather than settle for one measure of party follower, Kritzer produced no fewer than four: (1) Democratic identifiers who did not vote in the primaries, (2) Democratic identifiers who voted in the 1972 election, (3) all eligible voters regardless of party identification who did not vote in the Democratic primaries, and (4) persons who voted for McGovern in the general election. He found few noteworthy differences between primary voters and Democratic identifiers except that the former tended to be older and union members. Primary voters showed up as notably more liberal only when compared to nonvoters.[89]

Scott Keeter and Cliff Zukin drew on the 1980 ANES to define a party's following as *primary nonvoters plus party identifiers voting in the general election*. They found that primary voters were older, better educated, more affluent, and more likely to be white and Jewish than party followers. Even so, primary voters did not stand out as more liberal or conservative than party followers.[90]

William Crotty and John S. Jackson III drew on the 1980 ANES to compare *all primary voters regardless of party* in selected states with *all nonvoters of voting age*. They found the primary electorate to be more educated, affluent, white-collar, white, and ideological than the party following.[91]

Barbara Norrander took a different tack, viewing primary voters as a more active subset of the general electorate: "If we want to uncover distortions caused by the presidential primary system, and not those caused by patterns of participation in America, the correct comparison group is *general election voters who failed to vote in the primaries* [emphasis added]."[92] Norrander looked closely at three dimensions of ideology derived from 1980 NES questions: self-location on a scale measuring liberal and conservative extremes, abstract thinking and consistency in responses, and willingness to define oneself ideologically as well as to comment on the ideology of various groups and candidates. This rather complex analysis uncovered no significant differences between primary voters and party followers.

Michael Hagen relied on the Current Population Survey (CPS) of the U.S. Census to gather information about primary turnout in seven states. Like Crotty and Jackson, he aggregated all primary voters regardless of party registration into a single primary electorate for each state. He constructed not one but three comparison groups: (1) all voting-age adults, (2) all registered voters, and (3) all voters who turned out for the general election.[93] Hagen generally found that primary voters were older, more educated, and better off economically than the comparison groups.

In sum, we are left with the unsatisfying conclusion that different studies using different definitions have produced different findings. Those comparing primary voters with general election voters of the same party who had not voted in the primaries find few significant differences. Those comparing the primary electorate with party identifiers uncover substantial differences that implicitly support the Key thesis. Defining the party following in yet another way, Geer finds primary electorates demographically unrepresentative, but in ways contrary to the Key thesis.

THE CHANGING PRIMARY SYSTEM

Since its difficult delivery by progressive midwives, the presidential primary has come to dominate the choice of presidential nominees. After 1968, reform cast a big shadow over the delegate selection events of both parties. Democratic control of state legislatures meant that at least some of the McGovern-Fraser reforms became part of the election code, binding on Republicans as well. Local and state party leaders lost their power over delegate selection. Indeed, for a time, Democratic party officials and elected officeholders could not count on being a part of their state delegations. Except for superdelegates, Democratic rules require proportional allocation of delegates in accordance with the preference vote. The 15 percent threshold is now enforced by every primary and caucus-convention state. In precinct caucuses, for example, 15 percent is the minimum show of "viability" needed for a group of candidate supporters to elect a delegate. Republicans operate under looser rules allowing state parties considerably greater discretion in deciding how to allocate delegates. Yet Republicans, too, tie allocation to preference voting. Both parties have adopted "windows" within which all delegate selection must take place, with exemptions for Iowa and New Hampshire. At this writing, experts are still debating whether front-loading has increased or reduced the power of Iowa and New Hampshire to propel challengers like Hart and McCain all the way to the nomination.

The other major developments associated with reform include a dramatic increase in the number of primaries, the growing number of open and semi-open primaries, front-loading, enhancement of the invisible primary, and the failure of campaign finance reform to lessen the importance of big money. The presidential primary has proven far less perfect than its progressive creators promised. Big money matters more than it ever did. Media coverage of the nominating process is probably may be no more edifying than in the days of Norris and LaFollette. Other controversies endure as the present system has come under attack for alleged inequities, unrepresentativeness, and propensity to discourage a better class of politicians from running for president. Moreover, the system appears to be sliding toward a national primary. What does the future hold? Will the present system be transformed once again by a reform movement, or will change occur incrementally, at a pace and to a degree acceptable to state parties? What in the next system will be truly new?

CHAPTER 11

Why I Believe in the Direct Primary

George W. Norris

Our government is founded upon the theory that the people are sufficiently intelligent to control their own government. The argument I shall make is based upon the truth of this assumption. The direct primary is simply a method by which the will of the people can be ascertained in the selection of those who shall make and administer the laws under which all of the people must live. There is nothing sacred about it. If a better method can be devised I would not hesitate to abandon it and throw it aside. Neither will I claim that it is perfect. It has many weaknesses and imperfections. Until we can find a better system we ought to devote our energies toward its improvement by making whatever amendments experience demonstrates are necessary, always having in view the fundamental principle that we are trying to devise a plan by which the people will come as nearly as possible into the control of their own government. We must not expect perfection. We cannot hope to devise a plan that will make it impossible for mistakes to occur. We cannot by law change human nature. Selfish, designing, and even dishonest men will sometimes be able to deceive a majority of the people, however intelligent and careful they may be. Every government, whatever may be the system of nominating candidates for office, ought to provide by law for the recall of its officials by the people. If the people should make a mistake they will correct it. If a public

From the *Annals of the American Academy of Political and Social Science* 106 (1923): 22–30. A Nebraska progressive, Republican George William Norris (1861–1944) served in the U.S. House of Representatives (1903–1913) and U.S. Senate (1913–1943).

servant has been faithful and true to his trust it will not be necessary for him to seek the approval of party bosses and machine politicians for his own vindication. The direct primary is in fact a part of the system of our election machinery. It is just as important, and often more important, than the official election which follows. A people who are qualified to vote for candidates at the general election are likewise qualified to select those candidates at the primary election. It requires no more intelligence to vote at that election than it does at the regular election. To deny to the citizen the right to select candidates and to confine his suffrage rights solely to a decision as between candidates after they have been selected is, in reality, at least a partial denial of the right of suffrage. It very often means that the voter is given the right only to decide between two evils. The right, therefore, to select candidates is fundamental in a free government, and whenever this right is denied or curtailed, the government is being placed beyond the control of the people.

No better defense can be made of the direct primary than to consider the objections that are made to it. In doing this, it must be remembered that up to this time we have had but two systems. One is the old convention and the other is the newer and more modern system of the primary. Those who are opposed to the latter advocate the return to the convention system, and in doing this they point out various objections to the direct primary, which, they argue are sufficient reason for discrediting it. It is my purpose now to consider some of these objections. Some of them, instead of being objections to the direct primary, are in reality arguments in its favor. Other objections made are only partially sound, while some of them are untrue in fact. If we are seeking better government and have no ulterior motive whatever, we ought to be constructive in our criticism. [. . .] I am seeking to find the best system of nominating candidates. The defects of the direct primary system, even in its crude state, are so much less than the wrongs and evils of the convention system, that an intelligent people will not hesitate to adopt it rather than the long used and universally condemned convention system, and devote their energies in a fair and honest way to the enactment of laws that shall, as far as possible, eliminate the defects of the primary.

One of the objections that is always made to the direct primary is that it takes away party responsibility and breaks down party control. This objection is perhaps the most important of any that are made against the direct primary. Politicians, political bosses, corporations and combinations seeking special privilege and exceptional favor at the hands of legislatures and executive officials, always urge this as the first reason why the direct primary should be abolished. But this objection thus given against the direct primary I frankly offer as one of the best reasons for its retention. The direct primary will lower party responsibility. In its stead it establishes individual responsibility. It does lessen allegiance to party and increase individual independence, both as to the public official and as to the private citizen. It takes away the power the party leader or boss and places the responsibility for control upon the individual. It lessens party spirit and decreases partisanship. These are some of the reasons why the primary should be retained and extended. A party is only an instrumentality of government. Whenever, through party control, a public official casts any vote or performs any official act that is not in harmony with his own conscientious convictions, then the party spirit has become an instrument of injury to the body politic rather than a blessing. Laws enacted through such influences not only do not express the wishes and the will of the citizens, but it is in this way that bad laws are placed upon the statute book and good laws are often defeated. A public official should in the performance of his official duties be entirely nonpartisan. Whenever he is otherwise, he is in reality placing his party above his country. He is doing what he conscientiously believes to be wrong with the people at large, in order that he may be right with his party.

The country owes most of its progress to the independent voter, and it is a subject of great congratulation that his number is increasing at a wonderfully rapid rate. Partisanship blinds not only the public official but the ordinary citizen and tends to lead him away from good government. In a Republican stronghold, the machine politician deceives the people by asserting that he is an Abraham Lincoln Republican, while in the Democratic locality, the same class of official seeks to carry public favor by claiming a political relationship to Thomas Jefferson. It is the party spirit that enables these men to cover up their shortcomings. It is the party spirit on the part of the voter that causes him to be moved by such appeals. Party allegiance and party control if carried to their logical end, would eliminate the independent voter entirely; and incidentally, it ought to be said that the independent voter is always condemned by the politicians and those in control of political parties.

The direct primary is comparatively new. The one circumstance more than any other that brought it into life was the evil in our government that came from the spirit of party. This evil grew from a small beginning and gradually increased until it pervaded and controlled our government. The means through which this evil spirit could most successfully work was the party convention. Its danger was seen long before it had reached a point where its evil was felt. Its demoralizing influence upon popular government was forcibly predicted by George Washington. He warned his countrymen in the most solemn manner against the baneful effects of the spirit of party generally. In speaking of party spirit in his Farewell Address, he said:

> It exists under different shapes in all governments, more or less stifled, controlled, or repressed; but in those of the popular form it is seen in its greatest rankness, and is truly their worst enemy.

The alternate domination of one faction over another, sharpened by the spirit of revenge natural to party dissension, which in different ages and countries has perpetrated the most horrid enormities, is itself a frightful despotism. But this leads at length to a more formal and permanent despotism. The disorders and miseries which result, gradually incline the minds of men to seek security and repose in the absolute power of an individual; and, sooner or later, the chief of some prevailing faction, more able or more fortunate than his competitors, turns this disposition to the purpose of his own elevation on the seams of public liberty.

He declared it was not only the duty but to the interest of a wise people to discourage and to restrain the party spirit. Again he said:

And in governments of a monarchical cast, patriotism may look with indulgence, if not with favor, upon the spirit of party. But in those of the popular character, in governments purely elective, it is a spirit not to be encouraged. From their natural tendency, it is certain there will always be enough of that spirit for every salutary purpose. And there being constant danger of excess, the effort ought to be, by force of public opinion, to mitigate and assuage it. A fire not to be quenched, it demands a uniform vigilance to prevent it bursting into a flame, lest instead of warning, it should consume.

The direct primary does not seek the destruction of party, but it places its control directly in the bands of the voter. It lowers party responsibility, and to a certain extent takes away party government by placing country above party. If the primary had done nothing more than the one thing of substituting individual responsibility for party responsibility, thus doing away with party control, it would have given sufficient reason for its existence.

Another objection made to the direct primary is that it results in giving control over nominations to the newspapers. There is no doubt that the direct primary increases the influence and power of some newspapers. The newspaper that is true to its name, gives first of all, the news—unbiased, uncensored, and unprejudiced—and one whose editorial policy is open and fair will have its influence in political matters increased by the primary. This, however, is a good rather than a bad thing. The newspaper that publishes the truth and gives a true report of political news ought to have its power and its influence increased. The increase of influence on the part of such instrumentalities will tend toward a more intelligent selection of candidates, and therefore should be encouraged rather than condemned.

Another objection made to the direct primary is that it extends the campaign over an unnecessarily long time, and it is for that reason, and others, too expensive. It is probably true that in actual practice the direct primary extends the time of the campaign, although there is no limit of time that a candidate for office can spend in his campaign. He can put in all his time if he desires, whether he is campaigning for a nomination at a direct primary or for a nomination at the hands of a convention.

The advocates of the convention system claim that the convention is as representative of all the people as the direct primary. If this be true, then it will require as much time to secure a nomination at a convention as it would at a primary. If the convention is really representative of all the people, and carries out the wishes of the people, then the campaign in one case would be as long as in the other. The candidate, to get the nomination, would undertake to reach as many voters as possible, the difference being that in the case of the primary, when he had convinced the voter, he would have nothing further to do, while in the case of a convention nomination he would first convince the voter in order that the voter might select a favorable delegates and then put in a lot more time to see that the delegate carried out the wishes of those whom he represented. The result, therefore, so far as time is concerned, would be favorable to the direct primary. Of course, everybody knows this is not what actually occurs in the case of the convention system. The bosses who control conventions are the only ones necessary to secure the nomination. They manipulate the convention so as to bring about the desired result.

In actual practice it has been demonstrated that the direct primary is not expensive. The expenditure of enormous sums of money to secure the nomination deserves righteous condemnation, and there have been many glaring incidents where this condemnation has taken place. There is no doubt but that there are many cases both in the primary and under the convention system, and likewise at the election, where the expenditure of large sums of money has been instrumental, and in some cases the predominating influence, in securing nominations and elections. It is an evil that I do not believe can be entirely eliminated, but it is not confined to the primary. It applies equally to the convention and to the general election. The man with money has an advantage over the poor man. This is true in politics as it is in business. The remedy lies in the enactment of stringent corrupt practice acts. The law should limit the expenditure of money for the purpose of securing nominations either at a direct primary or at a convention. It should prohibit expressly the expenditure of money for some of the practices indulged in. It should provide for the most complete publicity of all expenditures. These publications should take place both before and after the election. The violation of any of these laws should make the nomination or the election absolutely void. Political advertisements should, in my judgment, be prohibited by law. Contributions to religious and charitable institutions should likewise be prohibited. Proper criminal penalties for violation of the law should be provided. It should perhaps be made the duty of some specific official to prosecute violations of this statute, not only against the successful candidate if he is properly charged, but in the same way against any other candidate at the direct primary, before the convention, or at the election. One of the difficulties with this kind of statute has been that prosecuting officials have not been called upon to act especially against the man who had been defeated, and it sometimes happens that the defeated candidate, being as guilty as the successful one, is so anxious to cover up his own violation of law that he is therefore not in very good condition to prosecute his opponent.

It might be a good precautionary measure to provide by law not only that reports shall be made but that candidates, officers of committees, and managers of campaigns should be required to submit themselves to cross-examination upon the filing of such reports, with a view of uncovering any violation of law that might have taken place. One of the difficulties in the enforcement of such laws at the present time is the party spirit and party responsibility. Where both parties are guilty, it is difficult to get anyone to father the responsibility for a prosecution. If party responsibility were eliminated, and party regularity not considered almost a divine attribute, many of these illegal acts would be brought to light that are otherwise concealed and covered up.

Complete publicity will go a long way toward relieving the evil. The intelligent citizen revolts at the expenditure of large sums of money for the purpose of controlling election, either direct primary or general, and the people themselves will do a great deal toward punishing those who are guilty of the offense. The expenditure of large sums of money in any honest campaign is not necessary, and the intelligent citizen knows this, and will condemn the man who indulges in it. From my personal acquaintance with public officials, I am satisfied that the direct primary has been instrumental in putting more poor men into office than the convention system. I have no doubt of the truth of this statement. I think the United States Senate is a demonstration of this proposition. There are a great many members of that body whom I could name, who would not be there if it were not for the direct primary, and most of them are poor. I have no doubt if the truth were really known, that candidates for office have spent more money under the convention system than under the direct primary. But that is not the only recommendation of the direct primary nor the only objection to the convention method. The public official who has to be nominated at a convention knows very well that in order to retain his place he must become a part if not the head of a political machine. He must keep this machine oiled all the time he is in office. He must obey the mandates of those above him in order to secure his share of patronage, and he must use this patronage to build up his machine. In other words, he trades public office for political support. It costs no small amount of both time and money to keep his machine oiled. He must either pay it himself or become obligated officially to someone who does. The result of it all is that the public gets the worst of the deal. Appointees are selected entirely upon their ability to control the politics of their communities, and not with regard to their qualifications for office. We have, therefore, poorer government at a greater expense. The public are paying the salaries of incompetent men who use their official positions to keep the machine in control. On the other hand, the public official who depends upon the direct primary for election is responsible to the rank and file of the people themselves. He can defy the machine and take the question directly to the people, and if he possesses the courage of his convictions, he will not do this in vain. This relieves him entirely during his occupancy of the office from the taking up of a large portion of his time in looking after his machine. He can devote his energies and his abilities entirely to the welfare of the country and to the performance of his official duties.

It might not be out of place in this connection to relate my own personal experience. I have been nominated several times for the House of Representatives and twice for the Senate. Both times when I was a candidate for the Senate I had very active and spirited opposition. My nominations cost me, as I remember it now, less than five hundred dollars on each of these occasions. I know that if I had undertaken to secure a nomination at the hands of a convention, I would have been defeated had I not spent many times this sum of money, and probably would have been defeated anyway. In neither of these campaigns, so far as I was able to see, was I handicapped on account of money. In looking back over it now, I do not see where I could have legitimately spent more than I did.

Another objection made to the direct primary is that it takes away the deliberation which the convention system affords, and that therefore the primary does not give the proper opportunity for an intelligent selection of candidates. This objection is not true. The convention does not afford any opportunity for deliberation. It is a place where trades are made and not where judicious selection of candidates is indulged in. In a state convention, for instance, where there are a large number of candidates to be nominated, a candidate having behind him the delegates of a county or a group of counties will throw these votes anywhere, to any candidate, for any office, except the one for which he is a candidate. The candidate who secures the nomination is the one whose manager has been the most successful in making these trades. This manager does not ask the delegates behind some candidate for some other office anything about the qualifications of their candidate. He wants to know how many votes he can get for his candidate if he will throw his delegation in favor of the candidate for some other office. No question is asked on either side as to qualifications. Political bosses are often instrumental in having candidates get into the field for some office, not because they want to nominate the candidate, but because they are anxious to fill a particular office with a particular man, and they therefore try their best to get as much trading stock in the field as possible. The convention usually does its work in one day. It would be an impossibility, even if delegates were seeking men with particular qualifications for particular offices, for them to ascertain the truth within the short time in which a decision must be made. A political convention is anything but a deliberative body.

There are always, of course, many delegates in all conventions moved by the highest of motives and doing their best to nominate good men for all the offices, but as a general rule they are in a small minority. The convention system has been condemned by an enlightened citizenship after a long and wearisome trial. This fact is so well known and understood by the people generally that its defense is almost a waste of words. The direct primary system, while by no means perfect, [provides] much more opportunity for intelligent selection. The citizen in his own home has weeks of time to inform himself upon the qualifications of the various candidates seeking the primary nomination. He does this deliberately. He has no opportunity to make a trade. He decides the question upon what to him seems to be the best evidence. As the citizen becomes used to the direct primary, he takes greater pains to inform himself. The direct primary tends to educate the people. They get together and discuss the qualifications of the various candidates at the meetings of different kinds of clubs and organizations. They do this in no partisan way, but in an honest effort to secure the best nominees. This means that the electorate is constantly improving itself, and while improving itself, is improving the government by selecting better candidates for office.

Another objection sometimes urged against the direct primary is that sometimes the nominee does not receive a majority of all of the votes. This is true. It is a defect that ought to be remedied, but those who urge this objection give it as one reason for abolishing the direct primary and going back to the convention system, and yet the same objection applies to the convention system. Who is able to say in any case that the nominee of a convention is a choice of the majority of the members of a party? There is no machinery in the convention that will disclose whether or not this is true. Why is it that those who are opposed to the primary will not be fair in their argument? If the direct primary should be abolished because the nominee is sometimes voted for by only a minority, then likewise, the convention should be abolished because there is no way of telling that the nominee is favored by a majority of the party. This objection applies both to the convention and to the direct primary. By what logic can it be urged therefore, that the primary should be abolished and the convention reestablished? As far as I am able to see there is no way of relieving this objection as far as it applies to the convention, but there is a way of at least reducing the probability of a minority nominee in the primary. If the primary law provided that the voter could express both a first and a second choice we would have gone a long way toward the elimination of this objection. If the law provided that in case no one received a majority of all the votes cast, that the second choice of the voters as to all candidates except the highest two should be counted, this would in most every case give the expression of a majority of the voters. In my judgment such a provision ought to be included in every primary law. Even without this provision this objection is no greater against the primary law than it is against the convention, but with it, it gives the primary a great advantage over the convention in this respect.

It is alleged that the direct primary has been abolished in several of the states after giving it a trial. The intention seems to be to convey to the public the idea that those who have given the direct primary a fair and honest trial, have reached the conclusion that it is not practical, that good results are not obtained therefrom, and that the people have voluntarily gone back to the convention on the theory that this system is after all superior to the direct primary. Those who offer this objection boastingly refer to New York, Idaho, South Dakota and Nebraska as instances where the direct primary has been discarded and the people have returned to the old convention system. Again our opponents are unfair, again they tell only half of the truth. [. . .] I know of no state that has given the direct primary a fair and honest test that does not consider it far superior to the old convention system. [. . .] While the people may not always be satisfied with a direct primary they are nevertheless much better pleased with it than with the convention system, and there is no danger after having once tried a fair primary that an intelligent people will take a step backward to the convention. The fight for the direct primary has always been a bitter one. Those who advocate it have at every step had to contest the way with political machines, and all of the power and resourcefulness of these machines has been used to defeat the direct primary. Where they have not been successful in defeating the law, they have sometimes succeeded in keeping in the law objectionable features, placed there often for the sole and only purpose of making the law objectionable.

It can be safely stated that the great majority of the American people are in favor of the direct primary, and that politicians, men seeking a selfish advantage, political machines, and combinations of special interests, constitute the vast majority of those who are opposed to it. It has some objectionable features, but upon examination it is found that practically every one of these applies with equal force to the convention. Many of these objections can be entirely eliminated as far as the direct primary is concerned, and practically all of them can be partially eliminated. The direct primary relieves the party and party machinery of a great deal of its responsibility, and places this responsibility upon the individual voter. The intelligent American citizen assumes this responsibility with a firm determination of performing his full duty by informing himself upon all the questions pertaining to government. It therefore results in a more intelligent electorate, and as this intelligence increases, it results in better government. Experience will bring about improvement as the necessity is shown to exist by practice. It will not bring the millennium and it will not cure all of the defects of government, but it will relieve many of the admitted evils and act as a great school of education for the common citizen. The artificial enthusiasm created by the convention system which makes it easy to deceive the people will give way to the enlightened judgment of reason that will pervade the firesides and homes of a thinking, patriotic people. A citizenship that is sufficiently intelligent to vote at a general election will never surrender to others the right to name the candidates at that election.

CHAPTER 12

What the Political Parties Are Not

E. E. Schattschneider

Whatever else the parties may be, they are not associations of the voters who support the party candidates. That is to say, the Democratic party is not an association of the 27 million people who voted for Mr. Roosevelt in November 1940. To describe the party as if it were this sort of association of voters is to produce confusion, and, moreover, to be victimized by a promotional device so old that it should deceive no one. The concept of the parties as a mass association of partisans has no historical basis and has little relation to the facts of party organization. It is only necessary to examine the platforms of the parties, however, to see how persistently the parties have tried to identify themselves with all voters who may have supported their candidates. [...]

The mental image behind these declarations is that of a huge association of partisan voters. The Republican party professes to be an association of all Republicans, i.e., of all partisans who vote for Republican candidates. It follows that these partisans are "members" of the Republican party. The parties have drawn this portrait of themselves so successfully that assumptions concerning the nature of the parties, wholly unjustified by the facts, have gained general

From *Party Government* (New York: Holt, Rinehart and Winston, 1942), 53–64, with the permission of Wadsworth, an imprint of the Wadsworth Group, a division of Thompson Learning. E. E. Schattschneider (1892–1971) taught political science at Wesleyan University; chaired the committee of political scientists that produced the 1950 report, *Toward a More Responsible Two-Party System;* and was president of the American Political Science Association in 1956–1957. His best-known book is *The Semi-Sovereign People* (New York: Holt, Rinehart, and Winston, 1960).

acceptance. One of the incidental consequences of the common notion that the parties are associations of large masses of partisans is that the states have enacted a large body of legislation regulating the internal processes of the parties in the interests of their "members." This is the surprising aftermath of something that seems to have been originally a mere promotional stunt invented by the party managers to emphasize the devotion of the parties to their followers.

It is, however, one thing to be a partisan and another thing to be a member of an association. Let us suppose that the owner of a professional baseball club issued a membership certificate with each ticket sold and that these certificates entitled each "member" of an imaginary association of patrons to buy tickets to all future games and to cheer lustily for the home team. How would the purely promotional "association" so created differ from the Republican and Democratic parties, conceived of as associations of partisans? The concept of membership has doubtless enabled parties to identify themselves with partisan voters more closely than they might have otherwise, but it has also evoked mental images of parties that are definitely misleading.

As a matter of fact, membership in a political party has none of the usual characteristics of membership in an association. In most states the party has no control over its membership. Any legal voter may on his own initiative and by his own declaration execute legal formalities before a duly designated public official making himself a registered member of the party. The party as such is not consulted. It does not accept the application; it does not vote the applicant into the association; it may not reject the application; and, finally, there is usually no recognized and authoritative procedure by which the party may expel a member.

Moreover, the member assumes no obligations to the party. He takes no oath prescribed by the party. He does not subscribe to a declaration of party principles and does not sign articles of incorporation. He does not pay membership dues, is not liable for the debts of the party, and has no equity in its property. He has no duties whatever to perform as a condition of membership. He is not required to solicit votes, is not required to participate in the campaign, need not attend party rallies, and need not vote for the party candidates. In fact, he need not vote at all. If he wishes to leave the party he does not resign. He does not even notify the party. He merely goes to the proper public authorities to register with another party. Membership in a political party is therefore highly unreal because the party has no control over its own membership and the member has no obligations to the party.

What the partisan has acquired as a consequence of the attempt of the parties to identify themselves with him is a highly declamatory set of "rights." In the spirit of pure unbounded extravagance, party managers have repeatedly "given" the party to the voters. The figure of speech by which the party managers have acted in the name of all past, present, and potential partisans should have been completely transparent. As a matter of fact the ordinary partisan has not known what to do with the gift; he has rarely exhibited a strong desire to run the party, any more than the ordinary baseball fan really wants to manage the club. It is a tribute to the histrionic talents of politicians that some people have taken their pronouncements seriously enough to write the whole concept into law and to try to do something about it.

Direct primary legislation is based on the mental image of the party as an association of which the partisans are members. The purpose of the legislation is to use the authority of the state to protect the right of the members to control the party, much as a statute might direct a merchant to please his customers. The member has therefore acquired the interesting status of belonging to an association in which he has nothing but rights.

Legislation designed to democratize the internal processes of the parties (based on the opinion that all partisans are "members" of a vast party association) has taken the form of statutory abolition of the convention system and the substitution therefor of another system. For that reason it is worth recalling that the convention system was itself established in the name of a movement to democratize the parties, to popularize control of the parties after the destruction of the undemocratic "King Caucus." There is, however, no satisfactory evidence that the direct primary has in fact produced a change in the character of the party system or that the internal processes of the party have in fact been democratized. In the opinion of one expert: "It appears that by of laws providing for the election of party officers we have given political bosses and their lieutenants a monopoly of the party and have provided them with a system which effectively shuts out opposition."[1] Are we now going to see a third attempt to "democratize" the internal processes of the parties by some new means designed to give control to the rank and file of the "members"?

It is not here contended that attempts to democratize the parties have done much harm. The whole episode has been innocent enough, but it has produced much confusion.[2] If the parties are thought of as vast associations of partisans, it follows that their internal processes must be described as oligarchic because the great mass of partisans most certainly do not control them. Thus we arrive at the "iron law of oligarchy" formulated by Robert Michels, who, however, wrote primarily about the parties in European multiparty systems. The party is divided into two entities: (1) an organized group of insiders who have effective control of the party, and (2) a mass of passive "members" who seem to have very little to say about it. It is manifestly impossible for 27 million Democrats to control the Democratic party. Neither the will nor the machinery, in spite of the direct primaries and the conventions, exists for this sort of democratization of the parties. No one has ever attempted to find out what a democratization of the parties in this sense would entail. There is no basis in reality for it, and the idea that a few party primaries might enable the rank and file of party membership to control the inner processes of the parties is fantastic. Will it be necessary to develop parties within the parties in order to simplify and define the alternatives for the members? Finally, no one has ever attempted to find out whether democratization, if it were possible, would be appropriate to the legitimate functions of the parties in a modern political system.

The unfortunate result of the confusion created by the concept of the party as a large association of partisans is that it blackens the name of the parties. The parties are the most important instrumentalities of democratic government. To call them oligarchies and thus to identify them with undemocratic tendencies is unfortunate. If it is true that the democratization of the parties is impossible, what is to be gained by insisting on it? Are we any better off than we would have been if we had decided long ago that the internal processes of the parties are the private affair of the managers? The relations of the party and the partisan are not oppressive. The hospitality of the parties has been practically unlimited; no one is forced to join a party and, if anyone does join, he assumes no obligations. In what sense is a partisan injured if he is deprived of the right to control an organization toward which he has no duties? The whole theory is chaotic.

A more realistic theory, closer to the facts, can relieve us of the nightmarish necessity of doing the impossible. Let us suppose that the concept of the party membership of the partisans is abandoned altogether. If the party is described as a political enterprise conducted by a group of working politicians *supported* by partisan voters who approve of the party but are merely partisans (not members of a fictitious association), the parties would seem less wicked. After all, we support many organizations without belonging to them and without asserting a right to control them. The partisans of a professional baseball team do not feel a sense of deprivation because they are not owners of the ball club. A person may speak of "his" doctor or "his" college without implying possession. Loyalty need not express itself in the form of a proprietary relationship. Whether or not a great injustice has been done to the partisans by the fact that they do not control the parties depends merely on how the parties are defined. If we abandon the concept of party membership and substitute a concept such as that of the "good will" relation of a merchant and his customers, much of the sense of immorality and deprivation associated with the member's lack of authority in the party will vanish. The partisan voter will lose merely imaginary rights but will also be relieved of merely imaginary injustices, if the nature of the parties as private associations is better understood.

Will the parties be less responsive to the needs of the voters if their private character is generally recognized? Probably not. The parties do not need laws to make them sensitive to the wishes of the voters any more than we need laws compelling merchants to please their customers. The sovereignty of the voter consists in his freedom of choice just as the sovereignty of the consumer in the economic system consists in his freedom to trade in a competitive market. That is enough; little can be added to it by inventing an imaginary membership in a fictitious party association. Democracy is not to be found in the parties but *between* the parties.

Once it is seen that the party as an association of all partisans is a mere fiction, a whole series of myths about the parties will be exploded. It is not true, for instance, that the party managers perform miracles of contrivance in keeping control of the parties by managing an obstreperous membership. The eager party member who must be managed by the political bosses is largely a figment of the imagination. Long disquisitions designed to illustrate the intricate processes by which the party bosses maintain their control of party against what is supposed to be the will of the rank and file of the members become irrelevant once it is realized that party membership is unreal. Equally doleful accounts of the indifference of party members toward their supposed party obligations are less exciting if the concept of party membership is simply dropped. The truth of the matter is that the partisan has nearly always been merely partisan, and that is about all. The more intensely partisan he has been, the less interested has he been in internecine warfare; his interest has been in party unity for the purpose of defeating the opposition party.

Would it not be to our advantage to abandon the whole concept of party membership, the mental image of the party an association of all partisans, and to recognize frankly that the party is the property of the "organization"? The voter might view the loss of his purely theoretical rights of ownership with equanimity because he would retain the privilege of being courted by *both* parties. [...]

The bid for power through elections [...] makes the nomination the most important activity of the party. In an election the *united front* of the party is expressed in terms of a nomination. For this reason nominations have become the distinguishing mark of modern political parties; if a party cannot make nominations it ceases to be a party.

What is a nomination? A nomination is the designation, by some process or other, of a candidate who is accepted as *the* candidate by the party, i.e., the designation is considered legitimate and binding by the whole party and results in the effective mobilization of the voting strength of the party. Whether or not a nomination is a real nomination depends on whether or not it is binding, whether it effectively commits the whole party to support it. If it is binding, if all other candidates within the party (for the office in question) are denied party support, and if the party is able to concentrate its strength behind the designated candidate, a nomination has been made *regardless of the process by which it is made*. The nomination may be made by a congressional caucus, a delegate convention, a mass meeting, a cabal, an individual, or a party election. The test is, does it bind? Not, how was it done? Unless the party makes authoritative and effective nominations, it cannot stay in business, for dual or multiple party candidacies mean certain defeat. As far as elections are concerned, the united front of the party, the party concentration of numbers, can be brought about only by a binding nomination. The nominating process thus has become the crucial process of the party. The nature of the nominating procedure determines the nature of the party; he who can make the nominations is the owner of the party.

This is therefore one of the best points at which to observe the distribution of power within the party.

CHAPTER 13

Party Reform: Revisionism Revised

Kenneth A. Bode and Carol F. Casey

The aftermath of the 1968 Democratic national convention ushered in a decade of party reform that has been the subject of controversy since its inception. What critics fail to note, however, is that this contemporary reform movement grew out of a long tradition of American politics.

Since our founding fathers first promised government "which derives all its powers directly or indirectly from the great body of the people,"[1] the American political system has undergone a number of changes instituted by those who wished to add meaning to that phrase. Some of these were the results of gradual change, such as the evolution of Madison's factions into the formal mechanisms we know as political parties. Others were specific reforms designed to cure perceived abuses. Among these:

• Presidential nominations passed from the hands of congressional caucuses to national party nominating conventions.

• American blacks were guaranteed the constitutional right to vote after a bitter civil war and were assured the right to exercise that vote only after hundred years of civil rights struggle.

From *Political Parties in the Eighties*, ed. Robert A. Goldwin (Washington, D.C.: AEI Press, 1980), 3–19, with permission of the American Enterprise Institute for Public Policy Research, Washington, D.C. This essay has been reformatted. Bode, an award-winning journalist and former dean of the Medill School of Journalism at Northwestern University, is now the Pulliam Distinguished Professor of Journalism at DePauw University. At one point, Carol F. Casey worked at the Democratic National Committee.

• Women obtained suffrage early in this century and are still seeking to have their full rights recognized through a constitutional amendment.

• The election of U.S. senators became the direct responsibility of the voters, not the state legislators.

• The poll tax was banned as a prerequisite for voting.

• The direct primary was instituted in many states as a means of taking the nomination of elected officials from the party bosses and giving the responsibility directly to the voters.

• Apportionment for representative bodies was based on the principle of one man, one vote.

• The voting age was lowered from twenty-one to eighteen years of age for all federal elections.

• Most recently, campaign finance laws have been rewritten ostensibly to ensure against the abuses uncovered during the Watergate scandals.

In each instance, somebody gains power and somebody loses. In all cases, the justification for reform is some variation on two themes: broadening the base of political participation and holding public officials more directly accountable to the electorate. Party reform was no exception.

If there can be said to have been a single, dominant theory behind the party reform movement of the last decade, it would be this: In a country in which two—and only two—political parties can elect a president, it is important that the nomination processes in both parties afford the possibility of a genuine test of the leadership and stewardship of candidates, even of an incumbent president. If such a test is precluded at the nominating stage, then the general election choice may be hollow for many participants.

The Democratic experience of 1968 clearly showed under circumstances of great stress that there was little accountability in the presidential nominating process. Party adherents who disagreed with their incumbent president on matters of major public policy had two very limited alternatives available to them: They could form a third party, or they could seek to influence the presidential nomination within their own party.

The first option was hardly viable. For more than a century, it has been evident that third-party movements have little chance to win the presidency. The American electoral system has increasingly institutionalized the two major parties as the only vehicles for obtaining office. In most states, the Democratic and Republican nominees—or the presidential electors designated on their behalf—are automatically and directly certified for ballot position in the November election. New and minor party candidates must mount a state-by-state effort to have their names placed on the ballot, a time- and money-consuming process usually involving the gathering of petition signatures under stringent procedural requirements within an extremely limited period of time. Although new and minor parties have won some gains in access to the ballot because of recent court cases growing out of George Wallace's 1968 presidential candidacy and Eugene McCarthy's 1976 presidential bid, those gains have been more than offset by public financing of presidential campaigns. Now, the Democratic and Republican presidential nominees are automatically given $20 million—adjusted for inflation—to mount their general election campaigns. In the nominating race, they benefit from the matching fund program, which doubles the value of every individual contribution of $250 or less. New and minor party candidates generally cannot reap these benefits, and if they can at all, it is only after the election is over.

In addition to the institutionalized bias in favor of the two-party system, the other obstacle to third-party success is the traditional pattern of voting behavior. Despite the growing number of Americans who claim to be "independents," the vast majority of these voters will cast their ballots for the major-party nominees. That was true when Maurice Duverger conducted his voting studies, and that remains the case today.

In 1968, the overriding issue for many Democrats was the Vietnam war. But those who sought to oppose President Johnson on this issue were often frustrated by structural barriers and procedural irregularities. Dissident Democrats, inspired almost entirely by opposition to the administration's Vietnam policies, were able to force Johnson's withdrawal. But because of Johnson's heavy hand on Humphrey's shoulder, along with the procedural chicanery the dissidents endured state-by-state during the caucuses and primaries, many of the 1968 insurgents were not attracted back into the party fold. The result was a Nixon victory and a serious examination of the party's nominating processes, which might not have otherwise occurred.

The earliest critics of party reform tended to judge the rules that came out of the successive Democratic party commissions only in terms of their ultimate result—the success of the party's presidential nominee in the general election—rather than viewing them in the broader context of the American political tradition. For the most part, the original eighteen guidelines adopted by the McGovern-Fraser Commission merely extended the concepts of fairness and equal protection to the presidential nominating process. These guidelines were developed in response to very real and serious flaws exposed in the tumultuous political arena of 1968. Without Vietnam, which divided the party so bitterly and stimulated previously inactive party members to attempt to express their opinions through the presidential nominating process, the party's internal decision-making processes probably would not have been subjected to such a close scrutiny. The year 1968 was not the first time that the party establishment had passed over the candidate with the best record in preferential primaries, in favor of a candidate of its own choosing. But in 1968, many who differed with the party establishment on issues and presidential candidate preferences found themselves deprived of an effective voice by a myriad of state laws and party traditions that worked against an election year challenge to an incumbent president.

Although the party reform rules are still hotly debated, mostly in academic circles, there is little attention to what the McCarthy and Kennedy supporters faced in 1968. The lessons they learned then bear repeating here.

In ten states, there simply were no rules: nothing whatsoever to regulate delegate selection procedures; to notify voters how, when, and where to participate in the presidential nominating process; and, most importantly, nothing to prevent party leaders from adjusting procedures when they found themselves under challenge. In at least ten additional states, rules existed but were inaccessible or grossly inadequate. In Rhode Island, for example, there were party rules, but it took a two-month search by the McGovern Commission (aided by U.S. Senator Claiborne Pell) to ferret out the single existing mimeographed copy from the files of a retired state chairman. Even where rules were readily available, important elements of the process were left to the discretion of local or state party officials. In Virginia, for example, mass meetings—the equivalent of precinct caucuses—constituted the first step of the process, and the only step generally open to rank-and-file Democratic participation. In 1968, the rules said that these were to be held sometime in April at a time and place determined by city and county committees and that notice was to be given in local newspapers. Seeking to turn out their supporters to these meetings, McCarthy organizers found that the typical notice was a small announcement in the legal section of the newspapers. Not infrequently, the mass meetings were convened on party-sponsored buses on the way to the state convention. Virginia party officials subsequently admitted that the most influential party reforms in their state were the requirements that meetings be held at uniform times and places and that adequate notice be given.

Missouri was one of the states with no rules at all. It also proved to be one of the most controversial battlegrounds in 1968 and provided a neatly contained laboratory for the McGovern Commission's analysis of the kinds of changes that might prevent a recurrence of the highhandedness and resulting divisiveness of that year. The only clues to the Missouri delegate selection puzzle were provided by the "Call to the State Convention," which left the dates, times, and places of ward and township conventions to each county chairman. The call was issued on April 15, 1968, and instructed each county to complete the first stage of the delegate selection process on or before May 3. As of April 30, according to the *St. Louis Post Dispatch*, seven of the eighteen townships in St. Louis County had made no arrangements for meetings, and, by the morning of May 3, the committeemen in four townships still refused to disclose to the newspaper the times or locations of the meetings they presumably intended to hold that day. In Concord Township, McCarthy organizers discovered the time and place of the meeting forty minutes before its scheduled beginning; by the time they arrived, the township convention was conducting its business.

At one township caucus, McCarthy supporters found themselves in a majority at the meeting, on the verge of electing some delegates. Suddenly, the party official chairing the caucus unpocketed 492 proxy votes—three times the total number of people in attendance—and cast them as a unit for his own slate.

At the other end of the state in Kansas City, a carefully selected list of party regulars (in many cases not the elected ward committeemen) received notices from Jackson County Chairman Frank Hughes instructing them to hold ward conventions at 8:00 p.m. on May 1, at places unspecified. Hughes published no notice of the time or place of these meetings nor of the persons he had designated as chairmen. On the night of April 29, he finally divulged his list of chairmen to McCarthy organizers, who then had to track down the chairmen on their own, to find out where the meetings would be held.

Where rules are vague, arbitrary fiddling with them is easy. This truth was not something new in 1968, of course. Four years before, Indiana's governor, a favorite-son stand-in for LBJ, lost one congressional district to Alabama's George Wallace. Embarrassed and chagrined, Indiana party leaders simply changed the party rules retroactively to provide that all delegates would be apportioned at large, thereby stripping Wallace of the convention delegates he had legitimately won.

Similarly, in 1968, rules were changed here and there. For example, in Comanche County, Oklahoma (home of Senator Fred Harris, then Humphrey's national cochairman and later chairman of the Democratic National Committee), the rules were changed at the last moment. Only delegates selected at earlier precinct meetings could vote legally at the county conventions, but at the Comanche County convention, State Senator James Taliaferro moved that these rules be suspended and all registered Democrats at the meeting be permitted to vote. Packed in preparation for that motion, the meeting quickly changed its own rules, and, by so doing, rendered the results of the precinct meetings meaningless.

Proxy voting, as we have seen in the case of Missouri, was a device frequently used to disfranchise Democrats who had the perseverance to attend their precinct meetings. In Hawaii, proxies that provided the margin of victory at the state convention were later discovered to have come from an urban redevelopment area in Honolulu, precincts consisting largely of vacant lots.

In many other convention states, the use of the winner-take-all system ensured that successive majorities at each level of the process stifled discussion, dissent, and the representation of divergent points of view. In Iowa, Senator Eugene McCarthy received about 40 percent of the vote at the precinct caucus level. By the time the national convention delegates were chosen in June, that proportion had dwindled to around 8 percent.[2] Those in the majority at county and district conventions could—and did—elect all the delegates to the next level of the process. The ultimate result was that the presidential preferences of a substantial minority of voters were underrepresented or unrepresented at the national convention.

The late professor Alexander Bickel served as a consultant to the McGovern Commission and profoundly shaped some of its conclusions. Looking at the question of representation of minority views in the process by which delegates are selected, Bickel concluded:

> If at such preliminary stages in the delegate selection process successive majorities are allowed to prevail and to represent only themselves, and if the representation of minorities is not carried forward to the national convention, then it is quite possible, it is in some circumstances likely, that the final majority of delegates which prevails at the convention will represent a minority, and not a majority, of the Democratic voters in the country at large.[3]

Even where the minority was permitted to elect some delegates to the convention at the next level, the imposition of the unit rule often prevented the expression of divergent points of view: a vote of the majority of the delegates at precinct and county conventions would bind all delegates—regardless of their presidential commitment—to vote for the candidate preferred by the majority. In Texas—the most notorious but by no means the only offender—the unit rule was applied in 224 of 254 county caucuses. In 1968, the unit rule was applied at Democratic party meetings in fifteen states using the caucus-convention system, including, besides Texas, Connecticut, Alaska, North Carolina, Tennessee, North Dakota, and several others.

Two primary states—Massachusetts and Oregon—had arrangements which permitted a unit-rule effect: delegates pledged to or favoring one candidate could be elected in a delegate primary and simultaneously be bound in a presidential preference primary to vote for an opposing candidate. In Oregon, Congresswoman Edith Green was cochairman of the Kennedy campaign and sought election as a delegate. She won, but Senator Eugene McCarthy carried the presidential preference poll, so Green was bound to vote for McCarthy at the national convention.

Other problems came to light in states with primaries in 1968. Fair representation of minority views was questionable in states that had winner-take-all primaries by statute (California, Oregon, South Dakota, Massachusetts, and Indiana), as well as those that were structured to have a district-by-district winner-take-all effect (Ohio, New Jersey, and Illinois).

In West Virginia, Illinois, Pennsylvania, Florida, New Jersey, and New York, primary laws permitted delegates to run with no notice to voters of their presidential preferences. How does a voter make an informed choice in a delegate primary, without knowing the candidates' stands on the central question before the convention? In New York, for local political reasons, the state law *precluded* candidates for delegate from listing a presidential preference. In other places, it was optional to list a preference, but official party slates traditionally ran uncommitted. In all these instances, the effect was essentially the same: Voters were required to cast a blind ballot.

In a number of other primary states—partially because of the divorce between popular presidential preference and selection of delegates with the blind ballot—the popular vote for a presidential candidate would have no bearing on the number of delegates won. In Pennsylvania, for example, Senator McCarthy won 78.5 percent of the preference vote, but only twenty-four of 130 delegates. The fifty-two at-large delegates had been elected three months before the primary by the state committee, well before any primaries or caucuses had been held anywhere in the country. And in the delegate primary, no presidential preference was listed by candidates. The result was a bitter party split and a credentials challenge on the charge that the delegation did not accurately reflect Democratic opinion in the state.

Democrats in other states faced even more serious barriers to participation. In Arizona, Arkansas, Georgia, Louisiana, Maryland, and Rhode Island, party members had no opportunity to participate in choosing their national convention delegates in the same year as the convention. In Georgia, the entire national convention delegation was chosen by the state party chairman, in consultation with the Democratic governor. In Louisiana, the governor made the choice, with the pro forma approval of the Democratic State Central Committee. In Arizona, Arkansas, Maryland, and Rhode Island, the national convention delegation was selected by party committees. Those committees, in turn, had been chosen in 1964 or 1966, thus denying the party's rank-and-file any voice in determining the 1968 presidential nominee. In fact, the McGovern-Fraser Commission found that, when Senator McCarthy announced his candidacy, nearly one-third of the delegates to the 1968 Democratic National Convention had, in effect, already been selected. By the time Lyndon Johnson announced his decision to withdraw from the presidential race, the delegate selection process had begun in all but twelve states.

The point of these observations is not that the McCarthy-Kennedy faction was discriminated against procedurally, nor that the deck was stacked against them—though in many instances they deeply believed that to be the case. The point instead is that, until 1968, one of the prime axioms of American politics was that a sitting president eligible for reelection could not be denied the nomination. The events of 1968 revealed some of the reasons this was so—reasons of rules and procedure extending beyond the vast patronage resources of the White House.

As the great battle for the nomination was being waged, another effort was being organized quietly. Challenges demanding some form of proportional representation were organized in Connecticut and Pennsylvania. A unit-rule challenge grew out of Texas. An apportionment challenge came from Minnesota. Objections were raised in Georgia to a racially imbalanced delegation hand-picked by the governor, and in Washington to delegates serving ex officio. Charges of racial discrimination or imbalance (or both) came from Mississippi, Georgia, and North Carolina. A loyalty oath challenge arose in Alabama. Virtually every question raised in the subsequent deliberations of the McGovern Commission was anticipated in the credentials and rules challenges of 1968.

The rules battles of 1968 were initially conceived as a means of winning more delegates for Senator Eugene McCarthy at the convention in Chicago. But what began as a partisan scrap evolved into a lengthy, serious, often acrimonious analysis of the presidential nominating process by party commissions, academic committees, state legislatures, and Congress. An ad hoc party committee of Democrats including Alexander Bickel, Senator Harold Hughes, and Congressman Donald Fraser examined the complaints and abuses of 1968, made recommendations to the convention, and concluded that "state systems for selecting delegates to the National Convention display considerably less fidelity to basic democratic principles than a nation which claims to govern itself can safely tolerate."[4]

Viewed within the context of the time, the eighteen guidelines adopted by the McGovern-Fraser Commission were a moderate response to very real problems within the Democratic party's nominating process. Generally, they sought to apply the routine standards of fairness, due process, and equal protection enjoyed by voters in general elections to the internal decision-making processes of the party. Over time, the reforms have been adopted, codified, and implemented. They have also attracted a not inconsiderable body of critics, many of whom do not know or remember the genuine procedural abuses and abridgement of the democratic process that characterized the party of Lyndon Johnson in 1968. Like every other political reform in this century, party reform involved a certain redistribution of power. It became an extension of the partisan split of 1968 and prolonged the divisiveness of that year. Among those who were "distributed" out of power, those who argued backwards from outcomes they did not like, and those whose political theories were offended, certain myths about party reform have become conventional wisdom.

Myth No. 1: The reforms were devised by Senator McGovern for his own benefit and for that of the liberal-activist wing of the Democratic party.

A look at the composition of the commission is enough to defuse this myth. Senator McGovern was chosen to chair the commission by Senator Humphrey, who viewed Senator Harold Hughes of Iowa as too liberal and too closely identified with the McCarthy-Kennedy forces. Humphrey directed Senator Fred Harris, then National Democratic Chairman, to appoint Mc-Govern. All appointments to the commission were made by Harris, a Humphrey backer, whose presidential ambitions were then tied to the Humphrey wing of the party. Commission members included three U.S. senators, one U.S. representative, four persons who were serving or had served as state party chairmen or vice-chairmen, one governor, one former governor, three current or past members of the Democratic National Committee, one state senator, one state treasurer, three labor union leaders, and two professors of political science. Overall, the majority of commission members were party regulars; most had supported Humphrey's 1968 presidential candidacy. As for McGovern, he knew no more about the presidential nominating process in fifty different states than did any other U.S. senator and proved to be an independent though somewhat tentative chairman, committed to democracy and fairness in party procedures, but dispositionally prone to compromise if the other side really dug in its heels.

It is conventional wisdom in some quarters that McGovern rigged the rules to his own benefit—some commentators even conjure a more elaborate scenario wherein the ouster of Mayor Daley from the 1972 convention was contrived years in advance—but they offer only their own phantoms for evidence. McGovern won the nomination not because the reforms gave him an edge but because in a span of less than a month he won primaries in New York, South Dakota, Oregon, California, Rhode Island, and New Jersey—all essentially unreformed, winner-take-all primaries conducted under the same rules as in 1968—and won thereby nearly half the votes he carried with him into the convention.

Myth No. 2: The membership of the commission is irrelevant: The important decisions were made by the commission staff—a staff dominated by young Mc-Carthy-Kennedy political activists who had little regard for the Democratic party as an institution.

Consider for a moment what that says about senators like Birch Bayh, Harold Hughes, and George McGovern, about Governor Calvin Rampton of Utah and former Governor LeRoy Collins of Florida, or about politicians as good as Louis Martin, Warren Christopher, Will Davis, Fred Dutton, and George Mitchell, not to mention Adlai Stevenson of Illinois, and about professors as astute as Sam Beer of Harvard and Austin Ranney of Wisconsin. This group was led around by a couple of thirty-year-old political activists and a band of college interns? Although the staff and consultants did formulate the first draft of the guidelines based upon the information collected from seventeen regional hearings and additional research into each state's 1968 delegate selection system, few of the original guidelines remained intact after the commission had finished its deliberations. The staff proposals were debated at the commission's September 1969 meeting. Then the commission's revised guidelines were circulated to more than 3,000 Democrats, drawn from every list then available, for their comments before the final decisions were made in November 1969—after an additional two days of deliberation.

In the main, the commission had a pragmatic bent and a penchant for fairness. Confronted with a mountain of evidence that revealed flaws in the democratic process, they absorbed an overwhelming amount of detail in a short time about the ways fifty-four jurisdictions chose and mandated delegates. They fashioned practical, straightforward remedies.

The commission's most controversial guidelines were those requiring state parties to encourage the representation of women, blacks, and young people on the national convention delegation in reasonable relationship to their presence in the population—otherwise known as the quota system. These were purely the product of the commission itself. The staff draft contained no such guarantees, merely requiring affirmative steps to overcome the effects of past discrimination. The "quota" language grew out of a motion by Professor Austin Ranney, as expanded by Senator Birch Bayh, and adopted by the full commission.

Myth No. 3: The guidelines eliminated party leaders from the national convention delegations, thereby depriving the convention of their judgment and experience.

There is some truth to this charge: The commission did prohibit party committees or party leaders elected before the year of the national presidential nominating convention from selecting delegates, and it did limit selection of delegates by any party committee to not more than 10 percent of the national convention delegation. However, the ban on national convention delegates being chosen by officials elected in an "untimely" fashion was merely a direct method of implementing the 1968 national convention's mandate; that mandate did not leave much leeway for interpretation. The 1968 convention said that delegates to the next convention had to be selected through "party primary, convention, or committee procedures open to public participation within the calendar year of the National Convention."

Those who argue that the new rules produced a lower-than-usual ratio of party and public officials in convention delegations tend to forget that politicians may have political reasons for avoiding party conventions. The list of those who did not show up at the 1968 convention contains many Democratic luminaries, including nearly all southern House Democrats who wanted to avoid any association with the national ticket. The list was long in 1972, too, in part because big-name Democrats in 1972 made an early swarm to the candidacy of Edmund Muskie. Not only were the big handicappers wrong, but so were the thousands of middle-level party regulars who went along with them and found themselves sidelined for the convention. In other words, the party's establishment was not at Miami Beach because they had backed the wrong horse.

Even so, data from the 1972 CBS convention survey indicates that the notion of the party convention without party leaders is largely the creation of the propagandists. Exactly one quarter of the delegates had held public office at one time or another, 38 percent had held party office, and 50 percent had been party officials at some time in their lives. Again, as evidence that the rules were not the problem, those same rules produced plenty of party leaders at the convention that nominated Governor Jimmy Carter in 1976.

The ignominy visited upon party leaders by the McGovern Commission guidelines was not that they were barred from participation, only that they were required to compete under the same rules as anyone else.

Myth No. 4: Reforms turned the nominating process over to activist elites whose views are unrepresentative of the total electorate, especially in states without primaries.

One of the fundamental objectives of the guidelines was to open the nominating process to broader participation. Particularly in convention states, the reformers were successful. Participation has jumped in every presidential nominating year so that caucus turnout now nearly rivals the average primary vote. Early results from the 1980 contest showed this trend: the Iowa Democratic precinct caucuses attracted nearly three times as many voters as they had in 1976. In Maine, turnout at the 1980 town caucuses was seven times as great as it was in 1976. Turnout has increased because Democrats have become more familiar with caucus procedures and because state Democratic parties have fulfilled their obligations of having published party rules, setting uniform times and dates for the first stage of the delegate selection process, and giving publicity to those events.

Critics, of course, contend that caucus participants are elites who do not represent the broader base of the Democratic party. Studies have shown, however, that those who attend caucuses are no more "elite" than those who vote in primaries. In both cases, persons with higher income and greater education are more likely to turn out. The same, in fact, is true in general elections. The reform rules are not to blame for the fact that participants in the presidential nominating process do not mirror the socioeconomic characteristics of the electorate as a whole. That is and has been true in every election held in the United States. The reform rules were designed merely to remove barriers to participation and give everyone equal access, not to guarantee advantages to any segment of the Democratic electorate.

Oddly enough, many of the persons who cry "elitism" also denigrate the party's affirmative action requirements as a quota system. The purpose of the outreach efforts imposed on state parties is to bring those groups that traditionally have low rates of political participation—blacks, Hispanics, and youth—into the active party ranks. Affirmative action (if it works) can only make the nominating process less elite.

What alternative do the "anti-elitists" offer? Basically, they suggest replacing one elite with another. Rather than permitting too much rank-and-file influence, they propose that elected Democratic party and public officials do a larger measure of the choosing. The professional functionaries of a party, notes Professor Bickel, maintain its continuity and play a role in its identity. Bickel goes on:

> The party's professional cadres should, no doubt, have a voice. The professionals are, if nothing else, a faction that deserves representation. Surely it is also sound institutional policy to reward their services with a measure of influence. Their greatest interest is the party's own institutional interest in winning—at least it is vouchsafed to them to see that interest over the long term. But if they lend the party its character of an "organized appetite" as Felix Frankfurter once wrote, their appetite is sometimes keener for power in the organization than for organizing to secure the power of government.[5]

It is also said the party professionals make well-informed and sophisticated judgments, tending to choose the abler rather than the more popular or glamorous candidate. When party leaders substitute their judgment for the popular view registered in primaries, however, they do not always produce

winners. Stevenson was the leaders' choice over Kefauver, the primaries'
choice, in 1952, as was Humphrey in 1968. Both lost.

Myth No. 5: Reforms spawned primaries.

Some even argue more specifically that "the controversial rules changes
that required a state's delegation to include minorities, young people, and
women in proportion to their respective numbers in the state led directly to
this proliferation of primaries. State party leaders fearing challenges to the
makeup of their delegations, opted for primaries whose results conventions
have traditionally been reluctant to upset."[6]

It is true that after the guidelines were adopted, many states enacted presidential primary laws. It is simplistic and inaccurate, however, to say that primaries were adopted *because* of the guidelines. Historically, the result of
public dissatisfaction with acrimonious, divisive nominating contests has
been the adoption of new primaries. Like it or not, primaries draw a favorable response from the general public. After the bitter Taft-Roosevelt battle in
1912, fourteen states instituted presidential primaries, bringing the total to
twenty-six—a record that was not matched until 1976. After the Stevenson-
Kefauver contest in 1952, states once again looked toward presidential primaries as a means of giving greater public legitimacy to the selection of
delegates. Thus, the adoption of new primaries after 1968 is in keeping with
the flux of American political history. By the time the McGovern Commission met for its first deliberative session in 1969, new presidential primaries
had been introduced in nine state legislatures. Before the guidelines had been
adopted, the number grew to thirteen.

The number of primaries has fluctuated in the past and is likely to do so
again. The primaries adopted during the Progressive period were in response
to a public desire to wrest control of nominations from the party bosses.
Often the primary laws did just the opposite—maintaining control in the
hands of party leaders, while providing the illusion of popular participation.
In time, dissatisfaction with the way the primaries worked led to their abandonment.

There were a number of reasons why states opted for presidential primaries in 1972 and thereafter. In Maryland, for example, it was merely a case of
returning to their usual system. Dismayed that George Wallace had won 43
percent of the 1964 presidential primary vote against LBJ stand-in Senator
Daniel Brewster, and fearful that the Alabama governor could equal or better
his showing in 1968, the Maryland Democratic party leadership abandoned
the primary in favor of a committee selection system for 1968; they reinsti-
tuted the primary for 1972. In some instances, primaries are enacted to benefit a potential presidential candidate. The Texas legislature adopted a primary

law when Senator Bentsen threw his hat in the presidential ring. This primary was so obviously a vehicle for Bentsen that it carried a self-destruct clause after 1976. The North Carolina primary was to provide a vehicle for Terry Sanford. Georgia became a primary state when Jimmy Carter sought the nomination. In other instances, income and attention are motivating factors: The candidates, their campaigns, and the press who cover them are known to spend a great deal of money in "crucial" primary states. Vermont adopted a primary in the hope of a financial "spillover" from New Hampshire and Massachusetts. States established primaries in cooperation with each other to set up mini-regional primaries that would focus media and candidate attention more sharply on their regional problems. Because New Hampshire would not yield its "first-in-the-nation" status, the New England regional primary never became a reality. In 1976, a de facto western primary occurred when Idaho, Nevada, and Oregon all held their primaries on the same day. In 1980, the Southern regional primary occurred on March 11 when Alabama, Florida, and Georgia Democrats all went to the polls.

In 1972, New Mexico designed a presidential primary—distributing its convention delegates between the top two vote-getters—and scheduled it for the same day as the California primary, hoping for some attention. Most of the state's leading Democrats lined up behind Senator Humphrey. By primary day, the Democratic contest in California had boiled down to a Humphrey versus McGovern shootout for that state's winner-take-all lode of 271 delegates. Neither the candidates nor the press bothered with New Mexico. McGovern came in first and Wallace second in the voting; most of the party's leaders stayed home, and the next time around the state abandoned its primary.

Aware that many new primaries were resting in legislative hoppers around the country, the McGovern Commission went out of its way to stress that it had no preference between primary and convention systems, and that, run properly, either system could provide an open, democratic selection contest. It was no easier to comply with the guidelines by adopting a presidential primary law than it was to amend a party constitution to bring a state convention process into conformity with the rules. Using state law as an excuse for noncompliance did not protect a state, as Mayor Daley learned at the 1972 Democratic National Convention. The 9–0 Supreme Court decision in *Cousins v. Wigoda* underscores both the national convention's willingness to overturn primary results supported by state law and its right to do so.

In 1980, for the first time in more than a decade, caucus procedures are beginning to get a good press. Voters have discovered that the process is not intimidating and caucus states—at least the early ones—have begun to attract the kind of attention that once made primaries so appealing to party leaders who wanted a larger spot on the national tote board. There is no guarantee of it, of course, but we may be on the verge of another period when the appeal of primaries begins to wane and a more even balance with caucus systems is established.

In any case, the new, post-1968 primaries have assimilated reform requirements that make them more representative of primary voters and of Democratic party members. Presidential candidates now receive national convention delegates in proportion to the votes they win in the primary. Now, only Democrats can vote in Democratic presidential primaries. When voters cast their ballots for candidates seeking to be convention delegates, they know which presidential aspirant the candidate supports. These are significant accomplishments when measured against the type of primaries that were held in 1968 and before.

Myth No. 6: Proportional representation is a notion of European origin that will fragment the American party system, exacerbate divisions, prolong the nominating contest, and make unity more difficult.

The early winnowing of the field in 1976 and the subsequent unity behind Jimmy Carter's nomination took much of the air out of this balloon. Common sense suggests that those who lose a fight fairly will be more likely to rally around the eventual winner than those who lose because they think the deck was stacked against them. Contrast 1976 with 1968.

Myths such as these have clouded a thoughtful evaluation of what party reform did, in fact, accomplish. The rules provided a convenient battleground for a spirited factional dispute within the party. The debate seemed to encourage exaggerations like the current notion that the reforms have made the contest so long and exhausting that only candidates without jobs can compete—witness Jimmy Carter and Ronald Reagan in 1976; George Bush, John Connally, and Reagan again in 1980. Candidates with a lot of time on their hands could do well under the old system, too, as Richard Nixon proved in the two years before 1968. And, as far back as 1959–1960, John Kennedy's attendance record in the Senate got no gold stars.

It is also said that the addition of twenty new presidential primaries has weakened the party system and that primaries are a bypass mechanism that saps the parties' vitality. If this is true (which it may not be), then the place to look to remedy the weakness is at the base of the pyramid where tens of thousands of municipal, county, district, and state primaries determine nearly every nomination of every party in the country.

Parties are getting weaker. Anyone would concede as much. But they have been eroding over the course of the past century, as David Broder points out in his perceptive study, *The Party's Over*. Public financing of elections, the movement of candidates away from political parties as organizing mechanisms to garner support in the electorate, the influence of television on our politics and its use in supplanting party organizations in get-out-the-vote drives—these, much more than the addition of a few presidential primaries, have been responsible for the weakening of the party system over the past decade.

After the revisionist bombast is cleared away, a few things become clear. First, the original McGovern reforms have undergone two lengthy, thoughtful reviews by follow-up party commissions not pre-disposed to accept the reforms as gospel. There have been some modifications, some tinkering, but the basic concepts that guided the original reform proposals have been endorsed by both commissions. Ninety percent of the original guidelines have been accepted and codified into party rules around the country. In 1980 we may see the second consecutive hard-fought presidential nomination conferred without procedural bitterness—not a bad accomplishment after 1968 and 1972. In other words, the basic principles of the reform movement have been accepted, and they are with us to stay.

Second, the people seem to be going for the reforms. Participation is up in both parties. In an era of cynicism about parties, a *Los Angeles Times* poll (December 16–18, 1979) found that 70 percent of Americans nationwide said the nominating system was "basically sound," compared with 62 percent for the political system as a whole and only 49 percent for the judicial system.

Finally, those who condemn the party reforms as too radical must at least concede that they headed off worse possibilities. Public opinion polls throughout the late 1960s and 1970s showed whopping majorities of Americans cynical about political parties, politicians, and institutions, and strongly in favor of a national primary, abolition of the electoral college, and establishing a binding national initiative.

The survival of political institutions lies in their adaptability. Party reform is the latest evidence of that.

PART V

Back to the Future? Proposals for Change

Emmett H. Buell Jr.

A S IN previous transitions, repudiation of past inequities heralded the emergence of the present system for choosing presidential nominees. Reform, however, has hardly put an end to criticism or the prospect of further change. Few if any who labored on the Hughes and McGovern-Fraser commissions anticipated a process that selects the vast majority of delegates in preference primaries, allocates more than half of the delegates only weeks after New Hampshire, and effectively ends before millions of primary voters have their say.

Controversy has dogged this system since its inception. Most of the early criticism fastened on Democratic reforms that stripped state party leaders of power over delegate selection, established racial and other preferences, and denied party officials and elected officeholders seats at the convention. The unseating of Mayor Richard J. Daley's slate of party regulars at the 1972 Democratic convention symbolized these developments, as did its replacement by an insurgent delegation that included Jesse Jackson. "Where are the rights of the people to elect who they want as delegates?" an exasperated Daley asked. "How can they be told they must have so many delegates who are women, who are black, and who are Spanish-speaking?" Left-wingers and antiwar zealots, he avowed, were "destroying" the Democratic party.[1] Academics similarly blamed reform for accelerating if not causing this decline. Jeane Kirkpatrick, for example, cited the proliferation of primaries, public financing of presidential campaigns, empowerment of ideological activists at the expense of party regulars, and proportional representation methods of delegate selection as particularly harmful.[2] Everett C. Ladd linked party takeover by ideologues and issue activists to a new dynamic, the "unnatural landslide," in which the nomination of an ideological extremist opposed by most of the party following suffers a crushing defeat in the fall.[3] Nelson W. Polsby argued that the new nominating process encouraged outsider candidates to play on party divisions by mobilizing ideological and issue factions, a strategy that hardly prepares a candidate to become an effective president.[4]

The Vanishing Voter Project of 2000 unearthed evidence of discontent with the way things are. Several of the polls conducted for this project found most voters unhappy with not only the length of nominating campaigns but also the premature ending induced by front-loading. When pollsters asked respondents to compare the present system with each of four alternatives, the present system lost out every time.[5] Marvin Kalb of Harvard's Kennedy School of Government avowed: "Americans now seem ready to go back to the old smoke-filled rooms and let the party pros do the selecting of the nominee."[6]

Back to the future? Part V introduces a series of proposals to revive old ideas or revitalize old institutions: the national convention, cluster primaries of one type or another, and the national primary. These proposals embody conflicting assumptions and priorities. Proponents of stronger national conventions seek to enhance representative decision making at the expense of direct democracy, while advocates of a national primary want to make the process even more democratic.[7] The most recent calls for rotating regional primaries arose out of concern about the inequities of front-loading.

PROPOSALS TO REVIVE THE NATIONAL CONVENTION

Efforts to strengthen the national convention date back at least to a 1950 report of the American Political Science Association, *Toward a More Responsible Two-Party System,* which E. E. Schattschneider directed and helped to write.[8] Operating on the assumption that the national convention would remain the principal organ of party representation and deliberation, Schattschneider and associates called for a reduction of delegates attending the national convention to about 525. "Rank-and-file" voters in state primaries would directly elect upwards of 350 delegates, while another 150 would consist of national committee members, state party chairmen, congressional leaders, and other ex officio members from party organizations. Twenty-five "prominent party leaders outside the party organization" would also attend.[9]

As always, the concept of party membership proved to be evanescent, as revealed by language in this report: "In electing these delegates it will be necessary to accept the existing definitions of party membership in the laws of the respective states. At the same time it will be possible to work toward a more satisfactory basis of membership."[10] This formulation dissatisfied many political scientists of the day, including Austin Ranney:

We have not been told who has a right to be considered a party member. Yet this consideration is fundamental to the committee's notion of "intraparty democracy"; for, if the members are to have the "right" of holding party leaders to account "in primaries, caucuses, and conventions," we must first know just who will be permitted to exercise this "right." Will the party leaders, for example, be "responsible" to all those persons who register as party members and vote in the closed primaries? Or will they be "responsible" to all those persons who vote for the party ticket?[11]

Thirty years later, Gov. Terry Sanford of North Carolina issued a call to return all of the nominating power to national conventions. Under his plan, the candidate preferences of primary voters would have no bearing on the selection of delegates to national conventions. No delegate would attend the convention pledged to a candidate. The delegates would subject each presidential aspirant to a thorough examination before settling on a nominee. This plan received little notice except in academic circles; not a trace of support showed up among presidential candidates, party officials, or primary voters. James W. Ceaser deemed the ideal of wholly uncommitted delegates highly improbable and expressed doubts about the kind of peer review that would result.[12]

Michael Walzer takes a similar tack derived from a "hankering for an older form of democracy, inappropriate to a mass society and insufficiently accessible to the mass media." Only party activists and government officials of the same party, presumably chosen in a caucus-convention process at the state level, would attend this convention. Like Sanford, Walzer wants to free delegates of the obligation to support any candidate. Recalling the 1980 Democratic debate over Carter's yank rule, he concludes: "It makes no sense to have primaries if the elected delegates can ignore the results. It makes no sense to have conventions if the delegates are nothing more than automatons, beyond the reach of argument and negotiation. But if both of these propositions are true, then we have to conclude that it makes no sense to have primaries." Like Polsby, Walzer regards Carter as typical of the kind of nominee likely to emerge from a primary-dominated process. Without support from state and national party leaders, presidential aspirants, and party activists, such proposals have gone nowhere.

Does this mean that nothing can be done to restore some of the convention's importance? When Woodrow Wilson asked Congress to enact a national primary system in 1913, he allowed that conventions might still have some use for writing platforms.[13] In 1950, the authors of *Toward a More Responsible Party System* melded this notion with a proposal to convene the convention every two years for purposes of formulating party policy. Democrats actually tried the idea in 1974, 1978, and 1982 by holding "mini" or "midterm" conventions. Each gathering drew several times the maximum number of delegates advocated in 1950. Presidential aspirants made the 1982 midterm convention into an invisible-primary event and, after mixed reviews, the project ended.[14]

Thomas Cronin and Robert Loevy chart a bolder course. Drawing on state experience, they propose a transformation of the convention into the great winnower of candidates. [15] That is, the convention rather than state primaries would reduce the field to a few finalists. A national primary would follow in which voters would choose among the top two or three. The scheme would also create a pool of losers at the convention, out of which the vice-presidential nominee must come. This plan could not be implemented without congressional enactment. Under the Cronin-Loevy proposal, every primary state must select its delegates in a caucus-convention process, all fifty states must revise their election laws, and both national parties must rewrite their rules of delegate selection. States wedded to a primary tradition would resist these changes, some ferociously. It seems unlikely that candidates would forfeit the prerogative of running with someone of their own choosing. Voters unhappy about the length of the present process might find this one even less tolerable. The invisible primary would go on pretty much as before, including fund raising to finance television ads for every state's caucuses. Moreover, the nominating process would carry over to the summer of each election year. Only two months after the national primary, voters would be called back to the polls for a general election. Although frequently reprinted, this proposal has attracted little notice and less support outside academic circles.

Everett C. Ladd also proposes to fold conventions into a national primary system, but by having the primary select two-thirds of all convention delegates. Ladd does not address the issue of whether primaries should be open or closed, but he does stipulate that delegates must mirror the voters' preferences, with 10 percent as the threshold. The remaining one-third of all delegates—consisting of governors, members of Congress, and national and state party officers— would attend in an ex officio capacity with full voting rights. Delegates selected in the primaries must vote for the candidates to whom they are committed on the first ballot, even if their candidate withdraws or supports someone else. Unless the national primary produced a majority of delegates favorable to one candidate, the convention would require two or more ballots to choose a nominee. In this way, as Ceaser notes, Ladd seeks to balance representative decision making at the convention with direct democracy in the national primary:

> The better a candidate does in the democratic contest, the less support he would need from ex officio delegates. As a practical matter, an extremely popular candidate, one winning 60 percent of the delegates from the primaries, probably would have little difficulty in securing enough support

from the uncommitted delegates to win the nomination. As the popular contest becomes closer, however, the chances for genuine representative decision making increase accordingly. The convention could exercise discretion, taking into account not only the popular vote total in the primary but also other considerations.[16]

Although unlikely to win acceptance for basically the same reasons raised against Cronin-Loevy, the Ladd plan underscores important differences in national primary proposals. A national primary that directly picks a party's presidential and vice-presidential nominees is not the same as one that selects delegates to a national convention empowered to make the nomination. The first type represents the full triumph of democracy over representative decision making; the second promotes representative decision making without threatening direct democracy. Other things being equal, any scheme that retains a major role for primary voters has a better chance of adoption than one that does not.

REGIONAL, CLUSTER, AND ROTATING PRIMARY PROPOSALS

Proposals to group state primaries by region or some other criterion go back at least to 1972, when Sen. Robert Packwood (R-Ore.) and Rep. Morris Udall (D-Ariz.) introduced their bills. Packwood tried again in 1973, 1975, and 1977, eventually picking up co-sponsors in senators Mark Hatfield (R-Ore.) and Ted Stevens (R-Alaska). Joined by Rep. John Ashbrook (R-Ohio), Udall offered a second version of his bill in 1977. None of these measures got out of committee. In 1976, Rep. Richard Ottinger (D-N.Y.) dropped his bill into the hopper.[17]

The Packwood proposal groups states into five regions, determines the order of regional voting by lot, and sets aside the first Tuesday in March, April, May, June, and July for regional primaries. State participation would be voluntary. The Federal Election Commission (FEC) would decide which names would appear on each regional ballot. Candidates winning 5 percent or more of the preference vote would divide up the delegates on a proportional basis. Delegates would be bound to support their candidate on the first two ballots, unless said candidate withdrew or fell below 20 percent in convention balloting.[18]

Seeking to shorten the primary process, Udall's first bill called for three cluster primaries in April, May, and June. States again could opt out of the scheme altogether, and those wanting to take part would do so in the cluster of their choice. While the plan hardly precluded regional configurations, it did not seek to create them. A special committee, consisting partly of party leaders, would decide such matters as candidates named on the ballot. Udall proposed to allocate delegates proportionally to all candidates receiving at least 10 percent of the preference vote. Any candidate winning 50 percent would get all of a state's delegates.

Unlike Packwood and Udall, Ottinger compelled every state to take part in one of five regional primaries scheduled from April to June. Under this plan, the Federal Election Commission would determine the order of regional voting by lot and would announce a date for each region only twenty days before the event. Every candidate eligible to receive federal matching funds would appear on the ballot. Each regional primary would be a closed affair, restricted to registered party supporters. Other features, such as proportional representation and a low threshold of 5 percent, gave it a superficial resemblance to the Packwood and Udall proposals. Yet the Ottinger plan was doomed from the outset because of the arbitrary dates, high costs, and other inconveniences imposed on the states.

Ceaser regards Udall's and similar proposals as rationalizations of the status quo, that is, as attempts to bring the system into some kind of order without diminishing current levels of democratic participation.[19] In this connection, note that the schemes outlined by Packwood, Udall, and Ottinger all maintain the national convention in its ratifying role. Indeed, some scenarios associated with these schemes raised the specter of convention deadlock. In this connection, James W. Davis warned that the lack of uncommitted delegates in Packwood's scheme might turn the clock back to the "bitter, multiballot conventions of yesteryear." Depending on the intensity of their beliefs and candidate commitments, delegates might lack the motive, the means, and the opportunity to break a deadlock. Then only the 20 percent rule would provide a way out of an impasse. Davis also speculated that the low qualifying thresholds set by Packwood and Udall would encourage minor candidates to run in hopes of emerging as the eventual nominee of a multiballot convention.[20]

All three plans contain design flaws likely to perpetuate unpopular aspects of the contemporary system. Packwood and Ottinger prescribe an even longer and perhaps even more expensive primary season, and, despite the random start, create the likelihood of regional bias. "For example," Ceaser noted in 1978, "it hardly would help a candidate from the West at the prime of his career if his region turns up fourth and fifth in the two elections in which he competes." The fairest system of sequenced contests, he added, would cluster states together from different regions.[21] The Udall plan obviously addresses this concern but gives rise to another problem, the likelihood that most primary states would choose to participate in the earliest cluster. After one or two trials, the Udall scheme would likely give way to a de facto national primary. We need not continue this line of conjecture, however, because developments since the

1970s have rendered these schemes irrelevant. Owing to front-loading, cluster and regional primaries have become staples of the present system.

Recently, however, Republican leaders have prescribed a system of rotating cluster primaries as an antidote to the ill effects of front-loading. Dissatisfied with the 1996 process, the Republican National Committee (RNC) threw its weight behind the so-called Delaware Plan, to take effect in 2004. This scheme would divide all fifty states, the federal territories, and the District of Columbia into four primary "pods" according to population size. The smallest states, the territories, and D.C. would lead off in March. The final vote would occur in June, when California, New York, Texas, Florida, Pennsylvania, Illinois, Michigan, Ohio, Georgia, Virginia, New Jersey, and North Carolina weighed in. Proponents argued that the plan would eliminate regional bias, attract better candidates, and give voters ample time to assess the candidates while reducing the early advantages enjoyed by candidates with greater name recognition and success at raising money. Conversely, the race would take longer to resolve and probably cost more. Doubtless it would increase the invisible primary's importance.[22]

Two days before the 2000 Republican convention met in Philadelphia, this writer watched the Committee on Rules and Order of Business vote down the Delaware Plan. Media reports attributed this turnabout wholly to a decree from George W. Bush, but the two-to-one vote, as well as the tenor of committee debate, indicated that Bush was not alone in expressing reservations. Some committee members decried the plan's infringement on state autonomy. One objector warned that failure to comply with the schedule would mean that delegations might not be seated at the next convention. Another maintained that the only realistic alternative in some states was to replace primaries with a caucus-convention process. Several speakers fastened on what would happen if the Democrats refused to go along with Republican scheduling changes. In that event, Republicans in states with Democratic legislatures would bear the cost of holding primaries on dates different from those set out in election statutes. Moreover, the Democrats would conclude their nominating races months before the Republican primaries ended. The idea of giving priority to the District of Columbia, a Democratic fiefdom, as well as to the territories, struck some committee members as absurd. New Hampshire members argued for retention of their first-in-the-nation primary and its tradition of retail politics. In sum, the Delaware Plan failed because the risk and costs of implementing it greatly outweighed perceived benefits.

Anticipating problems with the Delaware Plan, Ohio Republican chairman Bob Bennett stood ready to propose a regional primary scheme in which the voting order of grouped states would rotate. However, once the Bush camp made its preference for the status quo known to committee members, Bennett withdrew his "Ohio Compromise." This proposal bore some resemblance to the rotating regional primary plan promoted by the National Association of Secretaries of State (NASS) in 1999. Unlike the Delaware Plan, the NASS proposal had bipartisan origins. It, too, groups states by region, provides for a sequence of monthly voting, and sets out a plan for rotating the order of regional voting in future years. In a sop to Iowa and New Hampshire, the plan allows both states to hold their contests before any other delegate-selection event. Once again, the other states are asked to make major adjustments for the common good. After an initial burst of acclaim, the plan vanished from the public forum until a *New York Times* editorial touted it as an alternative to front-loading of the 2004 Democratic primaries.[23]

PROPOSALS FOR A DIRECT NATIONAL PRIMARY

No approach to changing the present system is more often proposed or more popular than the idea of substituting a direct national primary for the national convention. Congressman Richard Hobson (D-Ala.) introduced the first such bill in 1911, and a veritable flood of national primary proposals has inundated Congress since. As table 17 shows, a large proportion of these proposals have issued from relatively few sponsors. Sen. William Langer (R-N.D.)

Table 17
Direct National Primary Bills and Resolutions Introduced in Congress, 1911–1979

Years introduced	Proposals	Most frequent sponsors (number of proposals introduced)
1911–13	7	Britten (2), Cummins (2)
1920–29	4	Schall (2)
1931–37	5	Steiwer (3)
1944–49	9	Langer (5), Lemke (3)
1950–56	16	Langer (5), Celler (3), Kefauver (2)
1961–67	9	M. Smith (4), Kefauver (2), Smathers (2)
1968–69	27	Moss (4), Ullman (3), Waldie (3)
1971–72	23	Ullman (3), Conte (2)
1973–75	15	Ullman (4), Conte (2), Gaydos (2), Smith (2)
1976–79	11	Applegate (2), Bennett (2), Weicker (2)
Total	126	Langer (10), Ullman (10), Conte (4), Kefauver (4), Moss (4), M. Smith (4)

Source: Derived from Joseph B. Gorman, "Federal Presidential Primary Proposals, 1911–1979," Library of Congress, Congressional Research Service, Report 80-53 GOV, JK 2071 A (February 20, 1980).

introduced ten bills in the 1940s and 1950s, for example, as did Rep. Al Ullman (D-Ore.) in the 1960s and 1970s. More than half of the total number of such measures originated after 1967.

As for popularity, table 18 shows that in polls taken between 1952 and 1988 large majorities of Americans consistently preferred a direct national primary to national nominating conventions. Party breakdowns reveal only small differences in the percentage of favorable responses. Moreover, apparent swings in Democratic enthusiasm generally coincide with similar shifts among Republicans. These patterns differ markedly from the results Gallup obtained from infrequent samples of elites (not shown in the table). Only 52 percent of roughly 3,000 Democratic county chairmen sampled in 1972 wanted to replace national conventions with a direct primary. Similarly, a mere 47 percent took this position in a 1982 mail survey of "opinion leaders" drawn from *Who's Who in America*.[24]

No direct primary bill has come close to enactment in Congress or adoption by a national party. Because Gallup's question did not measure intensity of commitment or respondents' knowledge of presidential nominating politics, party leaders probably dismissed these majorities as shallow and uninformed.

Table 18

Popular and Partisan Support for a Direct National Primary in the Gallup Poll, 1952–1988

"It has been suggested that presidential candidates be chosen by the voters in a national primary instead of by political party conventions as at present. Would you favor or oppose this?"

Year	Total sample in favor (%)	Democrats in favor (%)	Republicans in favor (%)
1952 (February)	73	—	—
1952 (June)	73	72	70
1955	58	56	59
1956	58	57	57
1968	76	—	—
1972	72	72	66
1976	68	71	65
1980	66	64	62
1984	67	68	62
1988	65	66	60

Source: *The Gallup Poll: Public Opinion 1935–1971* (New York: Random House, 1971); *The Gallup Poll: Public Opinion 1972–1977* (Wilmington, Del.: Scholarly Resources, 1978); and volumes for 1980, 1984, and 1988 published by Scholarly Resources.

Note: Partisan breakdowns are not reported for February 1952 and 1968.

In some respects, however, even severe critics have acknowledged that a direct national primary would address important inequities in the present system. Ranney, for example, grants that a "one-day" national primary would bring unprecedented uniformity and simplicity to the nominating process. The undue advantage enjoyed by New Hampshire and a few other small states would vanish if every state voted on the same day. Ranney also argues that voters in a direct national primary would represent the party's following more so than national convention delegates.[25]

Conclusions about the representativeness of primary voters, of course, are inseparable from definitions of what constitutes a party following. The bill introduced by Rep. Albert Quie (R-Minn.) in 1977 restricted national primary voting to registered party adherents, while another brought forth by Sen. Lowell Weicker (R-Conn.) permitted independents to participate in either party's national primary. Quie's proposal, however, made no provision for federal enforcement of closed primary rules.

Like any other method choosing a presidential ticket, the direct national primary faces the problem of making legitimate and authoritative nominations. This means that the nominee must win a solid plurality, if not an outright majority, of the vote. Ranney argued that a vote based entirely on voters' first preferences would result in a choice less representative of the party following than an old-fashioned convention or sequence of state primaries. One way around this problem is to require a runoff between the top two candidates if none wins a specified proportion of the vote. The Quie plan called for a runoff if no candidate won 50 percent of the national primary vote, as did the Weicker proposal. Rep. Joseph Gaydos (D-Pa.) set 45 percent as the minimum vote needed to win on the first round in his plan. But the runoff option alters the strategic environment, encouraging candidates who have little chance of winning a first round to try anyway in hopes of getting into the runoff.[26] If the choice came down to two such candidates, one or both might lack credibility as the choice of a sincere majority.

Theoretically, as Ranney acknowledged in 1978, this problem can be resolved by adopting the "alternative vote" method used to elect Australian legislators. Alternative voting allows voters to rank candidates in order of preference, and, in the event that no one wins a majority on the first round, to have their second, third, or even fourth choices counted so that a majority accumulates for one candidate. Although Ranney proclaimed the concept worthy, he concluded its chances of implementation in the United States as minimal.[27]

Indeed, Ranney rejected all plans to replace national conventions with direct national primaries as mortal threats to political parties.

> The parties are very sick now. Some analysts believe their sickness is mortal, and they may be right. But if . . . the Quie Plan is adopted, they will

surely die. If we stay our hands from delivering the final blow, we at least leave open the possibility that some day they may recover. Believing, as I do, that political parties have been invaluable aggregating, moderating, consensus-building agencies in all democratic polities, especially our own, I can only conclude that dismantling them even further by a universal federalized primary would be a cost far greater than any benefit or set of benefits such a primary could possibly bring.[28]

Michael Nelson makes a strong case for a national primary in chapter 17. He emphasizes the simplicity and fairness of the procedure, arguing that most Americans want a national primary, that it would increase turnout, prove more representative of party identifiers, count all votes equally, oblige candidates to campaign on national rather than local issues, alter the strategic calculations of presidents seeking renomination, shorten the nominating process, and possibly revive parties rather than kill them off. On this last point, he recommends retaining national conventions for purposes of choosing vice-presidential nominees and writing platforms. In response to claims that a national primary would increase media power over nominations,[29] Nelson maintains that the press would be less influential. Moreover, every winner of a national primary would be chosen by the majority, albeit one derived from preferences of varying intensity.

Nagging issues remain, however. What about the great expense of campaign advertising in most or all of the nation's media markets? Who among the candidates could afford to compete in such a process? Would big money dominate even more in a national primary? Assuming that the invisible primary would remain the premier time for fund raising, would this make the process even longer?

CODA

If history is any guide, the next presidential nominating system will not come about by congressional statute. Nor is it likely to spring from sweeping reforms promulgated by national party councils. Rather, it will emerge piecemeal and as the result of decisions made at the state level. True, state parties have lost control over delegate selection, but they still retain control over the timing of their delegate-selection events. Moreover, they are free to shift from caucuses to primaries, or vice versa. It may take some time before key players realize that a de facto national primary has replaced the present system.

Republican elites seriously considered the Delaware Plan because they feared that still more front-loading would evolve into a national primary. One can easily construct a scenario by which fourteen primary states could have decided the 2000 Republican contest in a single day. If, for example, California,

Texas, New York, Florida, Pennsylvania, Illinois, Ohio, North Carolina, Michigan, Virginia, Indiana, Georgia, New Jersey, and Alabama had all agreed to hold their primaries on the same day, they would have selected 1,071 delegates, or thirty-seven more than needed for nomination.[30]

This is hardly what Gaydos, Quie, Weicker, or Nelson had in mind, but it is a national primary all the same. It resembles the Ladd plan in that voters would choose convention delegates rather than presidential nominees directly. Unlike Ladd, however, state participation in this national primary would be voluntary, perhaps involving no more than twenty states. Moreover, the lineup of states might well vary from one election year to the next. Nor would it prevent still earlier contests in Iowa, New Hampshire, and other states. Unlike the Quie proposal, the primary in each participating state would be open or closed as state law prescribes. Unlike the Gaydos, Quie, and Weicker plans, no runoff would follow. Clearly controversies over turnout, representativeness, and equality of voting power would endure. It is hard to imagine that national name recognition and money would matter less.

Once operational, of course, the de facto national primary would come under attack for not having solved perennial issues of nominating politics. This is the juncture at which national party intervention is most likely. Party councils might decree a common date, devise means of creating a sincere majority, establish uniform rules of primary voting for every state, and perhaps even do away with national conventions. Congress might intervene indirectly by legislating still more campaign finance reform. In any case, controversy over how we nominate our presidential candidates will endure.

CHAPTER 14

Democracy vs. Elections

Michael Walzer

Something is wrong with the way we choose presidents. I don't just mean that something went wrong in 1980. Something is structurally wrong. Columnists and editorial writers have been full of complaints. The process goes on too long, they say. It takes too much money, or more money than the candidates can raise legally. Running for president is incompatible with doing anything else, and so unemployed politicians have an advantage, even if they are unemployed for good reasons. A narrow victory in a small state where few people bother to vote makes too much of a difference. All these are justified complaints, but they don't get at the root of the matter, which is simply that the primary system is a disaster. Primaries are indeed a way of sorting out candidates, but they systematically leave us with the worst ones. Why?

Ostensibly, primaries are the democratic way of choosing candidates, and the fight for more primaries and for open primaries (in which people can vote for either Republican or Democratic candidates) has been a democratic fight. Once the voters could only choose between two candidates, themselves chosen by party bosses. Now, many reforms later, they choose among a large number; every would-be president in the country is running, men and women with se-

From *The New Republic* (January 3 and 10, 1981): 17–19, reprinted by permission of *The New Republic*, Inc.," 1981. Michael Walzer is a professor at the School of Social Science, Institute for Advanced Study, in Princeton, N.J. He has written extensively about political theory and moral philosophy, including questions of political obligation, nationalism and ethnicity, and just and unjust war.

rious ambitions, single-issue candidates, politicians speculating on the future. The people have broken into the innermost citadel of the parties; there are no back rooms left for the bosses. The reform movement has been driven by a simple creed: the more primaries, the more participants, the more democracy. If the resulting process is exhausting, then we can simplify it and make it even more democratic by eliminating the states with their uneven populations and uneven political effects, and establishing regional or national primaries. This would only make things worse. But the problem is not too much democracy.

The defenders of primaries never have come to grips with the requirements of a party system, even of a party system as attenuated as ours is (or was, for now it is not so much attenuated as disintegrated). Democratic politics generated parties for a reason. The purpose of a party system is to provide us with candidates who represent a certain set of interests, not some random, self-selected portion of the general electorate. Its purpose is also to provide us with candidates whose positions are widely and dependably known and who are likely to stand by those positions because they are tied into a stable network of commitments and alliances. A democracy needs candidates of this sort, or the election loses all political form, and degenerates into a public relations contest. And only candidates like this can govern effectively. Only candidates who have support within their party and who can mobilize its members, both during and after the campaign, can attempt serious political initiatives once they are in office (or, out of office, lead an effective opposition).

If this is right, then the candidates must be chosen by the active members and the local and national leaders of the party. After that the citizens as a whole, those who have been involved in the nominating process and those who have not, choose between (or among) the parties and their leaders rather than among some assortment of would-be leaders. Leaders come with labels attached, testifying to their commitments and associates. The citizens act, then, exactly as President Carter, in the last week of his campaign, asked the American people to act: pay attention, he told us, to my party label. But he had not been chosen by any such process as I have just described, and hardly looked like a Democrat. Nor did any of us have any clear sense of how he would act if reelected.

American parties always were loosely organized, the national organization little more than an alliance of state parties, urban machines, national and local notables, and so on, most often without a strong center. Still, it makes sense to say that there once were, parties—parties capable of sustaining loyalty. Sometimes the local organizations were run by local tyrants, party bosses who ruled by patronage and corruption and turned the courts and the police into partisan weapons. But there also are examples of democratically integrated and disciplined parties—the Democratic (Farmer-Labor) parties of Wisconsin and

Minnesota, for example, which produced a succession of politicians who were (mostly) faithful party men and women, and among the most attractive recent American leaders.

Sometimes, at least, the party provided a local presence, a place to work, a source of services. And beyond that there was some sort of articulated structure reaching toward the national level, so that one might hope that attending a ward committee meeting was an act not totally meaningless in terms of the politics of the country as a whole. The leaders of the ward had connections among the leaders of the city, and they in turn were connected to state leaders, who had connections in Washington. No doubt it never worked quite like that, or not only like that. American politics always has had room for celebrities, coteries, informal alliances. But the party provided one network, however rough and ready, for choosing and controlling political leaders and for mobilizing followers. The very existence of bosses testified that there was something of value to be had through party organization. Where there was a boss, there was something to be hoped for by his overthrow. But today there is hardly any party organization at all, nothing to be bossed, nothing to be taken over by citizen-reformers.

The decline of party in the United States antedates the recent upsurge in primary democracy. It has many causes, which I cannot take up here. But the new centrality of primaries in the selection of presidential candidates clearly has accelerated the decline. Once primaries are established, and especially once open primaries are established, the state and local organizations lose their hold. The candidate makes his appeal, not through an articulated structure but through the mass media. He doesn't negotiate with local leaders, speak to caucuses, form alliances with established interest groups. Instead, he solicits votes, as it were, one by one. And he solicits votes among all the registered voters, without regard to their attachment to the party, interest in or loyalty to its programs, or willingness to work for its success. In turn, the voters encounter the candidate only in their living rooms, on the television screen, without political mediation. Voting itself is lifted out of the context of parties and platforms. It is more like impulse buying than political decision-making. The expert in advertising is the most important adviser a candidate can have.

A primary campaign is like a raid. The candidate and his personal entourage, together with a few attached professionals, make-up artists for the face and mind, descend upon a state. No local ties are necessary. The endorsement of state notables is of little importance; increasingly it only demonstrates the weakness or disconnection of the notables themselves. Money is crucial, and so is the kind of organization that might be put together for any advertising campaign. What seems to me dangerous about all this is not that I don't know the candidate who invades my state in search of my vote: people like me never knew him. What is dangerous is that no one that I know knows him. We have no firm expectations as to how he will behave once in office. We have no way of enforcing whatever expectations—pious hopes, leaps of faith—we allow ourselves. For it is not his party loyalty, his stand on issues, his ties to other politicians (whose support he will need later on) that count, but only his "personality"—the image he projects, the mask he wears.

Television debates, it is now clear, make all this much worse, both at the primary and then at the electoral level. The candidates stand before us as individuals in a contest, not as spokesmen for factions, parties, or interests. The format of the debate and the necessary time constraints of state or national television virtually preclude serious discussion of the issues. We are invited, again, to focus on images: how the candidates look; how much they sweat; how confident, calm, and cool they appear to be. And the nature of the contest makes every slip of the tongue so dangerous and every candidate so careful that these television spectaculars are unutterably boring, a profound discouragement from politics. I would prefer a torchlight parade to a television debate: at least I would learn something about the candidate from the men and women with whom he chooses to march.

This description of the primary process fits most closely, I suppose, the Carter campaign of 1976, the seizure of the Democratic party by the gang from Georgia. But it also helps explain the success of Senator McGovern, who grasped the possibilities of the new system before anyone else, and of Ronald Reagan, media candidate and harbinger of things to come. And it suggests some of the reasons for the persistent disappointments of well-established party leaders: Humphrey, Muskie, Jackson, Bayh, Baker, and on—the sorts of men who might have been chosen the choice been left up to their colleagues and peers.

How should the choice be made? I am not a political engineer, and it may be that I shall manage to express only a certain hankering for an older form of democracy, inappropriate to a mass society and insufficiently accessible to the mass media. But it is worth asserting as a fundamental principle that parties and countries are different sorts of organizations and that their leaders should be chosen by different procedures and by different groups of people. The leaders of the country should be chosen by its citizens: here the goal is the largest possible participation of informed men and women. The leaders of the party should be chosen by a much smaller group: here the goal is to represent those men and women who are actually tied to the party and who play some part in its life between elections. American parties are not, and are most unlikely to be turned into, membership organizations. They are unlikely, that is, to become parties on the European model. It makes no sense, then, to propose primaries or caucuses limited to party members. In general, closed primaries, in which only registered Democrats, say, can vote for Democratic candidates, are better than open primaries. And caucuses, in which some further token of commitment is required—namely, a willingness to come to a meeting—are better than primaries of any sort. But the preferred procedure, it seems to me, at both the state and national level, is the old-fashioned party convention.

I mean party convention with all its festive and ritual character as well as its deep political purpose—with its convention floor and its back rooms, too. Ideally two different groups of people should be present at the convention: party activists, chosen in precinct, town, and city caucuses; and elected officials, councilors, mayors, governors, representatives, and senators. (In the Democratic party it probably would make sense to find some way of representing labor unions too, though their members might do well enough in the caucuses.) Since the activists tend to be overbalanced toward the left among the Democrats, or toward the right among the Republicans, the elected officials provide a kind of ballast. They represent a larger constituency and are sensitive to the requirements of electoral, as well as of ideological, politics. On the other hand, the activists embody the possibility of party rebellions against elected officials, even against a standing president. It is important to keep that possibility open if the rule of bosses is to be avoided. In the recent past, it has been the primary system that has enabled ambitious politicians or candidates committed on some issue or set of issues to challenge a standing president: thus McCarthy in 1968 and Kennedy in 1980. These were dramatic moments in the history of the Democratic party. But though I was a supporter of both challengers, I am not inclined to say that the primary system provided Democrats with the best chance actually to debate the issues or to find their way to a resolution that served the interests of the party (or the country) as a whole. Open caucuses at the local level and open conventions at the state and national level might well have been better.

Of course, the conventions must be open—not in the sense that anyone can attend, but in the sense that delegates are not bound in advance to vote for any particular candidate. The debate over this issue at the last Democratic convention was a wonderful piece of collective idiocy, not least because both sides had a perfectly valid point. It makes no sense to have primaries if the elected delegates can ignore the results. It makes no sense to have conventions if the delegates are nothing more than automatons, beyond the reach of argument and negotiation. But if both these propositions are true, then we have to conclude that it makes no sense to have primaries. For argument and negotiation are the very essence of any intelligible political process. What ought to happen at a convention is that the leaders and activists of the party, responsible to different groups within it, meet and argue about issues and personalities, about running a successful campaign and exercising power after that. They bargain over issues and offices. Some of this should go on in public; some of it shouldn't. That is not because the bargains are necessarily sordid but simply because they are bargains. The men and women who work them out need a chance to explain them to their supporters—and to put the best possible color on them too—before they are broadcast to the country at large. They know that the argument will be renewed another time, but they are prepared not to say that in public for the sake of the celebrations on the floor and the coming campaign.

A convention is a mixture—a politic mixture—of publicity and concealment, festival and negotiation. I don't doubt that it can go badly sometimes, but one possible result is a candidate capable of rallying the party and committed to behave in a certain ways, to press certain policies, if he wins. In primaries, by contrast, there can be no mixture. Everything goes on in public, and so the candidate is a public relation—really related, that is, to no one. We have aimed at a perfectly transparent political process, and the result is that we are ruled by masked men and movie actors. We need a process within which real people can function, within which policies can be worked out and alliances forged before the election itself—so that when we finally vote we have some firm sense of what we are doing.

CHAPTER 15

The Case for a National Pre-Primary Convention Plan

Thomas Cronin and Robert Loevy

Our presidential nominating process has changed dramatically since the 1960s when John F. Kennedy entered just four contested state primaries. Once shaped mainly by state and national party leaders, it is increasingly shaped by single-interest groups and the media.

The formal nominating process begins with the Iowa caucus in January of an election year and lumbers through more state caucuses and conventions and thirty-six primary elections before candidates are finally selected at national party conventions in July and August.

Nobody [...] seems happy with the present nominating system—especially the patchworky maze of presidential primaries. The process strains patience and, critics say, eliminates good candidates. The current primary system plainly favors well-heeled out-of-office individuals who can devote their full attention to selected early state nominating battles. Thus Carter in 1976, and Reagan in 1980, could spend up to a hundred days in Iowa, New Hampshire, and Florida, while officeholders such as Udall, Baker, Anderson, Kennedy, and the sitting presidents had to remain on their jobs.

Our present nominating process has become a televised horse race focus-

From *Public Opinion* 5 (December/January 1983): 50–53, reformatted and reprinted with permission of the American Enterprise Institute for Public Policy Research, Washington, D.C. Thomas E. Cronin is president of Whitman College and the author of numerous publications on the presidency and American politics. Robert Loevy has taught political science at Colorado College since 1968.

ing more on media appeal than on the competing ideas, programs, or character of the candidates. More voters, to be sure, take part in primary elections than in caucuses and conventions. But what about the *quality* of that participation? Primary voters often know little about the many candidates listed on the ballot. Popularity polls, slick spot ads, and television coverage of the early primaries offer episodes and spectacles, and the average citizen is hard pressed to separate significance from entertainment.

"Winners"—sometimes with only 20 percent of the vote—in the early small state nomination contests are given undue media coverage. For example, Jimmy Carter's victories in Iowa and New Hampshire in 1976 led to an outpouring of cover and human-interest stories on him.

Voters in New Hampshire and a few other early primaries often virtually get the right to nominate their party's candidate. Candidates who do not do well in these early states get discouraged, and their financial contributors and volunteers desert them. In most presidential years, the nominees of both major parties are decided much too early in the process.

Critics are also concerned, rightly we believe, about the declining importance of the national conventions. Now that nominations are often "sewed up" by early primaries, the national conventions have become *ratifying* rather than *nominating* conventions. Most delegates, bound by various state and party election rules, have little more to do than cast their predetermined required vote, enjoy a round of cocktail parties, pick up local souvenirs, and go home. It is little wonder that the networks are moving away from gavel-to-gavel coverage.

A further complaint is that the current nominating system has diminished the role of party and public officials, and concomitantly increased the role of candidate loyalists and issue activists. Primaries bypass the local party structure by encouraging candidates and their managers to form candidate-loyalist brigades several months before the primaries. Elected officials generally are unwilling to become committed to one candidate or another until well along in the election year and hence they are often excluded from the process. But because most serious candidates for national office hold (or have held) elective office, the views of their peers can be particularly insightful. Because elected officials, especially members of Congress, have some obligation to implement the goals and platform of their party, they should participate in the development of the party positions.

Elected officials plead to be brought back into the system; to be given incentives for involvement; to be given responsibility in selecting candidates and writing the platform. Let us integrate the national presidential party and the congressional party as one working unit where all the various components have some status and voice in the processes and outcomes.

Strengthening the party role in the nominating process does not require that elected or party leaders dominate or control nominations. Rather, it would encourage peer review and ensure that a reasonable number of elected officials are allowed to participate. Political scientist Everett Ladd suggests that the person who successfully "passes muster in a peer review process, if elected, comes into office with contacts and alliances that he needs if he is to govern successfully."

United States Senator Alan Cranston (D-Calif.) raises objections to the present system. He claims that few, if any, of the qualities that bring victory in primaries are the qualities the presidency demands:

> Primaries do not tell us how well a candidate will delegate authority. Nor do they demonstrate his ability to choose the best people for top government posts. . . . Primaries don't tell us how effective a candidate will be in dealing with Congress, nor how capable a candidate will be at moving the national power structure, nor how good an educator of the American public a candidate would really be as president. . . . Primaries do not adequately test courage and wisdom in decision making—yet those are the ultimate tests of a good president.

We are more than a little aware that no procedure is neutral, that any system has various side effects and unanticipated consequences. Further, we know that no method of nominating presidential candidates guarantees good candidates or good presidents. (The nominating method used in selecting Lincoln also gave us Buchanan. The methods that nominated Eisenhower and Kennedy nominated Richard Nixon as a member of the national ticket on five different occasions.) Plainly, no procedure can substitute for rigorous screening and the exercise of shrewd judgment at every step.

We think there is an intriguing alternative to the present system of nominating presidential candidates. Known as the National Pre-primary Convention Plan, it would reverse the present order of things. It would replace thirty-six individual state primaries with a caucus and convention system in all states, to be followed by a national convention, which in turn would be followed by a national Republican presidential primary and a national Democratic presidential primary to be held on the same day in September.

Although this proposal challenges the prevailing notion that the presidential primary should occur before the convention, there are working precedents at the state level. The proposal is new only when applied at the national level. At the state level, it has been well tested. Colorado, for example, has used this system since 1910 and has found it a good way to retain the strengths of both the party convention and the party primary election.

A National Pre-primary Convention Plan starts with nationwide party caucuses on the first Monday in May of the presidential year. Any citizen would be eligible to attend a particular party caucus, but, in order to vote there, he would have to register at the caucus as a member of that political party. By national law, those who register in a political party at the precinct caucus could vote only in that particular party's national primary the following September.

Party members at the party caucus would be eligible to run for delegate to the county party convention. Those candidates for delegate who wished to identify themselves as supporting a particular candidate for president could do so, and they would be bound to vote for that candidate when they attended the county convention.

The county conventions would be held on the second Saturday in May. County convention delegates would elect delegates to the state party conventions, which would be held on the first Saturday in June. The state conventions would elect the state delegations to the national party conventions, which would be held in July.

Similar to the procedure at the precinct caucuses, candidates for delegate at the county and congressional district conventions would state their preferences among competing presidential candidates, or state their preferences to remain uncommitted. Those stating a preference would then be committed or "bound" only on the first ballot at the national conventions.

We propose, and the National Pre-primary Convention Plan would readily accommodate, the selection at the state party convention of 25 percent of the state's delegation to the national convention as "unbound" delegates. These persons so designated might be nominated by the state central committees from available state elected and party leaders who have demonstrated strong commitment to their party. Such officials might include several members of the state's congressional delegation, statewide elected officers such as governor and attorney general, a few big-city mayors, and state legislators as well as state party leaders. These unbound delegates would sometimes mirror local and state caucus results. They would have an obligation to exercise their best political judgment, not simply to abide by public opinion and the temporary wishes of their supporters. Their presence and their perspective should help make national conventions more deliberative and more occasions for party renewal than has been the case in recent years. These officials could also take into consideration late-breaking events or reflect current opinion in July as opposed to the public moods earlier in the spring. States would be prohibited by national law from holding any form of official preconvention presidential primary election. Throughout the entire process, the emphasis would be on selecting party members as delegates.

Voting procedures and other operational details at the party caucus, the county convention, congressional districts, and the state conventions would be left to individual state laws and national political party rules. The structure, organization, and scheduling of the Democratic and Republican national conventions would be the same as they are now, with the exception that both conventions would be held in July instead of one in July and the other in August.

The major task, as always, of the national convention would be to nominate candidates for the national party primary the following September. On the first of two ballots, bound delegates would vote for their declared choice, and unbound delegates could vote for any candidate. After the first ballot, all candidates except the top three finishers would be eliminated. The top three candidates would then run against each other on the second ballot, at which time all delegates would be unbound and could vote their preference.

The authors are of two minds about what should happen at this point. One of us believes that only the top two remaining candidates (so long as each receives a minimum of 30 percent from the convention) should be placed on the national primary ballot.

The other one believes that the endorsement threshold should be lowered to 25 percent, with the possibility that three candidates be allowed on the national primary ballot. If three candidates are placed on the primary ballot, a procedure called "approval voting" would come into effect. Under approval voting, voters can vote for as many candidates as they like. Thus if Reagan, Bush, and Baker were on the national Republican primary ballot in September 1984, a moderate Republican might vote for both Baker and Bush, while a conservative Republican might decide to vote for Reagan, or to vote for both Bush and Reagan. Approval voting is, in part, an insurance plan preventing an unrepresentative or least preferred candidate from winning in the three-person race.

Regardless of which formula is used to get two or three candidates in the party's national primary, only those candidates among the top three who received 25 percent of the vote or more on the second ballot would appear on the September primary ballot.

In certain presidential years, a candidate might be so strong at the convention that he would not have to face a national primary election. This would occur when, on the second ballot, neither the second-place nor the third-place candidate had 25 percent of the convention vote (or under our other alternative, when the second of two top finishers had less than 30 percent). Some states which use the Pre-primary Convention Plan also declare that the candidate who receives 70 percent of the state convention automatically receives the party's nomination. This same stipulation should apply at the national level. It would be expected, for instance, that a popular incumbent president with strong support from his own party could avoid the strain of a September primary.

The final duty of the national party convention would be to create a pool of acceptable vice-presidential prospects from which the eventual presidential nominee would make a choice following the national primary in September. All of the candidates who qualify for the second ballot at the convention would automatically be in this vice-presidential pool. The convention could add up to three more vice-presidential candidates. Immediately following the party presidential primary election in September, the winning candidate would select his vice-presidential nominee from the candidates in the pool.

The National Democratic Presidential Primary and the National Republican Presidential Primary would both be held on the same day, the second Tuesday after the first Monday in September (after August vacations and Labor Day weekend).

Any voter who was registered in a particular party by July 1 of the presidential year would be eligible to vote in that party's national presidential primary. The date of July 1 is suggested because it is late enough that those citizens who have had their partisan interests stimulated by the local precinct caucuses and state and county conventions still will be able to register in a particular political party. The goal here is to prevent partisan voters whose party is not having a presidential primary in a particular year from switching their registration in order to vote for the weakest opposition candidate.

If there are, or should be in the future, states that do not provide under state law for voter registration in the two major political parties, the United States Congress should pass any necessary national laws to guarantee that all United States citizens have the right to register in a particular political party and vote in the September presidential primary.

The one candidate who gets the most votes in the September primary would be the party candidate in the November general election. A plurality of votes rather than a majority would be sufficient to declare the winner. In case of a tie, or in case of a close race where large numbers of ballots were contested, or if the winning candidate dies or becomes functionally disabled, the party national committee shall decide the official party candidate for the November election.

As noted above, the first official event following the national primary would be the selection of the vice-presidential candidate by the presidential nominee. Note that the presidential candidate will have considerable latitude in selecting his [. . .] running mate. If it appears propitious to select one of his defeated opponents and thereby mend party fences, he is free to do so. If he wishes not to choose a defeated opponent, however, he has three candidates available who have been officially approved by the candidate.

The National Pre-primary Convention Plan is designed to eliminate the more criticized characteristics of the present presidential nominating system and also to provide some positive additions not found in the present system:

- Replacement of the present six-month series of thirty-six individual state primaries by a single national primary election campaign that would last only six to eight weeks
- Increased voter interest (and turnout) generated by a single national party primary election
- Reduction of the media's tendency to concentrate on political "momentum" rather than a candidate's character and issue positions in the early small state primaries
- Elimination of regional advantages for those candidates who are lucky enough to have strong support in early state primaries
- A return to the *nominating* rather than ratifying convention
- Reemphasis on the importance of party membership and influence of party caucuses and conventions
- A strengthening of the average voter's role in the final decision
- Increased incumbent responsibility to his own party
- Increased role for party and elected officials

No plan is perfect, and there are some possible defects in the National Pre-primary Convention Plan. Here are likely concerns and our discussion of them.

Having all the local caucuses and state conventions taking place at the same time would make it more difficult for less known and less well-financed candidates to attract attention (and money). Our response in favor of the Pre-primary Convention Plan is that the cost of entering state caucuses is significantly, perhaps four times, lower than entering state primaries as a serious candidate. Second, a candidate need do well in only a handful of states to prove his or her abilities and capture at least some national delegates. Since the nomination would not usually be decided on the first ballot, a number of worthy candidates would be able to survive and thus obtain peer review and political scrutiny before the convention makes its final determination.

Some will contend that the National Pre-primary Convention Plan is too national, too rigid, and too mechanistic. They might add that it diminishes federalism, at least to the extent it tells states when and how they will select delegates. Our response is that the presidency is a national office. Further, it is clear that the national parties have both the responsibility and the authority to decide on the procedure for the nomination of a presidential candidate. Finally, this new plan will strengthen the party at the state level, and it treats all states as equals.

Critics are likely to say that the national primary feature of this new plan will encourage television and media events of the worst possible kind. Our plan will actually diminish much of the negative influence of television in the preconvention stage of a campaign. It will require presidential candidates to meet with party and elected local leaders and to build coalitions at the grass-roots level—not just appear in television spot ads.

Some critics may fear this will diminish the role of minorities and lessen the affirmative action gains of the past decade—especially gains made in the Democratic Party. We do not think this will be the case. Existing affirmative action rules may just as easily apply. Indeed, the increased turnout at the national primaries should enhance minority participation.

What about its effect on third or minor parties? Third parties would still have their national conventions, but they would seldom need a national primary. A rule could be devised so that any national party receiving at least 5 percent of the vote in the past presidential election could participate in the national primary arrangements.

Wouldn't the national primary be an even greater expense to the states? Perhaps. But conducting the national primary in fifty states in the fall as opposed to thirty-six in the spring is not really much different.

Here is a plan, we think, that shortens the formal election season and simplifies it so the average voter can understand its operations. More than the present system, it will test the political coalition-building skills of serious candidates—those skills so needed to win the general election and to govern; allow for sensible participation from all segments of the party; promote revitalized parties that are subject to popular control; facilitate and encourage the best possible candidates, including busy officeholders, to run for the presidency; encourage participatory caucuses and conventions at all levels of our system; and finally, it will go a long way toward rescuing the all but doomed national conventions and help make them more of an occasion for reflective societal leadership.

CHAPTER 16

Model Legislation for a Rotating Regional Primary Scheme in 2004

SECTION 1

1. The people of the state of _____ acting through their elected legislative representation find and declare that:

a. The quadrennial election of the president and vice president of the United States is among the most important civic acts of the voters of the state of _____.

b. The process leading to the nomination of candidates for president and vice president should be as open and participatory as possible.

c. It will enhance voter participation, strengthen the political process and protect the rights of all states and their citizens to have a coordinated, orderly and defined electoral schedule.

d. The state of _____ will participate in a rotating regional presidential primary system as defined herein.

e. Understanding the historically important role that smaller states have played in the presidential selection process in terms of "retail politics" the states of New Hampshire and Iowa shall be allowed to conduct their primary election or caucus prior to the commencement of the rotation schedule.

SECTION 2

"Presidential Primary" is the official primary election conducted or sanctioned by the state of _____ held in any year that is even divisible by the number four at which delegations to national party conventions are to be chosen.

Approved by the National Association of Secretaries of State (NASS), February 12, 1999, and kindly provided by New Hampshire Secretary of State William Gardner.

SECTION 3

Notwithstanding any other provision of law to the contrary, the state of _____, consistent with its decision to affiliate with Region _____, as defined by the National Association of Secretaries of States, shall holds its presidential primary not sooner than the first Tuesday after the first Monday in March, April, May and June, 2004, but in no case later than six (6) days after said Monday in the order defined below in Section 4; and shall rotate in subsequent presidential election years as specified in Section 5.

SECTION 4

For the purposes of presidential primaries the following states should be grouped as follows:

1. Eastern Region: Connecticut, Delaware, Maine, Maryland, Massachusetts, New Jersey, New York, Pennsylvania, Rhode Island, Vermont, West Virginia and the District of Columbia.

2. Southern Region: Alabama, Arkansas, Florida, Georgia, Kentucky, Louisiana, Mississippi, North Carolina, Oklahoma, South Carolina, Tennessee, Texas, Virginia, Puerto Rico and the Virgin Islands.

3. Midwestern Region: Illinois, Indiana, Kansas, Michigan, Minnesota, Missouri, Nebraska, North Dakota, Ohio, South Dakota, and Wisconsin.

4. Western Region: Alaska, Arizona, California, Colorado, Hawaii, Idaho, Montana, Nevada, New Mexico, Oregon, Utah, Washington, Wyoming and Guam.

It is the intent that Region 1 begin in March 2004, with other regions [following] in numerical sequence in April, May and June 2004. In subsequent cycles, the first region to hold its primary would move to last and all others in sequence shall move up.

SECTION 5

In the presidential primary elections subsequent to the year 2004, the date of the election shall be the first Tuesday of the month preceding the month of the most recent presidential primary election, except that if the most recent presidential primary election was conducted on the first Tuesday of March the date of the election shall be the first Tuesday of June.

CHAPTER 17

Two Cheers for the National Primary

Michael Nelson

We need a clearer, simpler, and more democratic presidential nominating system, one that would grow from the adoption of two or perhaps three measures: one of them old, one of them new, one of them borrowed.

The old idea—70 or more years old now—is for a national primary method of nominating party candidates for president. Since 1911 and shortly after, when Representative Richard Hobson of Alabama introduced the first piece of national primary legislation and Woodrow Wilson endorsed the concept, some 125 such bills have been offered in Congress. Most have been close kin to the one introduced by Republican U.S. Senator Lowell Weicker, which would work like this: Each major party's supporters, along with interested independents, would choose their nominee for president directly, with their votes.[1] To get on the primary ballot, a candidate would have until June 30 to round up valid signatures equal in number to 1 percent of the turnout in the most recent presidential election (around 800,000 in 1980)—a high enough standard to screen out frivolous candidacies, but not "outsider" ones. Ballots would be cast on the first Tuesday in August. If no candidate in a party got 50 percent, there would be a runoff between the top two finishers three weeks later.[2]

From *Rethinking the Presidency*, ed. Thomas E. Cronin (Boston: Little, Brown, 1982), 55–64, with the permission of the author. Michael Nelson teaches political science at Rhodes College and has authored and edited many books on the presidency and presidential selection, including *The Presidency and the Political System*, 7th ed. (Washington, D.C.: Congressional Quarterly Press, 2003).

By definition, a national primary would be a simpler system than the present one, or any other that has been proposed: the candidate who received a majority of votes would win. It offers the clearest connection between popular votes and outcome as well.

It was characteristic of the political theories of the framers that the electoral role of the citizen in the complex political process was to be clear, if not direct, and comprehensive to him and to those who represent him. First among those principles of constitutional government that the framers subscribed to, writes Clinton Rossiter, was that "government must be plain, simple, and intelligible. The common sense of a reasonably educated man should be able to comprehend its structure and functioning."[3] Henry Mayo notes in his *Introduction to Democratic Theory* that simplicity and clarity are hallmarks of all representative electoral processes: "If [the] purpose of the election is to be carried out—to enable the voter to share in political power—the voter's job must not be made difficult and confusing for him. It ought, on the contrary, to be made as simple as the electoral machinery can be devised to make it."[4]

It may be argued that the framers of the Constitution did not have candidate nominations in mind, that their notion of where citizens fit into the governing process was much more constricted. That is true, but beside the point. The framers also did not envision direct election of United States senators or universal adult suffrage. But, by allowing for amendments and for state discretion, their Constitution left open the possibility that the boundaries of popular political participation might expand. What remained constant was the principle that whatever doors of influence were opened to citizens, it should be clear to them how they could walk through.

Democratic theory, in mandating simplicity and clarity in citizen participation, treats elections as a process. But, especially to the extent that electoral rules become subjects of political controversy and government regulation, that process also should be thought of as public policy. (Certainly elections have been treated that way in the history of nominating politics.) It is useful, then, to consult the literature of policy analysis as well as that of democratic theory for guidance.

Again, one finds simplicity and clarity valued, this time as essential ingredients to sound implementation. In this case the policy is that some public officials be chosen democratically; the selection system is the method of implementation. "[A]n appreciation of the length and unpredictability of necessary decision sequences in implementation should lead the designers of policy to consider more direct means for accomplishing their desired ends," wrote Jeffrey Pressman and Aaron Wildavsky. They add that "simplicity in policies is much to be desired. The fewer the steps involved in carrying out the program, the fewer the opportunities for a disaster to overtake it. The more directly the policy aims at its target, the fewer the decisions involved in its ultimate realizations."[5]

But what other consequences might we reasonably expect of a national primary?

1. *Voter participation in the nominating process would rise substantially.*[6] In part this is almost tautologically true. In 1976, for example, 28.9 million people voted in thirty state primaries, a turnout rate of 28.2 percent of the voting age population in those states. If all the other states had held primaries, and if voters in those states also had turned out at a rate of 28.2 percent, some 38.5 million people would have participated in the process, an additional 9.6 million.[7]

Actually, it seems likely that the turnout rate would rise in a national primary as well. Austin Ranney has found that voters in states whose primary results are binding on delegates—where there is, in short, a direct causal relationship between votes and outcomes—turn out at a higher rate than voters in states whose primaries are advisory.[8] In a national primary, cause and effect not only would be direct, but obvious: there would be no delegates or other intermediaries between voters and candidates. Presumably, voter turnout would reflect this.

In addition, the replacement of state primaries with a national primary would mean that there no longer would be any such thing as an early or late primary, with the corrosive effects that order has on electoral participation. Specifically, all the candidates would be on the ballots of all the voters (no one's choice would be circumscribed by anyone else's) and no candidate would be prematurely declared the winner (no voter would feel that his or her vote was coming after the fact). Interestingly, in 1980 voter turnout rose substantially from 1976 levels in the early primaries, when the nomination contests still were up in the air (51 percent in 1980 v. 48 percent in 1976 in New Hampshire; 35 percent v. 25 percent in Vermont; 43 percent v. 33 percent in Massachusetts)[9] but fell precipitately after that. Richard Stearns of the Edward Kennedy campaign reported that: "According to the polling we've done, a large part of the explanation for the declining rate of participation after the early primaries has been a growing assumption among voters that the races effectively had been decided. Television and newspaper reporters told them, in effect, that their votes no longer had any particular value."[10]

2. *Participants would be more representative of ordinary party identifiers.* In nomination politics, it seems, there is a direct linear relationship between the volume of participation and its representativeness. Caucus participants are substantially more affluent, educated, and ideological than their fellow partisans. Similarly, Ranney found, "each party's [state] primary voters are unrepresentative of its rank-and-file identifiers in the same ways as the caucus-

convention activists but not to the same degree."[11] The effect in some cases is that candidates for a party's nomination must make ideological or special-interest appeals that will harm them in the general election campaign. Having a larger, more representative national primary electorate would reduce this dysfunction.

Other consequences probably would follow from adoption of a national primary, some of which also would stimulate turnout.

3. *Votes would count equally.* The advantage, or disadvantage, of living in a particular state or voting on a particular date vanishes when everyone votes at the same time. The present violations—in spirit if not in letter—of the "one person, one vote" standard no longer would exist under a national primary.

Not everyone sees the elimination of bias as an advantage. Jeane Kirkpatrick, citing arguments by opponents of direct election of the president to the effect that minority groups receive advantages under the electoral college system, maintains that the present nominating process has an identical bias that would, in the same way, be vitiated by a national primary. But other scholars question her very premise, arguing that the electoral college actually places disadvantages on blacks and some other minorities.[12]

4. *Campaigns would change.* It is too much to say, as some advocates do, that a millennium of rational debate on national issues would follow adoption of a national primary.[13] But it does seem likely that candidates would place less emphasis on local issues that are disproportionately important to crucial early states, such as gun control in New Hampshire and old-age benefits in Florida. And if, as is proposed and predicted below, nationally televised debates become an institutional feature of presidential nominating politics, voters would have a greater opportunity to hear and assess directly candidates' stands on national issues.

The campaign period also presumably would shorten. Strenuous campaigning that now begins a year before the Iowa caucus in January might start seven months later if the only voting day was in August. It might begin even later: local publicity in key early states can be obtained as a reward for campaigning in the pre-election year; publicity in the national media, the most valuable kind for a national primary, would not be so easy to come by that far ahead of the election. Candidates still would have to have the physical endurance of athletes to survive their campaigns, but perhaps not of marathon runners.

5. *The strategic position of the incumbent would change.* The shift from local arenas of conflict to a national one would, on the one hand, make it difficult for the challenger to a sitting president to concentrate his or her efforts and other resources in a small state like New Hampshire in order to gain credibility for other challenges elsewhere, as McCarthy did in the 1968 New Hampshire pri-

mary. On the other hand, the president's ability to gain an advantage by redistributing federal grant and contract monies to key states would disappear if there were no key states.[14]

6. *The press's influence in the nominating process would diminish.* Not disappear; diminish. Clearly the press still would have to decide which candidates it is going to take more seriously than others; its resources for campaign coverage are not unlimited. Clearly, too, reporters would continue to write and talk about who is ahead and who is behind. But a national primary offers its own scoreboard, which the present system does not. Polls provide relatively objective measures of how the candidates are faring prior to voting day. So the existing need for reporters to decide, as well as report, the shape of the race no longer would be present.

Historically, opposition to the national primary has come from those who feel that it would have another, less desirable consequence. According to Ranney:

> National primaries would be the final nail in the coffin of the party system. What they would do is eliminate any possibility that the parties might come back. National parties have never been tremendously strong in this country, but at least there was an event every four years—the nominating convention that brought together party leaders from around the country who would meet in private and wheel and deal and decide who the nominee would be and maybe even who the Cabinet would be.[15]

One can concede and even endorse the argument that the parties should not willfully be destroyed without accepting the corollary that a national primary would do so. Richard Scammon, for example, argues that with the parties already comatose, a national primary could only help them, "especially from the standpoint of reducing divisiveness. A series of bitterly fought state primaries and caucuses is like a series of wounds; it usually inflicts greater damage than one wound. And as the examples of the states and cities that choose their local candidates by primary show, a single primary settles things. It's clear; it's public; it's open. The verdict is accepted. You don't have people arguing about caucuses being packed or conventions being rigged."[16] Scammon's argument directs our attention to a related point, which is that direct primary nomination of candidates, far from being a bizarre, untested idea whose consequences are beyond anticipation, is the practice for virtually all other elected offices at all other levels of government in all states and regions of the United States. "Many of the strongest party machines in the country thrived in primary systems: Boss Crump in Memphis, Harry Byrd in Virginia, and Dick Daley in Chicago, among others."[17]

Would national party conventions become extinct if candidates for president were not chosen there? Not necessarily; there still would be the need to nominate vice-presidential candidates, make party rules, and, potentially most important, write the platforms. F. Christopher Arterton suggests that these latter activities, so central to the health of the party as an enduring organization, are not performed well in present-day "candidate-centered conventions": "[I]n a candidate-centered convention, platform writing and party governance issues will naturally and inextricably become linked to the nomination question. Although the platform and rule issues do provide real and symbolic prizes, useful for unifying the party around the nomination outcome, we need to consider the consequences of having all party business determined by the nomination struggle. Such a system is tantamount to parties being no more than arenas for candidate competitions."[18]

If, as James David Barber has suggested, "Purpose comes first, then party . . . themes of unity so compelling that they will attract allies whose allegiance might survive the selection" of this year's candidate, then divorcing conventions from the nominating process well might free them to become idea and theme-setting forums whose products the parties now seem to need.[19]

Another oft-predicted consequence of a national primary system is that it would limit the field of contenders to the already famous and close out the possibility of a less well-known candidate ever gaining the resources to mount an effective campaign. Bruce Adams, issues director of Common Cause, asks: "How could Jimmy Carter have convinced the press and the financial contributors that he was a serious candidate in 1976 if he hadn't had a chance to prove himself in a couple of small states first?"[20]

Adams's objection is a strong one. Just as the present system seems biased toward out-of-office politicians with unlimited time to campaign, the pre-reform system leaned too heavily toward Washington politicians, and a national primary system might swing the pendulum back too far in their favor. An ideal system would not place handicaps on any reasonable candidate. To help approach this ideal, we need to add a borrowed idea to our old one: debates before the primary among all candidates who qualify for the ballot. Debates already are close to being a routine practice in the present nominating system—the Democrats held several in 1976 and the Republicans did in 1980—and their track record of bringing outsider candidates before the public on equal footing with their opponents is well-established. John Anderson, for example, rose to public prominence largely on the strength of his performances in a pre-Iowa caucus debate, where he alone endorsed a tax on gasoline, and a pre–New Hampshire primary debate, in which he spoke out for gun control. He did so even though neither of these debates was nationally televised, as they almost certainly would be if a national primary were in operation. At the same time, the presidential candidacies of incumbent officeholders who can spare time for debates but not for daily campaigning would not be at a disadvantage.

A further objection to the national primary proposal generates our third, more tentative proposal, this one for something new. A primary, writes Ranney, "has no way of identifying, let alone aggregating, [voters'] second and third choices so as to discover the candidate with the broadest—as well as the most intense—support."[21] Thus, a candidate of the left and a candidate of the right, even though opposed by a majority of voters in a party, might end up facing each other in the runoff because each has the ardent support of a faction of zealous ideologues. This is not a truly serious problem—few have found cause to complain about it at the state or local level, where all candidates are nominated by primary—but it would be nice to solve it.

Interestingly, Australia has come up with a novel and time-tested solution in its legislative elections. Since 1918, voters there have been called upon to number their candidate preferences on the election ballot—first choice, second choice, and so on. If no candidate receives a majority of first-choice votes, the lowest ranking candidate is dropped, and voters' second and if need be third and fourth choices are divvied up until someone has a total of 50 percent or more. Thus, the extreme candidate who leads on the first count because he has the support of an intense but relatively small minority, but who gets few second choice votes, will not be elected; a candidate with more broadly based support will. No runoff at all is needed. Leon Epstein notes that the Australian "preferential voting" system "has proved to be entirely compatible with stable, majority-party control of the House of Representatives" in that nation.[22] Nor is it wholly foreign to the United States. Cambridge, Massachusetts, for example, has used a ranked-vote system to choose its city council since 1940. Some years ago, Cleveland tried preferential voting in its mayoral election, and Ann Arbor, Michigan, did so in 1975. Both cities rapidly abandoned the system when it resulted in seemingly anomalous outcomes.[23]

Steven Brams advocates a variation on the Australian method that he calls "approval voting."[24] Brams's proposal would allow primary participants to vote for as many candidates as they liked in a given field, though not more than once for each candidate. Brams who campaigned strenuously but unsuccessfully to persuade the New Hampshire legislature to adopt his system for the 1980 primary, argues that approval voting has all the purported advantages of the Australian system, yet is more likely to result in the choice of the candidate acceptable to most voters than either it or the runoff system. Brams offers the following hypothetical example:

> It is entirely possible in a three-candidate plurality race in which A wins 25 percent of the vote, B 35 percent and C 40 percent that the loser, A, is the

strongest candidate who would beat B in a separate two-way contest (because C supporters would vote for A), and would beat C in a separate two-way contest (because B supporters would vote for A). Even a runoff election between the two top vote-getters (B and C) would not show up this fact. On the other hand, approval voting in all likelihood would reveal A to be the strongest candidate because some B and C supporters—who liked A as much or almost as much—would cast second approval votes for A, who would thereby become the winner. . . . The Australian system] has a major drawback: it may eliminate the candidate acceptable to the most voters. . . . [Candidate] A would have been eliminated at the outset.[25]

Approval voting also has the advantage over the Australian system of being easily comprehended by voters. They do not have to express a preference—even a fourth-place preference—for a candidate they despise. And the candidate with the most votes wins. Part of the problem in the Cleveland and Ann Arbor elections was that second-place finishers ended up being elected, a result that, though "logical," runs against grain of experience with voting.

Approval voting, however imaginative a proposal it may be, is an idea whose time admittedly has not yet come—the more achievable task is to get a national primary law enacted, one that not only will simplify and clarify the nominating process for voters but make it more responsive to them as well. Distressingly, a major short-run obstacle seems to be the lack of seriousness of the proposal's present sponsor in Congress. To wit: When I called Senator Weicker's office in March 1980 to ask for an interview with the senator about his national primary bill, his press secretary's honest response was: "Do we have a national primary bill?" And when I sat down with Weicker in his office the following week, he told me that he did not know if his bill had attracted any co-sponsors, did not know if there were comparable bills being looked at in the House of Representatives, and was not sure whether hearings had been scheduled on it in the Senate or not. He thought there might be hearings in 1981. (Hearings were to be held by the Senate Committee on Rules and Administration on September 10, 1980.)

Nonetheless, the national primary has the kind of popular support among voters that may eventually win it serious consideration in Congress. The Gallup Poll, which has been asking people what they think of the idea every election year since 1952, has discovered bipartisan support ranging from two to one to almost six to one; its January 1980 survey found 66 percent supporting the national primary—62 percent of all Republicans, 65 percent of Democrats, and 72 percent of the Independents—and only 24 percent opposed. The level of support also was almost uniform across educational, regional, sexual, occupational, and religious lines, as well as those of age, income, and place of residence. George Gallup included the national primary in a *Reader's Digest* article he authored on the "Six Political Reforms Americans Want Most."[26] With even doubters like Austin Ranney conceding that a national primary "certainly would be better than what we have now," they someday may get it.

But the American political system still is best conceived as being invested with all the qualities of Newton's First Law of Motion. When it comes to existing programs and policies, American government tends to stay in motion; almost nothing is undone, even in conservative periods. But in treating new proposals for action, American government tends to stay at rest, except in times of crisis. Thus, there is any number of ideas kicking around Washington that, although an overwhelming majority of the public favors them and has for some time, show little sign of becoming law. Sometimes the reason is that of the many people who favor these ideas, only a small number have a strong enough personal commitment to them to push fervently for their enactment. As a result, the few who are ardently opposed triumph, taking advantage of the built-in inertia of our checked and balanced, separated-powers constitutional system. At other times, strong advocates of change, because they disagree on what the nature or method of change should be, "hang separately." One thinks of gun control, national health insurance, direct election of the president—and the national primary.

A reasonable forecast, then, is for more of the same. [. . .] This will remain the case unless and until some significant segment of the presently apathetic, pro-national primary majority becomes active on behalf of its cause. Given the history of nominating politics in the United States, this seems most likely to occur as an outgrowth of some decisive intraparty factional clash resembling those that have preceded and produced our previous nominating systems.

Notes

Part I: Introduction

1. See also Nelson W. Polsby, *Consequences of Party Reform* (New York: Oxford University Press, 1983); and W. Wayne Shannon, "Evaluating the New Nominating System: Thoughts After 1988 from a Governance Perspective," in *Nominating the President*, ed. Emmett H. Buell Jr. and Lee Sigelman (Knoxville: University of Tennessee Press, 1991), 250–77.

2. David S. Broder, *The Party's Over: The Failure of Politics in America* (New York: Harper Colophon, 1972).

3. Xandra Kayden and Eddie Mahe Jr., *The Party Goes On: The Persistence of the Two-Party System in the United States* (New York: Basic Books, 1985), 29–30.

4. Norman H. Nie, Sidney Verba, and John R. Petrocik, *The Changing American Voter*, enl. ed. (Cambridge: Harvard University Press, 1976), 47.

5. Kayden and Mahe, *The Party Goes On*, 94–122. For more recent assessments of organizational health, see John F. Bibby, "State Party Organizations: Coping and Adapting to Candidate-Centered Politics and Nationalization," in *The Parties Respond*, 3rd ed., ed. L. Sandy Maisel (Boulder, Colo.: Westview, 1998): 23–49; see also Paul S. Herrnson, "National Party Organizations at the Century's End," in ibid., 50–82.

6. See Alan I. Abramowitz and Kyle L. Sanders, "Party Polarization and Ideological Realignment in the U.S. Electorate, 1976–1994," in *The Parties Respond*, 3rd ed., 128–43; *American Political Parties: Decline or Resurgence?*, ed. Jeffrey E. Cohen, Richard Fleisher, and Paul Kantor (Washington, D.C.: Congressional Quarterly Press, 2001); *Responsible Partisanship: The Evolution of American Political Parties Since 1950*, ed. John C. Green and Paul S. Herrnson (Lawrence: University Press of Kansas, 2002); *Diverging Parties: Social Change, Realignment, and Party Polarization*, ed. Jeffrey M. Stonecash, Mark D. Brewer, and Mack D. Mariani (Boulder, Colo.: Westview Press, 2003).

7. On early establishment support for George W. Bush, for example, see Harold M. Stanley, "The Nominations: The Return of the Party Leaders," in *The Elections of 2000*, ed. Michael Nelson (Washington, D.C.: Congressional Quarterly Press, 2001), 27–53; see also William G. Mayer, "The Presidential Nominations," in *The Election of 2000*, ed. Gerald M. Pomper (New York: Chatham House/Seven Bridges Press, 2001), 12–45.

8. Bruce E. Keith et al., *The Myth of the Independent Voter* (Berkeley: University of California Press, 1992).

9. Warren E. Miller, "Party Identification, Realignment, and Party Voting: Back to the Basics," *American Political Science Review* 85 (June 1991): 557–68 (a revised version appears in several editions of *The Parties Respond*, ed. Maisel). The argument summarized here was updated by Kenneth Goldstein and Mark Jones as "Party Identification and the Electorate at the Start of the Twenty-First Century," in *The Parties Respond*, ed. Maisel, 4th ed. (Boulder, Colo.: Westview, 2002), 79–98. See also Warren E. Miller and J. Merrill Shanks, *The New American Voter* (Cambridge: Harvard University Press, 1996).

10. James W. Ceaser and Andrew E. Busch, *The Perfect Tie: The True Story of the 2000 Presidential Election* (Lanham, Md.: Rowman and Littlefield, 2001), 166.

11. Miller, "Party Identification and the Electorate at the Start of the Twenty-First Century," 89.

12. Joel H. Sibley, "From 'Essential to the Existence of Our Institutions' to 'Rapacious Enemies of Honest and Responsible Government': The Rise and Fall of American Political Parties, 1790–2000," in *The Parties Respond*, ed. Maisel, 4th ed., 17–18. See also Daniel Wirls, "Voting Behavior: The Balance of Power in American Politics," in *The Election of 2000*, ed. Pomper, 93–108.

13. See, for example, Thomas E. Patterson, *The Vanishing Voter: Public Involvement in an Age of Uncertainty* (New York: Knopf, 2002).

14. William G. Mayer, "Caucuses: How They Work, What Difference They Make," in *In Pursuit of the White House: How We Choose Our Presidential Nominees*, ed. Mayer (Chatham N.J.: Chatham House, 1996), 118.

15. Early work on presidential primaries suggested a direct correlation between the margin of victory in a primary and the general election outcome in the same state. See, for example, James I. Lengle, "Divisive Presidential and Party Electoral Prospects, 1932–1976," *American Politics Quarterly* 8 (July 1980): 261–77; and James I. Lengle, Diana Owen, and Molly W. Sonner, "Divisive Nominating Mechanisms and Democratic Party Electoral Prospects," *Journal of Politics* 57 (May 1995): 370–83. More recent scholarship points to existing cleavages rather than the primaries themselves as the source of fall setbacks. See William G. Mayer, *The Divided Democrats: Ideological Unity, Party Reform, and Presidential Elections* (Boulder, Colo.: Westview Press, 1996): 43–71. See also Lonna Rae Atkinson, "Divisive Primaries and General Election Outcomes: Another Look at Presidential Campaigns," *American Journal of Political Science* 42 (January 1998): 256–71.

1. Political Parties and Presidential Ambition

1. See Austin Ranney, *Curing the Mischiefs of Faction* (Berkeley: University of California Press, 1975), 188–210.

2. See Alexander Bickel, *The New Age of Political Reform* (New York: Harper and Row, 1968), 74–79.

3. *Federalist Papers*, no. 10, in Alexander Hamilton, James Madison, and John Jay, *The Federalist Papers*, ed. Clinton Rossiter (New York: New American Library, 1961), 79.

4. Nelson Polsby and Aaron Wildavsky, *Presidential Elections*, 3rd ed. (New York: Charles Scribner's Sons, 1971), 238.

5. V. O. Key, *The Responsible Electorate* (New York: Random House, 1966), 6–7.

6. John S. Saloma III and Frederick H. Sontag, *Parties* (New York: Random House, 1973), 7, 374.

7. Hugh Heclo, "Presidential and Prime Ministerial Selection," in *Perspectives on Presidential Selection*, ed. Donald R. Matthews (Washington, D.C.: Brookings, 1973), 32–37.

8. Erwin C. Hargrove, "What Manner of Man?" in *Choosing the President*, ed. James D. Barber (Englewood Cliffs, N.J.: Prentice-Hall Inc., 1974), 31–33.

9. James Sterling Young, *The Washington Community* (New York: Harcourt Brace, 1966), 245–49.

10. *Federalist*, nos. 68 and 10, in *The Federalist Papers*, 414, 82.

11. See the debates of June 1, July 17, and July 19 in James Madison, *Notes of Debates in the Federal Convention*, ed. Adrienne Koch (New York: Norton, 1969); see also *Federalist Papers*, no. 49 and 72, for references to a favorite.

12. See Gordon Wood, *The Creation of the American Republic, 1776–1787* (New York: Norton, 1969), 475–83.

13. *Federalist Papers,* nos. 10, 64.

14. *Federalist Papers,* nos. 43, 68.

15. *Federalist Papers,* no. 27.

16. *The Writings of James Madison,* ed. Gaillard Hunt, 9 vols. (New York: G. P. Putnam, 1903), 4:126.

17. Quoted in Madison, *Notes of Debates in the Federal Convention,* 306 (July 17).

18. *The Writings of James Monroe,* ed. S. M. Hamilton (New York: G. P. Putnam, 1902), 6:289; Harry Jaffe, "The Nature and Origin of the American Party System," in *Political Parties U.S.A.,* ed. Robert Goldwin (Chicago: Rand McNally, 1964), 65.

19. Letter to Charles Dudley, January 10, 1832, in Catherina Bonney, *A Legacy of Historical Gleanings* (Albany: J. Munsell, 1875), 382–84; letter to Thomas Ritchie, January 13, 1827, Van Buren Papers, Library of Congress.

20. Madison, *Notes of Debates,* 324 (July 19).

21. Ibid., 589–96 (September 6, 7).

22. Cited in Arthur Schlesinger Jr., ed., *History of American Presidential Elections,* 4 vols. (New York: Chelsea House, 1973) 1:618–19.

23. Martin Van Buren, *The Autobiography of Martin Van Buren,* ed. John C. Fitzpatrick; Annual Report of the American Historical Association of 1918, 115–16.

24. Martin Van Buren, *Inquiry into the Origin and Course of Political Parties in the United States* (New York: Hurd and Houghton, 1867), 3–4.

25. Van Buren to Ritchie, January 13, 1827; *The Virginia Enquirer,* December 23, 1823; January 3, 1824.

26. Van Buren to Ritchie, January 13, 1827.

27. Van Buren, *Inquiry,* 5.

28. *The Works of Thomas Jefferson,* ed. Paul L. Ford, 12 vols. (New York: G. P. Putnam, 1905), 7:154–55.

29. Van Buren, *Autobiography,* 125.

30. Woodrow Wilson, *Leaders of Men,* ed. T. H. U. Matter (Princeton: Princeton University Press, 1952), 42, 45.

31. Wilson, *The New Freedom* (Englewood Cliffs, N.J.: Prentice-Hall, 1966), 81.

32. Wilson, *Constitutional Government in the United States* (New York: Columbia University Press, 1908), 108–9.

33. Ibid., 199–200.

34. See Arthur M. Schlesinger Jr., *The Imperial Presidency* (Boston: Houghton Mifflin, 1973); Theodore Lowi, *The End of Liberalism* (New York: Norton, 1969), 187–93.

35. Wilson, "Cabinet Government in the United States," in *College and State,* ed. Ray S. Baker and William E. Dodd, 2 vols. (New York: Harper and Brothers, 1925), 1:36–37.

36. Herbert Croly, *Progressive Democracy* (New York: Macmillan, 1914), 337–46.

37. Wilson, "Leaderless Government," in *College and State,* ed. Baker and Dodd, 1:339.

38. Wilson, *Leaders of Men,* 45–46.

39. Polsby and Wildavsky, *Presidential Elections,* 234–52; James W. Davis, *Presidential Primaries* (New York: Crowell, 1967), 252–70.

40. Heclo, "Presidential Selection," 29.

41. *Report on the Commission on the Democratic Selection of Presidential Nominees,* 90th Cong., 2nd sess., *Congressional Record* 114: 31546–47.

42. *Mandate for Reform,* a report of the Commission on Party Structure and Delegate Selection (Washington, D.C.: Democratic National Committee, April 1970), 49.

43. Alexis de Tocqueville, *Democracy in America,* trans. George Lawrence (Garden City, N.J.: Doubleday, 1969), 135.

44. Normal J. Ornstein, Robert Peabody, and David W. Rhode, "The Changing Senate: From the 1950s to the 1970s," in *Congress Reconsidered*, ed. Lawrence Dodd and Bruce Oppenheimer (New York: Praeger, 1977), 17.

45. V. O. Key, *Southern Politics in State and Nation* (New York: Vintage, 1949), 302–06.

46. See William R. Keech and Donald R. Matthews, *The Party's Choice* (Washington, D.C.: Brookings, 1976), 156.

47. William Schneider, "Brown Exposes Democratic Splits," *Los Angeles Times*, May 23, 1976.

48. Schlesinger, *Imperial Presidency*, 206.

Part II: Presidential Nominations of the Pre-Convention Era

1. In 2000 the "in such manner as the Legislature thereof may direct" clause figured prominently in the protracted dispute over Florida's electoral votes. See Richard A. Epstein, "'In Such Manner as the Legislature Thereof May Direct': The Outcome in *Bush v. Gore* Defended," in *The Vote: Bush, Gore and The Supreme Court*, ed. Cass R. Sunstein and Richard A. Epstein (Chicago: University of Chicago Press, 2001), 13–37.

2. *Federalist Papers*, no. 39, in Alexander Hamilton, John Jay, and James Madison, *The Federalist*, Gideon Edition, ed. George W. Carey and James McClellan (Indianapolis: Liberty Fund, 2001), 197.

3. Article II also prescribed a contingency procedure for selection of the vice president: "In every Case after the Choice of the President, the Person having the greatest Number of Votes of the electors shall be the Vice President. But if there should remain two or more who have equal Votes, the Senate shall choose from them by Ballot the Vice President."

4. Max Farrand, *The Framing of the Constitution of the United States* (New Haven: Yale University Press, 1913), 167.

5. Calvin C. Jillson, *Constitution Making: Conflict and Consensus in the Federal Convention of 1787* (New York: Agathon, 1988), 179.

6. Paul Schumaker, "Analyzing the Electoral College and its Alternatives," in *Choosing A President: The Electoral College and Beyond*, ed. Schumaker and Burdett A. Loomis (New York: Chatham House/Seven Bridges Press, 2002), 14.

7. Hamilton also tried to manipulate the voting of Federalist electors in 1796 and 1800 so that Adams would finish second to his vice-presidential running mate.

8. Richard P. McCormick, *The Presidential Game: The Origins of American Presidential Politics* (New York: Oxford University Press, 1982), 27–30, 33–34.

9. William Nisbet Chambers, *Political Parties in a New Nation: The American Experience, 1776–1809* (New York: Oxford University Press, 1963), 10–12. See also Stanley Elkins and Eric McKitrick, *The Age of Federalism: The Early American Republic, 1788–1800* (New York: Oxford University Press, 1993), 257–302.

10. Wilfred E. Binkley, *Political Parties: Their Natural History*, 4th ed. (New York: Knopf, 1965), 78.

11. James Sterling Young, *The Washington Community 1800–1828* (New York: Harvest/Harcourt Brace Jovanovich, 1966), 114.

12. McCormick, *The Presidential Game*, 63–64.

13. James S. Chase, *Emergence of the Presidential Nominating Convention 1789–1832* (Urbana: University of Illinois Press, 1973), 19.

14. *Guide to U.S. Elections* (Washington, D.C.: Congressional Quarterly Press, 1976), 2.

15. Ibid., 27.

16. Chase, *Emergence of the Presidential Nominating Convention*, 20; McCormick, *The Presidential Game*, 91.

17. Binkley, *Political Parties*, 98–99.

18. See, for example, Robert V. Remini's account in *Henry Clay: Statesman for the Union* (New York: Norton, 1991), 235–36.

19. This paragraph draws heavily on Chase, *Emergence of the Presidential Nominating Convention;* and McCormick, *The Presidential Game.*

20. Chase, *Emergence of the Presidential Nominating Convention*, 25–26.

21. McCormick, *The Presidential Game*, 91.

22. Remini, *Henry Clay*, 236.

23. Chase, *Emergence of the Presidential Nominating Convention,* 60.

24. Quoted in Norvall Neil Luxon, *Niles' Weekly Register: News Magazine of the Nineteenth Century* (Baton Rouge: Louisiana State University Press, 1947), 129–30.

25. Merrill D. Peterson, *The Great Triumvirate: Webster, Clay, and Calhoun* (New York: Oxford University Press, 1987), 118.

Evolution of the Presidential Selection Process During the Constitutional Convention

1. This account is based principally on *The Records of the Federal Convention of 1787*, 4 vols., ed. Max Farrand (New Haven: Yale University Press, 1937). I have cited specific quotations or arguments but not discussions of general activity on dates given in the text. See also Shlomo Slonim, "The Electoral College at Philadelphia: The Evolution of an Ad Hoc Congress for the Selection of a President," *Journal of American History* 73 (June 1986): 35–58; John D. Ferrick, "The Electoral College: Why It Was Created," *American Bar Association Journal* 54 (March 1968): 249–55; Forrest McDonald, *Novus Ordo Seclorum: The Intellectual Origins of the Constitution* (Lawrence: University Press of Kansas, 1985), 240–53; and McDonald, *The American Presidency: An Intellectual History* (Lawrence: University Press of Kansas, 1994), chap. 7; Richard P. McCormick, *The Presidential Game: The Origins of American Presidential Politics* (New York: Oxford University Press, 1982), chap. 2; Jack N. Rakove, "The E-College in the E-Age," in *The Unfinished Election of 2000*, ed. Rakove (New York: Basic Books, 2001), 201–34; and Rakove, *Original Meanings: Politics and Ideas in the Making of the Constitution* (New York: Knopf, 1996), chap. 9.

2. Farrand, *Records of the Federal Convention of 1787,* 2:109; 2:501.

3. For the full text of the Virginia resolutions, see ibid., 1:18–23.

4. Ibid., 1:68.

5. For those who may be unfamiliar with the Convention's rules and procedures, it is worth noting that all voting in the Convention was by states, with each state having a single vote, no matter how many actual delegates it had in attendance. It is, in most cases, not possible to translate an 8–2 or 9–0 vote into the precise number of delegates who voted for or against a given motion.

6. Farrand, *Records of the Federal Convention of 1787,* 2:50.

7. When taking a vote upon the subject, the delegates split the proposal in two. The first part, which asked whether the national executive should be selected by electors, was approved 6–3. The second half, asking whether the electors should be chosen by the state legislatures, passed 8–2.

8. Farrand, *Records of the Federal Convention of 1787,* 2:95, 2:99.

9. Ibid., 2:103, 102.

10. Ibid., 3:403. The quotation comes from a report on an 1803 debate in the U.S. Senate.

11. This point is emphasized in MacDonald, *American Presidency*, chap. 7.

12. John P. Roche, "The Founding Father: A Reform Caucus in Action," *American Political Science Review* 55 (December 1961): 810–11.

13. In some forms of negotiation analysis, this is known as a "zone of agreement." See, for example, Howard Raiffa, *The Art and Science of Negotiation* (Cambridge: Harvard University Press, 1982), chap. 4. The very quantity of scholarly literature on negotiation is testimony to the fact that compromises are not random acts and can be studied from a variety of perspectives.

14. For further details, see the Maryland Constitution of 1776, articles XIV–XIX. There is apparently very little historical or contemporary analysis of the Maryland Senate. For one of the few exceptions, see John V. L. McMahon, *An Historical View of the Government of Maryland* (Baltimore: F. Lucas Jr., Cushing and Sons, and William and Joseph Neal, 1831), chap. 9.

15. Jonathan Elliot, ed., *The Debates in the Several State Conventions on the Adoption of the Federal Constitution*, 5 vols. (New York: Burt Franklin, 1888), 2:127–28.

16. See Farrand, *Records of the Federal Convention of 1787*, 2:113–14.

17. Ibid., 2:30.

18. See ibid., 1:68.

19. See, in particular, M. J. C. Vile, *Constitutionalism and the Separation of Powers* (Oxford: Clarendon Press, 1967), chaps. 1–6; and W. B. Gwyn, *The Meaning of the Separation of Powers*, Tulane Studies in Political Science, vol. 9 (New Orleans: Tulane University Press, 1965).

20. According to Donald Lutz, who counted references to political thinkers in 916 books, pamphlets, and newspaper articles published between 1760 and 1805, Montesquieu was the most often cited political writer, particularly in the decades when state and federal constitutions were written. See Lutz, "The Relative Influence of European Writers on Late Eighteenth-Century American Political Thought," *American Political Science Review* 78 (March 1984): 189–97.

21. See Bernard Bailyn, *The Ideological Origins of the American Revolution* (Cambridge: Harvard University Press, 1967), 55–60, 144–59. Many of the same themes are stressed in Gordon S. Wood, *The Creation of the American Republic, 1776–1787* (New York: Norton, 1969), chap. 1.

22. Farrand, *Records of the Federal Convention of 1787*, 2:109–10.

23. On the use of viva voce voting, see Robert J. Dinkin, *Voting in Provincial America: A Study of Elections in the Thirteen Colonies, 1689–1776* (Westport, Ct.: Greenwood Press, 1977), 133–40; and Dinkin, *Voting in Revolutionary America: A Study of Elections in the Thirteen Colonies, 1689–1776* (Westport, Ct.: Greenwood Press, 1982), 101–4.

24. The proposal for multiple votes was originally made by Hugh Williamson of North Carolina, who recommended that each person vote for three candidates. Gouverneur Morris immediately amended Williamson's suggestion, reducing the number to two and adding the explicit stipulation that at least one of the two "should not be of his own state."

25. J. Allen Smith, *The Spirit of American Government* (Cambridge: Harvard University Press, 1965 [1907]), 134–35. See also Charles A. Beard, *An Economic Interpretation of the Constitution of the United States* (New York: Macmillan, 1960 [1913]), 159–62.

26. Even this proposal could perhaps be considered as republican, though perhaps minimally so, since the executive was elective rather than hereditary and was liable to impeachment.

27. Besides Gerry and Mason, the other opponents of popular election were Roger Sherman of Connecticut and Charles Pinckney of South Carolina. The six in favor were James Wilson, Gouverneur Morris, Rufus King, James Madison, John Dickinson, and Daniel Carroll.

28. Unlike Gerry, Mason had "argued strongly" for having the House of Representatives elected directly by the people.

3. The Origin and Development of the Congressional Caucus

1. See Joseph Charles, *The Origins of the American Party System* (Williamsburg: Institute of Early American History and Culture, 1956); Noble E. Cunningham Jr., *The Jeffersonian Republicans: The Formation of Party Organization 1789–1801* (Chapel Hill: University of North Carolina

Press, 1957); and William Nisbet Chambers, *Political Parties in a New Nation: The American Experience 1776–1809* (New York: Oxford University Press, 1963).

2. John Quincy Adams, *Memoirs of John Quincy Adams, Comprisng Portions of His Diary from 1795 to 1848*, ed. Charles Francis Adams (Philadelphia: J. B. Lippincott, 1874–1877), 242.

3. John Adams, *The Works of John Adams, Second President of the United States*, ed. Charles Francis Adams (Boston: Little, Brown, 1850–1856), 2:687.

4. See William Gordon, *The History of the Rise, Progress and Establishment of the Independence of the United States of America*, 4 vols. (London 1788), 1:365n [Ann Arbor: University Microfilms (American Culture Series, Reel 21, no. 208).

5. Chambers, *Political Parties in a New Nation*, 21.

6. *Webster's New Twentieth Century Dictionary of the English Language* (New York: 1951), 272.

7. Richard Hildreth, *The History of the United States of America* (New York: Harper, 1851), 4:687.

8. James A. Woodburn, *Political Parties and Party Problems in the United States* (New York, G. P. Putnam, 1903), 285; Thomas H. McKee, *National Conventions and Platforms* (Baltimore: Friedenwald, 1901), 6.

9. John B. McMaster, *History of the People of the United States, From the Revolution to the Civil War*, 8 vols. (New York: D. Appleton, 1883–1913), 2:490n; Stuart Lewis, *Party Principles and Practical Politics* (New York: Prentice-Hall, 1928), 172; Wilfred E. Binkley, *The Man in the White House: His Powers and Duties* (Baltimore: Johns Hopkins Press, 1959), 80; Chambers, *Political Parties in a New Nation*, 114–17; Cunningham, *The Jeffersonian Republicans*, 91, 62.

10. William Smith to Ralph Izard, May 18, 1796, in "The South Carolina Federalist II," ed. Ulrich B. Phillips, *American Historical Review* 14 (July 1909): 731–43.

11. George Gibbs, ed., *Memoirs of the Administrations of Washington and John Adams, Edited from the Papers of Oliver Wolcott* (New York: W. Van Norden, 1846), 1:387; William Vans Murray to James McHenry (photocopy), September 9, 1796, James McHenry Papers, Library of Congress; Svend Peterson, *A Statistical History of the American Presidential Elections* (New York: Ungar, 1963), 12.

12. James McHenry to John McHenry, May 20, 1800, in *Memoirs of the Administrations of Washington and John Adams*, ed. Gibbs, 347.

13. David H. Fischer, "The Myth of the Essex Junto," *William and Mary Quarterly* 21 (April, 1964): 226; Peterson, *A Statistical History of the American Presidential Elections*, 13.

14. Statement of James Nicholson, December 26, 1803, DeWitt Clinton Papers, Columbia University.

15. Albert Gallatin to his wife, May 12, 1800, in Henry Adams, *The Life of Albert Gallatin* (Philadelphia: J. B. Lippincott, 1879), 243.

16. *Niles' Weekly Register*, October 2, 1824, 66; Peter Freneau to Thomas Jefferson, December 2, 1800, in Richard B. Davis and Miledge B. Siegler, "Peter Freneau, Carolina Republican," *Journal of Southern History* 13 (August 1947): 395–405; Peterson, *A Statistical History of the American Presidential Elections*, 13.

17. John Randolph to James Monroe, February 28, 1804, James Monroe Papers, Library of Congress; John Randolph to Littleton W. Tazewell, February 26, 1804, Tazewell Family Papers, Virginia State Library; *National Intelligencer*, February 29 and March 2, 1804; see also *Niles' Weekly Register*, December 27, 1823, 258, and January 17, 1824, 306.

18. DeWitt Clinton to George Clinton, April 3, 1808, DeWitt Clinton Papers; James Lennox to James Madison, January 28, 1808, James Madison Papers; George Clinton to DeWitt Clinton, January 12, 1808, DeWitt Clinton Papers.

19. George Joy to James Madison, January 28, 1808, James Madison Papers; see again Lennox to Madison, January 28, 1808, James Madison Papers.

20. Harry Ammon, "James Monroe and the Election of 1808 in Virginia," *William and Mary Quarterly* 20 (January 1963), 33–56; *Colvin's Weekly Register*, January 23, 1808, 32; *National Intelligencer*, March 16, 1808, 3; *Colvin's Weekly Register*, February 6, 1808, 32; *Niles' Weekly Register*, February 24, 1824, 402.

21. Morgan Lewis to James Madison, January 9, 1808, James Madison Papers.

22. *National Intellingcer*, January 25, 1802, 2; *Memoirs of John Quincy Adams*, ed. Adams, 1:504–07; *Colvin's Weekly Register*, February 6, 1808, 63.

23. *National Intelligencer*, January 27, 1808, 3, and January 29, 1808, 3; *Colvin's Weekly Register*, February 6, 1808, 63–64; Ammon, "James Monroe and the Election of 1808 in Virginia," 39–46.

24. George Clinton to DeWitt Clinton, February 13, 1808, DeWitt Clinton Papers.

25. George Clinton to Pierre Van Cortlandt, February 20, 1808, Pierre Van Cortlandt Papers, New York Public Library.

26. George Clinton to Pierre Van Cortlandt, March 10, 1808, and February 5 and 20, 1808, Van Cortlandt Papers; George Clinton to DeWitt Clinton, February 26, 1808, DeWitt Clinton Papers.

27. DeWitt Clinton to George Clinton, April 3, 1808; George Clinton to DeWitt Clinton, April 10, 1808, DeWitt Clinton Papers.

28. Henry Lee to James Madison, February 10, 1808, James Madison Papers.

29. Reprinted in the *New York Evening Post*, June 1, 1808, 2; John Taylor to James Monroe, March 20, 1808, James Monroe Papers.

30. Samuel Eliot Morison, "The First National Nominating Convention, 1808," *American Historical Review* 17 (July 1912): 744–63.

31. J. H. Douglass to James Madison, June 17, 1808, James Madison Papers; *New York Evening Post*, September 28, 1808, 3; James Monroe to L. W. Tazewell, October 30, 1808, in *The Writings of James Monroe, Including a Collection of His Public and Private Papers and Correspondence*, ed. Stanlislaus Murray Hamilton (New York: G. P. Putnam's Sons, 1903), 5: 72–81.

32. Lyon to Bradley, *The Northern Post*, February 24, 1808, 2.

33. *National Intelligencer*, March 7, 1808, 2–3; *Colvin's Weekly Register*, March 12, 1808, 129–31.

34. *The Northern Post*, 3 March 1808, 3.

35. *Colvin's Weekly Register*, January 23, 1808, 32; February 20, 1808, 90–91.

36. Ibid., March 12, 1808, 132–46.

37. Peter B. Porter to DeWitt Clinton, 27 July 1808, DeWitt Clinton Papers.

38. William Lowndes, letter quoted in Irving Brant, *James Madison: The President* (Indianapolis: Bobbs-Merrill, 1956), 391.

39. Calhoun to James Macbride, April 18, 1812, in *The Papers of John C. Calhoun*, ed. Robert L. Meriwether (Columbia: University of South Carolina Press, 1959), 1:99–100.

40. Brant, *James Madison*, 421–36.

41. Augustus Foster to Lord Castlereagh, May 3, 1812, in Henry Adams, *The History of the United States* (New York: Charles Scribner's Sons, 1891), 6:212–14.

42. John Randolph to Joseph H. Nicholson, February 2, 1812, Bruce-Randolph Collection, Virginia State Library.

43. Littleton W. Tazewell to James Monroe, January 17, 1812, James Monroe Papers.

44. *National Intelligencer*, May 19, 1812, 3; *Niles' Weekly Register*, May 30, 1812, 192–93, June 27, 1812, 276.

45. Elbridge Gerry to James Madison, May 20, 1812, and John McKinley to Madison, June 1, 1812, James Madison Papers.

46. Benjamin Ferris et al., circular letter from the New York committee of correspondence, August 18, 1812, DeWitt Clinton Papers.

47. *Niles' Weekly Register*, September 12, 1812, 17–19.

48. *Niles' Weekly Register*, May 30, 1812, 196.

49. Elbridge Gerry to James Monroe, August 24, 1812, James Monroe Papers; Rufus King, "Notes on the Federal Convention," September 15–17, 1812, Rufus King Papers, New York Historical Society; John S. Murdock, "The First National Nominating Convention," *American Historical Review* 1 (July 1896): 680–83.

50. Samuel R. Betts to Martin Van Buren, January 19, 1816, Martin Van Buren Papers, Library of Congress.

51. John W. Taylor to E. Cowen, March 4, 1816, John Taylor Papers, New York Historical Society; *National Intelligencer*, March 6, 1816, 3.

52. *National Intelligencer*, March 12, 14, and 18, 1816, 2.

53. Crawford to Albert Gallatin, May 10, 1816, in *The Writings of Albert Gallatin*, ed. Adams, 1:702.

54. *Annals of Congress*, 13th Cong., 1st sess., January 3, 1814, 842–3; ibid., 14th Cong., 2nd sess., December 17, 1816, 310.

55. *Aurora*, September 7 and 24, October 31, and November 1, 1816.

56. January 8, 1816, 73.

57. January 22, 1816, 97; see also issues of March 4, 11, and 25, 1816.

58. *Niles' Weekly Register*, February 28, 1824, 402, contrasted with statement of March 23, 1816, 59.

59. *National Intelligencer*, March 29, 1816, 3.

60. Smith Thompson to Martin Van Buren, April 9, 1820, Martin Van Buren Papers.

61. Jackson to John Overton, December 21, 1823, and March 23, 1824, John Overton Papers, Claybrooke Collection, Tennessee Historical Society.

62. See William G. Morgan, "The Decline of the Congressional Nominating Caucus," *Tennessee Historical Quarterly* 24 (Fall 1965): 245–55.

63. Thomas Hart Benton, *Thirty Years View* (New York: D. Appleton, 1854), 1:49.

Part III: The National Nominating Convention

1. Lyn Ragsdale, *Vital Statistics on the Presidency: Washington to Clinton* (Washington, D.C.: Congressional Quarterly Press, 1996), 40.

2. *Presidential Elections, 1789–1996* (Washington, D.C.: Congressional Quarterly Press, 1997).

3. Ibid.

4. Theodore H. White, *The Making of the President 1968: A Narrative History of American Politics in Action* (New York: Atheneum, 1969), 273.

5. For different perspectives on these events and their consequences, see Byron E. Shafer, *Quiet Revolution: The Struggle for the Democratic Party and the Shaping of Post-Reform Politics* (New York: Russell Sage, 1983); Nelson W. Polsby, *Consequences of Party Reform* (New York: Oxford University Press, 1983); William Crotty, *Party Reform* (New York: Longman, 1983); Howard L. Reiter, *Selecting the President: The Nominating Process in Transition* (Philadelphia: University of Pennsylvania Press, 1985); and Michael G. Hagen and William G. Mayer, "The Modern Politics of Presidential Selection: How Changing the Rules Really Did Change the Game," in *In Pursuit of the*

White House 2000: How We Choose Our Presidential Nominees, ed. Mayer (New York: Chatham House/Seven Bridges Press, 2000), 1–55.

6. James S. Chase, *Emergence of the Presidential Nominating Convention 1789–1832* (Urbana: University of Illinois Press, 1973), ix–x.

7. Gerald M. Pomper, *Nominating the President: The Politics of Convention Choice* (New York: Norton, 1966), 22.

8. Paul T. David, Ralph M. Goldman, and Richard C. Bain, *The Politics of National Party Conventions*, cond. by Kathleen Sproul (New York: Vintage Books, 1964), 54.

9. Ibid., 53–54; see also *National Party Conventions, 1831–2000* (Washington, D.C.: Congressional Quarterly Press, 2001), 38.

10. *National Party Conventions, 1831–2000*, 38; see also David et al., *Politics of National Party Conventions*, 54.

11. Chase, *Emergence of the Presidential Nominating Convention*, 263.

12. Carl Becker, "The Unit Rule in National Nominating Conventions," *American Historical Review* 5 (October 1899): 64–82.

13. William Crotty, *Decision for the Democrats: Reforming the Party Structure* (Baltimore: Johns Hopkins Press, 1978), 87–88, 288–90.

14. *National Party Conventions, 1831–2000*, 52–53.

15. Becker, "The Unit Rule."

16. This paragraph draws on *National Party Conventions, 1831–2000*; Herbert Eaton's account of the 1880 convention in *Presidential Timber: A History of Nominating Conventions, 1868–1960* (New York: Free Press, 1964), 67–100; and Kenneth D. Ackerman, *Dark Horse: The Surprise Election and Political Murder of President James A. Garfield* (New York: Carroll and Graf, 2003).

17. Crotty, *Decision for the Democrats*, 11.

18. Pomper, *Nominating the President*, 182–83; for another typology, see William R. Keech and Donald R. Matthews, *The Party's Choice* (Washington, D.C.: Brookings, 1976).

19. Eaton, *Presidential Timber*, 321–24.

20. Sidney Hyman, "Nine Tests for the Presidential Hopeful," *New York Times Magazine*, January 4, 1959, 11.

21. David et al., *Politics of National Party Conventions*, 144.

22. See James E. Campbell, *The American Campaign: U.S. Presidential Campaigns and the National Vote* (College Station: Texas A&M University Press, 2000), 175–76.

23. On the southern factor in Sen. Richard Russell's failed bid for the 1952 Democratic nomination, see Robert A. Caro, *Master of the Senate: The Years of Lyndon Johnson* (New York: Alfred A. Knopf, 2002), 463–73.

24. Hyman, "Nine Tests."

25. Hyman, *The American President* (New York: Harper, 1954), 231–32.

26. The small-town tally does not include nominees brought up in relatively isolated rural settings such as farms or plantations.

27. Three governors of New York also won Republican nominations: Theodore Roosevelt, Charles Evans Hughes, and Thomas E. Dewey.

28. For a contrary analysis of presidents and prime ministers, see Hugh Heclo, "Presidential and Prime Ministerial Selection," in *Perspectives on Presidential Selection*, ed. Donald R. Matthews (Washington, D.C.: Brookings, 1973), 19–48.

29. Harold J. Laski, *The American Presidency: An Interpretation* (New York: Harper, 1940), 49–50.

30. See Aaron Wildavsky, "On the Superiority of National Conventions," *Review of Politics* 24

(July 1962): 307–19; Herbert McClosky, "Are Political Conventions Undemocratic?" *New York Times Magazine,* August 4, 1968, 10.

31. Murray Edelman, *The Symbolic Uses of Politics* (Urbana: University of Illinois Press, 1985), 94.

32. Eaton, *Presidential Timber,* 244–45.

33. Eugene H. Roseboom and Alfred E. Eckes Jr., *A History of Presidential Elections,* 4th ed. (New York: Collier Books, 1970), 182–83.

34. Ibid., 485.

35. David et al., *Politics of National Party Conventions,* 145–46. This book's claim that lack of geographical balance spells defeat was mistaken at the time of publication: regional duplication did not prevent the election of Grant and Colfax in 1868 or stop Truman and Barkley in 1948; subsequently, Clinton and Gore won in 1992 and 1996.

36. N's omit the Democratic ticket of 1840 and the Republican ticket of 1864. The 1840 Democratic convention refused to make a vice-presidential nomination as a show of contempt for Vice President Richard Johnson. The 1864 Republican convention picked Andrew Johnson of Tennessee, a war Democrat, as Lincoln's running mate. Tennessee, however, had forfeited its electoral votes by seceding.

37. Eaton, *Presidential Timber,* 387.

38. Jack W. Germond and Jules Witcover, *Whose Broad Stripes and Bright Stars? The Trivial Pursuit of the Presidency 1988* (New York: Time-Warner, 1989), 346.

39. This figure is derived from analysis of the candidates named as receiving votes on at least one convention ballot. See Richard C. Bain and Judith H. Parris, *Convention Decisions and Voting Records,* 2nd ed. (Washington, D.C.: Brookings, 1973), App. C; and *National Party Conventions 1831–2000* (Washington, D.C.: Congressional Quarterly, 2001).

40. Jack W. Germond and Jules Witcover, *Blue Smoke and Mirrors: How Reagan Won and Why Carter Lost the Election of 1980* (New York: Viking, 1981), 169.

41. Eaton, *Presidential Timber,* 67–86.

42. Jules Witcover, *Marathon: The Pursuit of the Presidency 1972–1977* (New York: Viking, 1977), 509.

43. Barton J. Bernstein, "Election of 1952," in *The Coming to Power,* ed. Arthur M. Schlesinger Jr. (New York: Chelsea House, 1972), 402.

44. Witcover, *Marathon,* 357–70; Germond and Witcover, *Whose Broad Stripes and Bright Stars?,* 346; William G. Mayer, "The Presidential Nominations," in *The Election of 2000,* ed. Gerald M. Pomper (New York: Chatham House/Seven Bridges Press, 2001), 39.

45. Barbara Slavin and Susan Page, "Cheney Rewrites Roles in Foreign Policy," *USA Today,* July 29, 2002, 1A.

46. Roseboom and Eckes describe English as a banker with a "barrel" in *History of Presidential Elections,* 99; on Davis's selection, see William H. Harbaugh, "Election of 1904," in *History of American Presidential Elections,* ed. Arthur M. Schlesinger (New York: Chelsea House, 1971), 3:1982–83.

47. On Morton's selection, see Robert F. Wesser, "Election of 1888," in *History of American Presidential Elections,* 2:1635; Paolo E. Coletta describes "Sunny Jim" Sherman as "rich" and "close to corporations" ("Election of 1908," in ibid., 3:2074).

48. Jack W. Germond and Jules Witcover, *Mad as Hell: Revolt at the Ballot Box, 1992* (New York: Time-Warner, 1993), 331–32.

49. James Madison, *Federalist Papers,* no. 58, in Alexander Hamilton, John Jay, and James Madison, *The Federalist,* ed. George W. Carey and James McClellan (Indianapolis: Liberty Fund, 2001), 304; see also *Federalist Papers,* no. 55.

50. See Joseph M. Bessette, *The Mild Voice of Reason: Deliberative Democracy and American National Government* (Chicago: University of Chicago Press, 1994), 46–48.

51. James Bryce, *The American Commonwealth* (Chicago: Charles H. Sergel, 1891), 2:216.

52. William Allen White, *The Autobiography of William Allen White* (New York: Macmillan, 1946), 588.

53. Will Rogers, *Convention Articles of Will Rogers,* ed. Joseph A. Stout (Stillwater: Oklahoma State University Press, 1976), 56.

54. Bain and Parris, *Convention Decisions and Voting Records,* App. C; *National Party Conventions 1831–2000,* 21.

55. R. Craig Sautter, *Philadelphia Presidential Conventions* (Highland Park, Ill.: December Press, 2000).

56. Pendleton Herring, *The Politics of Democracy: American Parties in Action* (New York: Norton, 1940), 226.

57. Ibid., 229.

58. Clinton Rossiter, *The American Presidency,* intro. by Michael Nelson (Baltimore: Johns Hopkins University Press, 1987), 178.

59. "Are Political Conventions Undemocratic?" *New York Times Magazine,* August 6, 1968, 63.

60. Democratic and Republican platform language quoted in *Toward a More Responsible Two-Party System: A Report of the Committee on Political Parties,* special supplement to the *American Political Science Review* 44 (1950): 52.

61. Gerald M. Pomper and Susan S. Lederman, *Elections in America: Control and Influence in Democratic Politics,* 2nd ed. (New York: Longman, 1980), 129–53; Jeff Fishel, *Presidents and Promises* (Washington, D.C.: Congressional Quarterly Press, 1985).

62. Quoted in Bryce, *The American Commonwealth,* 191.

63. Nelson W. Polsby and Aaron B. Wildavsky, "Uncertainty and Decision-Making at National Conventions," in *Politics and Social Life: An Introduction to Political Behavior,* ed. Nelson W. Polsby, Robert A. Dentler, and Paul A. Smith (Boston: Houghton Mifflin, 1963), 378–89.

64. Eaton, *Presidential Timber,* 238–39.

65. David et al., *The Politics of National Conventions,* 245.

66. James Q. Wilson, *The Amateur Democrat: Club Politics in Three Cities* (Chicago: University of Chicago Press, 1962), 3.

67. Ibid., 4.

68. Aaron B. Wildavsky, "The Goldwater Phenomenon: Purists, Politicians, and the Two-Party System," *Review of Politics* 27 (July 1965): 386–413.

69. Nelson W. Polsby and Aaron B. Wildavsky, *Presidential Elections: Strategies of American Electoral Politics,* 3rd ed. (New York: Charles Scribner's Sons, 1971), 35–59; John W. Soule and Wilma E. McGrath, "A Comparative Study of Presidential Nomination Conventions: The Democrats of 1968 and 1972," *American Journal of Political Science* 19 (August 1975): 501–19.

70. See, for example, Walter J. Stone and Alan I. Abramowitz, "Winning May Not Be Everything, but It's More Than We Thought: Presidential Party Activists in 1980," *American Political Science Review* 77 (December 1983): 945–56.

71. Hanna Fenichel Pitkin, *The Concept of Representation* (Berkeley: University of California Press, 1967), 38–39.

72. *Toward A More Responsible Two-Party System,* 28–29.

73. Crotty, *Party Reform*; Shafer, *Quiet Revolution.*

74. Pitkin, *The Concept of Representation,* 92–111.

75. See esp. Bryon E. Shafer, *Bifurcated Politics: Evolution and Reform in the National Party Convention* (New York: Russell Sage, 1988).

76. John Adams, quoted in Pitkin, *The Concept of Representation*, 60.

77. Barbara Farah, "Delegate Polls: 1944–1984," *Public Opinion* (August/September 1984): 43–45.

78. David et al., *Politics of National Party Conventions*, 229–47.

79. Jeane Kirkpatrick, *The New Presidential Elite: Men and Women in National Politics* (New York: Russell Sage, 1976), 63; see also Emmett H. Buell Jr. and John S. Jackson III, "The National Conventions: Diminished but Still Important in a Primary-Dominated Process," in *Nominating the President*, ed. Emmett H. Buell Jr. and Lee Sigelman (Knoxville: University of Tennessee Press, 1991), 230–31.

80. "Convention Delegates: Who They Are," *New York Times*, August 14, 2000, A19.

81. Buell and Jackson, "National Conventions," 230; *Washington Post/ABC News* polls, repr. in *Washington Post Weekly Edition*, August 12–18 and August 26–September 1, 1996; "Convention Delegates: Who They Are."

82. Herbert McClosky et al., "Issue Conflict and Consensus Among Party Leaders and Followers," *American Political Science Review* 54 (June 1960): 406–27.

83. Everett C. Ladd, *Where Have All the Voters Gone?* (New York: Norton, 1977); John S. Jackson III, Jesse C. Brown, and Barbara L. Brown, "Recruitment, Representation, and Political Values: The 1976 Democratic Convention Delegates," *American Politics Quarterly* 6 (April 1978): 187–212; Commission on Presidential Nominations and Party Structure, *Openness, Participation, and Party-Building: Reforms for a Stronger Democratic Party* (Washington, D.C.: Democratic National Committee, 1978).

84. Shafer, *Bifurcated Politics*, 104; see also John S. Jackson III, Jesse C. Brown, and David Bositis, "Herbert McClosky and Friends Revisited: 1980 Democratic and Republican Party Elites Compared to the Mass Public," *American Politics Quarterly* 10 (April 1982): 158–80.

85. Warren E. Miller, *Without Consent: Mass-Elite Linkages in Presidential Politics* (Lexington: University Press of Kentucky, 1988), 87–88.

86. "Convention Delegates: Who They Are."

87. *1996 Washington Post/ABC News* polls; "Convention Delegates: Who They Are."

88. Polsby, *Consequences of Party Reform*, 77.

89. Polsby and Wildavsky take strong exception to this claim in "Uncertainty and Decision-Making at the National Convention," 386.

90. See Shafer, *Bifurcated Politics*, 17–39; David B. Truman, "Party Reform, Party Atrophy, and Constitutional Change: Some Reflections," *Political Science Quarterly* 99 (Winter 1984–85): 637–55.

91. On partisan bias in television news stories, see Stephen J. Farnsworth and S. Robert Lichter, *The Nightly News Nightmare: Network Television's Coverage of U.S. Presidential Elections, 1988–2000* (Lanham, Md.: Rowman and Littlefield, 2003), 112–26. This study found that Democratic candidates got more favorable coverage than Republicans in general election campaigns but not during the primary season.

92. See Larry David Smith and Dan Nimmo, *Cordial Concurrence: Orchestrating National Party Conventions in the Telepolitical Age* (Westport, Conn.: Praeger, 1991).

93. Martin P. Wattenberg, *The Rise of Candidate-Centered Politics: Presidential Elections of the 1980s* (Cambridge: Harvard University Press, 1991), 57–58.

94. Harold W. Stanley and Richard G. Niemi, *Vital Statistics on American Politics 2001–2002* (Washington, D.C.: Congressional Quarterly Press, 2002), 191.

95. "Frontloading, Progressive Disengagement Creates Second Lowest Turnout," Committee for the Study of the American Electorate, August 31, 2002, posted on www.gspm.org/csae/cgans/html.

96. Frank Newport, "From the Editor: Volatility in the Polls, Bush's Bounce, and What Gore Needs," Gallup News Services, August 14, 2000; David W. Moore, "Poll Analyses: Major Turning Points in 2000 Election: Primary Season, Party Conventions, and Debates," Gallup News Services, November 7, 2000, both on http://www.gallup.com/poll/releases.

97. Lydia Saad, "Poll Analyses: Average Convention 'Bounce' Since 1964 Is Six Points," Gallup News Services, July 26, 2000; http://www.gallup.com/poll/releases.

98. Ibid. Saad also reports averages for first and second conventions as well as for incumbent and challenger conventions.

99. Randal C. Archibold, "For 2004 Convention, G.O.P. Raises $91 Million in a Hurry," *New York Times*, June 19, 2003, A24.

100. Diana Dwyre and Robin Kolodny, "Throwing Out the Rule Book: Party Financing of the 2000 Elections," in *Financing the 2000 Election*, ed. David B. Magleby (Washington, D.C.: Brookings, 2002), 137.

5. The First National Nominating Convention

1. John S. Murdock, "The First National Nominating Convention," *American Historical Review* 1 (July 1896): 680–83.

2. Morison uses the terms *Democrat* and *Republican* interchangeably (editor's note).

3. Timothy Pickering to C.W. Hare, January 16, 1808, Pickering Papers, 14:177.

4. Timothy Pickering to George Rose, March 13, 1808, Pickering Papers, 14:197.

5. Timothy Pickering, *A Letter from the Hon. Timothy Pickering . . . Addressed to his Excellency James Sullivan*, Boston, March 9, 1808.

6. Pickering's complaint in 1804, in *Documents Relating to New England Federalism, 1800–1815*, ed. Henry Adama (Boston: Little, Brown, 1905), 352.

7. C. W. Hare to H. G. Otis, Otis papers in the author's possession.

8. Christopher Gore to Rufus King, Boston, June 8 and 16, 1808, in Charles R. King, *The Life and Correspondence of Rufus King* (New York: G. P. Putnam's Sons, 1894–1900; repr. Da Capo, 1971), 5:100–02.

9. I take it that the Essex junto, from 1800 to 1815, should be defined as the Massachusetts Federalist leaders who opposed John Adams in 1800, who condoned the Chesapeake outrage and who squinted at secession in 1814.

10. Christopher Gore to Rufus King, Boston, June 16, 1808, in King, *The Life and Correspondence of Rufus King*, 5:101.

11. So far as appears from the available sources. The idea was probably discussed by H. G. Otis with politicians in New York and Philadelphia on a visit to those cities in May 1808.

12. Curiously [. . .] the Federalists held one of the first conventions that nominated candidates for office (in Pennsylvania, 1788). Joseph S. Walton, "Nominating Conventions in Pennsylvania," *American Historical Review* 2 (June 1897): 262–78.

13. C. W. Hare to H. G. Otis, July 12, 1808, Otis papers.

14. George Cabot to H. G. Otis, two letters of August 14, 1808, Otis papers.

15. W. M. Meigs, "Pennsylvania Politics Early in This Century," *Pennsylvania Magazine of History and Biography* 17 (1893–94): 462–90.

16. The resolutions are printed in the Boston *Columbian Centinel*, July 20, 1808, quoted from *U. S. Gazette*.

17. Abraham Van Vechten to H. G. Otis, July 21, 1808; see index to De Alva Alexander, *Political History of New York* (New York: Henry Holt, 1906).

18. Letter of New York Federalist committee of correspondence (which was evidently ap-

pointed by the convention to a position corresponding to the modern Committee on Notifications), to the Charleston Federalist committee, September 1808. Manuscript copy enclosed in letter of October 9 from the New York committee to the Boston committee.

19. Letter of the Philadelphia committee to the New York committee, quoted in "To the Honble Harrison G. Otis Esquire and the Gentlemen of the Federal Committee in Boston," October 6, 1808.

20. Rufus King to Christopher Gore, September 27, 1808; King, *Rufus King*, 5:104.

21. Theophilus Parsons, "An Address to the Citizens of Rhode Island, on the Choice of Electors of President and Vice-President of the United States," Providence, November 1808, 13–14, also in the *Providence Rhode-Island American*, November 17, 1808.

22. James B. Mason to H. G. Otis, November 21, 1808, Otis papers.

7. The National Convention

1. Ostrogorski qualified this claim with a footnote about the 1896 Democratic convention, which, dominated by "silverites," rejected the committee's "gold-bug" candidate for temporary chairman.

2. Ostrogorski cites a "well known American journalist" who recall the sounds of an 1860 convention: "Imagine all the hogs ever slaughtered in Cincinnati giving their death squeals together."

8. Rationality and Uncertainty at National Nominating Conventions

1. See William H. Riker, *The Theory of Political Coalitions* (New Haven: Yale University Press, 1962), 78; also Anthony Downs, *An Economic Theory of Democracy* (New York: Harper, 1957), 135–36.

2. See Nelson W. Polsby and Aaron B. Wildavsky, "Uncertainty and Decision-Making at the National Conventions," in *Politics and Social Life: An Introduction to Political Behavior*, ed. Nelson W. Polsby, Robert A. Dentler, and Paul A. Smith (Boston: Houghton Mifflin Co., 1963), 370–89.

3. Ibid., 378–79.

4. Ibid., 375.

5. William A. Gamson, "Coalition Formation at Presidential Nominating Conventions," *Journal of Sociology* 68 (September 1962): 157–51, esp. 166.

6. These cases are adapted from Nelson Polsby and Aaron Wildavasky, *Presidential Elections*, 2nd ed. (New York: Scribner, 1968), 87–90. See also Gerald Pomper, *Nominating the President: The Politics of Convention Choice* (Evanston: Northwestern University Press, 1963), 45.

7. Polsby and Wildavsky, "Uncertainty and Decision-Making," 387.

8. See John Soule and J. W. Clarke, "Amateurs and Professionals: A Study of Delegates to the 1968 Democratic National Convention," *American Political Science Review* 64 (September 1970): 888–98.

9. Polsby and Wildavsky, "Uncertainty and Decision-Making," 380.

10. Factionalism figures importantly in presidential nominating conventions. See Frank Munger and James Blackhurst, "Factionalism in the National Conventions, 1940–1964: An Analysis of Ideological Consistency in State Delegation Voting," *Journal of Politics* 27 (May 1965): 375–93.

11. When there are two major contenders for each of the seventeen nominations, eleven correct guesses is nearly a 30 percent improvement on random guessing; when there are three major contenders, eleven correct guesses is nearly a 95 percent improvement on random guessing; and when there are four major contenders, eleven correct guesses is over a 150 percent improvement.

12. Paul T. David, Ralph M. Goldman, and Richard C. Bain, *The Politics of National Party Conventions*, cond. by Kathleen Sproul (New York: Vintage, 1964), 121; Mark Sullivan, *Our Times: The United States 1900–1925* (New York: Scribner, 1935), 121.

13. V. O. Key Jr., *Politics, Parties, and Pressure Groups*, 5th ed. (New York: Thomas Y. Crowell, 1964), chap. 14.

14. Pomper, *Nominating the President*, 143–53. Pomper mentions three classic strategies which occur at conventions, two of which have been considered earlier in this research: the band-wagon, the deal, and the test of strength. While the bandwagon and the deal are strategies designed to increase a candidate's strength, the test of strength may well be the most important because it is a means whereby candidates can gain additional information about the relative strengths of proto-coalitions. On this basis, candidates can assess the advantages of a deal and the chances of a successful bandwagon.

10. Television's Great Leap Forward

1. Jack Gould, "The X of the Campaign—TV Personality," *New York Times*, June 22, 1952, in James Fixx, *The Mass Media and Politics* (New York: Arno Press, 1972), 22.

2. Several years later I discovered that the microphone behind the drape in the meeting room had not been placed there by NBC. At a news broadcasters' convention I was introduced to a news director from a 250-watt radio station in Houston owned by Roy Hofheinz, one-time mayor of that city. He reminded me that we had met in the Conrad Hilton Hotel in Chicago during the 1952 Republican convention. Our rooms had been on the same corridor. I remembered that as I walked down the corridor, I had seen a man, sitting beside an open door, wearing a headset and listening intently to something I could not hear. I asked him if he happened to be the man with the headset. He replied affirmatively, so I went on to ask what he had been listening to so patiently for hours at a time. His answer: he had been monitoring the proceedings of the credentials committee through a microphone he had placed behind a drape in the committee room.

3. Kurt Lang and Gladys Lang, *Politics and Television* (Chicago: Quadrangle Books, 1968), 137.

4. "After Chicago," *New York Times*, July 26, 1952, in Fixx, *The Mass Media and Politics*, 23.

Part IV: The Rise of a Primary-Dominated Process

1. For more on primary origins, see Austin Ranney, *Curing the Mischiefs of Faction: Party Reform in America* (Berkeley: University of California Press, 1975), 121.

2. Louise Overacker, *The Presidential Primary* (New York: Macmillan, 1926), 15.

3. Nancy C. Unger, *Fighting Bob LaFollette: The Righteous Reformer* (Chapel Hill: University of North Carolina Press, 2000), 109.

4. James W. Davis, *Presidential Primaries: Road to the White House*, rev. ed. (Westport, Conn.: Greenwood, 1980), 42–43; *Presidential Elections 1789–1996* (Washington, D.C.: Congressional Quarterly Press, 1997), 149–50.

5. Overacker, *The Presidential Primary*, 164.

6. David Bruce Johnson, *National Party Platforms*, vol. 1, *1840–1956* (Urbana: University of Illinois Press, 1978), 170, 176.

7. Letter to A. Mitchell Palmer, February 5, 1913, 63rd Cong., 1st sess., *Congressional Record* 53 (1913): 12620.

8. Woodrow Wilson, Annual Address to Congress, December 2, 1913, in americanpresidency.org: State of the Union Addresses and Messages, http://www.presidency.uscb.edu.

9. Strong party advocates of that day also denigrated reformers as feckless and hypocritical. Former president William Howard Taft hit upon this theme in a 1916 lecture at Columbia Uni-

versity: "We find that often the difference between political machines and a party organization for reform is only determined by the question, 'Is it for you or against you?' If it is for you and your ideas, it is a justifiable organization, and the more effective you can make it, the better. If it is against you, it is a low political machine and ought to be condemned out of the mouths of all decent people." William Howard Taft, *Our Chief Magistrate* (New York: Columbia University Press, 1924), 68.

10. M. Margaret Conway, *Political Participation in the United States*, 3rd ed. (Washington, D.C.: Congressional Quarterly Press, 2000), 9.

11. Norman J. Ornstein, Thomas E. Mann, and Michael J. Malbin, *Vital Statistics on Congress 2001–2002* (Washington, D.C.: AEI Press, 2002), 81.

12. Austin Ranney, "Turnout and Representation in Presidential Primary Elections," *American Political Science Review* 66 (March 1972): 35.

13. Ronald D. Hedlund and Meredith W. Watts, "The Wisconsin Open Primary: 1968 to 1984," *American Politics Quarterly* (January–April 1986): 55–74.

14. *Cousins v. Wigoda*, 419 U.S. 477. This case arose out of a challenge to the Illinois delegation at the 1972 Democratic convention. The justices upheld the right of the national party to impose standards for delegate selection upon state parties, regardless of state laws to the contrary, on grounds that the national party and its adherents enjoy a First Amendment right of political association, which presupposes freedom to designate appropriate voters and devise rules governing their participation in this association. See Gary D. Wekkin, *Democrat versus Democrat: The National Party's Campaign to Close the Wisconsin Primary* (Columbia: University of Missouri Press, 1984).

15. Rhodes Cook, *Race for the Presidency: Winning the 1988 Nomination* (Washington, D.C.: Congressional Quarterly Press, 1987), 83–84.

16. These were the results of exit polls posted on CNN.com/allpolitics. Scheduled for the same day, the Michigan Democratic primary was of no consequence, since it did provide for separate tabulation of the vote for Gore and Bradley. Michigan Democrats held precinct caucuses on March 11.

17. Bruce E. Cain and Elisabeth R. Gerber, *Voting at the Political Fault Line: California's Experiment with the Blanket Primary* (Berkeley: University of California Press, 2002), 5.

18. *California Democratic Party v. Jones*, 530 U.S. 567 (2000).

19. Richard M. Scammon, Alice V. McGillivray, and Rhodes Cook, *America Votes 22: A Handbook of Contemporary American Election Statistics* (Washington, D.C.: Congressional Quarterly, 1998); *America Votes 24* (Washington, D.C.: Congressional Quarterly, 2001).

20. Walter Lippmann, *Public Opinion* (New York: Macmillan, 1922).

21. For examples of how news media "frame" candidates and issues, see Marjorie Random Hershey, "The Campaign and the Media," in *The Election of 2000*, ed. Gerald M. Pomper (New York: Chatham House/Seven Bridges Press, 2001), 46–72; see also Michael J. Robinson and Margaret A. Sheehan, *Over the Wire and On TV: CBS and UPI in Campaign '80* (New York: Russell Sage, 1983).

22. Larry J. Sabato, *Feeding Frenzy: How Attack Journalism Has Transformed American Politics* (New York: Free Press, 1993); Thomas E. Patterson, *Out of Order* (New York: Vintage Books, 1994); Stephen J. Farnsworth and S. Robert Lichter, *The Nightly News Nightmare: Network Television's Coverage of U.S. Presidential Elections, 1988–2000* (Lanham, Md.: Rowman and Littlefield, 2003).

23. See, for example, Emmett H. Buell Jr., "Meeting Expectations," in *Nominating the President*, ed. Emmett H. Buell Jr., and Lee Sigelman (Knoxville: University of Tennessee Press, 1991), 150–95.

24. Patterson, *Out of Order.*

25. Alexander Heard, *The Costs of Democracy* (Chapel Hill: University of North Carolina Press, 1960), 321–22.

26. See John C. Green and Nathan Bigelow, "The 2000 Presidential Nominations: The Costs of Innovation," in *Financing the 2000 Elections,* ed. David B. Magleby (Washington, D.C.: Brookings, 2002), 49–78; and Diana Dwyre and Robin Kolodny, "Throwing Out the Rule Book: Party Financing of the 2000 Elections," in ibid., 133–62.

27. See Nelson W. Polsby, "Money in Presidential Campaigns," in *New Federalist Papers: Essays in Defense of the Constitution,* ed. Alan Brinkley, Nelson W. Polsby, and Kathleen M. Sullivan (New York: Norton, 1997), 51–58; and Bradley A. Smith, *Unfree Speech: The Folly of Campaign Finance Reform* (Princeton: Princeton University Press, 2001).

28. See Seth Gitell, "The Democratic Party Suicide Bill," *Atlantic Monthly* (July–August 2003): 106–13.

29. See, for example, Scott Keeter and Cliff Zukin, *Uninformed Choice: The Failure of the New Presidential Nominating System* (New York: Praeger, 1983); Samuel L. Popkin, *The Reasoning Voter: Communication and Persuasion in Presidential Campaigns* (Chicago: University of Chicago Press, 1991); and Thomas E. Patterson, *The Vanishing Voter: Public Involvement in an Age of Uncertainty* (New York: Knopf, 2002).

30. On state rules for presidential primaries during this time, see Davis, *Presidential Primaries.*

31. David E. Price, *Bringing Back the Parties* (Washington, D.C.: Congressional Quarterly Press, 1984), 146–48.

32. Quoted in Robert E. DiClerico, "Evolution of the Presidential Nominating Process," in DiClerico and James W. Davis, *Choosing Our Choices: Debating the Presidential Nominating Process* (Lanham, Md.: Rowman and Littlefield, 2000), 20.

33. Ibid, 19.

34. Austin Ranney, "Changing the Rules of the Nominating Game," in *Choosing the President,* ed. James David Barber (Englewood Cliffs., N.J., 1974), 73–74.

35. This paragraph draws heavily on William G. Mayer, "Caucuses: How They Work, What Differences They Make," in *In Pursuit of the White House: How We Choose Our Presidential Nominees,* ed. Mayer (Chatham, N.J.: Chatham House, 1996), 105–57.

36. Hugh Winebrenner, *The Iowa Precinct Caucuses: The Making of a Media Event* (Ames: Iowa State University Press, 1998), 35–56. Winebrenner also details how caucuses work in both parties.

37. Nelson W. Polsby, "The Democratic Nomination," in *The American Elections of 1980,* ed. Austin Ranney (Washington, D.C.: American Enterprise Institute, 1981), 47–48.

38. Susan Berry Casey, *Hart and Soul: Gary Hart's New Hampshire Odyssey and Beyond* (Concord, N.H.: NHI Press, 1986), 202.

39. See *Media and Momentum: The New Hampshire Primary and Nomination Politics,* ed. Gary R. Orren and Nelson W. Polsby (Chatham, N.J.: Chatham House, 1987); see also Emmett H. Buell Jr., "The Changing Face of the New Hampshire Primary," in *In Pursuit of the White House 2000,* ed. Mayer, 87–144. On New Hampshire primary activists, see Emmett H. Buell Jr., "Divisive Primaries and Participation in Fall Presidential Campaigns: A Study of 1984 New Hampshire Primary Activists," *American Politics Quarterly* 14 (October 1986): 376–90; see also Dayton Duncan, *Grass Roots: One Year in the Life of the New Hampshire Presidential Primary* (New York: Viking, 1991); and Niall Palmer, *The New Hampshire Primary and the American Electoral Process* (Boulder, Colo.: Westview, 1997).

40. Walter F. Mondale, *The Accountability of Power: Towards a Responsible Presidency* (New York: David McKay, 1975), 41–42.

41. Emmett H. Buell Jr., "First-in-the-Nation: Disputes Over the Timing of Early Democratic Presidential Primaries and Caucuses in 1984 and 1988," *Journal of Law and Politics* 4 (Fall 1987), 311–42.

42. Dennis Roddy, "Mondale May Be the Candidate Before April 10," Greensburg (Pa.) *Sunday Tribune-Review,* February 26, 1984.

43. On front-loading and related changes, see Michael G. Hagen and William G. Mayer, "The Modern Politics of Presidential Selection: How Changing the Rules Really Did Change the Game," in *In Pursuit of the White House 2000*, ed. Mayer, 1–56; see also Andrew E. Busch and William G. Mayer, *The Front-loading Problem in Presidential Nominations* (Washington, D.C.: Brookings, 2004).

44. Arthur T. Hadley, *The Invisible Primary* (Englewood Cliffs, N.J.: Prentice-Hall, 1976), xiii. For a critique of Hadley's argument, see Emmett H. Buell Jr., "The Invisible Primary," in *In Pursuit of the White House,* ed. Mayer, 1–43. James W. Ceaser and Andrew E. Busch provide a detailed account of the 2000 invisible primary in *The Perfect Tie: The True Story of the 2000 Presidential Election* (Lanham, Md.: Rowman and Littlefield, 2001), 49–76.

45. On poll standings during the invisible primaries of 1972–1992, see Buell, "The Invisible Primary," 16–20; Buell discusses polling during the 1996 invisible primary in "Some Things Are Predictable: Nominating Dole, Clinton, and Perot" in *Politics in Era of Divided Government: Elections and Governance in the Second Clinton Administration,* ed. Harvey L. Shantz (New York: Routledge, 2001), 1–41.

46. Quoted in Buell, "The Invisible Primary," 12.

47. Herbert E. Alexander, *Financing the 1968 Election* (Lexington, Mass.: Lexington Books, 1971), 50–51.

48. Herbert E. Alexander and Brian A. Haggerty, *Financing the 1984 Election* (Lexington, Mass.: Lexington Books, 1987), 200.

49. Barbara Norrander, quoted in Patterson, *The Vanishing Voter*, 115.

50. On the BCRA, see Michael J. Malbin, ed., *Life After Reform: When the Bipartisan Campaign Reform Act Meets Politics* (Lanham, Md.: Rowman and Littlefield, 2003).

51. This paragraph draws on findings reported in studies by Emmett H. Buell Jr.: "'Locals' and 'Cosmopolitans': National, Regional, and State Newspaper Coverage of the New Hampshire Primary," in *Media and Momentum,* ed. Orren and Polsby, 60–103; "Meeting Expectations," in *Nominating the President,* 154–56; "The Invisible Primary," 24–32; "The 'Invisible Primary' Revisited," presented at the annual meeting of the Southern Political Science Association, Atlanta, November 9, 1996; analysis of ABC, CBS, CNN, and NBC stories mentioning each candidate from July 1, 1998, to January 24, 2000, as summarized by the Vanderbilt Television News Archive.

52. Ceaser and Busch, *The Perfect Tie,* 66–67.

53. Mark J. Rozell, "The Christian Right in the 2000 GOP Presidential Campaign," in *Piety, Politics, and Pluralism,* ed. Mary C. Segers (Lanham, Md.: Rowman and Littlefield, 2002), 57–72; Ceaser and Busch, *The Perfect Tie*, 92–93.

54. Richard L. Berke, "Surprising Straw Poll Gives Dole a Glimpse of the Battles Ahead," *New York Times,* August 21, 1995, A1; Hugh Winebrenner, correspondence with the author, September 28, 1995.

55. James A. Barnes, "The Invisible Primary and the Hidden Campaign," in *The State of American Politics,* ed. Byron E. Shafer (Lanham, Md.: Rowman and Littlefield, 2002), 59–61.

56. David Yepsen, "Straw Poll Solidifies Bush Lead," *Des Moines Register,* August 15, 1999, 1A.

57. Buell, "The 'Invisible Primary' Revisited."

58. See Tami Buhr, "What Voters Know About the Candidates and How They Learn It: The 1996 New Hampshire Republican Primary as a Case Study," in *In Pursuit of the White House 2000*, ed. Mayer, 203–53; see also Samuel J. Best and Clark Hubbard, "The Role of Televised Debates in the Presidential Nominating Process," in ibid., 255–84.

59. "Frontloading, Progressive Disengagement Creates Second Lowest Primary Turnout," Committee for the Study of the American Electorate, August 31, 2000.

60. Patterson, *The Vanishing Voter*, 111–12.

61. See also Martin P. Wattenberg, *Where Have All the Voters Gone?* (Cambridge: Harvard University Press, 2002), 7. Wattenberg downplays the distortion factor, arguing that removing noncitizens from turnout estimates does not alter the trend for voting in presidential elections.

62. Everett C. Ladd quotes Curtis Gans and responds in "The Turnout Muddle," *America at the Polls 1994* (Storrs, Conn.: Roper Center for Public Opinion Research, 1995), 15.

63. On this point, see Mayer's account in "The Presidential Nominations," 15–16.

64. Ceaser and Busch, *The Perfect Tie*, 52.

65. For example, I excluded New York from this overview because Republican primary rules did not allow a direct preference vote. Likewise, I included Texas because both parties held preference primaries on the same day, even though Texas Democrats chose their delegates later in caucuses restricted to voters who had participated in the primary.

66. Ceaser and Busch, *Upside Down and Inside Out*, 67.

67. See ibid., 41; also Ryan J. Barilleaux and Randall E. Adkins, "The Nominations: Process and Patterns," in *The Elections of 1992*, ed. Michael Nelson (Washington, D.C.: Congressional Quarterly Press, 1993), 44–45.

68. See table 2.5 in Ross K. Baker, "Sorting Out and Suiting Up: The Presidential Nominations," in *The Election of 1992*, ed. Gerald M. Pomper (Chatham, N.J.: Chatham House, 1993), 39–73.

69. See Harold W. Stanley, "The Nominations: Republican Doldrums, Democratic Revival," in *The Elections of 1996*, ed. Michael Nelson (Washington, D.C.: Congressional Quarterly Press, 1997), 32. Ceaser and Busch write that all doubt of Dole's victory had ended by mid-March. See James W. Ceaser and Andrew E. Busch, *Losing to Win: The 1996 Elections and American Politics* (Lanham, Md.: Rowman and Littlefield, 1997), 89. Mayer argues that the cutoff date is really March 2, the day of Dole's resounding victory over Buchanan in South Carolina: "Never again would Dole's quest for the nomination be seriously challenged." See William G. Mayer, "The Presidential Nominations," in *The Election of 1996*, ed. Gerald M. Pomper (Washington, D.C.: Congressional Quarterly Press, 1997), 21–76.

70. Overacker, *The Presidential Primary*, 143.

71. See, for example, Thomas B. Edsall and Mary D. Edsall, *Chain Reaction: The Impact of Race, Rights, and Taxes on American Politics* (New York: Norton, 1991); and David G. Lawrence, *The Collapse of the Democratic Presidential Majority: Realignment, Dealignment, and Electoral Change from Franklin Roosevelt to Bill Clinton* (Boulder, Colo.: Westview, 1997); see also Ceaser and Busch, *The Perfect Tie*, 1–14; Daniel Wirls, "Voting Behavior: The Balance of Power in American Politics," in *The Elections of 2000*, ed. Michael Nelson (Washington, D.C.: Congressional Quarterly Press, 2001), 93–108.

72. Paul Abramson, John H. Aldrich, and David W. Rohde, *Change and Continuity in the 2000 Elections* (Washington, D.C.: Congressional Quarterly Press, 2002), 168–91.

73. See esp. Earl Black and Merle Black, *The Rise of Southern Republicans* (Cambridge: Belknap Press, 2003).

74. Chandler Davidson, *Race and Class in Texas Politics* (Princeton: Princeton University Press, 1990), 221–39.

75. Charles Prysby, "Realignment among Southern Party Activists," presented at the annual meeting of the American Political Science Association, Chicago, 1992.

76. This paragraph draws from Taylor E. Dark, *The Unions and the Democrats*, rev. ed. (Ithaca: Cornell University Press, 1999); and Herbert E. Asher et al., *American Labor Unions in the Electoral Arena: People, Passions, and Power* (Lanham, Md.: Rowan and Littlefield, 2001).

77. Ceaser and Busch, *The Perfect Tie*, 109–32; Barnes, "The Invisible Primary and the Hidden Campaign"; Emmett H. Buell Jr., "Some Things Are Predictable," 1–41.

78. Brooks Jackson, "Financing the 1996 Campaign: The Law of the Jungle," in *Toward the Millennium: The Elections of 1996*, ed. Larry Sabato (Boston: Allyn and Bacon, 1997), 237.

79. *Washington Post/ABC News* telephone polls of 506 Republican delegates and 508 Democratic delegates summarized in national convention supplements of the *Washington Post National Weekly Edition*, August 12–18 and August 26–September 1, 1996.

80. This account of the 2000 pre-convention phase relies principally on Ceaser and Busch, *The Perfect Tie*, 109–32.

81. Barbara Norrander, "Selective Participation: Presidential Primary Voters as a Subset of General Election Voters," *American Politcs Quarterly* 14 (January–April 1986): 35–54.

82. V. O. Key Jr., *Southern Politics in State and Nation* (New York: Knopf, 1949), 526.

83. V. O. Key Jr., *American State Politics: An Introduction* (New York: Alfred A. Knopf, 1956), 152–53.

84. Ibid.

85. Ranney, "Turnout and Representation in Presidential Primary Elections."

86. James I. Lengle, *Representation and Presidential Primaries: The Democratic Party in the Post-Reform Era* (Westport, Conn.: Greenwood Press, 1981)

87. John G. Geer, *Nominating Presidents: An Evaluation of Voters and Primaries* (Westport, Conn.: Greenwood Press, 1989).

88. V. O. Key Jr., *The Responsible Electorate: Rationality in Presidential Voting, 1936–1960* (Cambridge: Belknap Press, 1966).

89. Herbert M. Kritzer, "The Representativeness of the 1972 Presidential Primaries," in *The Party Symbol: Readings on Political Parties*, ed. William Crotty (San Francisco: Freeman, 1980), 148–54.

90. Keeter and Zukin, *Uninformed Choice*, 25–52.

91. William Crotty and John S. Jackson III, *Presidential Primaries and Nominations* (Washington, D.C.: Congressional Quarterly Press, 1983), 85–97.

92. Barbara Norrander, "Ideological Representativeness of Presidential Primary Voters," *American Journal of Political Science* 33 (August 1989): 571.

93. Michael G. Hagen, "Voter Turnout in Primary Elections," in *The Iowa Caucuses and the Presidential Nominating Process*, ed. Peverill Squire (Boulder, Colo.: Westview, 1989), 51–87.

12. What the Political Parties Are Not

1. E. B. Logan, ed., *The American Political Scene* (New York: Harper, 1936), 72.

2. There were better reasons for the development of the convention systems and the direct primary than the democratization of the internal processes of the parties. Destruction of the Congressional Caucus became necessary when the Era of Good Feeling produced a one-party system. After 1896 one-party areas deprived people of an alternative in state and local elections in some regions. The direct primary did something to restore the alternative. In a decentralized party system some formal means of settling internecine party conflicts must be provided.

13. Party Reform: Revisionism Revised

1. James Madison, *Federalist Papers,* no. 39, in *The Federalist Papers,* ed. Clinton Rossiter (New York: Mentor, 1961), 241.

2. William Crotty, *Decision for the Democrats* (Baltimore: Johns Hopkins University Press, 1978), 45.

3. Alexander Bickel, *Reform and Continuity* (New York: Harper Colophon, 1971), 54.

4. "Hughes Committee Report. The Democratic Choice," *Congressional Record* 114, 90th Cong., 2nd sess. (October 14, 1968), E9172.

5. Bickel, *Reform and Continuity,* 41–42.

6. "Reform: What Works?" *Washington Post,* February 16, 1980.

Part V: Back to the Future? Proposals for Change

1. Adam Cohen and Elizabeth Taylor, *American Pharaoh: Mayor Richard J. Daley—His Battle for Chicago and the Nation* (Boston: Little, Brown, 2000), 521–23.

2. Jeane Kirkpatrick, *Dismantling the Parties; Reflections on Party Reform and Party Decomposition* (Washington, D.C.: American Enterprise Institute, 1978).

3. Everett Carll Ladd Jr., with Charles D. Hadley, *Transformations of the American Party System,* 2nd ed. (New York: Norton, 1978), 359.

4. Nelson W. Polsby, *Consequences of Party Reform* (New York: Oxford University Press, 1983).

5. Vanishing Voter Project, "The Public's Response to the 2000 Nominating Process: Implications for Alternative Nominating Systems," in *Nominating Future Presidents: A Review of the Republican Process* (Washington, D.C.: Republican National Committee, 2000), 151–58.

6. Quoted in "Poll: Americans Unhappy with How Nominees are Chosen," CNN.com/allpolitics, April 6, 2000.

7. See James W. Ceaser, *Reforming the Reforms: A Critical Analysis of the Presidential Selection Process* (Cambridge: Ballinger, 1982), 113–53.

8. *Toward A More Responsible Two-Party System* (Washington, D.C.: American Political Science Association, 1950), supplement to the *American Political Science Review* 44 (September 1950).

9. Ibid., 38, 73.

10. Ibid., 73.

11. Austin Ranney, "Toward a More Responsible Two-Party System: A Commentary," *American Political Science Review* 45 (June 1951): 490.

12. Ceaser, *Reforming the Reforms,* 148.

13. Similarly, a 1972 joint resolution introduced by senators Mike Mansfield (D-Mont.) and George Aiken (R-Vt.) called for a constitutional amendment establishing a direct national primary for any party that received 10 percent of the popular vote in the preceding presidential election. Nonetheless, this measure also provided for a national convention to write the platform and choose a vice presidential running mate. See James W. Davis, *National Conventions in an Age of Party Reform* (Westport, Conn.: Greenwood, 1983), 222.

14. Ibid., 255–63. On how political parties have evolved since publication of *Toward A More Responsible Two-Party System,* see *Responsible Partisanship? The Evolution of American Political Parties Since 1950,* ed. John C. Green and Paul S. Hernson (Lawrence: University Press of Kansas, 2002).

15. On "endorsement conventions" in gubernatorial nominations, see Malcolm E. Jewell, *Parties and Primaries: Nominating State Governors* (New York: Praeger, 1984).

16. Ceaser, *Reforming the Reforms,* 145.

17. Austin Ranney, *The Federalization of Presidential Primaries* (Washington, D.C.: American Enterprise Institute, 1978), 1; Davis, *National Conventions*, 233.

18. This paragraph and subsequent ones on the Packwood, Udall, and Ottinger bills draw from Ranney, *The Federalization of Presidential Primaries*; Ceaser, *Reforming the Reforms*, 138; and Davis, *National Conventions*, 229–30.

19. *Reforming the Reforms*, 137.

20. Davis, *National Conventions*, 230–31.

21. Ceaser, *Reforming the Reforms*, 132.

22. The same problems arise in consideration of even more recent cluster-primary schemes like the one offered by Rep. Sander M. Levin (D-Mich.) in which six clusters, consisting of states from each of six regions, would hold primaries on six dates in March, April, May, and June. See Kevin Coleman, "Presidential Nominating Process: Current Issues and Legislation in the 106th Congress," Library of Congress, Congressional Research Service (May 16, 2000).

23. "Primary Mischief," *New York Times*, March 14, 2003, A26.

24. *The Gallup Poll: Public Opinion 1972–1977* (Wilmington, Del.: Scholarly Resources, 1978), 1:32; *The Gallup Poll: Public Opinion 1982*, 291.

25. Ranney, *The Federalization of Presidential Primaries*, 8–32.

26. V. O. Key Jr., *Southern Politics in State and Nation* (New York: Knopf, 1949), 416–23.

27. Ranney, *The Federalization of Presidential Primaries*, 21.

28. Ibid., 35–36.

29. Ibid, 37.

30. Based on delegate votes reported in *National Party Conventions 1831–2000* (Washington, D.C.: Congressional Quarterly Press, 2001), 234.

17. Two Cheers for the National Primary

1. Minor parties, that is, those that received less than 5 percent of the popular vote in the most recent presidential election, would not be covered by the national primary requirement.

2. Other recent versions of the national primary proposal, such as those offered by Senators Mike Mansfield (D-Mont.) and George Aiken (R-Vt.) in 1972, and by Representative Albert Quie (R-Minn.) in 1977 differed from Weicker's in that they would not have allowed independent voters to participate. The Mansfield-Aiken bill also would have defined 40 percent as sufficient for victory in the first primary.

3. Clinton Rossiter, *1787: The Grand Convention* (London: MacGibbon and Kee, 1968), 63.

4. Henry Mayo, *Inrtroduction to Democratic Theory* (New York: Oxford University Press, 1960), 73. Among the definitional characteristics of "polyarchal democracy," as Robert Dahl defines it, are these: "In tabulating . . . votes, the weight assigned to the choice of each individual is identical." "The alternative with the greatest number of votes is declared the winner" (*A Preface to Democratic Theory* [Chicago: University of Chicago Press, 1956], 67). As argued above, the present nominating system fails to meet the first standard, and, on occasion, could fail to meet the second as well.

5. Jeffrey Pressman and Aaron Wildavsky, *Implementation* (Berkeley: University of California Press, 1973), 143, 147.

6. High levels of political participation, though only among those considered eligible to vote and in those governing processes to which citizens were invited to participate, also was desired by the framers, as evidenced in their concepts of "Republican Virtue." See Robert Salisbury, "Republican Virtue and Affirmative Citizenship," presented at the Foundation of Political Theory meeting, held in conjunction with the annual meeting of the American Political Science Association, Washington, D.C., August 1980.

7. Austin Ranney, *Participation in American Presidential Nominations, 1976* (Washington, D.C.: American Enterprise Institute), 20.

8. Ibid., 27–28.

9. "The Voters Turn Out," *Newsweek,* March 17, 1980, 36.

10. "Primaries '80." According to Rhodes Cook, "Generally the turnouts increased in states that received heavy attention from candidates and media" ("Carter, Reagan Exhibit Similar Approach in Preference Primaries," *Congressional Quarterly Weekly Report,* July 5, 1980, 1875).

11. Austin Ranney, *The Federalization of Presidential Primaries* (Washington, D.C.: American Enterprise Institute, 1978), 16; see also Ranney, "Turnout and Representation in Presidential Primary Elections," American *Political Science Review* 66 (1972): 21–37.

12. Jeane Kirkpatrick, *Dismantling the Parties* (Washington, D.C.: American Enterprise Institute, 1978), 24–27. Cf. Lawrence Longley, "Minorities and the 1980 Electoral College," presented at the annual meeting of the American Political Science Association, Washington, D.C., August 1980.

13. See, for example, the remarks of Rep. Lee Hamilton, *Congressional Record* (February 9, 1977): H1026–27.

14. Cf. Peter Goldman, "See Jimmy Run-in-Place," *Newsweek,* February 18, 1980, 45.

15. Austin Ranney, interview with the author, March 7, 1980; see also Kirkpatrick, *Dismantling the Parties,* 27–28.

16. Richard Scammon, interview with the author, March 6, 1980.

17. Ibid.

18. F. Christopher Arterton, "Strategies and Tactics of Candidate Organizations," *Political Science Quarterly* (Winter 1977–78): 671.

19. James D. Barber, *Pulse of Politics: The Rhythm of Presidential Elections in the Twentieth Century* (New York: Norton), 1980.

20. Bruce Adams, interview with the author, March 7, 1980.

21. Ranney, *The Federalization of Presidential Primaries,* 20.

22. Leon Epstein, "The Australian Political System," in *Australia at the Polls,* ed. Howard Penniman (Washington, D.C.: American Enterprise Institute, 1977), 33.

23. Malcolm Browne, "Can Voting Become Safer for Democracy?" *New York Times,* June 1, 1980; George N. Hallett, "Reply to Approval Voting," *National Civic Review* 69 (1980): 10.

24. Steven J. Brams, *The Presidential Election Game* (New Haven, Conn.: Yale University Press, 1978).

25. Drawing from an ABC News poll of New Hampshire primary voters that asked them which candidates were acceptable to them, Brains deduced that under an approval voting system, Reagan would have risen eight percentage points, from 50 percent to 58 percent; Bush sixteen points, from twenty-three to thirty-nine; and Baker twenty-eight points, from thirteen to forty-one—and second place ("Baker Could Have Survived N.H.," *Concord Monitor,* March 8, 1980). For an even more speculative treatment of the 1976 contest, see John Kellett and Kenneth Mott, "Presidential Primaries: Measuring Popular Choice," *Polity* 9 (1977): 528–37.

26. George Gallup, "Six Political Reforms Americans Want Most," *Reader's Digest,* August 1978, 59–62.

Index